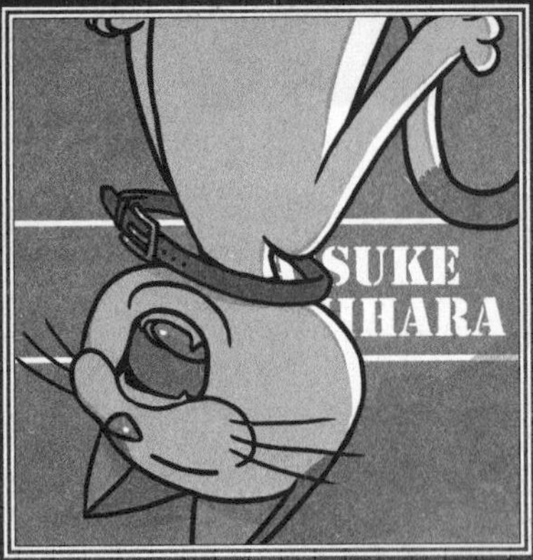
SUKE
IHARA

The author smoothly tumbling off the chair when he heard ***World Trigger*** would be an anime.

–Daisuke Ashihara, 2014

Daisuke Ashihara began his manga career at the age of 27 when his manga ***Room 303*** won second place in the 75th Tezuka Awards. His first series, ***Super Dog Rilienthal***, began serialization in ***Weekly Shonen Jump*** in 2009. ***World Trigger*** is his second serialized work in ***Weekly Shonen Jump***. He is also the author of several shorter works, including the one-shots ***Super Dog Rilienthal***, ***Trigger Keeper*** and ***Elite Agent Jin***.

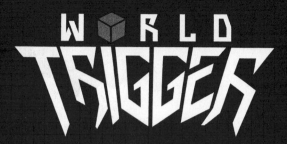

WORLD TRIGGER VOL. 6
SHONEN JUMP Manga Edition

STORY AND ART BY DAISUKE ASHIHARA

Translation/Lillian Olsen
Touch-Up Art & Lettering/Annaliese Christman
Design/Sam Elzway
Editor/Hope Donovan

WORLD TRIGGER © 2013 by Daisuke Ashihara/SHUEISHA Inc.
All rights reserved.
First published in Japan in 2013 by SHUEISHA Inc., Tokyo.
English translation rights arranged by SHUEISHA Inc.

The stories, characters and incidents mentioned
in this publication are entirely fictional.

Printed in the U.S.A.

Published by VIZ Media, LLC
P.O. Box 77010
San Francisco, CA 94107

10 9 8 7 6 5 4 3 2 1
First printing, July 2015

www.viz.com

THE WORLD'S MOST POPULAR MANGA
SHONEN JUMP
www.shonenjump.com

SHONEN JUMP MANGA EDITION

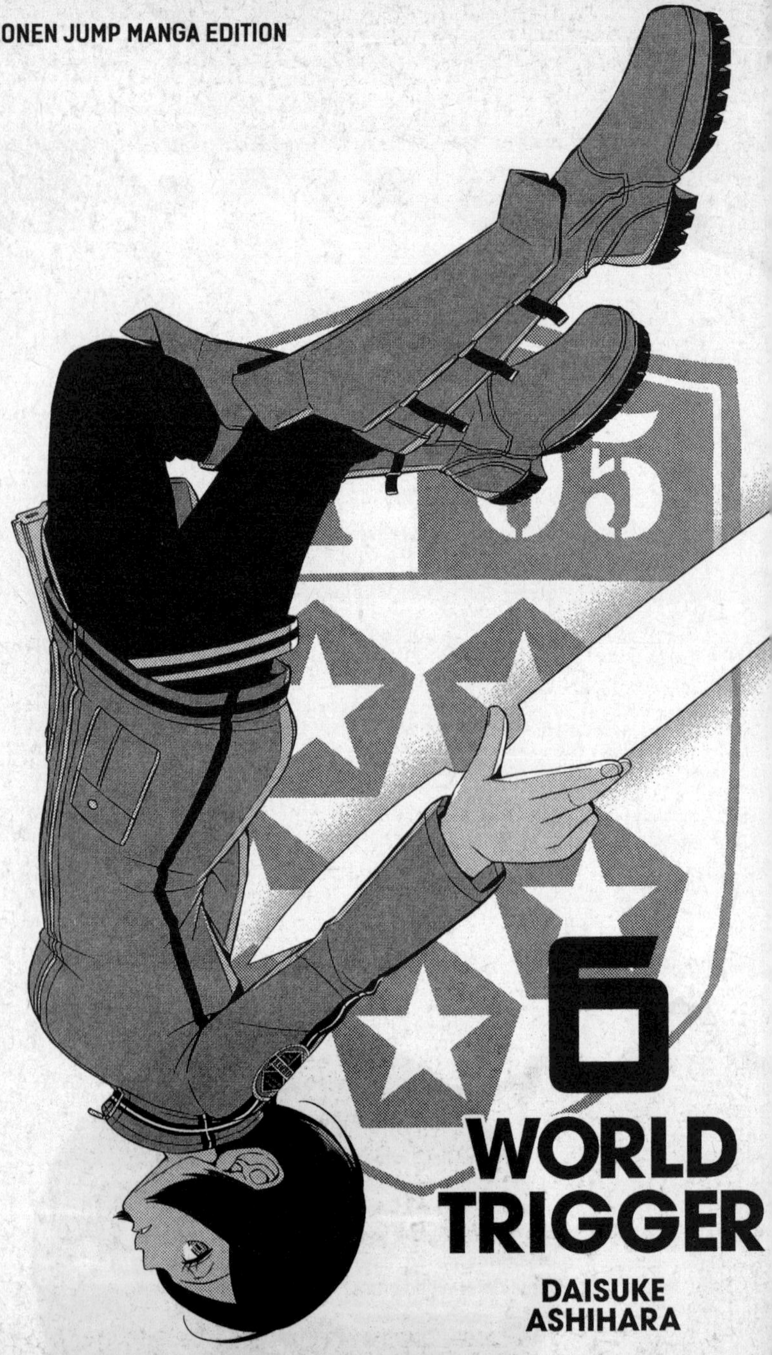

6
WORLD TRIGGER

DAISUKE ASHIHARA

WORLD TRIGGER DATA BASE

sion NEIGHBOR

Invaders from another dimension that enter Mikado City through Gates. Most "Neighbors" here are Trion soldiers built for war. The Neighbors who actually live on the other side of the Gates are human, like Yuma.

H-HEY, IT'S COMING THIS WAY!!
DRMN
WHOA...
WAAAA

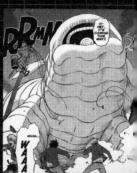

Trion solider built for war.

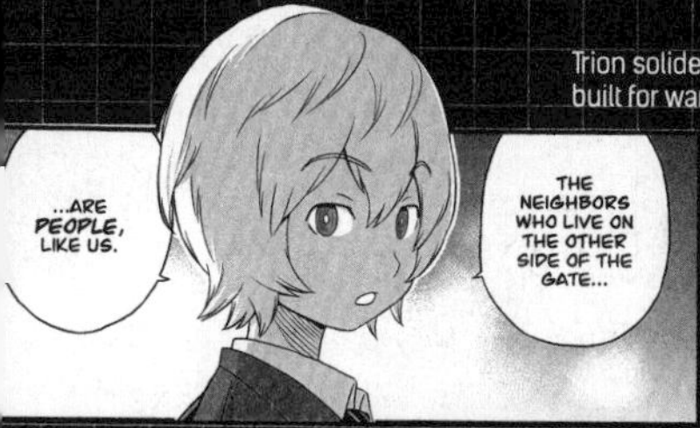

THE NEIGHBORS WHO LIVE ON THE OTHER SIDE OF THE GATE...
...ARE PEOPLE, LIKE US.

NEIGHBORHOOD

The Neighbor world. Mostly the darkness of space, with individual countries floating like stars.

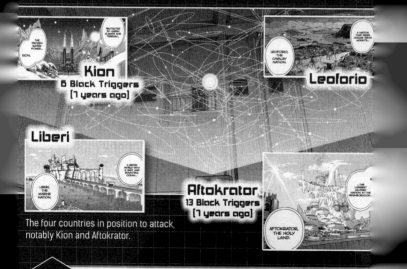

PROTECTED BY HARSH CLIMATE AND TERRAIN...
THE FROZEN SUPER-POWER...
KION.

Kion
6 Black Triggers
(7 years ago)

A NATION THAT RIDES UNIQUE TRION MOUNTS...
LEOFORIO, THE CAVALRY NATION.

Leoforio

Liberi

A WATER WORLD WITH A VAST AND BOUNTIFUL OCEAN...
LIBERI, THE MARINE NATION.

...THE LARGEST MILITARY NATION IN THE NEIGHBORHOOD...
AFTOKRATOR, THE HOLY LAND.

Aftokrator
13 Black Triggers
(7 years ago)

The four countries in position to attack, notably Kion and Aftokrator.

Planet-Nations

Neighbor countries are called "planet-nations" because they traverse the darkness on their own orbits. Many of them brush by this world as they travel along their paths. Some, called "errant nations," fly about freely, without determined orbits.

BORDER

An agency founded to protect the city from Neighbors. Agents are classified as follows: C-Rank for trainees, B-Rank for main forces, A-Rank for elites and S-Rank for those with Black Triggers. A-Rank squads get to go on away missions to the Neighborhood.

Resistanc

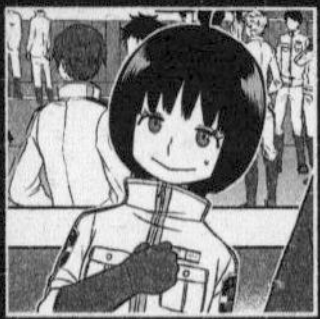

C-Rank: Chika

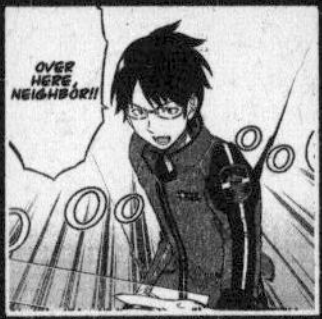
OVER HERE, NEIGHBOR!!

B-Rank: Osamu

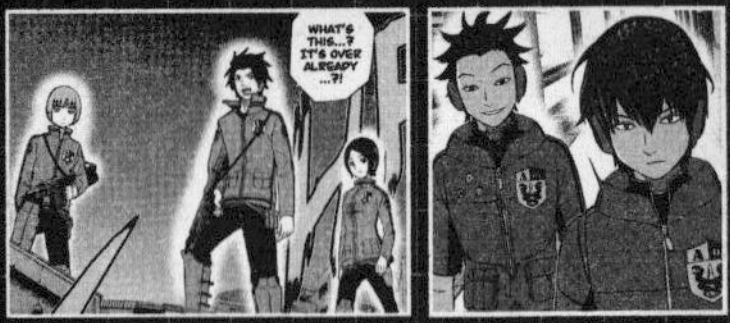
WHAT'S THIS...? IT'S OVER ALREADY ...?!

A-Rank: Arashiyama Squad, Miwa Squad

Trigger

A technology created by Neighbors to manipulate Trion. Used mainly as weapons, Triggers come in various types. Border classifies them into three groups: Attacker, Gunner, and Sniper.

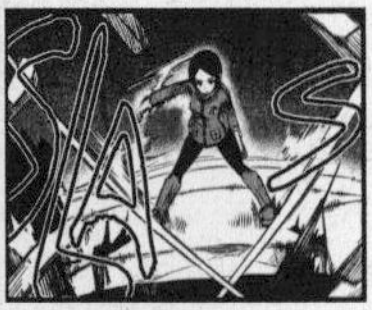

▲ Attacker Trigger

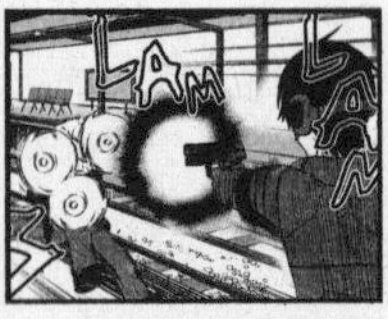

▲ Gunner Trigger

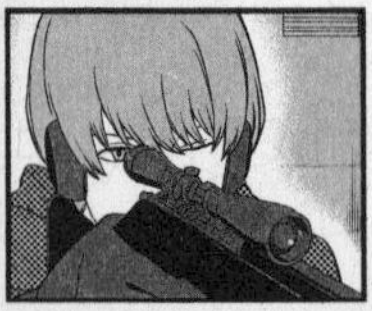

◀ Sniper Trigger

Black Trigger

A special Trigger created when a skilled user pours their entire life force and Trion into a Trigger. Outperforms regular Triggers, but the user must be compatible with the personality of the creator, meaning only a few people can use any given Black Trigger.

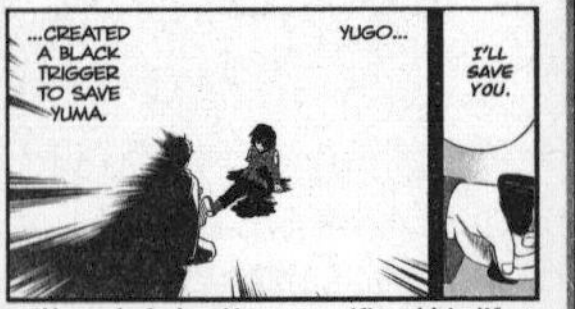
I'LL SAVE YOU.
YUGO...
...CREATED A BLACK TRIGGER TO SAVE YUMA.

▲ Yuma's father Yugo sacrificed his life to create a Black Trigger and save Yuma.

STORY

About four years ago, a Gate connecting to another dimension opened in Mikado City, leading to the appearance of invaders called Neighbors. After the establishment of the Border Defense Agency, people were able to return to their normal lives.

Osamu Mikumo is a junior high student who meets Yuma Kuga, a Neighbor. Yuma is targeted for capture by Border, but Tamakoma Branch agent Yuichi Jin steps in to help. He convinces Yuma to join Border instead, then gives his Black Trigger to HQ in exchange for Yuma's enlistment. Now Osamu, Yuma and Osamu's friend Chika work toward making A-Rank together. When the intrepid new team visits HQ, Border's number two Attacker, Kazama, challenges Osamu to a practice match. Though Osamu loses 24 of 25 rounds, everyone only remembers that the final round ended in a tie! Meanwhile, the long-feared Neighbor large-scale attack begins...

WORLD TRIGGER CHARACTERS

TAMAKOMA BRANCH

Understanding toward Neighbors. Considered divergent from Border's main philosophy.

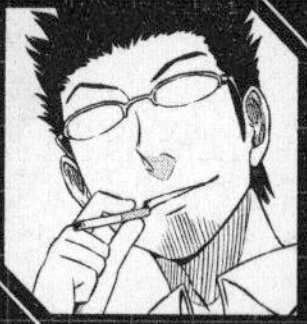

TAKUMI RINDO

Tamakoma Branch Director

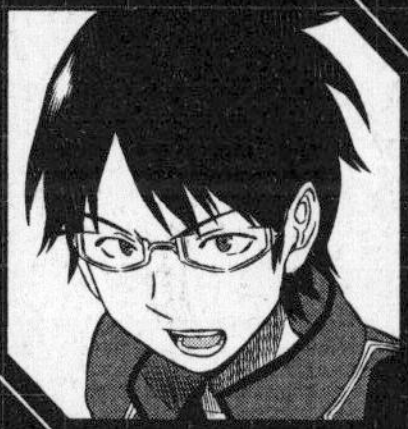

OSAMU MIKUMO

Ninth-grader who's compelled to help those in trouble. Border agent.

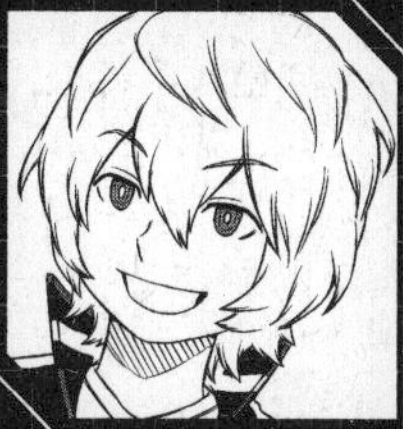

YUMA KUGA

Since he's a Neighbor, he lacks common sense. Has a Black Trigger.

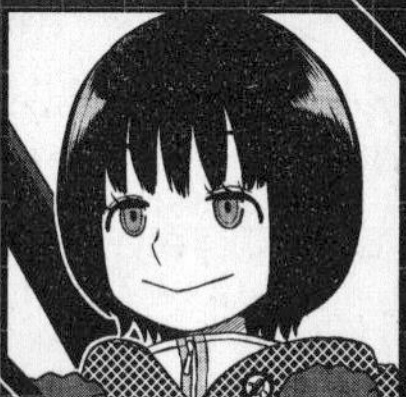

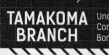

CHIKA AMATORI

Targeted by Neighbors because of her high Trion levels.

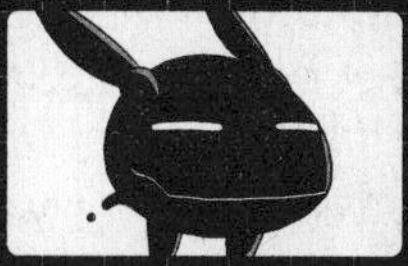

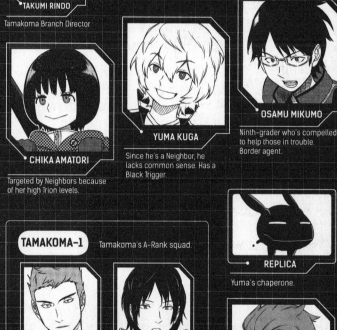

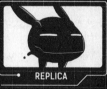

REPLICA

Yuma's chaperone.

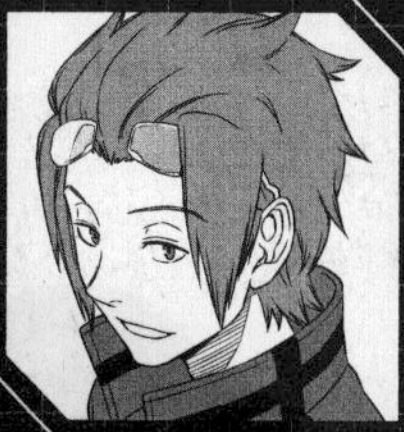

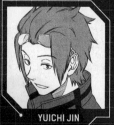

YUICHI JIN

Former S-Rank Black Trigger user. His Side Effect lets him see the future.

TAMAKOMA-1

Tamakoma's A-Rank squad.

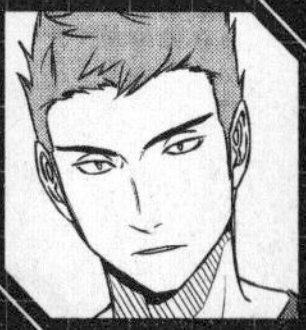

REIJI KIZAKI

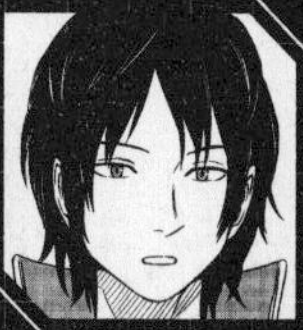

KYOSUKE KARASUMA

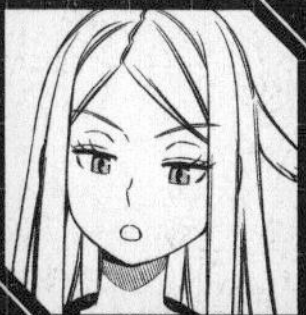

KIRIE KONAMI

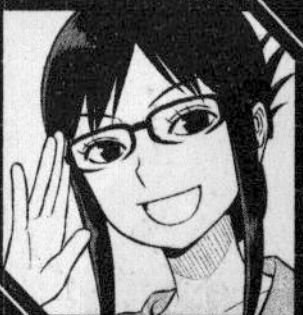

SHIORI USAMI

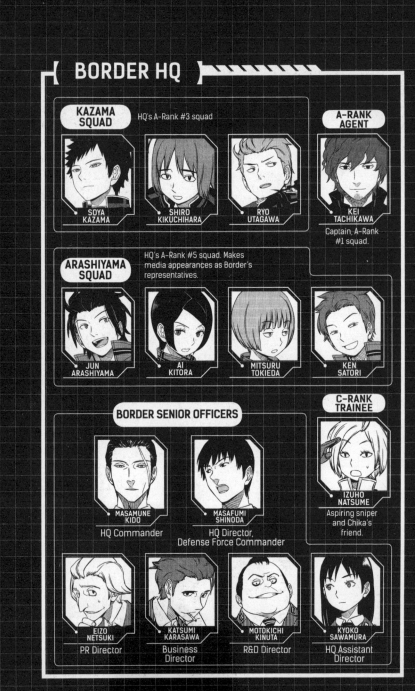

BORDER HQ

KAZAMA SQUAD

HQ's A-Rank #3 squad

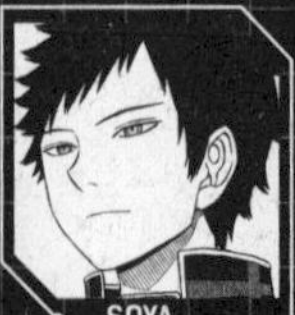

SOYA KAZAMA

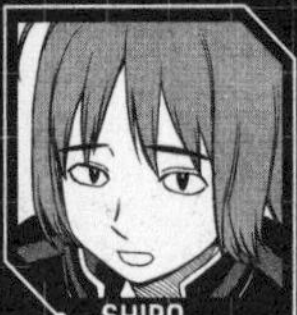

SHIRO KIKUCHIHARA

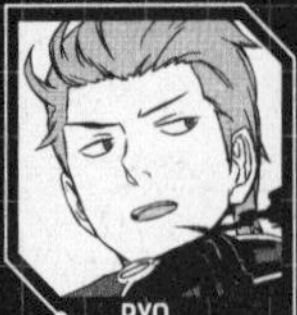

RYO UTAGAWA

A-RANK AGENT

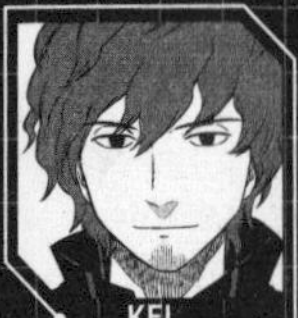

KEI TACHIKAWA

Captain, A-Rank #1 squad.

ARASHIYAMA SQUAD

HQ's A-Rank #5 squad. Makes media appearances as Border's representatives.

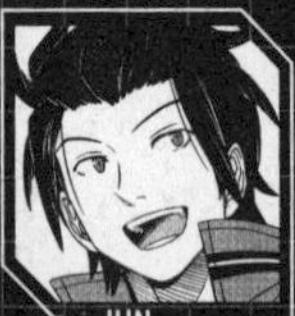

JUN ARASHIYAMA

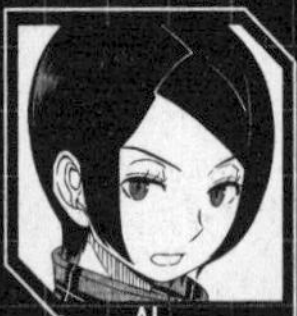

AI KITORA

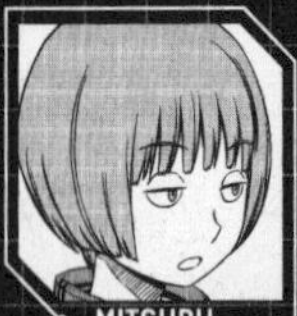

MITSURU TOKIEDA

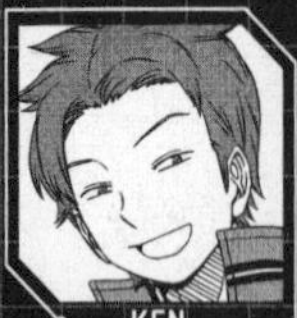

KEN SATORI

C-RANK TRAINEE

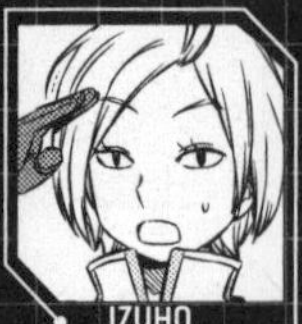

IZUHO NATSUME

Aspiring sniper and Chika's friend.

BORDER SENIOR OFFICERS

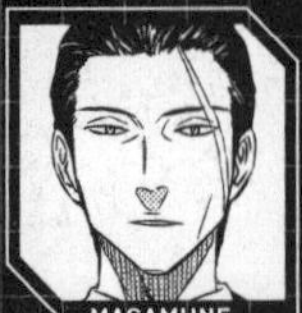

MASAMUNE KIDO

HQ Commander

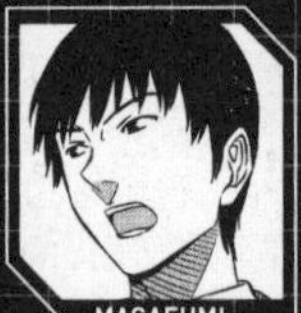

MASAFUMI SHINODA

HQ Director, Defense Force Commander

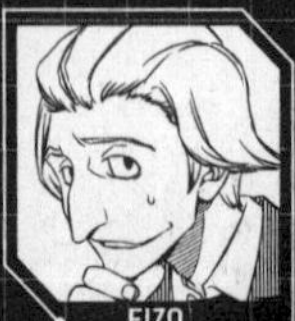

EIZO NETSUKI

PR Director

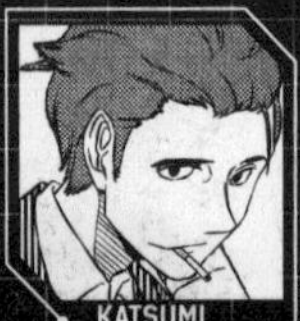

KATSUMI KARASAWA

Business Director

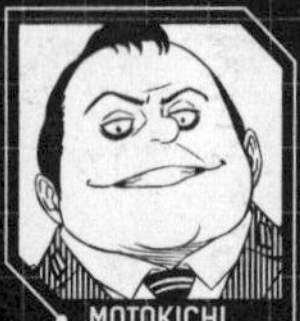

MOTOKICHI KINUTA

R&D Director

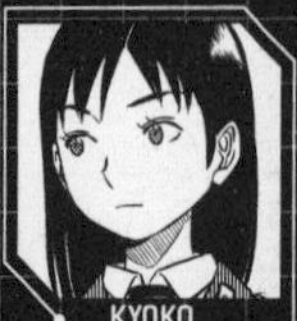

KYOKO SAWAMURA

HQ Assistant Director

WORLD TRIGGER
CONTENTS

6

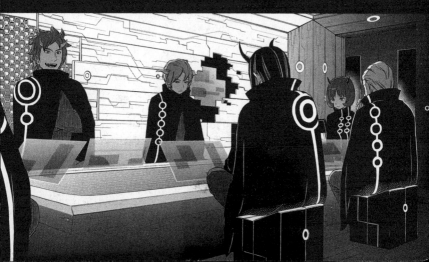

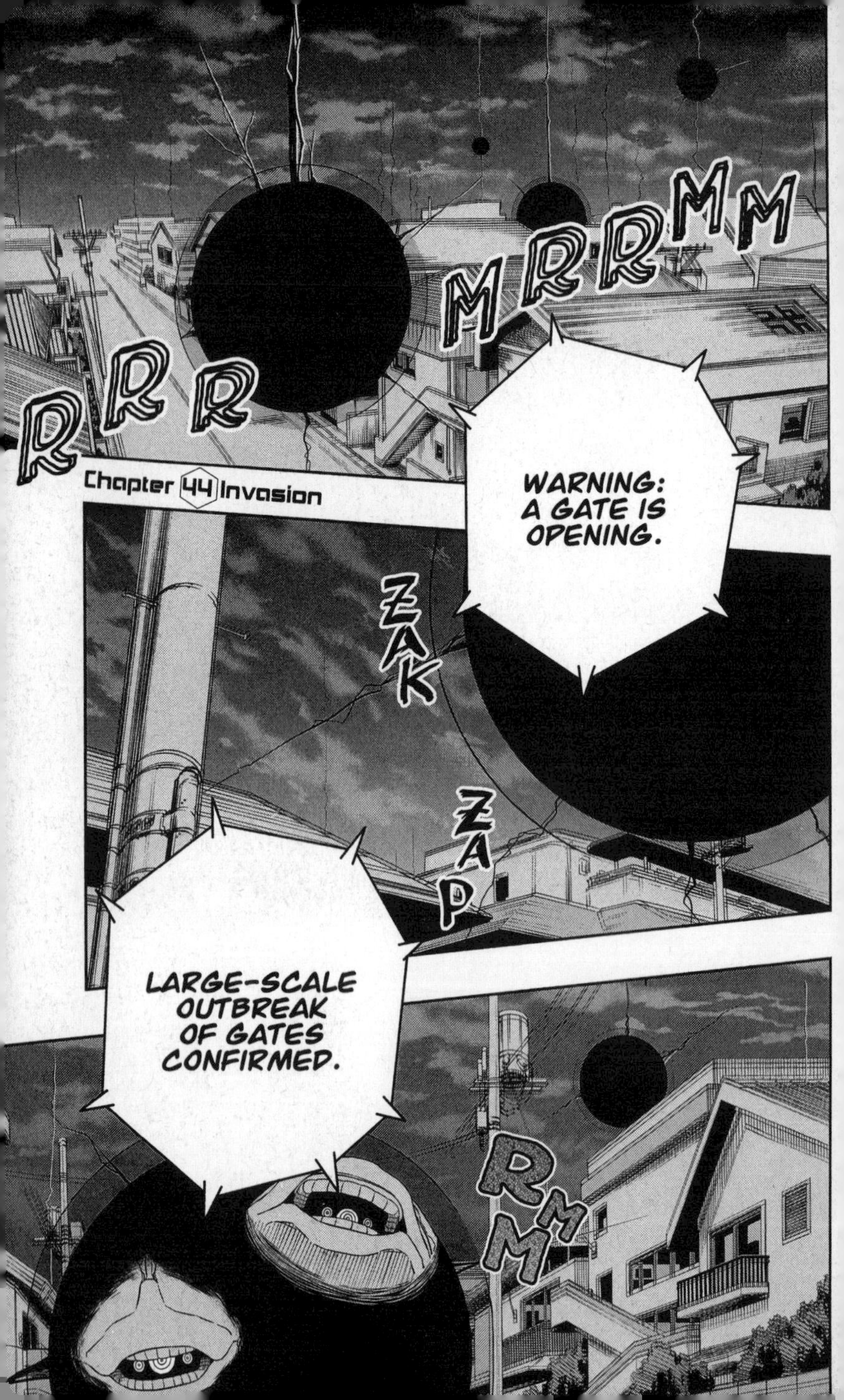
RRRRMRRRMMM
Chapter 44 Invasion
WARNING: A GATE IS OPENING.
ZAK
ZAP
LARGE-SCALE OUTBREAK OF GATES CONFIRMED.
RMMM

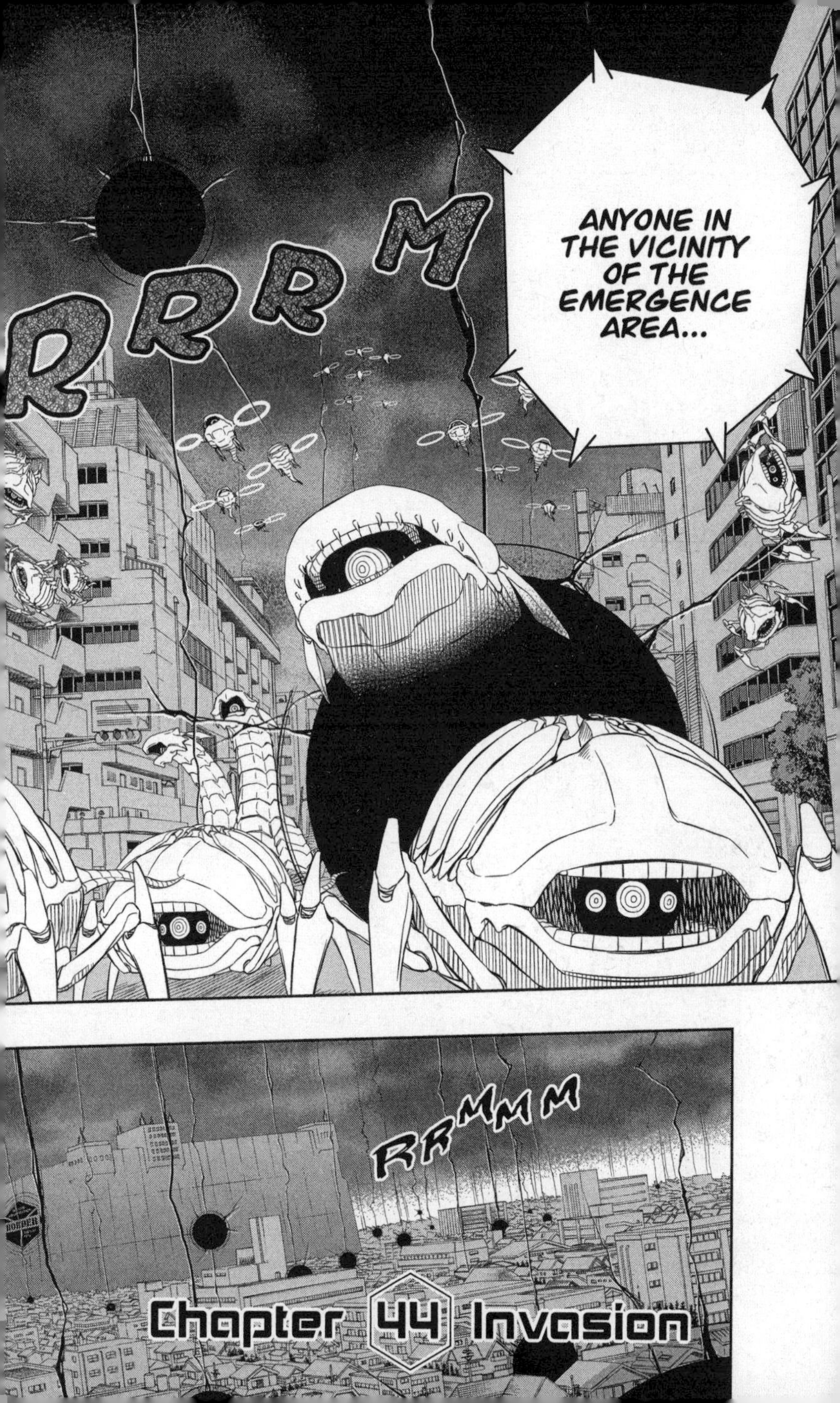
RRRRM
ANYONE IN THE VICINITY OF THE EMERGENCE AREA...
RRMMMM
Chapter 44 Invasion

READ THIS WAY

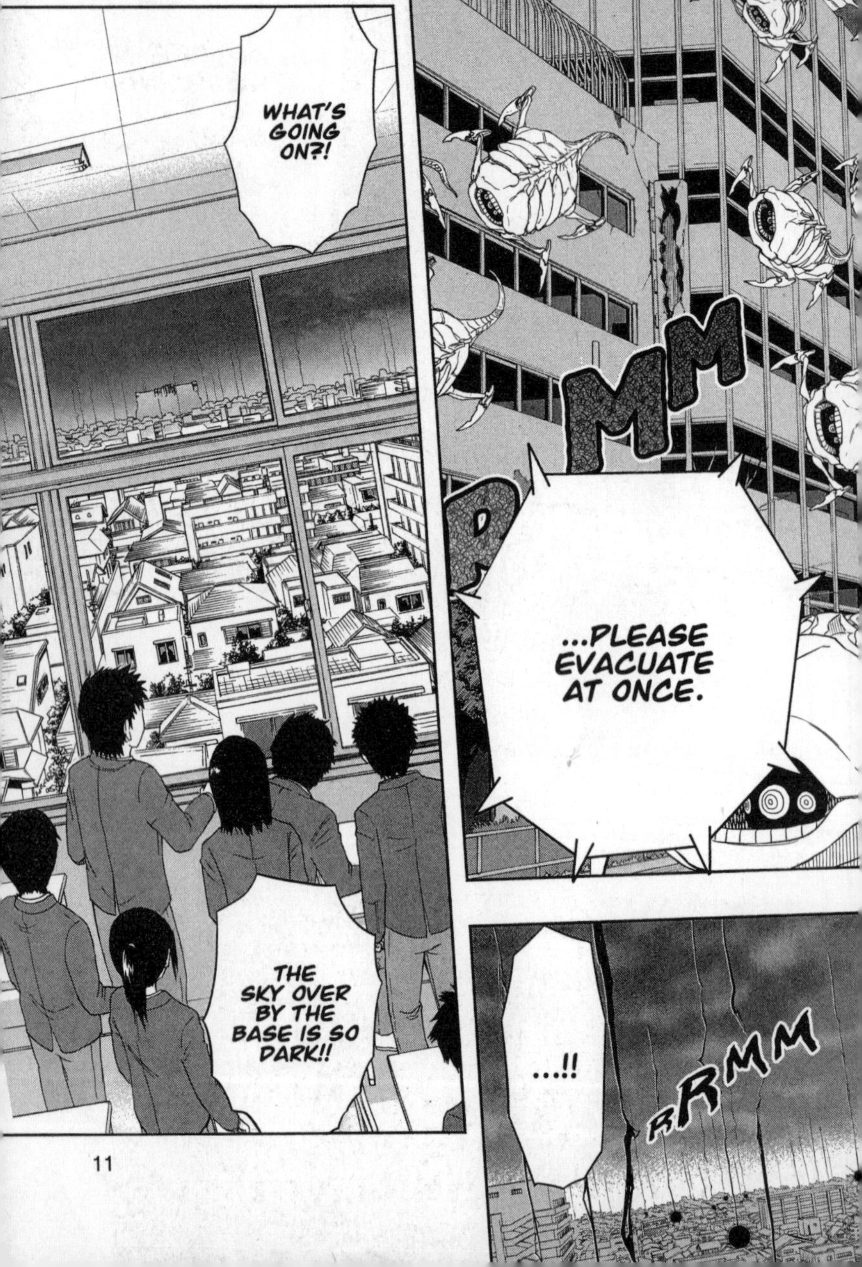
RMM
...PLEASE EVACUATE AT ONCE.
...!!
RRMM
WHAT'S GOING ON?!
THE SKY OVER BY THE BASE IS SO DARK!!

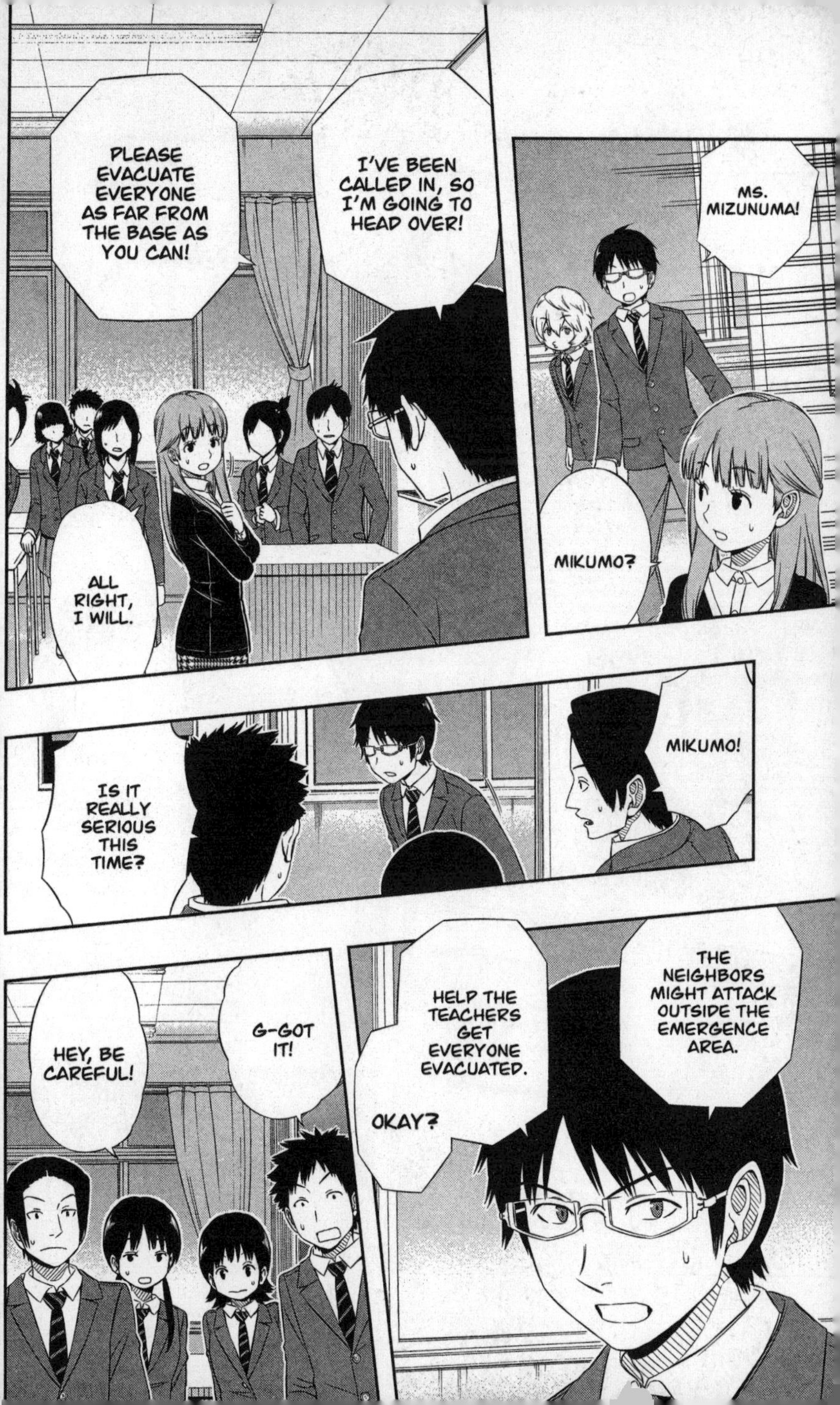
MS. MIZUNUMA!
MIKUMO?
I'VE BEEN CALLED IN, SO I'M GOING TO HEAD OVER!
PLEASE EVACUATE EVERYONE AS FAR FROM THE BASE AS YOU CAN!
ALL RIGHT, I WILL.
MIKUMO!
IS IT REALLY SERIOUS THIS TIME?
THE NEIGHBORS MIGHT ATTACK OUTSIDE THE EMERGENCE AREA.
HELP THE TEACHERS GET EVERYONE EVACUATED.
OKAY?
G-GOT IT!
HEY, BE CAREFUL!

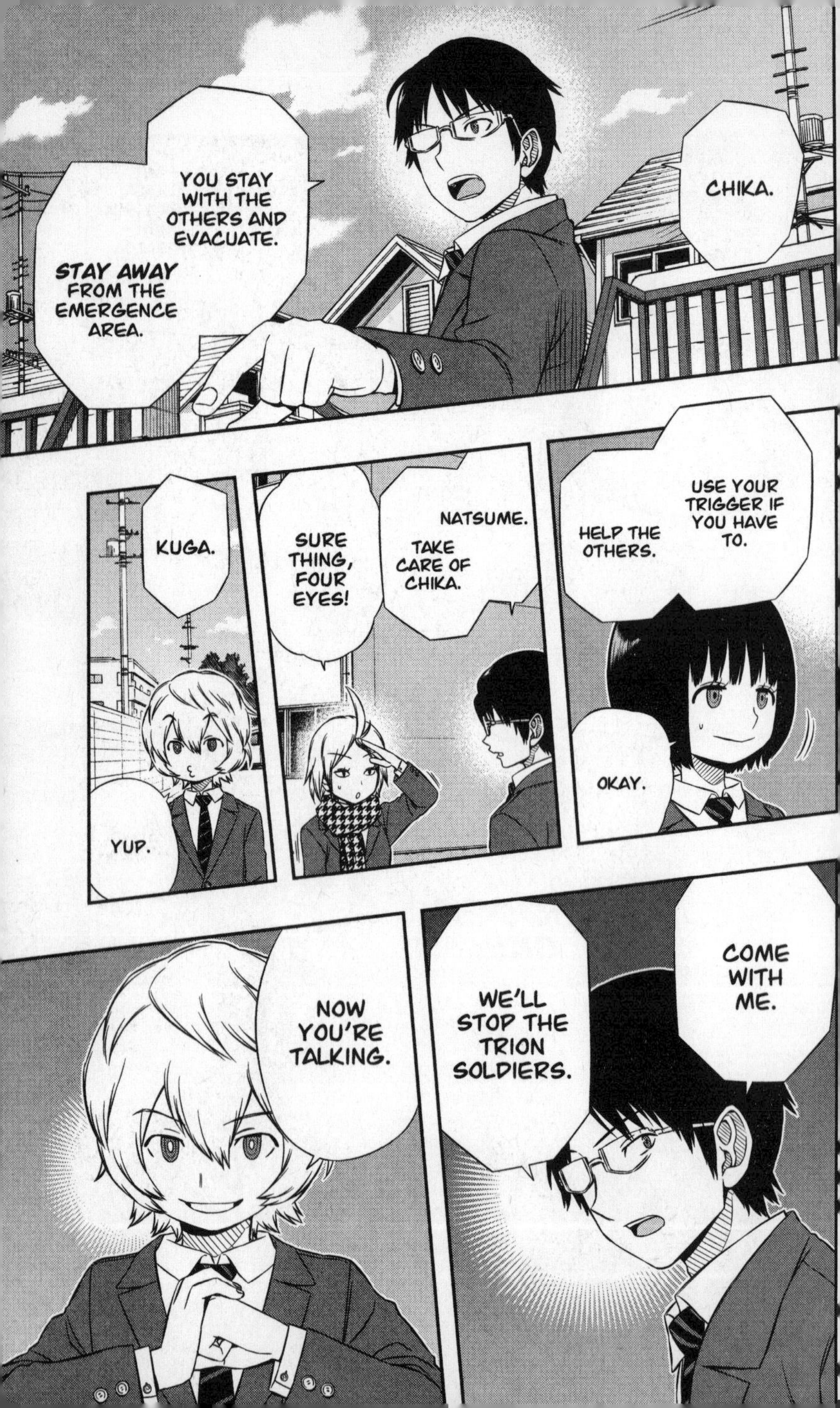
CHIKA.
YOU STAY WITH THE OTHERS AND EVACUATE.
STAY AWAY FROM THE EMERGENCE AREA.
USE YOUR TRIGGER IF YOU HAVE TO.
HELP THE OTHERS.
OKAY.
NATSUME.
TAKE CARE OF CHIKA.
SURE THING, FOUR EYES!
KUGA.
YUP.
COME WITH ME.
WE'LL STOP THE TRION SOLDIERS.
NOW YOU'RE TALKING.

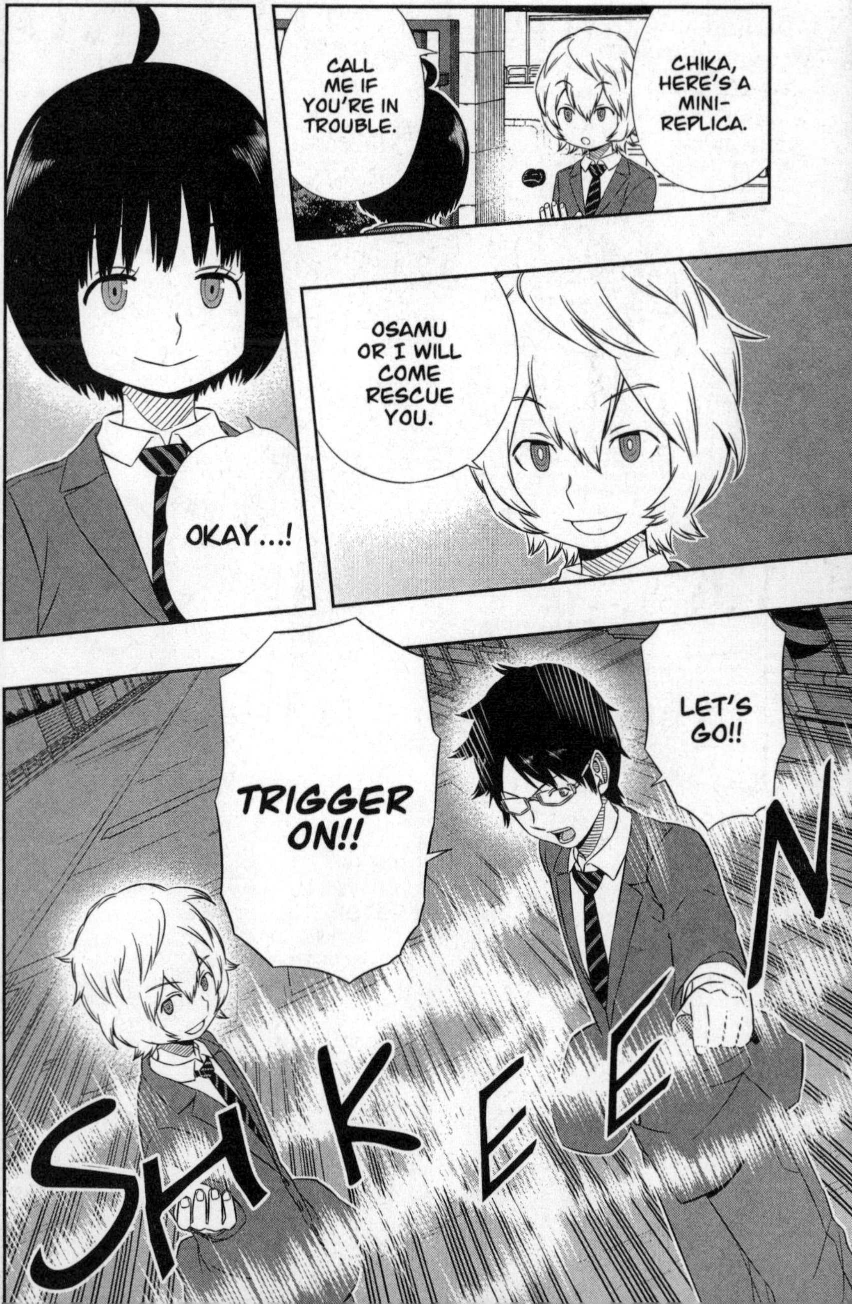
CHIKA, HERE'S A MINI-REPLICA.
CALL ME IF YOU'RE IN TROUBLE.
OSAMU OR I WILL COME RESCUE YOU.
OKAY...!
LET'S GO!!
TRIGGER ON!!
SHKEEEN

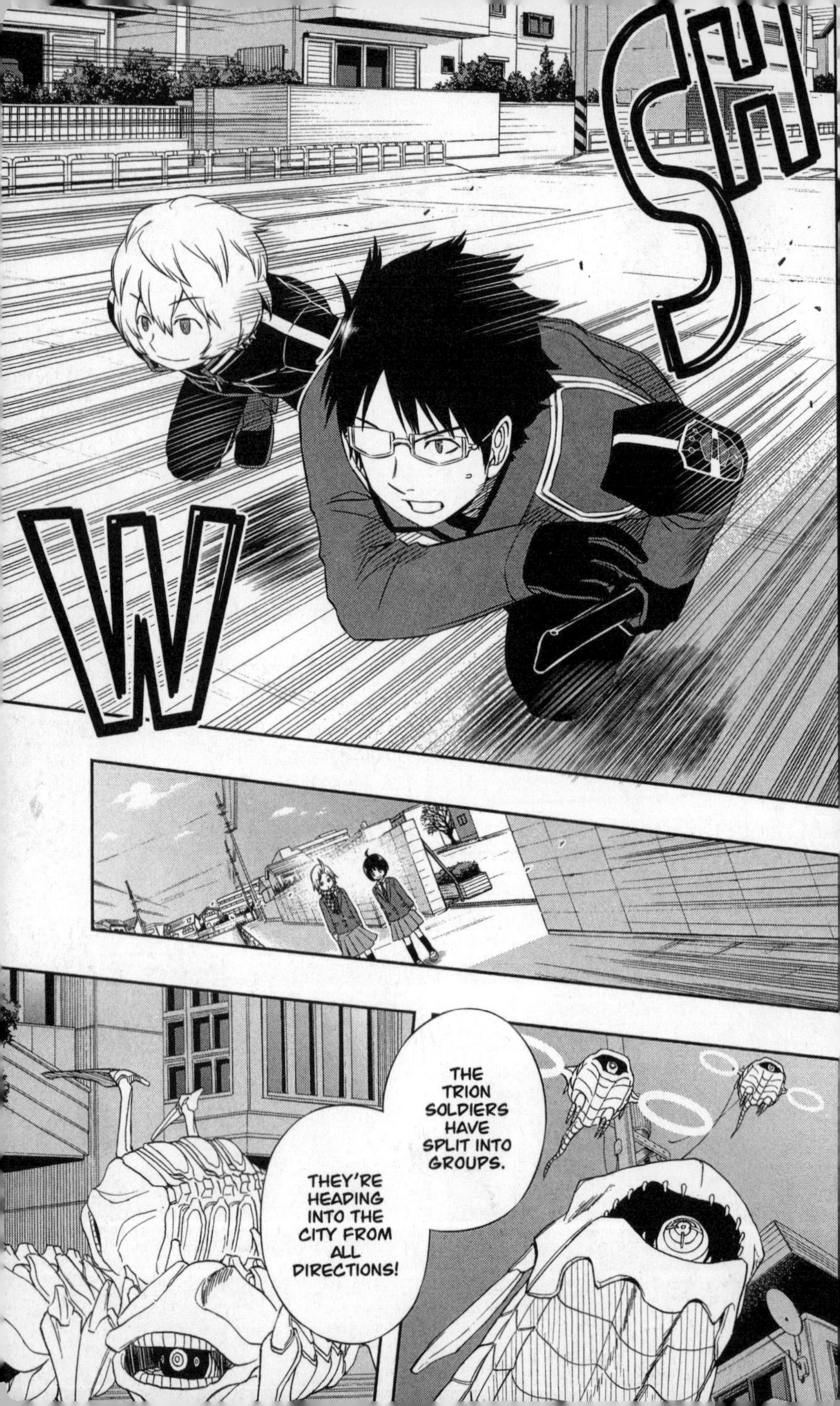
SH
W
THE TRION SOLDIERS HAVE SPLIT INTO GROUPS.
THEY'RE HEADING INTO THE CITY FROM ALL DIRECTIONS!

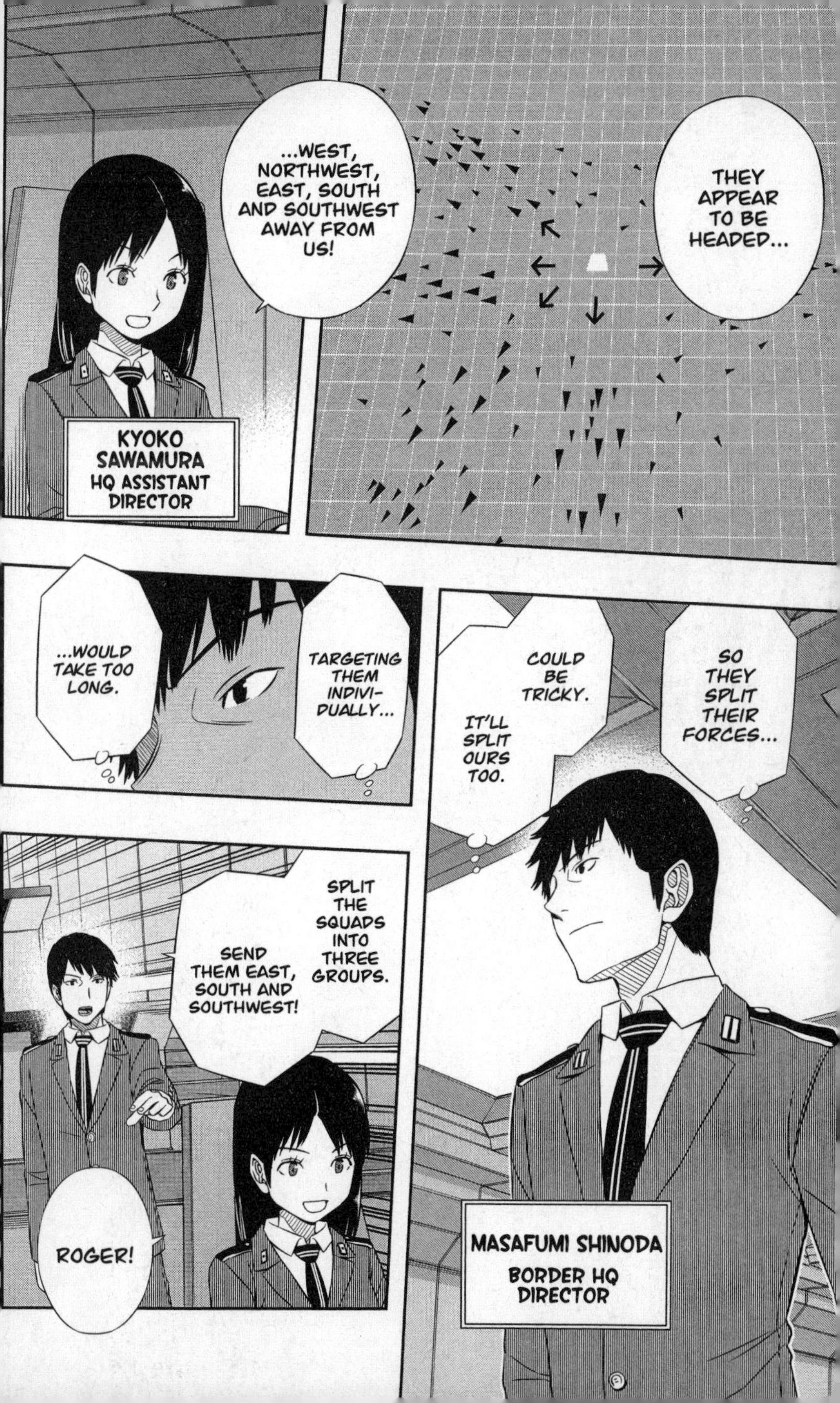
THEY APPEAR TO BE HEADED...
...WEST, NORTHWEST, EAST, SOUTH AND SOUTHWEST AWAY FROM US!
KYOKO SAWAMURA HQ ASSISTANT DIRECTOR
SO THEY SPLIT THEIR FORCES...
COULD BE TRICKY.
IT'LL SPLIT OURS TOO.
MASAFUMI SHINODA BORDER HQ DIRECTOR
TARGETING THEM INDIVIDUALLY...
...WOULD TAKE TOO LONG.
SPLIT THE SQUADS INTO THREE GROUPS.
SEND THEM EAST, SOUTH AND SOUTHWEST!
ROGER!

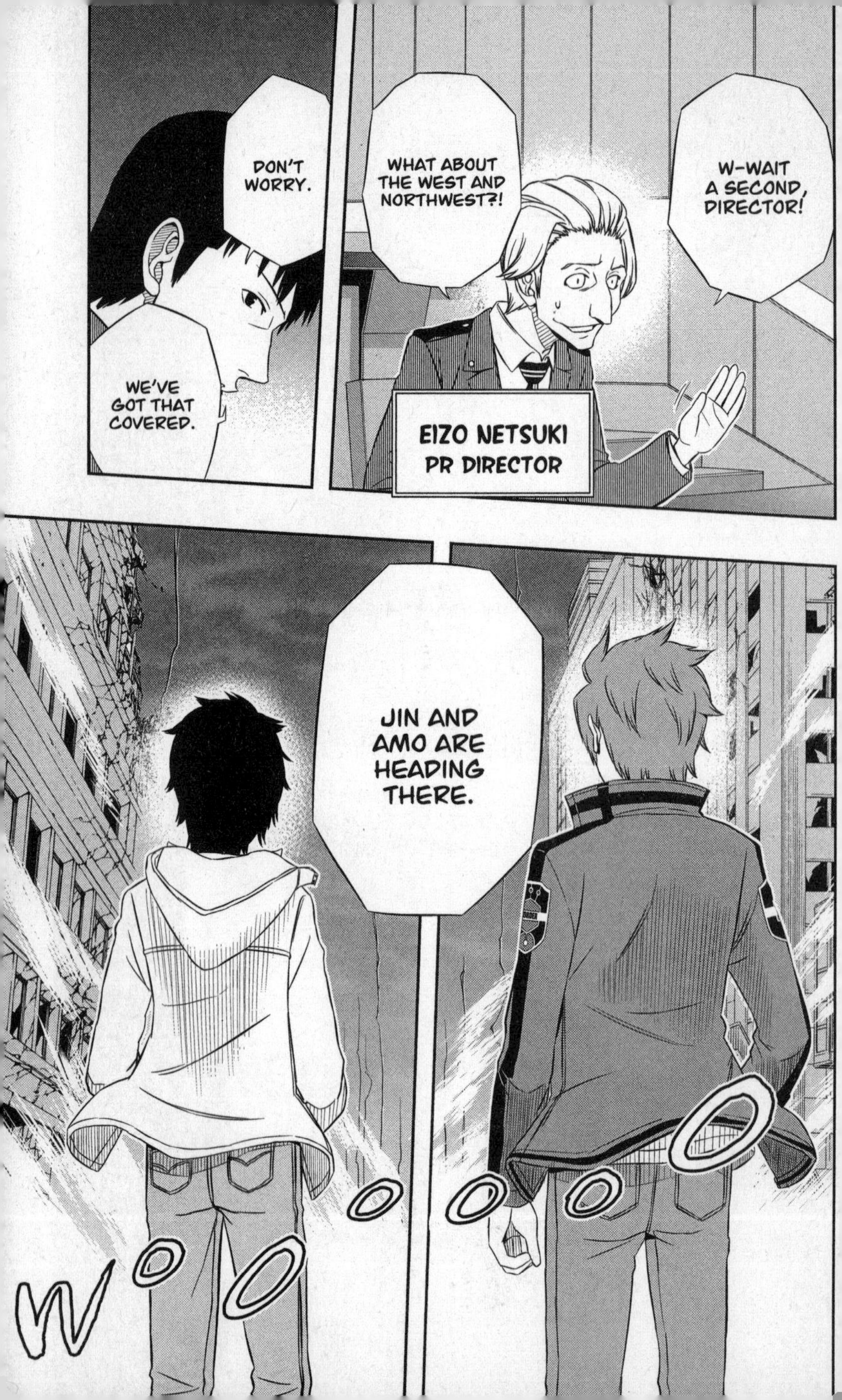
W-WAIT A SECOND, DIRECTOR!
WHAT ABOUT THE WEST AND NORTHWEST?!
EIZO NETSUKI
PR DIRECTOR
DON'T WORRY.
WE'VE GOT THAT COVERED.
JIN AND AMO ARE HEADING THERE.
WOOOOOO

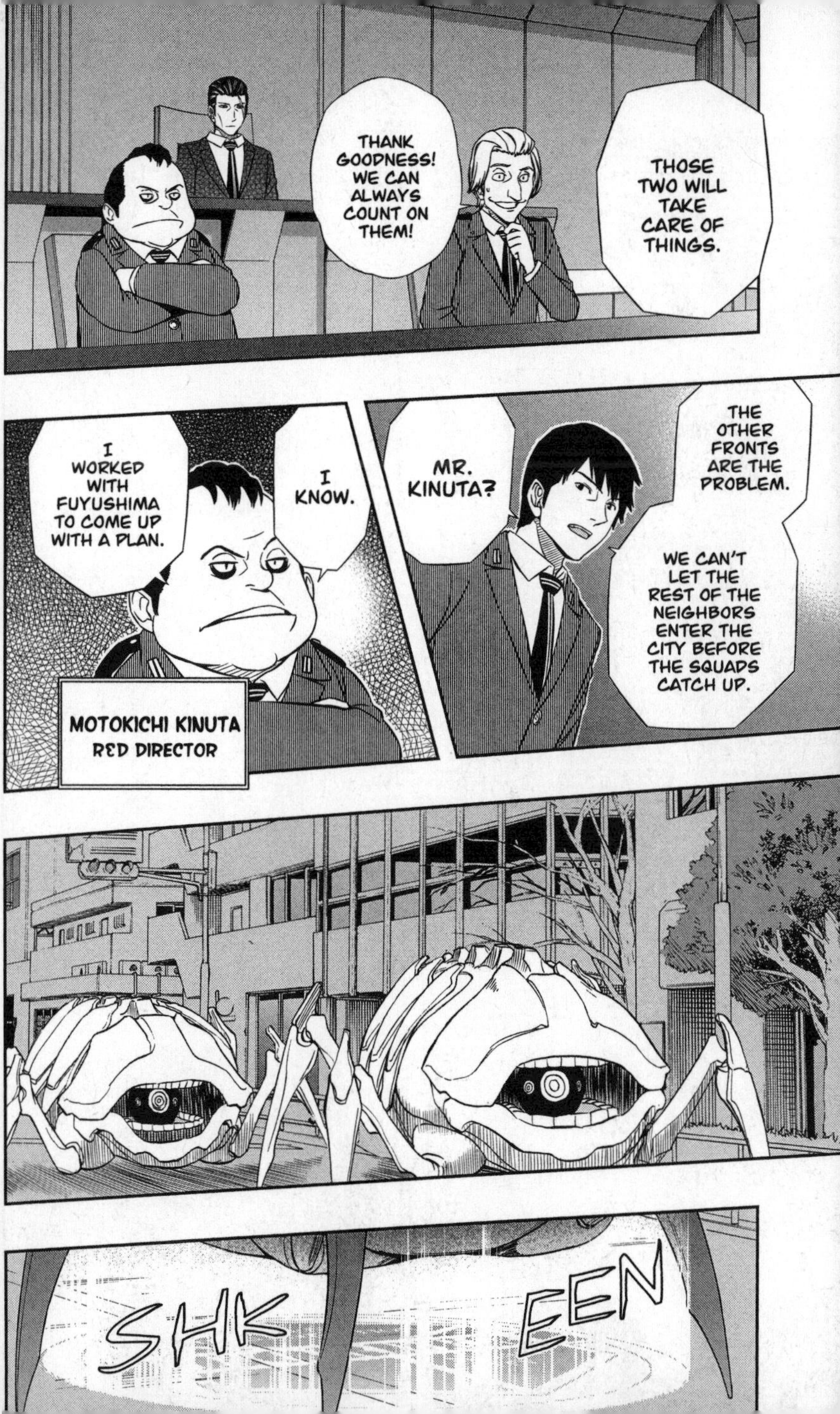
THOSE TWO WILL TAKE CARE OF THINGS.
THANK GOODNESS! WE CAN ALWAYS COUNT ON THEM!
THE OTHER FRONTS ARE THE PROBLEM.
WE CAN'T LET THE REST OF THE NEIGHBORS ENTER THE CITY BEFORE THE SQUADS CATCH UP.
MR. KINUTA?
I KNOW.
I WORKED WITH FUYUSHIMA TO COME UP WITH A PLAN.
MOTOKICHI KINUTA
R&D DIRECTOR
SHK EEN

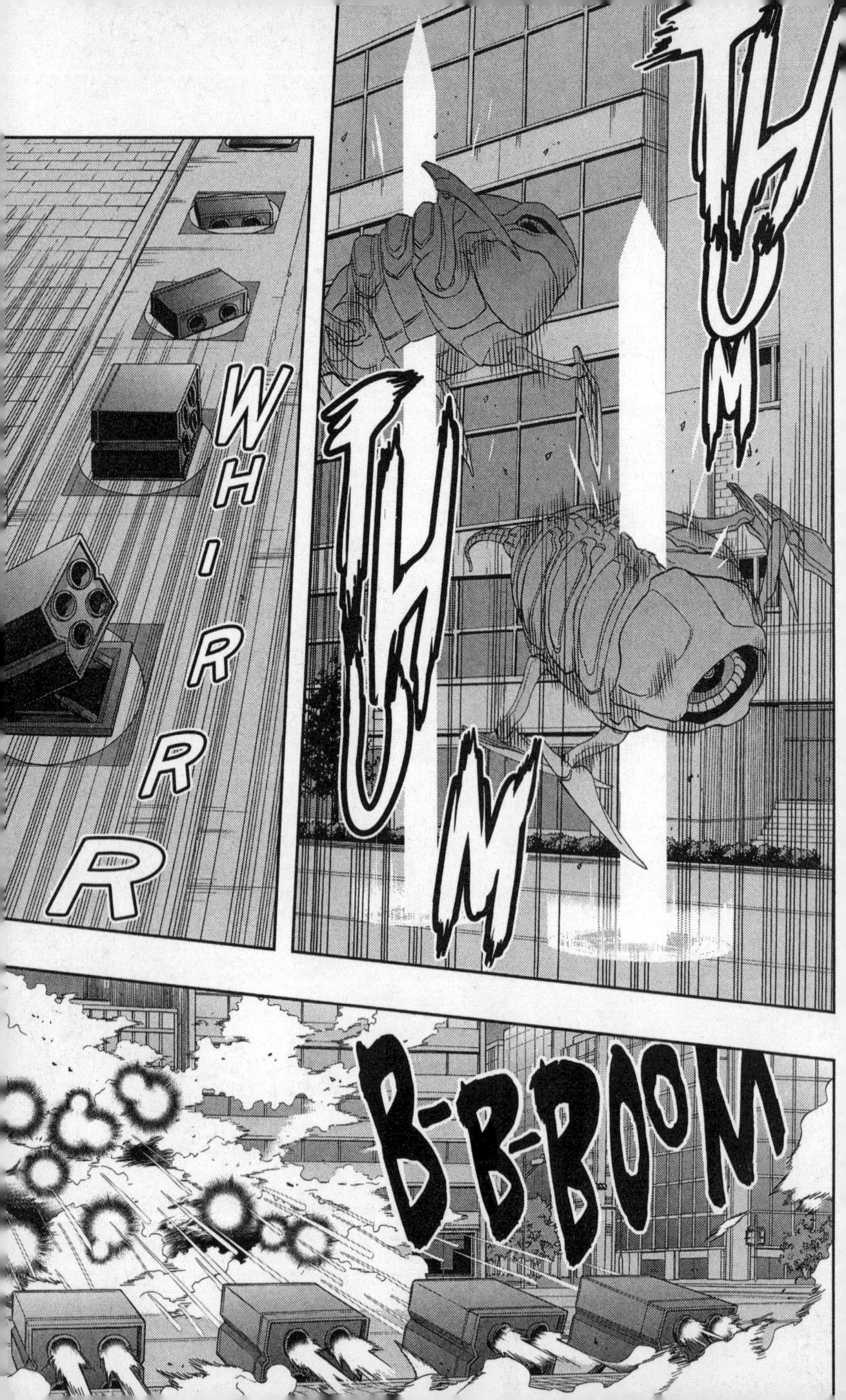
THUM
THUM
WHIRRR
B-B-BOOM

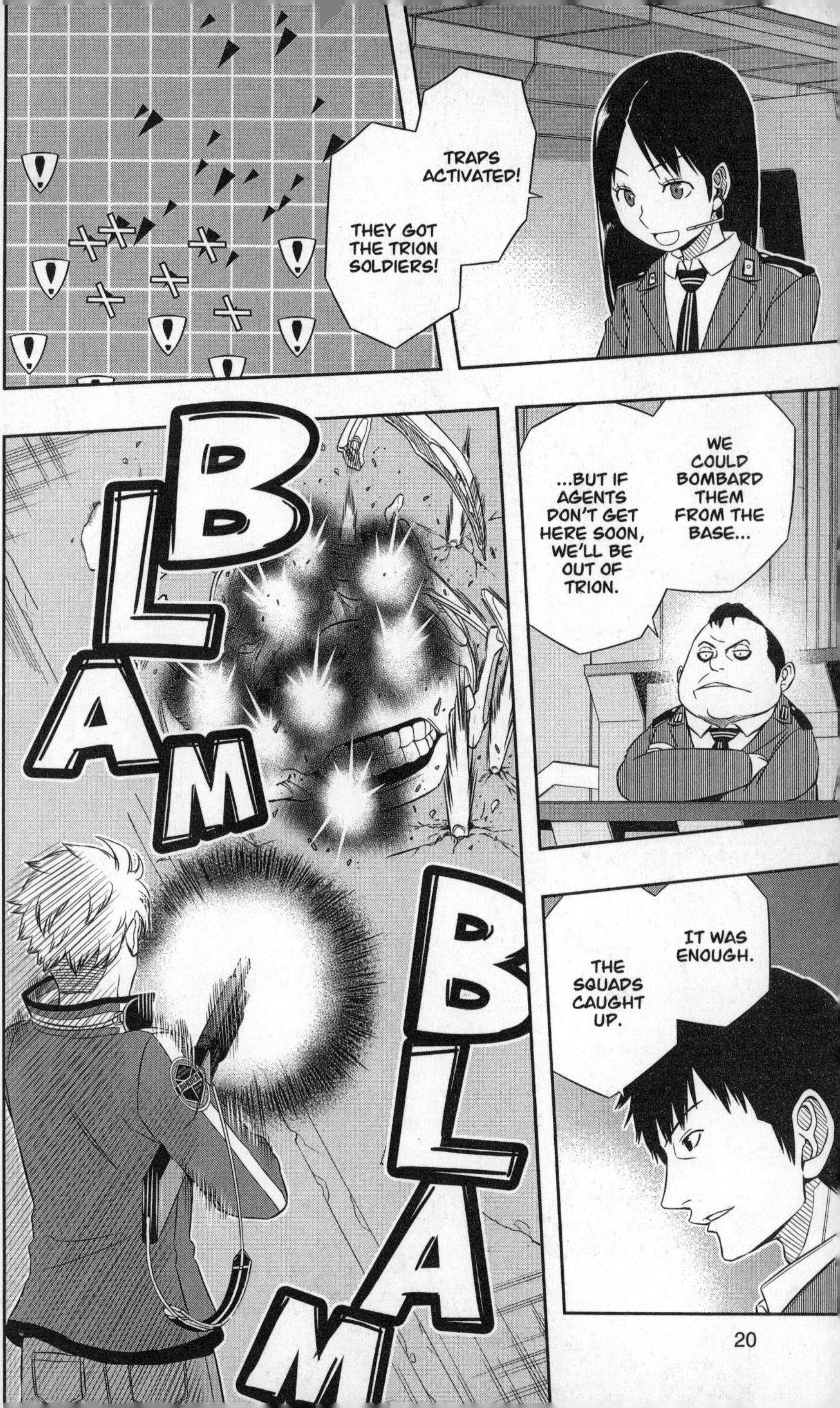
TRAPS ACTIVATED!
THEY GOT THE TRION SOLDIERS!
WE COULD BOMBARD THEM FROM THE BASE...
...BUT IF AGENTS DON'T GET HERE SOON, WE'LL BE OUT OF TRION.
IT WAS ENOUGH.
THE SQUADS CAUGHT UP.
BLAM
BLAM

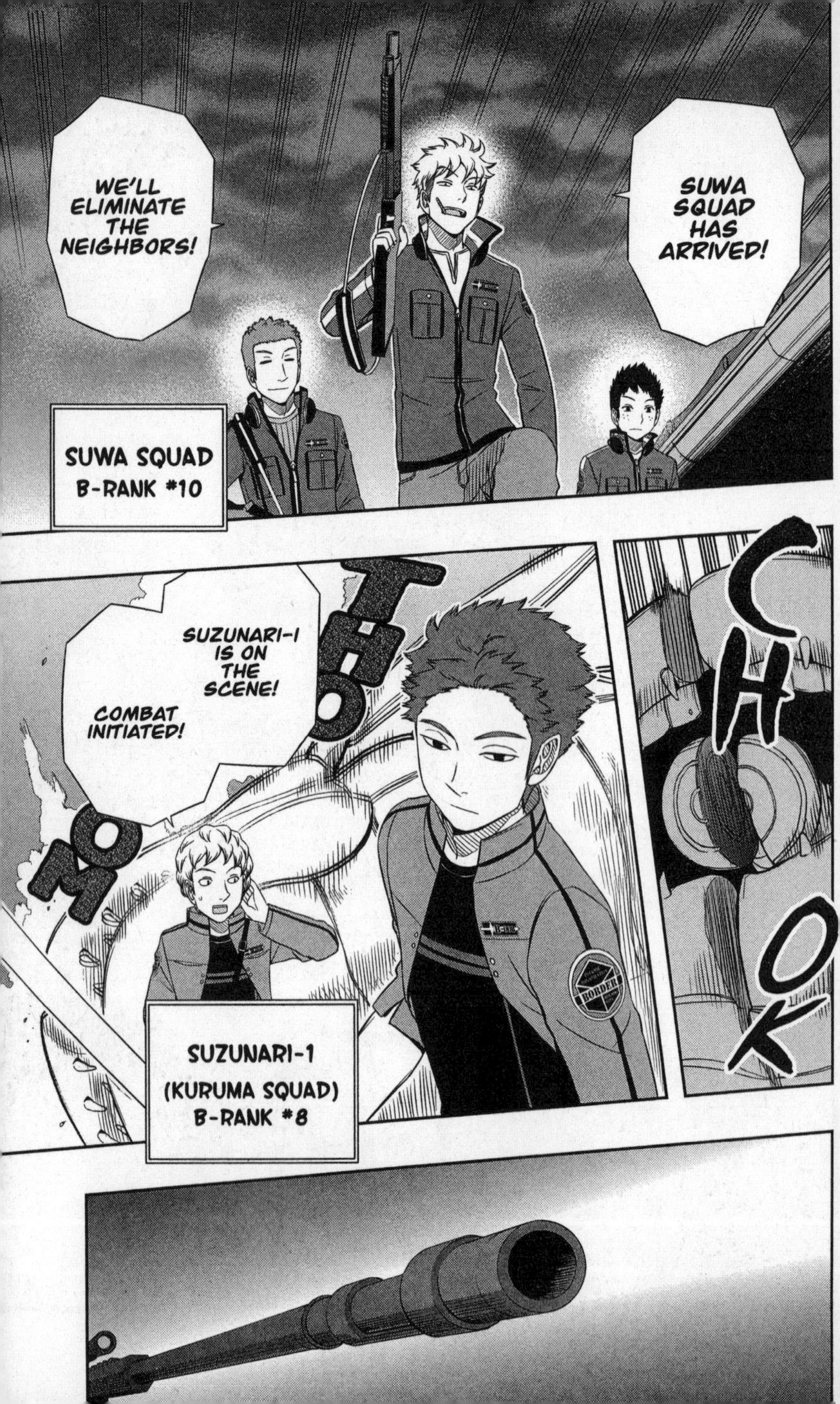
SUWA SQUAD HAS ARRIVED!
WE'LL ELIMINATE THE NEIGHBORS!
SUWA SQUAD B-RANK #10
CHOK
THOOM
SUZUNARI-1 IS ON THE SCENE!
COMBAT INITIATED!
SUZUNARI-1 (KURUMA SQUAD) B-RANK #8

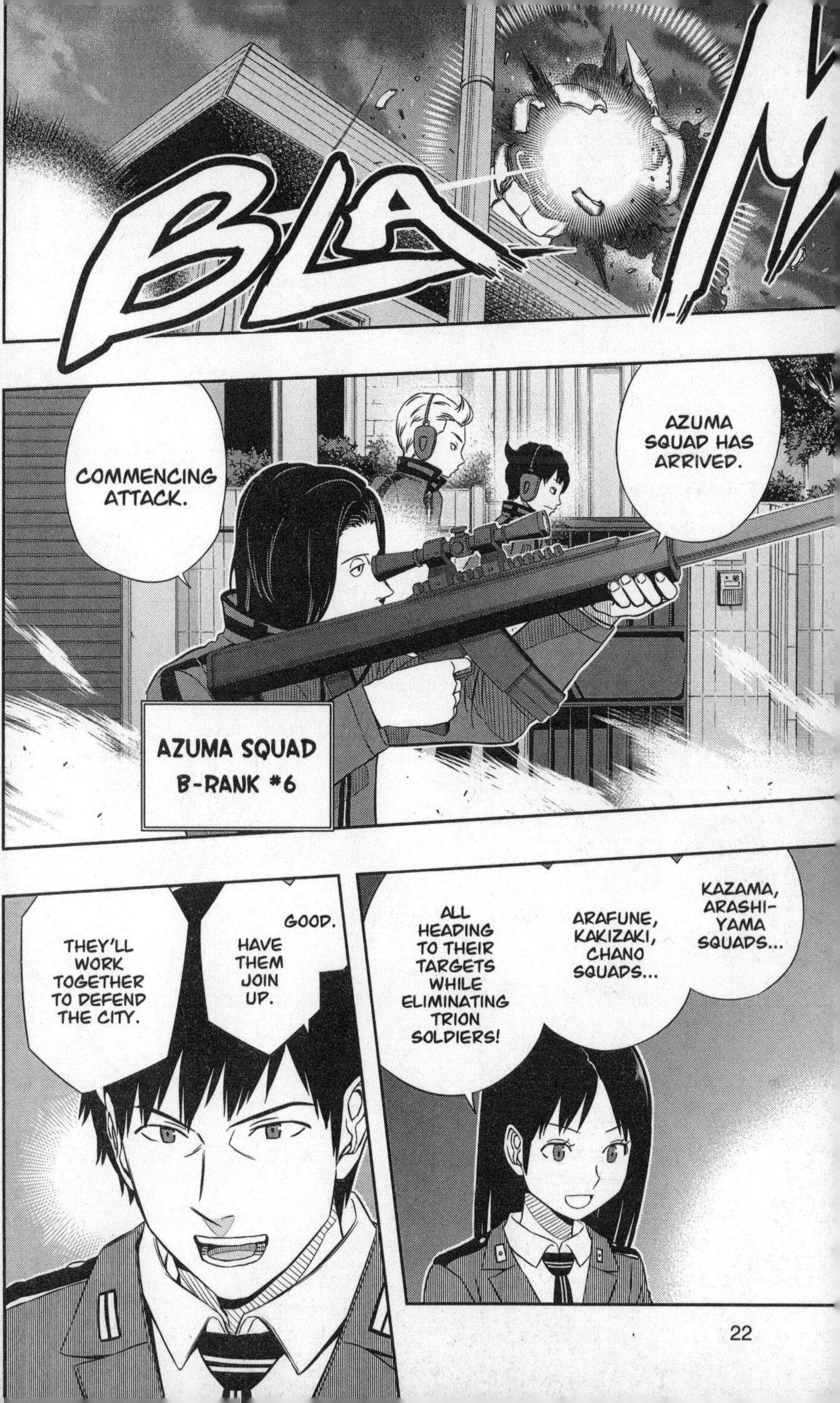
BLAM
AZUMA SQUAD HAS ARRIVED.
COMMENCING ATTACK.
AZUMA SQUAD B-RANK #6
KAZAMA, ARASHI-YAMA SQUADS...
ARAFUNE, KAKIZAKI, CHANO SQUADS...
ALL HEADING TO THEIR TARGETS WHILE ELIMINATING TRION SOLDIERS!
GOOD.
HAVE THEM JOIN UP.
THEY'LL WORK TOGETHER TO DEFEND THE CITY.

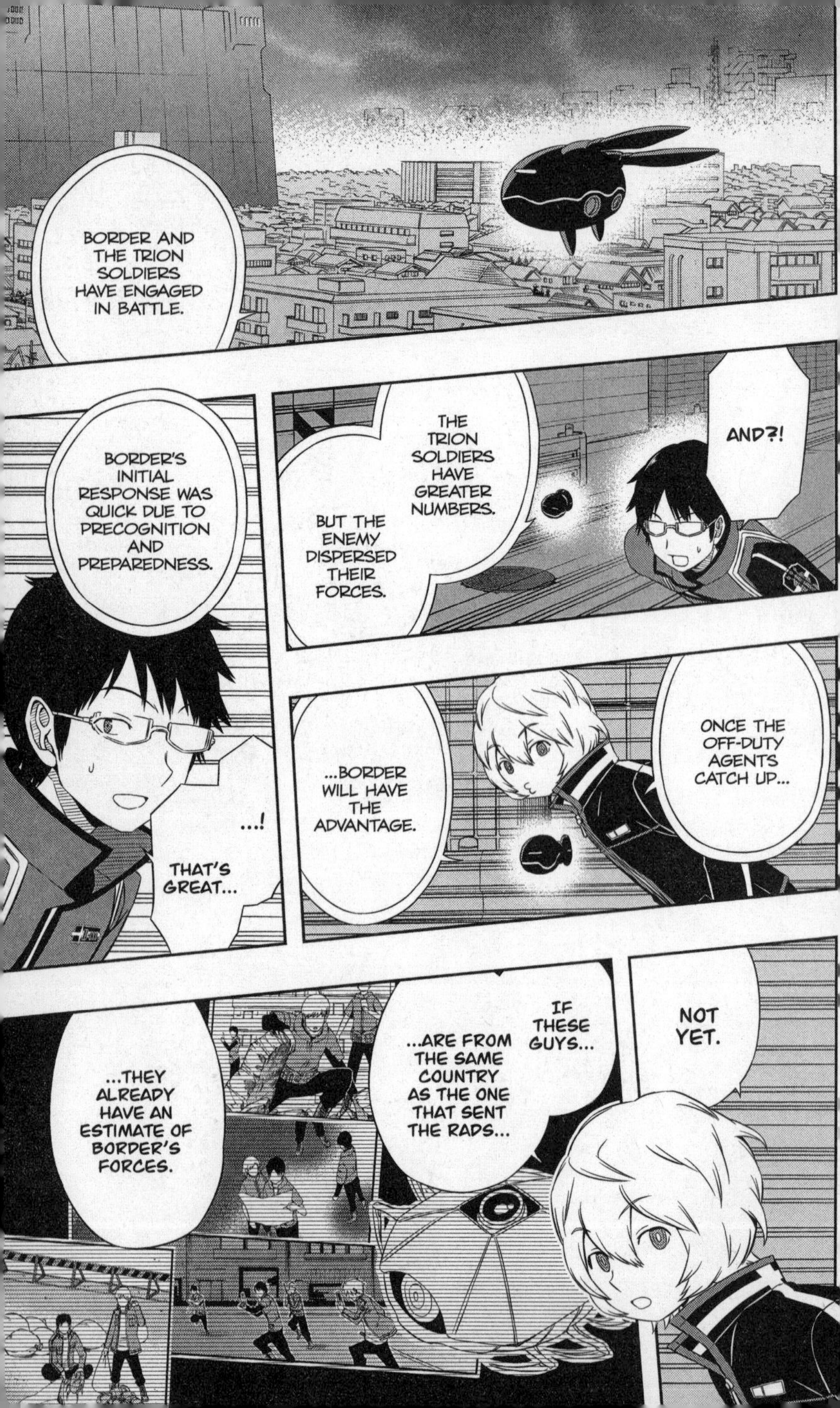
BORDER AND THE TRION SOLDIERS HAVE ENGAGED IN BATTLE.
AND?!
THE TRION SOLDIERS HAVE GREATER NUMBERS.
BUT THE ENEMY DISPERSED THEIR FORCES.
ONCE THE OFF-DUTY AGENTS CATCH UP...
...BORDER WILL HAVE THE ADVANTAGE.
BORDER'S INITIAL RESPONSE WAS QUICK DUE TO PRECOGNITION AND PREPAREDNESS.
...!
THAT'S GREAT...
NOT YET.
IF THESE GUYS...
...ARE FROM THE SAME COUNTRY AS THE ONE THAT SENT THE RADS...
...THEY ALREADY HAVE AN ESTIMATE OF BORDER'S FORCES.

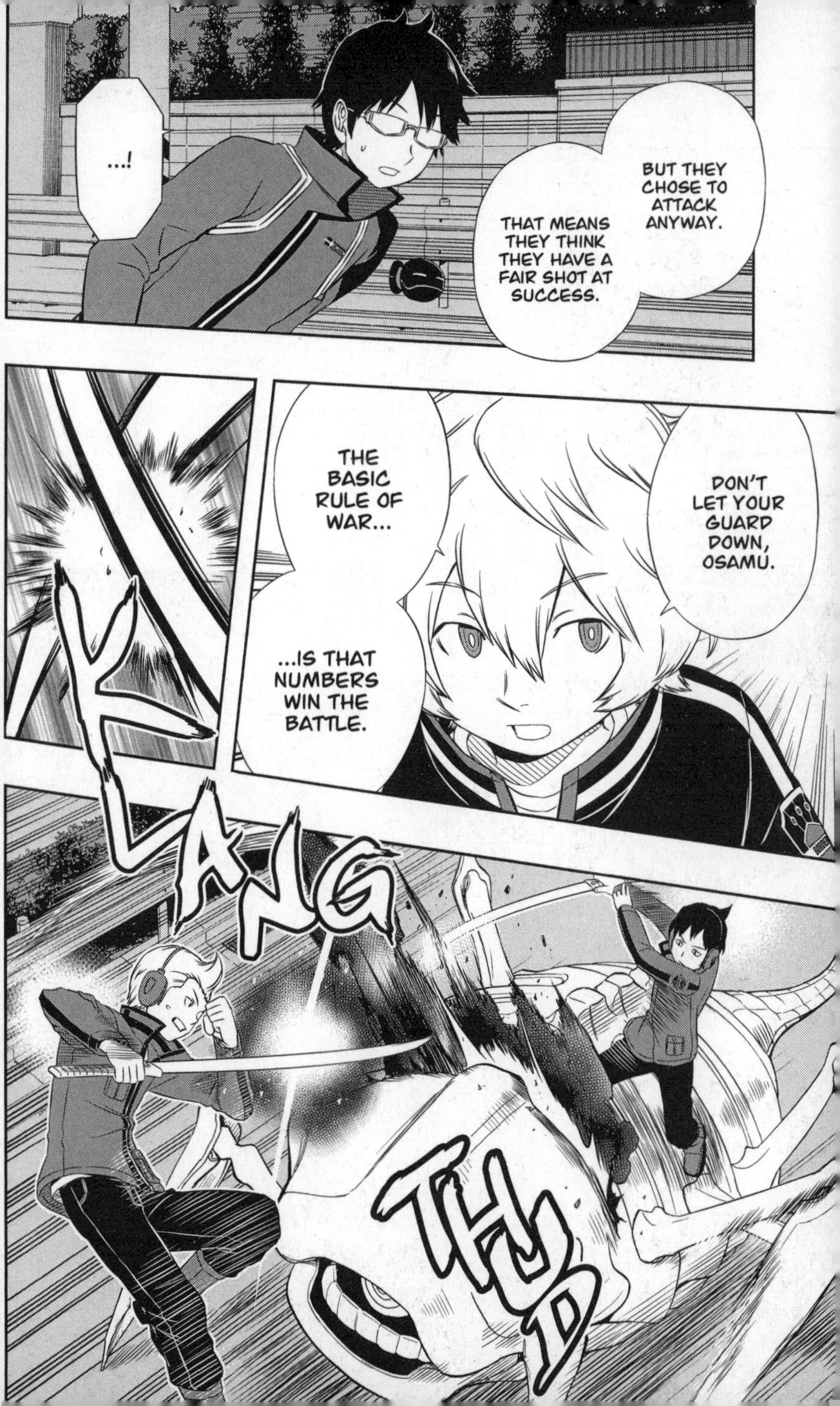
BUT THEY CHOSE TO ATTACK ANYWAY.
THAT MEANS THEY THINK THEY HAVE A FAIR SHOT AT SUCCESS.
...!
DON'T LET YOUR GUARD DOWN, OSAMU.
THE BASIC RULE OF WAR...
...IS THAT NUMBERS WIN THE BATTLE.
KLANG
THUD

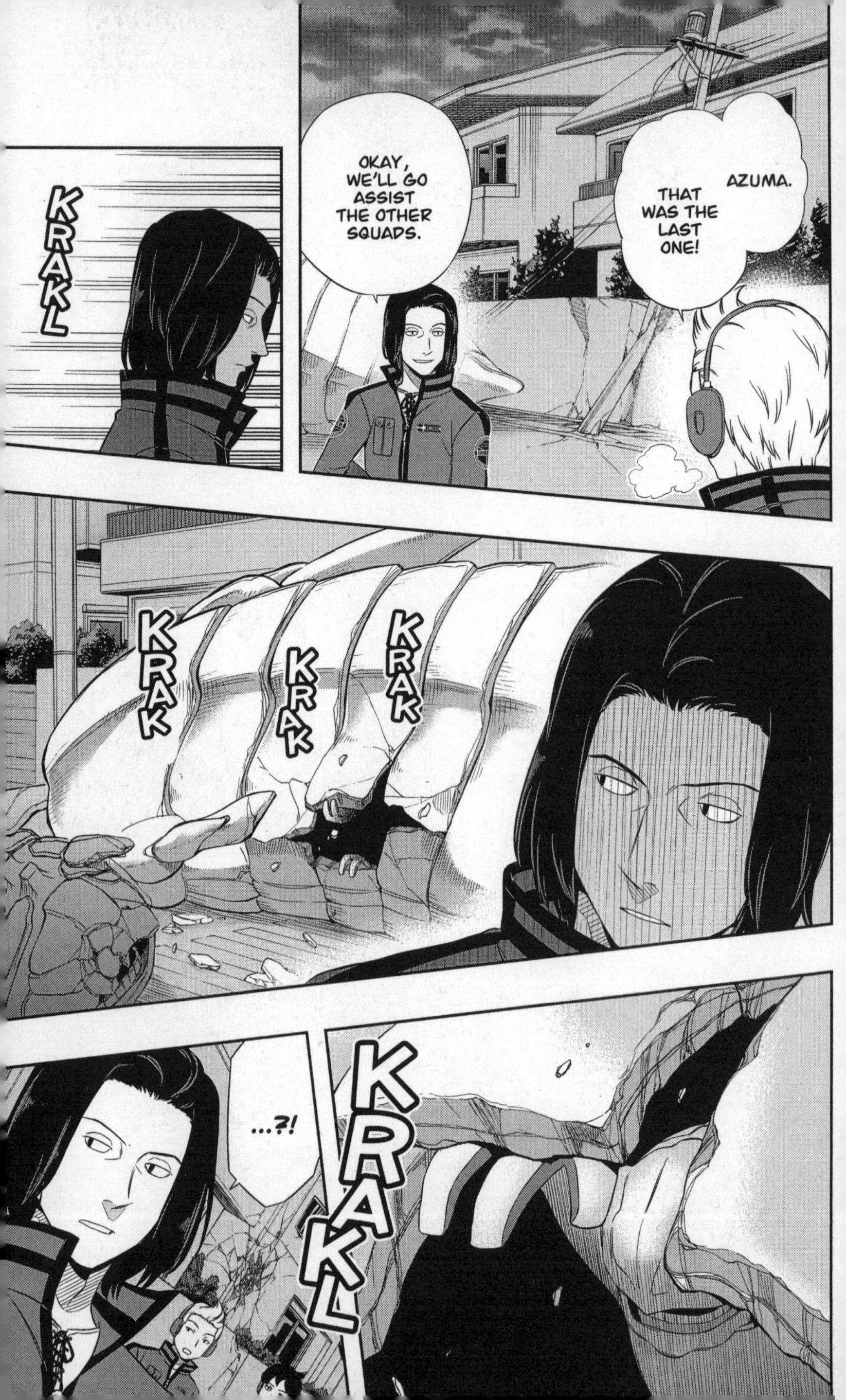
AZUMA. THAT WAS THE LAST ONE!
OKAY, WE'LL GO ASSIST THE OTHER SQUADS.
KRAKL
KRAK
KRAK
KRAK
KRAKL
...?!

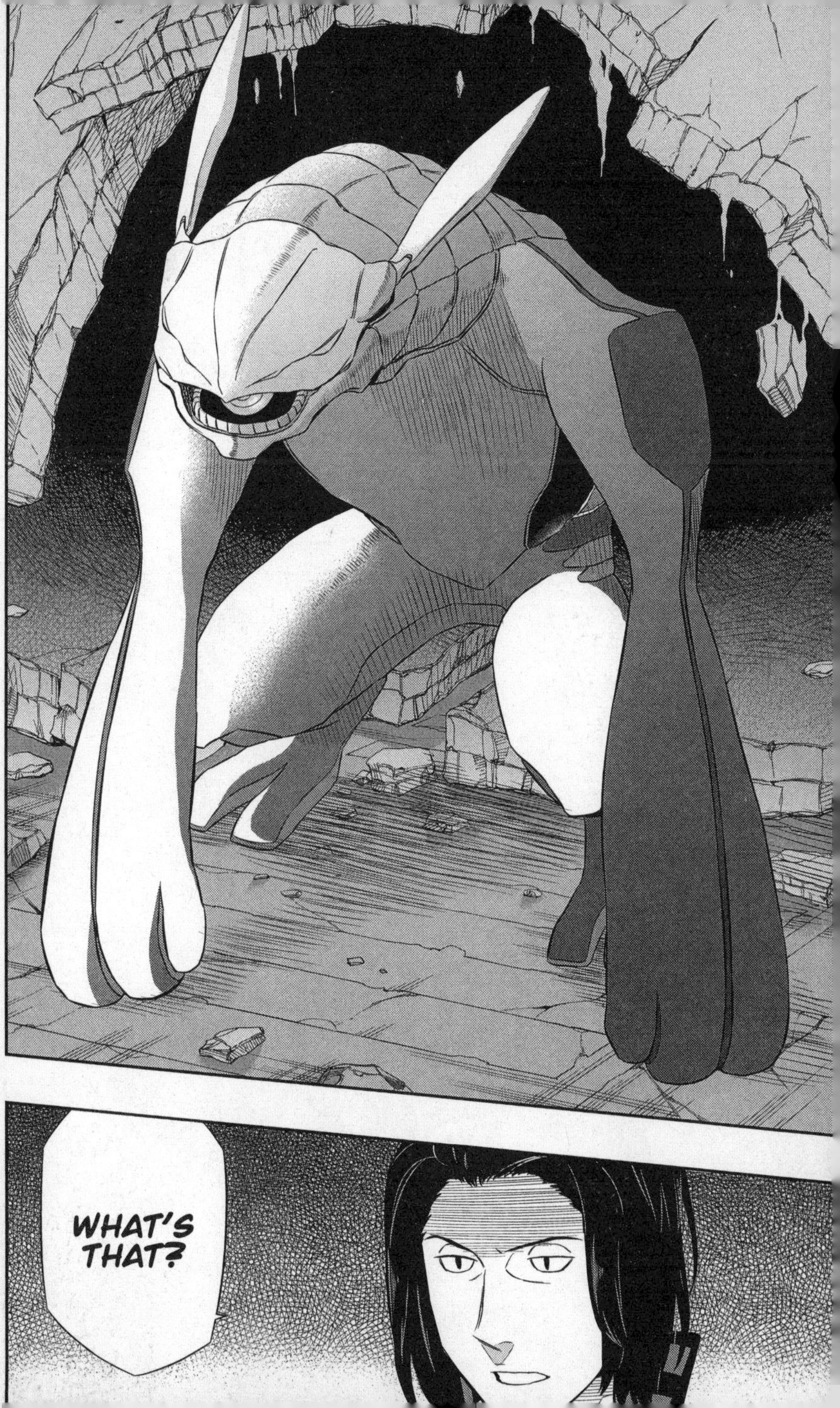
WHAT'S THAT?

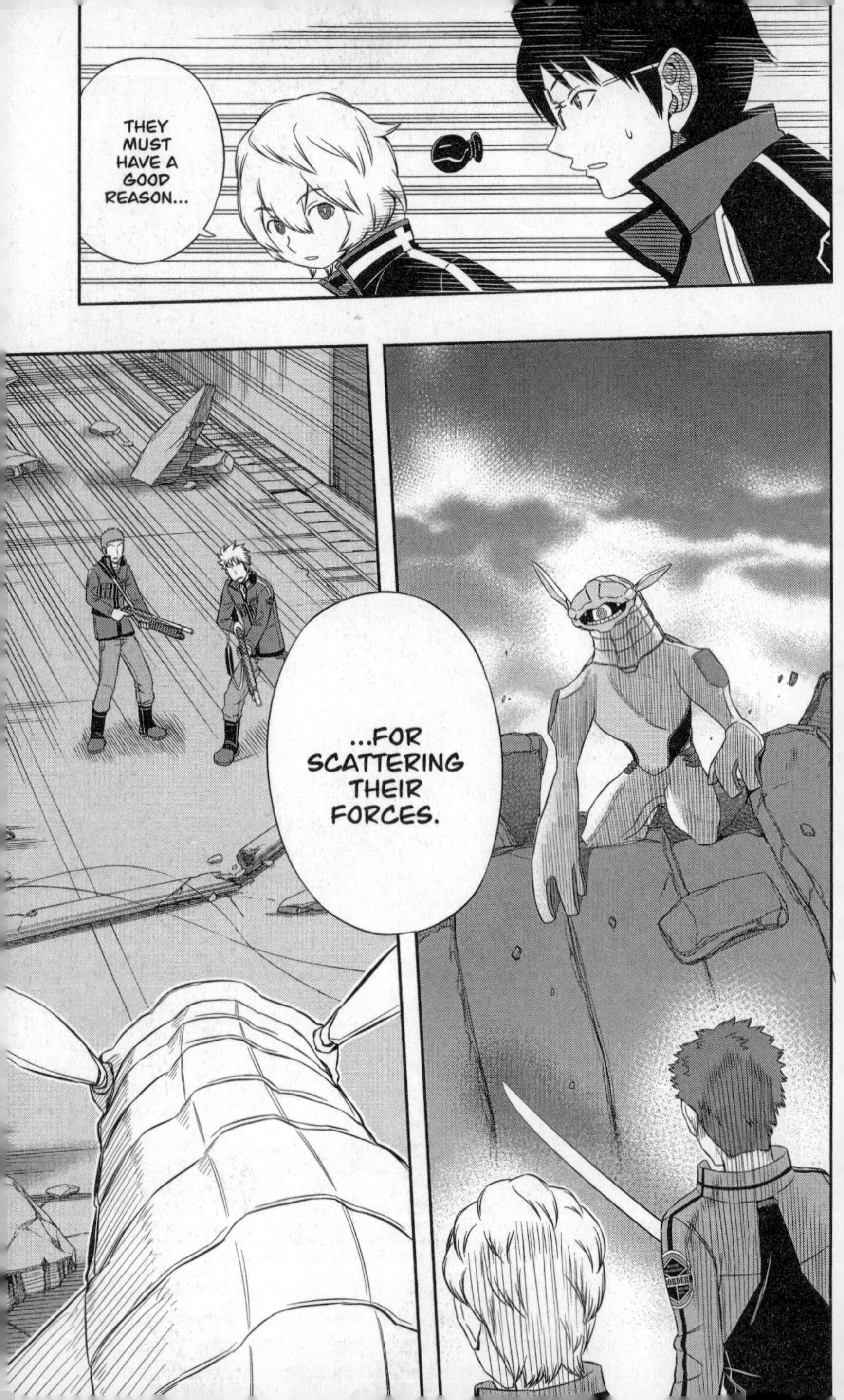
THEY MUST HAVE A GOOD REASON...
...FOR SCATTERING THEIR FORCES.

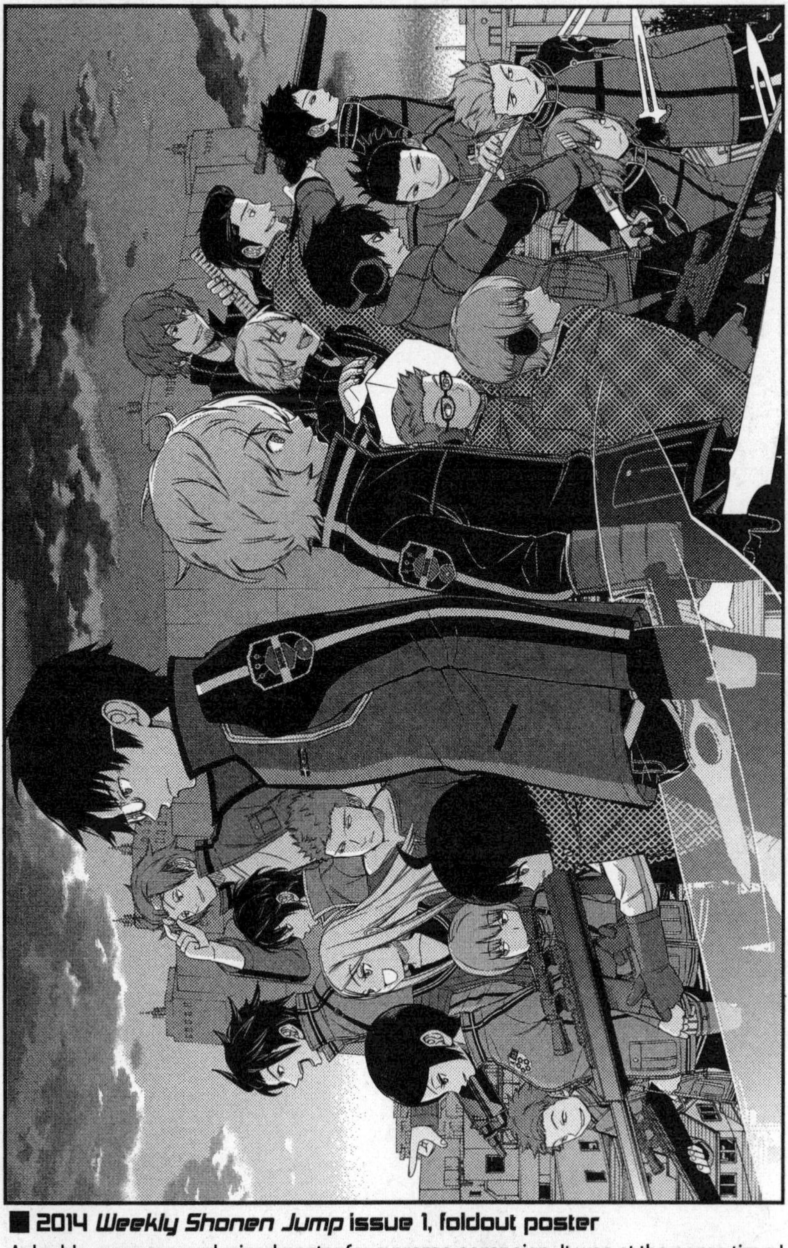

■ 2014 *Weekly Shonen Jump* issue 1, foldout poster

A double-page-spread-sized poster for a promo campaign. It was at the same time I was working on the center color page, so I had zero time, but my editor suggested an "everyone together!" kind of thing. So it became the piece with the most characters I've ever done at once. There are no women on the right side.

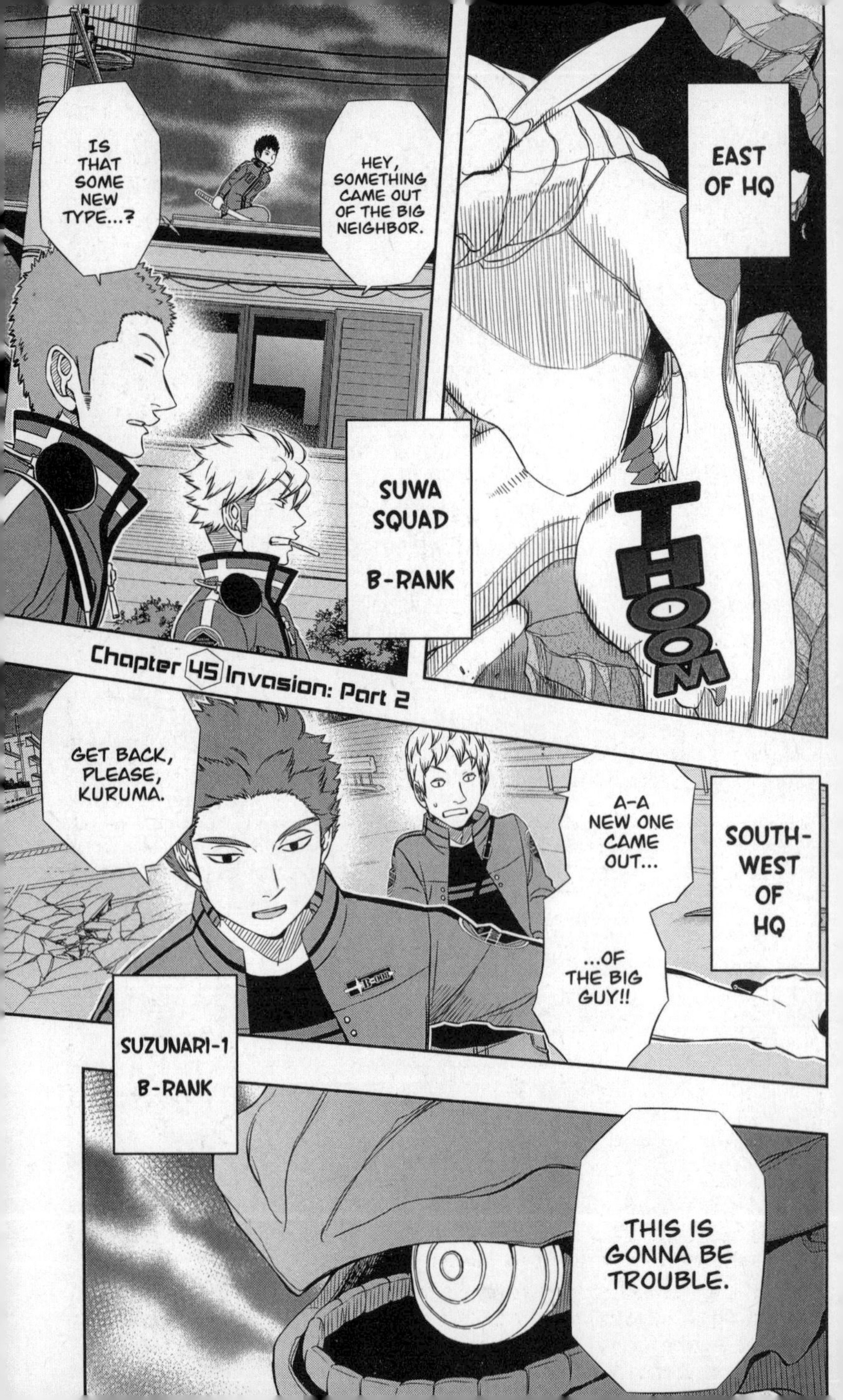
EAST OF HQ
THOOM
HEY, SOMETHING CAME OUT OF THE BIG NEIGHBOR.
IS THAT SOME NEW TYPE...?
SUWA SQUAD
B-RANK
Chapter 45 Invasion: Part 2
SOUTH-WEST OF HQ
A-A NEW ONE CAME OUT...
...OF THE BIG GUY!!
GET BACK, PLEASE, KURUMA.
SUZUNARI-1
B-RANK
THIS IS GONNA BE TROUBLE.

Chapter 45 Invasion: Part 2

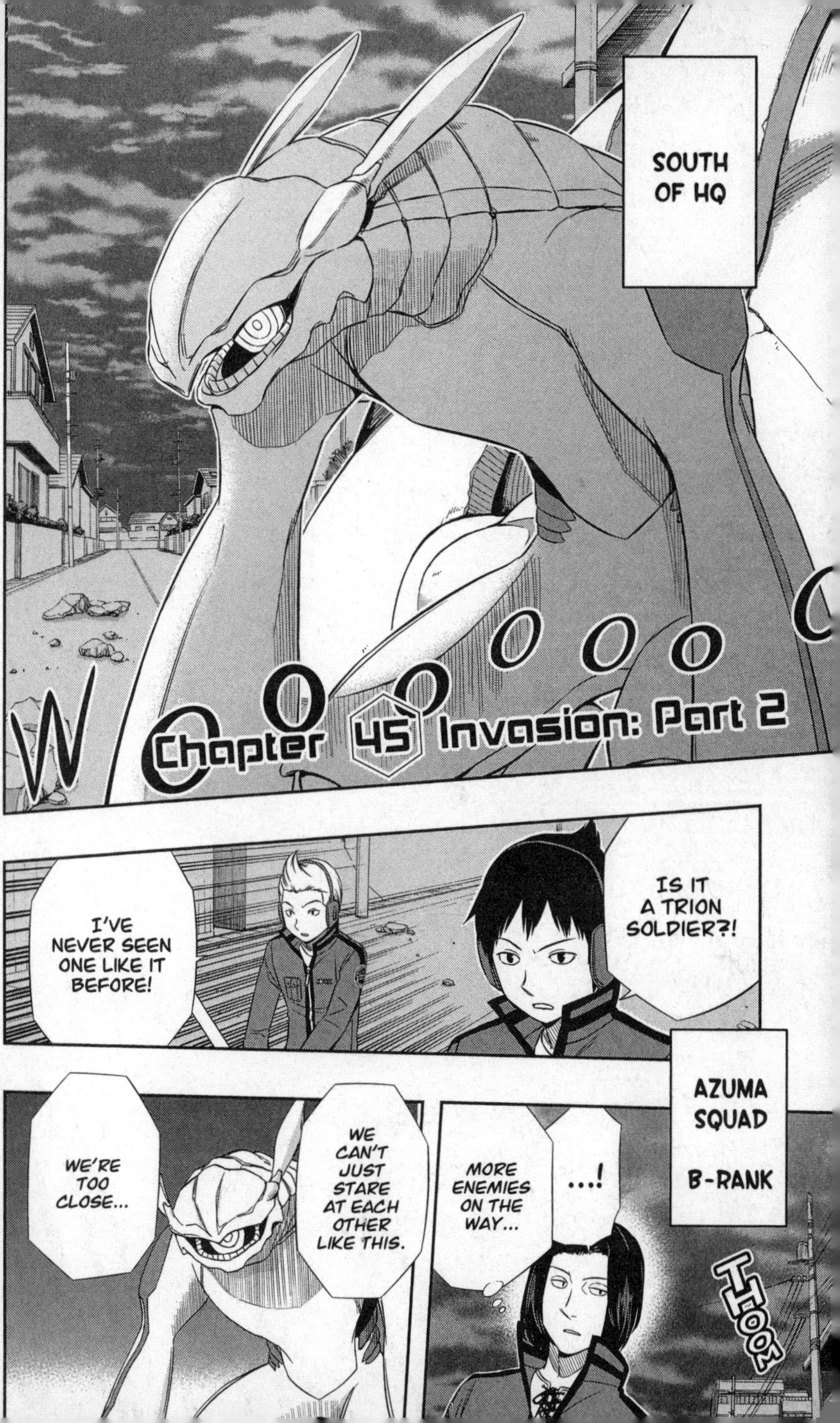
SOUTH OF HQ
WOOOOOOO
IS IT A TRION SOLDIER?!
I'VE NEVER SEEN ONE LIKE IT BEFORE!
AZUMA SQUAD
B-RANK
...!
MORE ENEMIES ON THE WAY...
THOOM
WE CAN'T JUST STARE AT EACH OTHER LIKE THIS.
WE'RE TOO CLOSE...

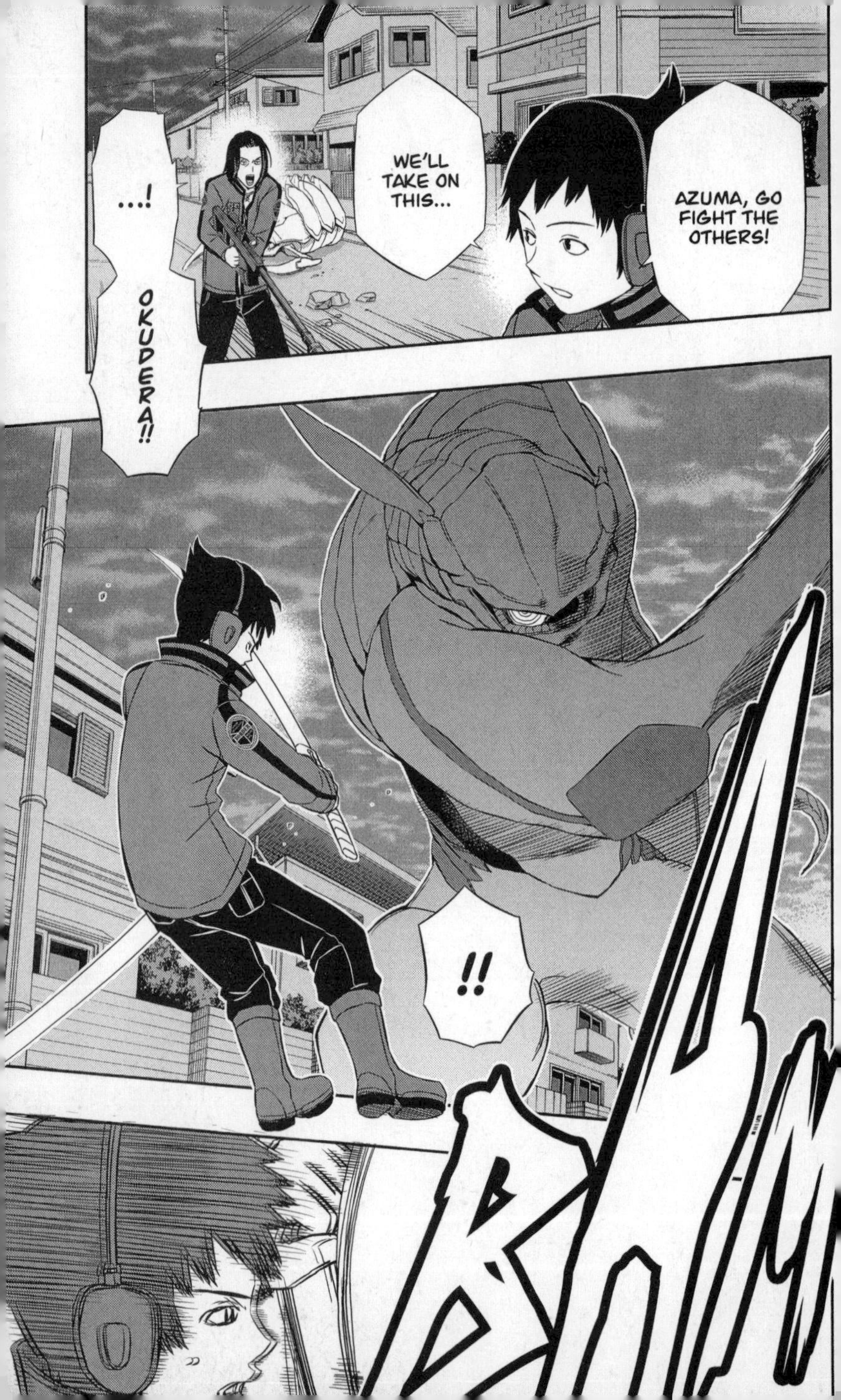
AZUMA, GO FIGHT THE OTHERS!
WE'LL TAKE ON THIS...
...!
OKUDERA!!
!!

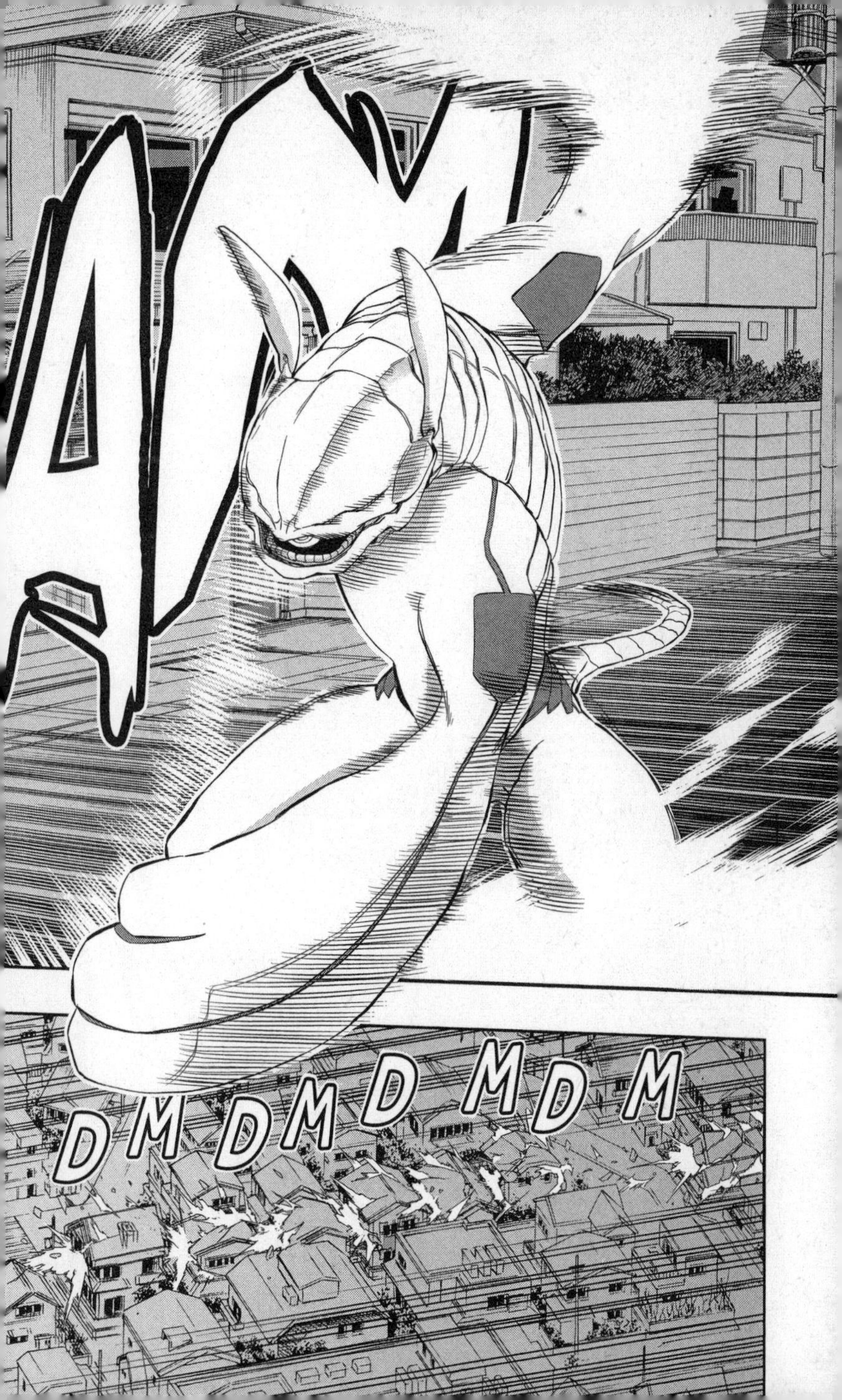
DMDMD MDM

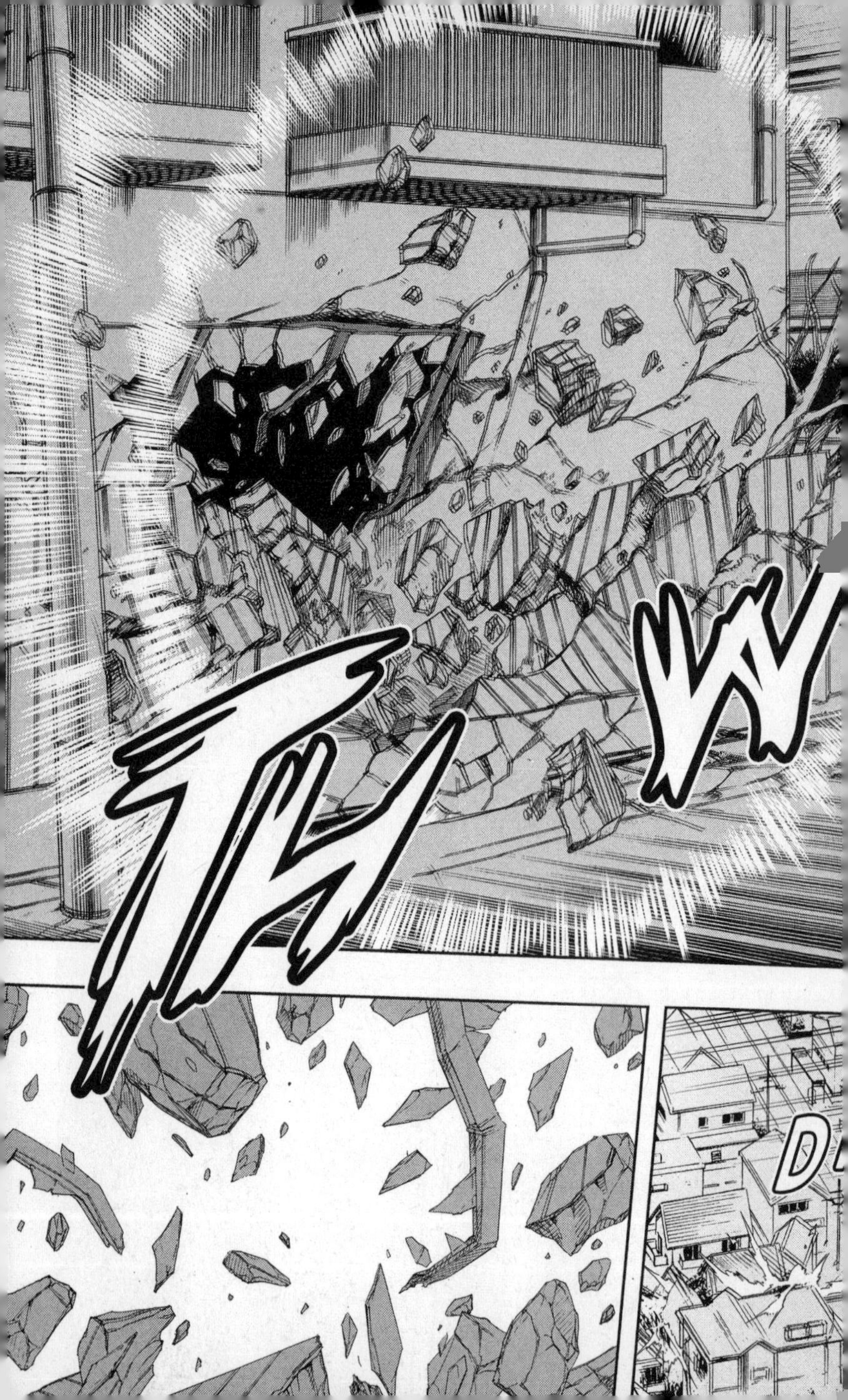

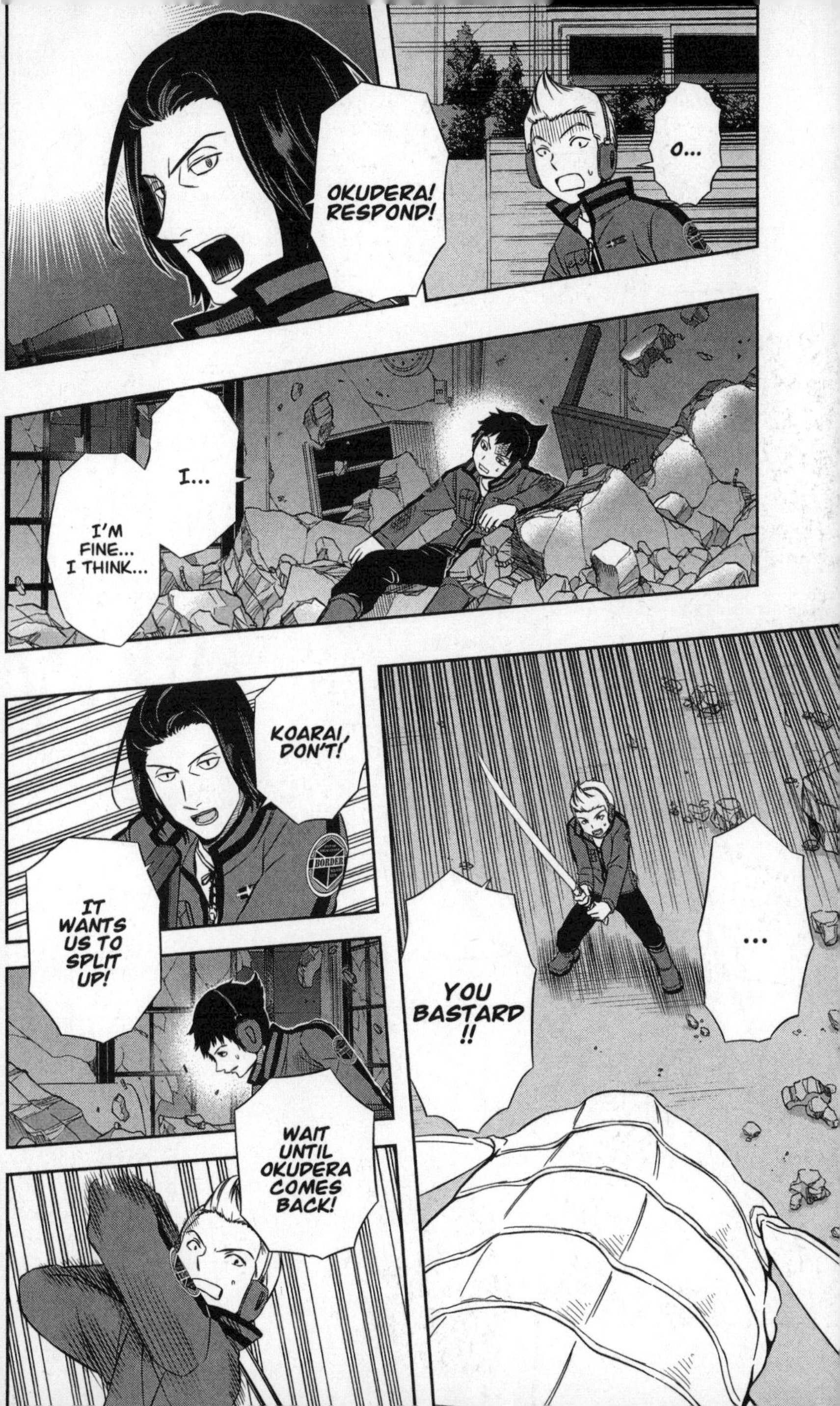
O...
OKUDERA! RESPOND!
I...
I'M FINE... I THINK...
...
YOU BASTARD!!
KOARAI, DON'T!
IT WANTS US TO SPLIT UP!
WAIT UNTIL OKUDERA COMES BACK!

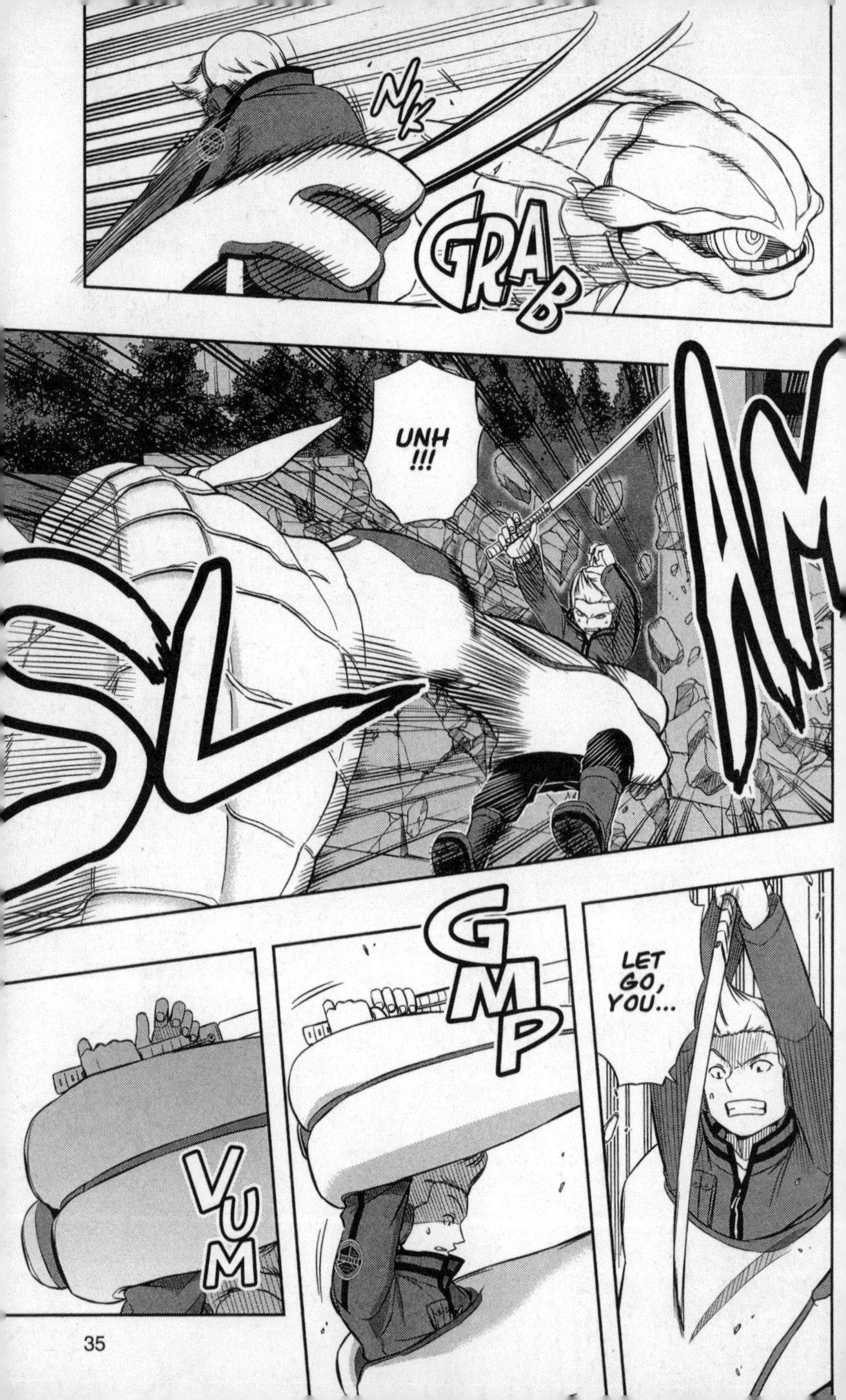
NK
GRAB
UNH !!!
LET GO, YOU...
GMP
VUM

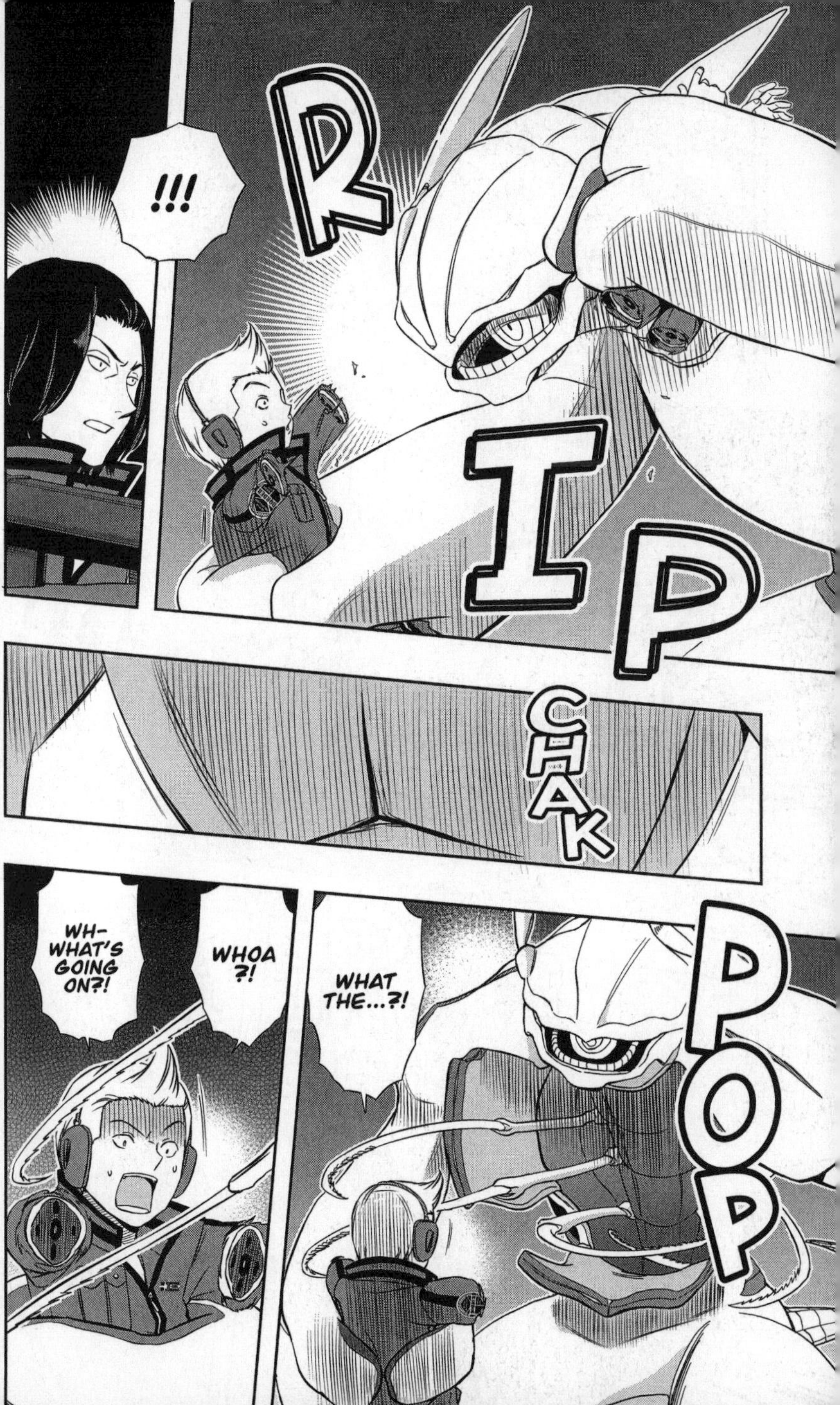
RIP
!!!
CHAK
POP
WHAT THE...?!
WHOA ?!
WH- WHAT'S GOING ON?!

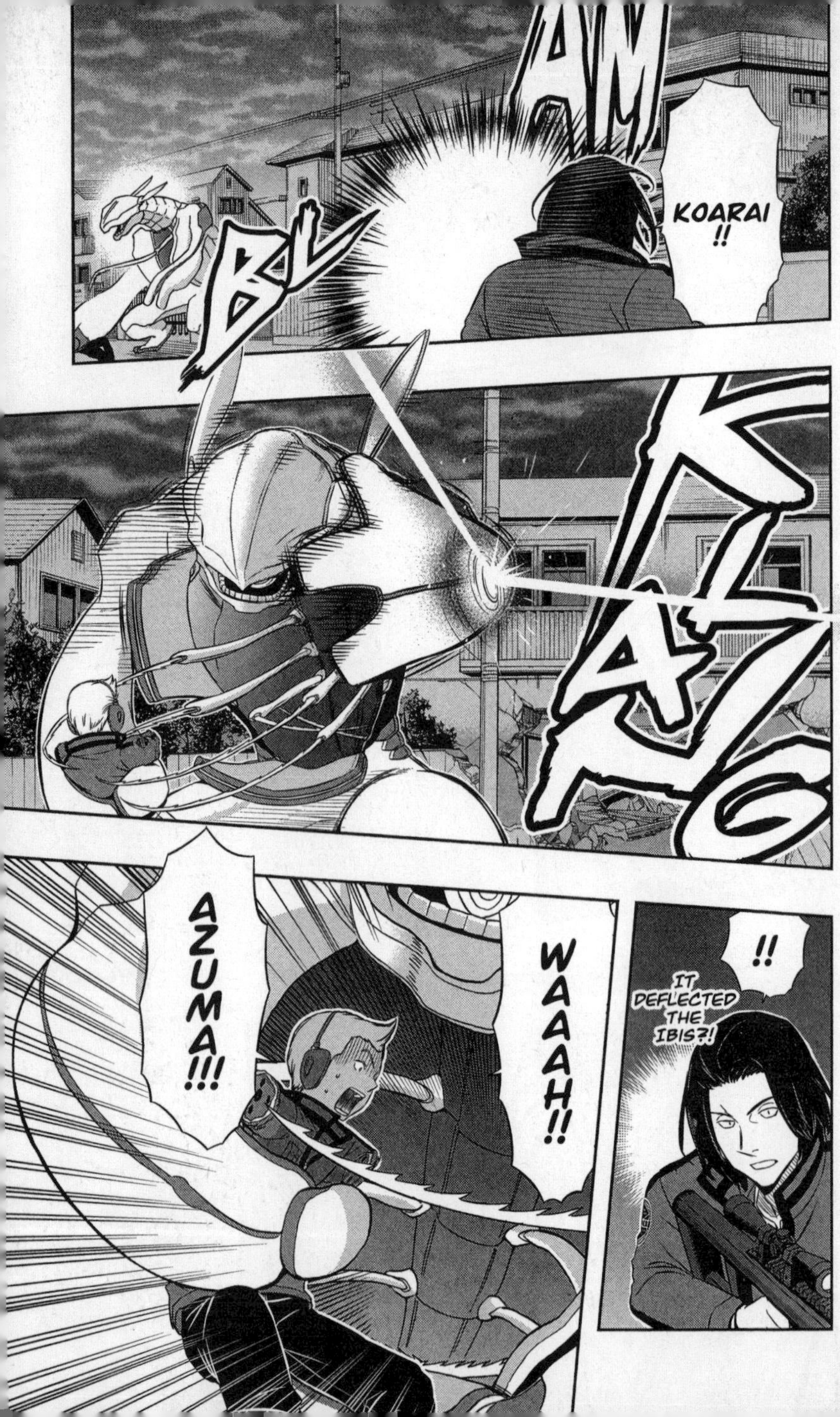
KOARAI !!
!!
IT DEFLECTED THE IBIS?!
WAAAAH!!
AZUMA!!!

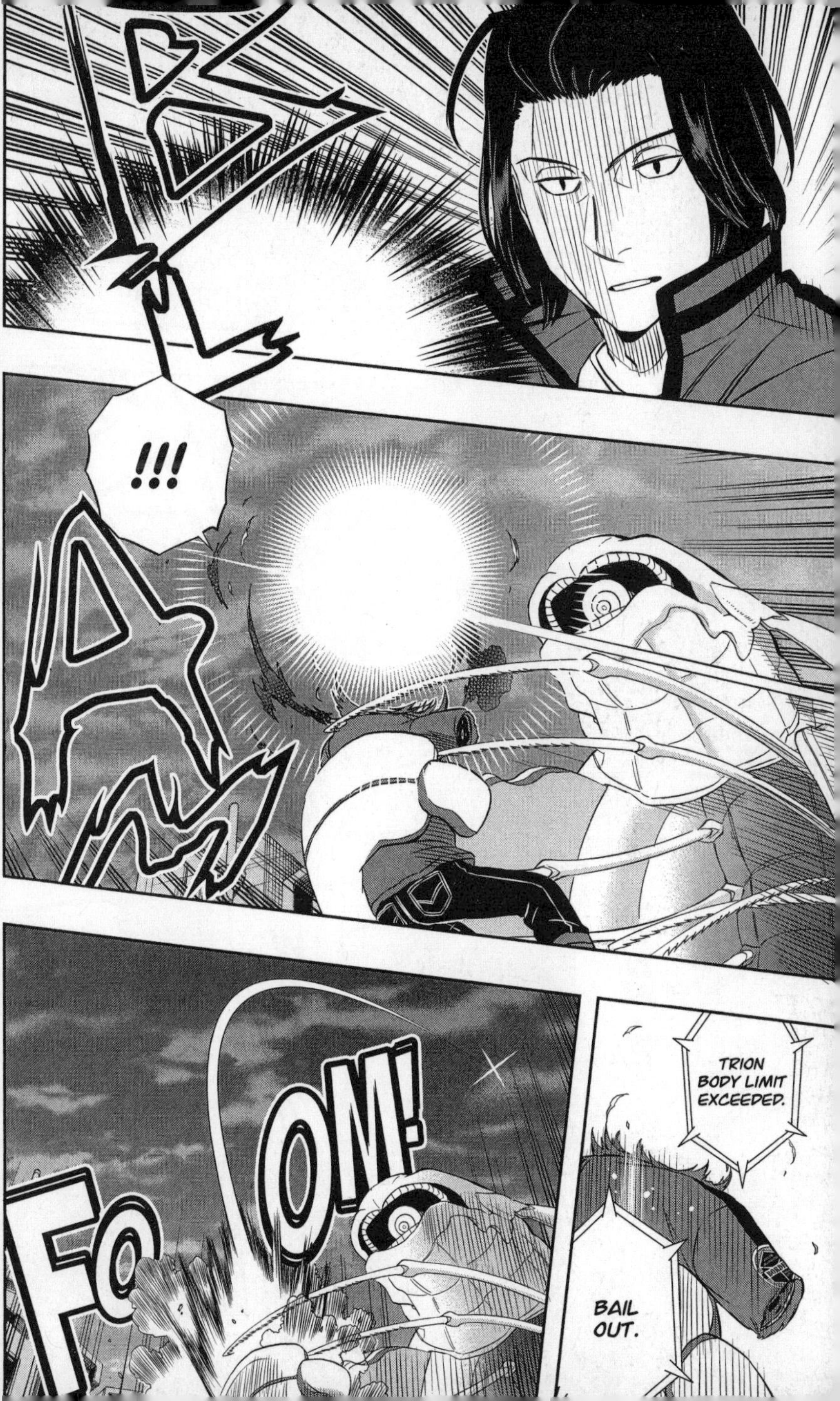
!!!
TRION BODY LIMIT EXCEEDED.
BAIL OUT.
FOOM!

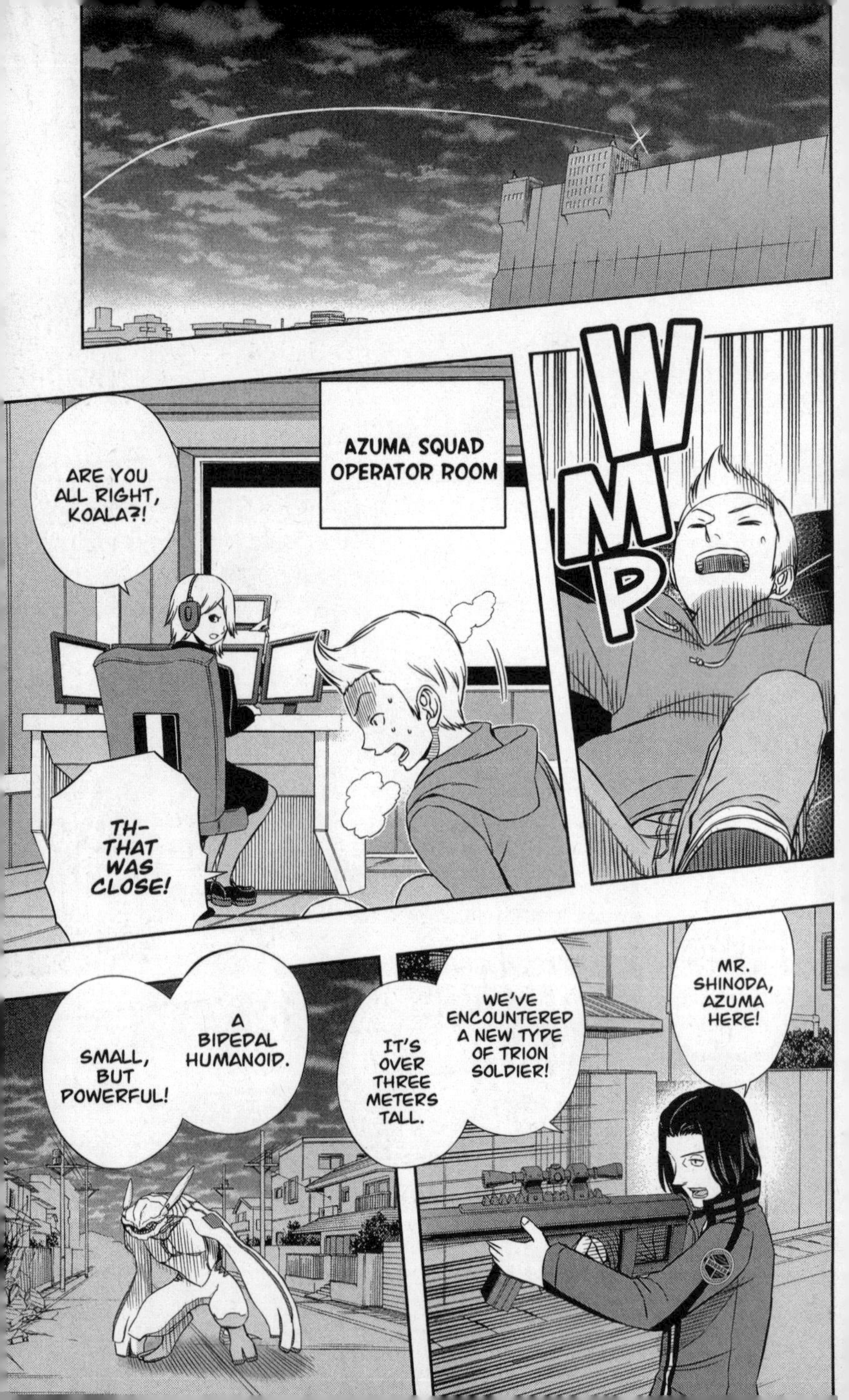
WMP
AZUMA SQUAD OPERATOR ROOM
ARE YOU ALL RIGHT, KOALA?!
TH-THAT WAS CLOSE!
MR. SHINODA, AZUMA HERE!
WE'VE ENCOUNTERED A NEW TYPE OF TRION SOLDIER!
IT'S OVER THREE METERS TALL.
A BIPEDAL HUMANOID.
SMALL, BUT POWERFUL!

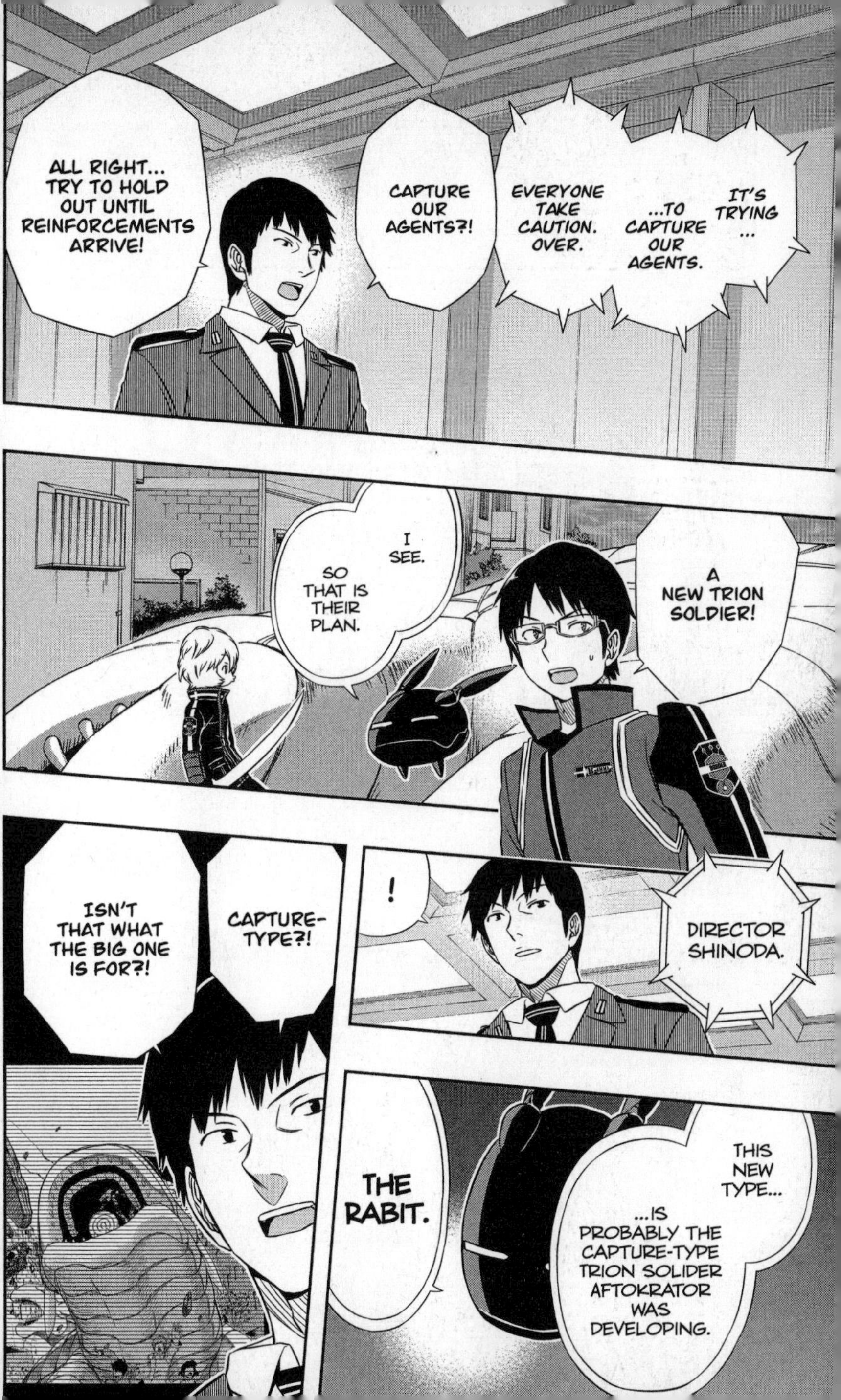
IT'S TRYING ...
...TO CAPTURE OUR AGENTS.
EVERYONE TAKE CAUTION. OVER.
CAPTURE OUR AGENTS?!
ALL RIGHT... TRY TO HOLD OUT UNTIL REINFORCEMENTS ARRIVE!
A NEW TRION SOLDIER!
I SEE.
SO THAT IS THEIR PLAN.
DIRECTOR SHINODA.
!
CAPTURE-TYPE?!
ISN'T THAT WHAT THE BIG ONE IS FOR?!
THIS NEW TYPE...
...IS PROBABLY THE CAPTURE-TYPE TRION SOLIDER AFTOKRATOR WAS DEVELOPING.
THE RABIT.

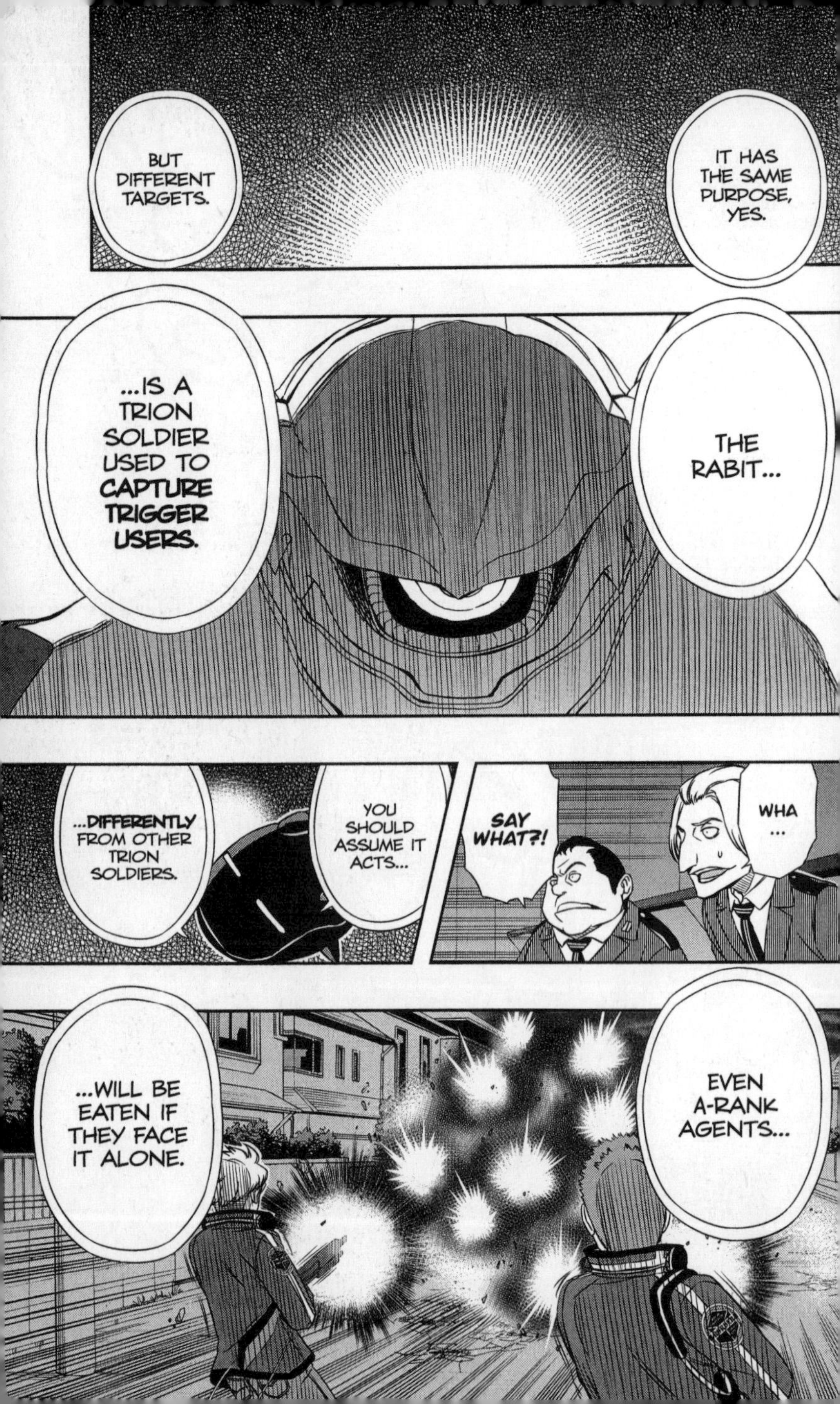
IT HAS THE SAME PURPOSE, YES.
BUT DIFFERENT TARGETS.
THE RABIT...
...IS A TRION SOLDIER USED TO **CAPTURE TRIGGER USERS.**
WHA ...
SAY WHAT?!
YOU SHOULD ASSUME IT ACTS...
...**DIFFERENTLY** FROM OTHER TRION SOLDIERS.
EVEN A-RANK AGENTS...
...WILL BE EATEN IF THEY FACE IT ALONE.

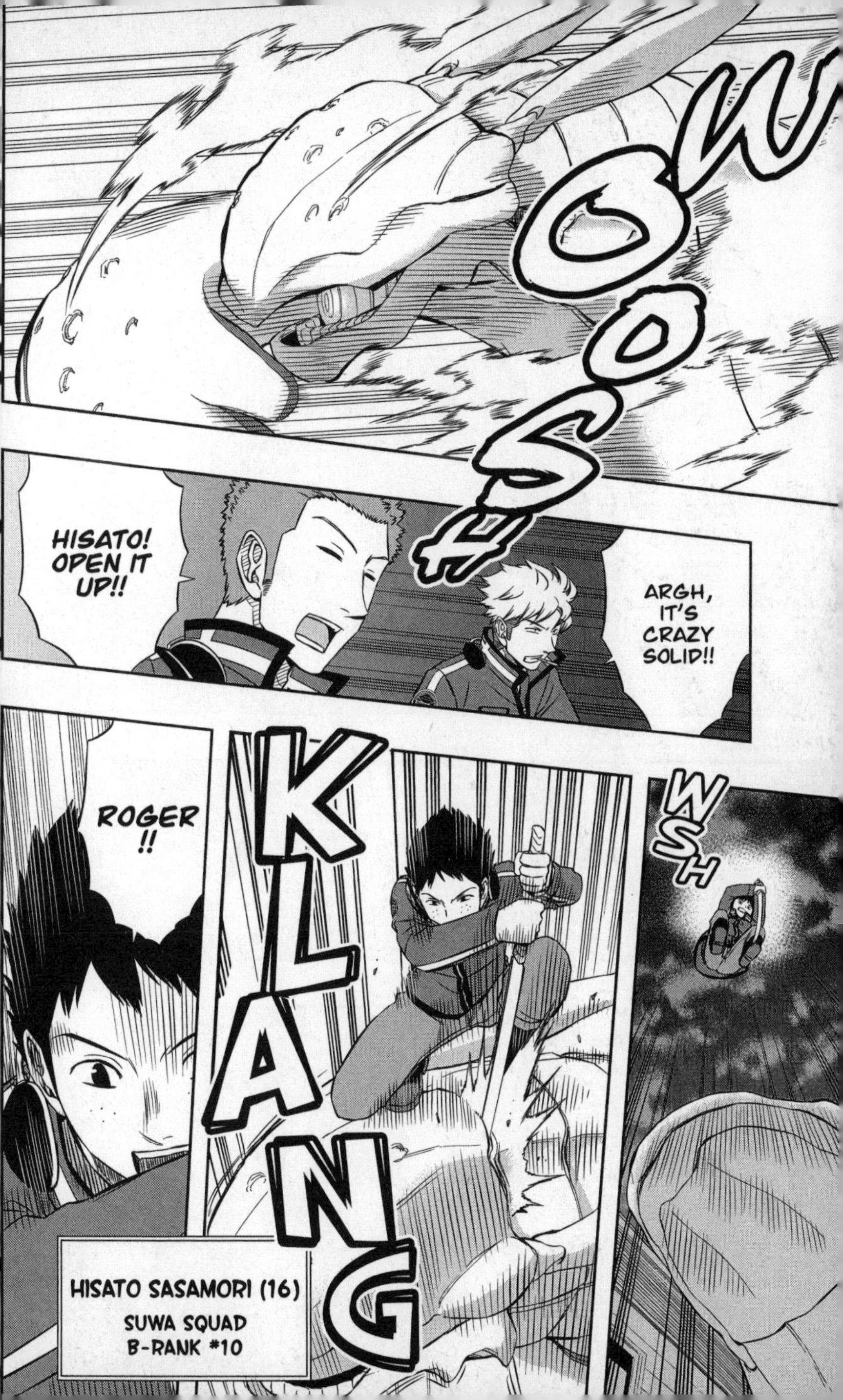
WHOOSH
ARGH, IT'S CRAZY SOLID!!
HISATO! OPEN IT UP!!
WSH
KLANG
ROGER!!
HISATO SASAMORI (16)
SUWA SQUAD
B-RANK #10

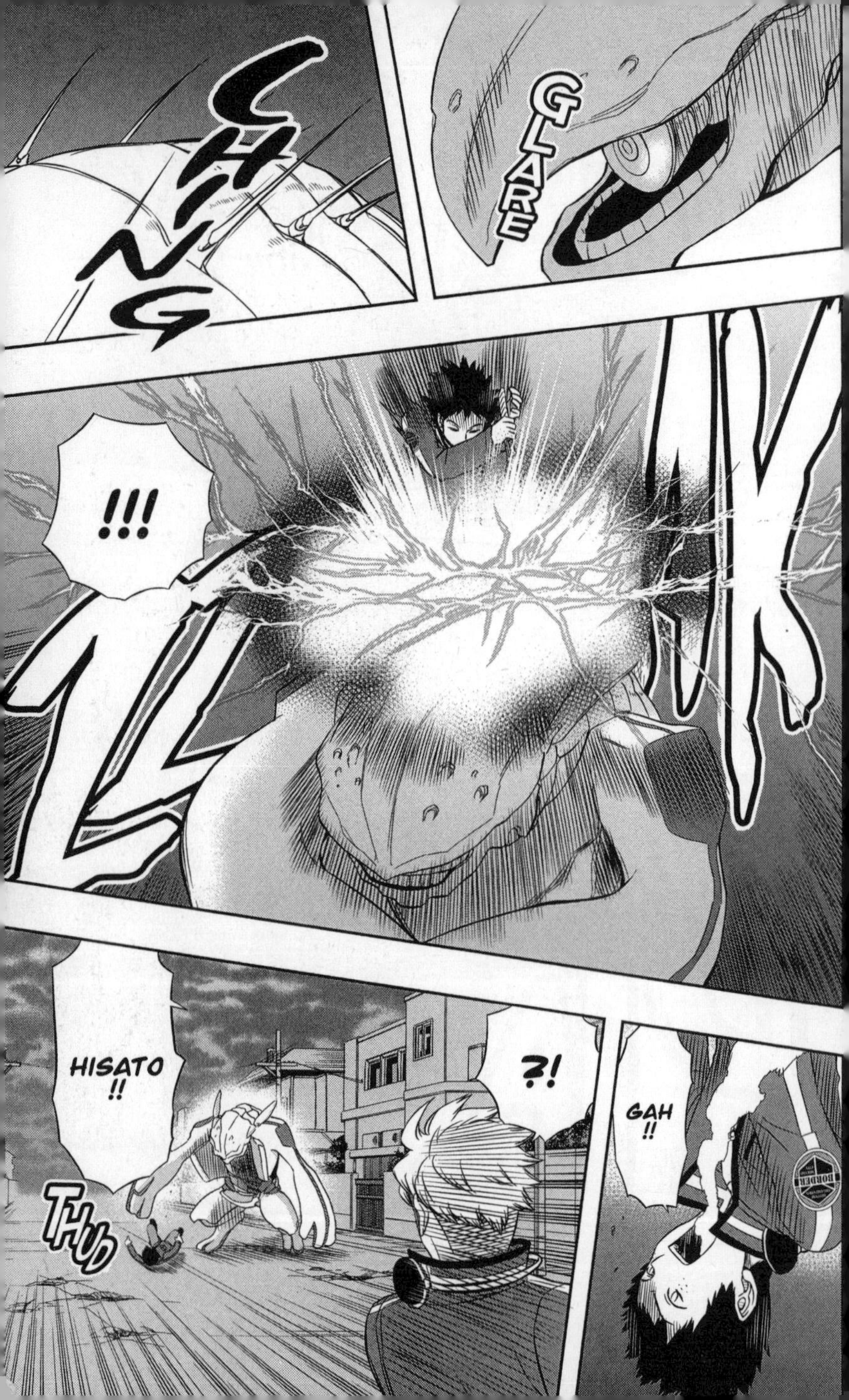
GLARE
CHING
!!!
GAH!!
?!
HISATO!!
THUD

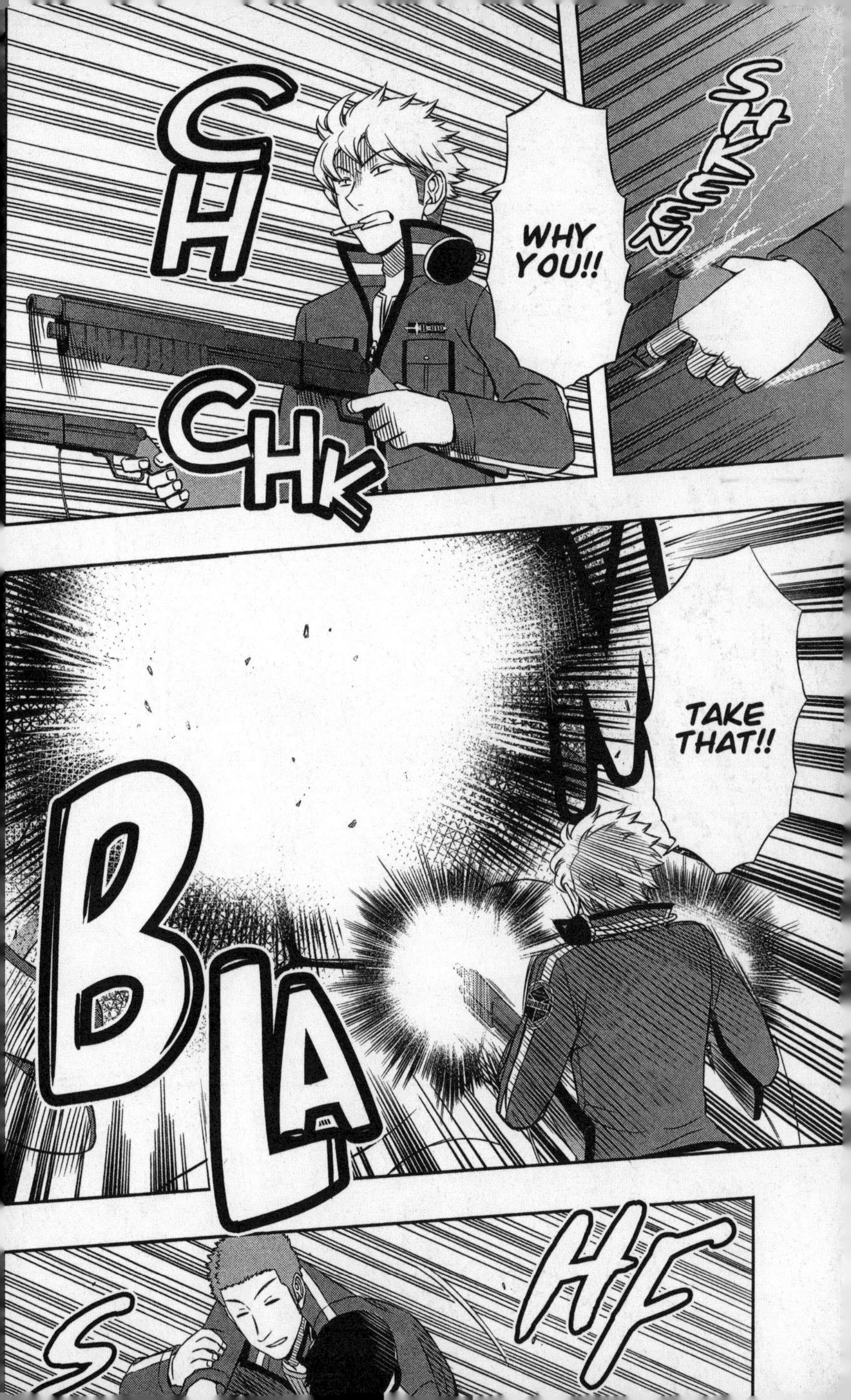
SHKEEN
WHY YOU!!
CH
CHK
TAKE THAT!!
BLA
HF
S

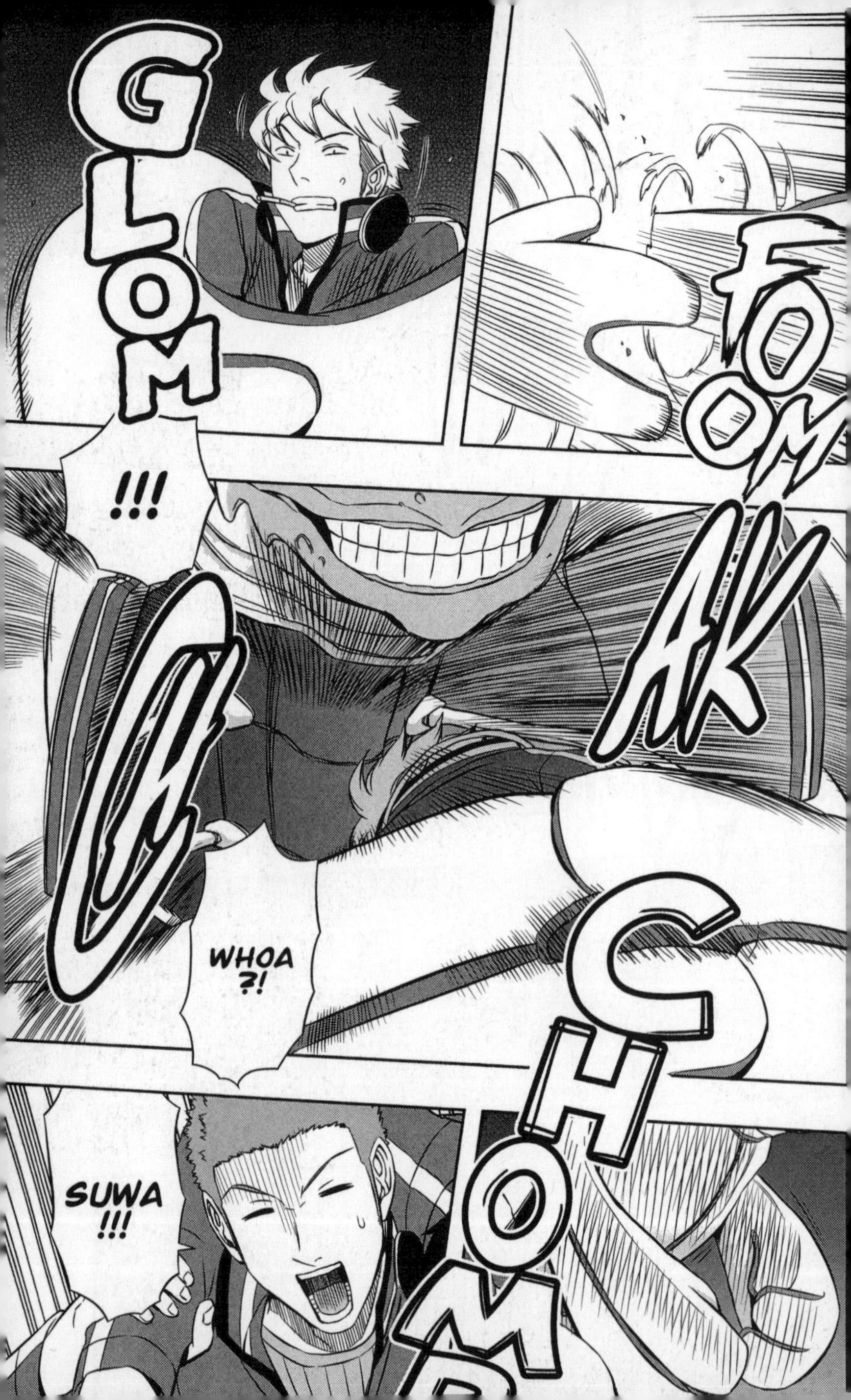
FOOM
GLOM
!!!
AK
WHOA ?!
CHOM
SUWA !!!

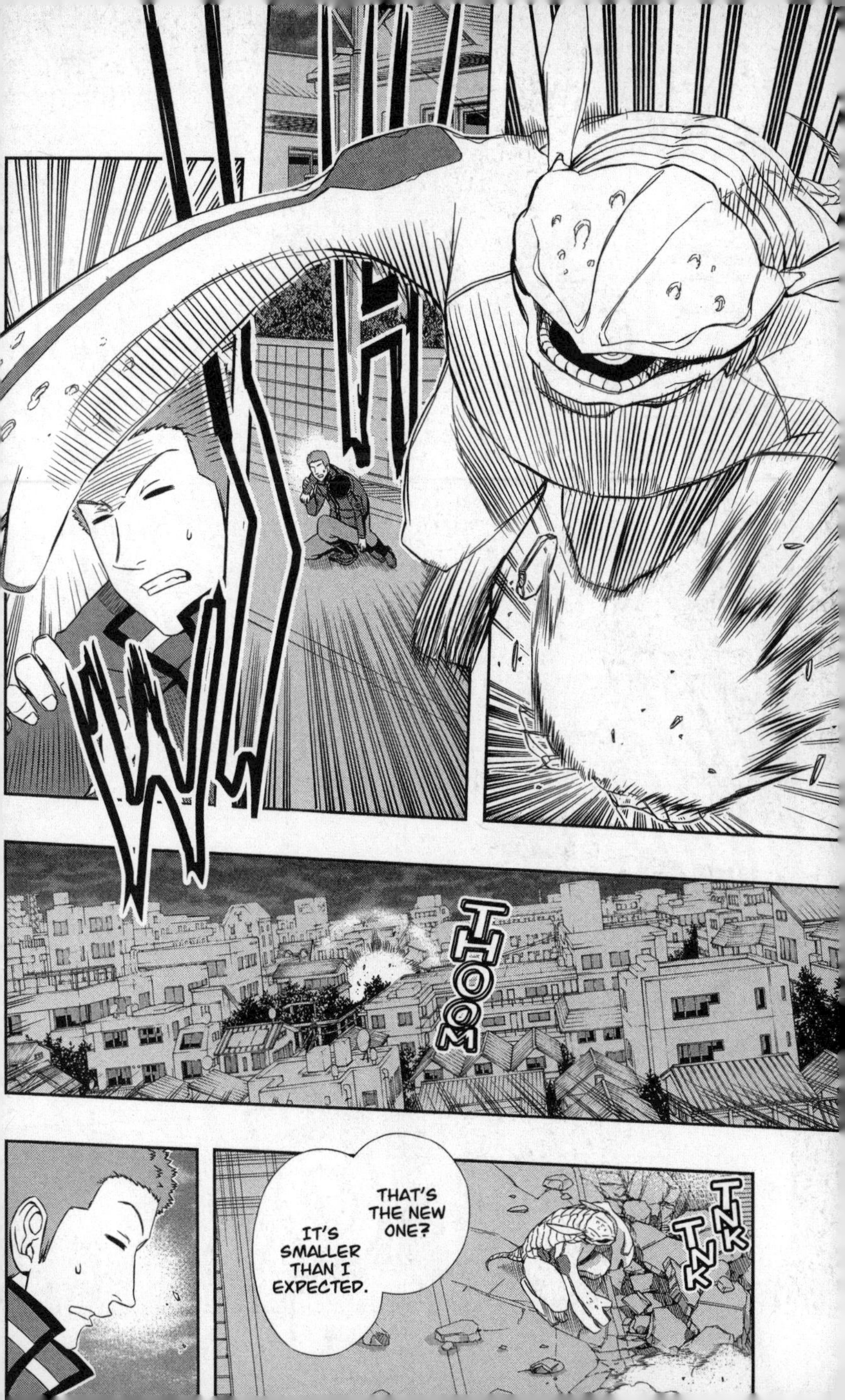
THOOM
TNK TNK
THAT'S THE NEW ONE?
IT'S SMALLER THAN I EXPECTED.

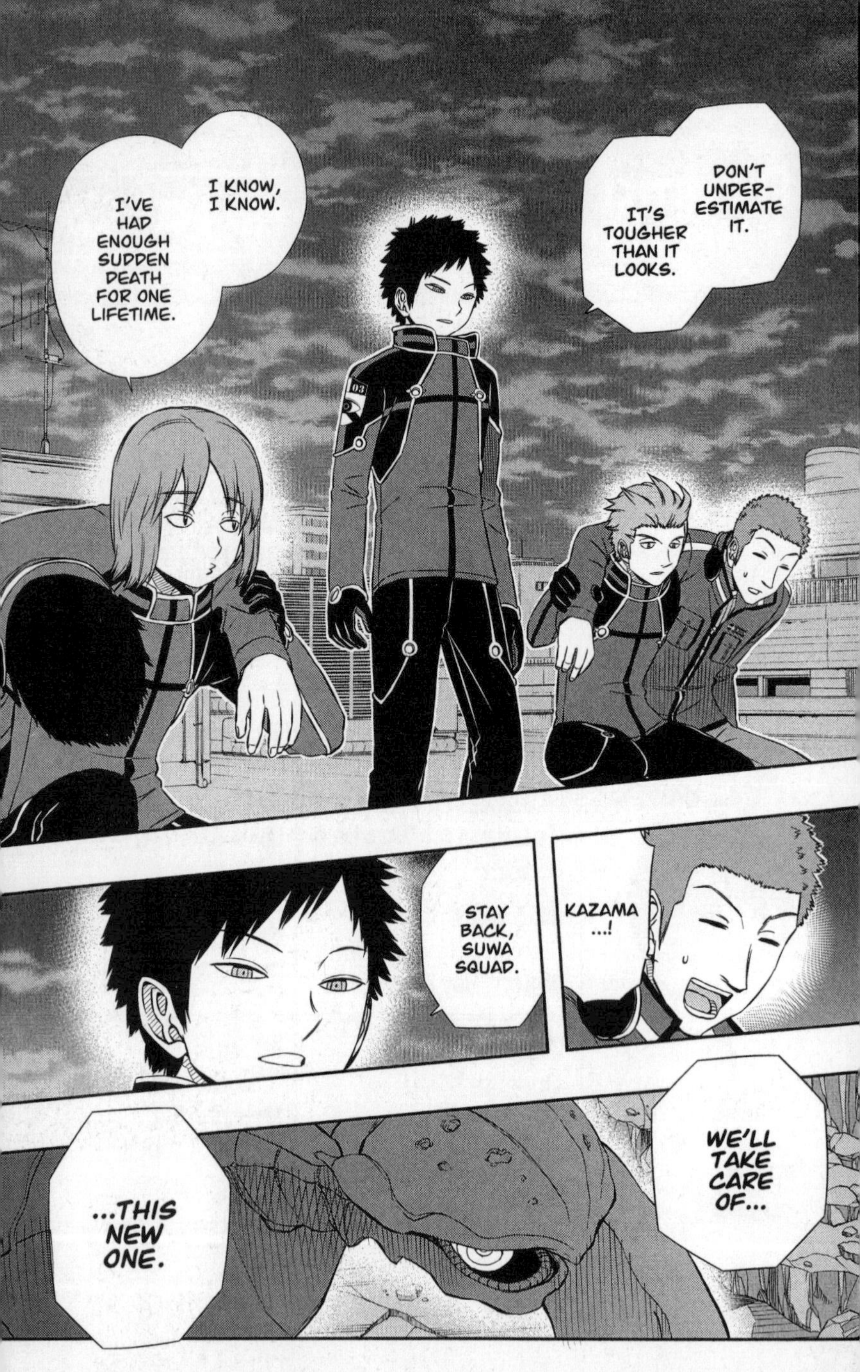
DON'T UNDER-ESTIMATE IT.
IT'S TOUGHER THAN IT LOOKS.
I KNOW, I KNOW.
I'VE HAD ENOUGH SUDDEN DEATH FOR ONE LIFETIME.
KAZAMA ...!
STAY BACK, SUWA SQUAD.
WE'LL TAKE CARE OF...
...THIS NEW ONE.

Azuma Squad

Border HQ B-Rank #6

B-006

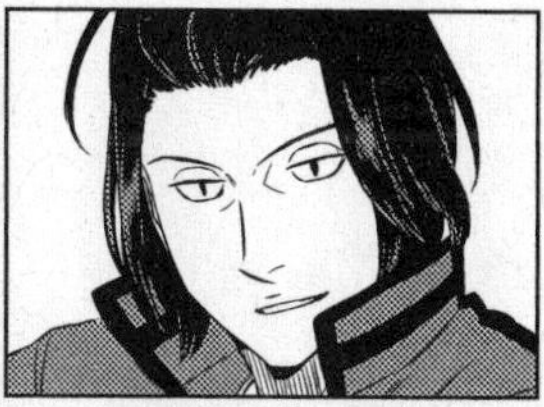

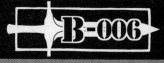

Haruaki Azuma

Captain, Sniper

■25 years old (grad student)
■Born Jan. 3
■Clavis, Blood type A
■Height: 6′1″
■Likes: Fishing, camping, sashimi, tempura

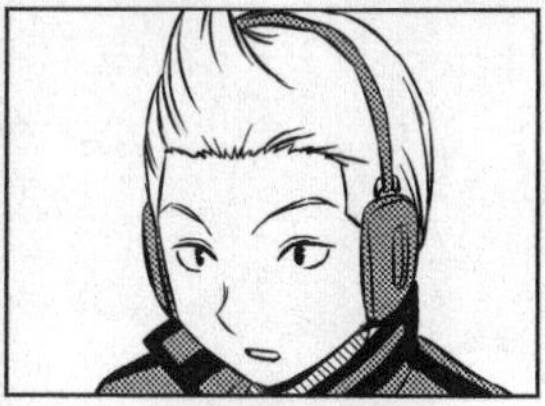

Noboru Koarai

Attacker

■16 years old (high school student)
■Born April 24
■Felis, Blood type O
■Height: 5′5″
■Likes: Soccer, fried chicken

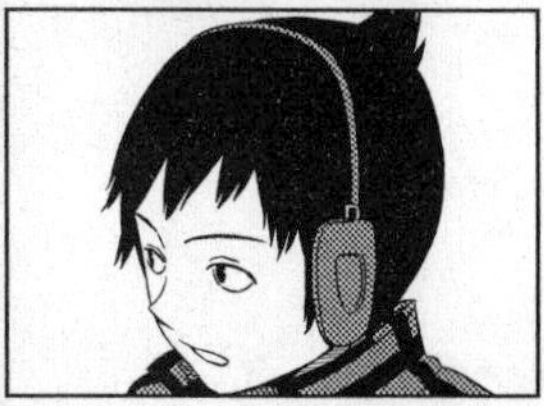

Tsuneyuki Okudera

Attacker

■16 years old (high school student)
■Born May 20
■Felis, Blood type A
■Height: 5′6″
■Likes: Soccer, ramen

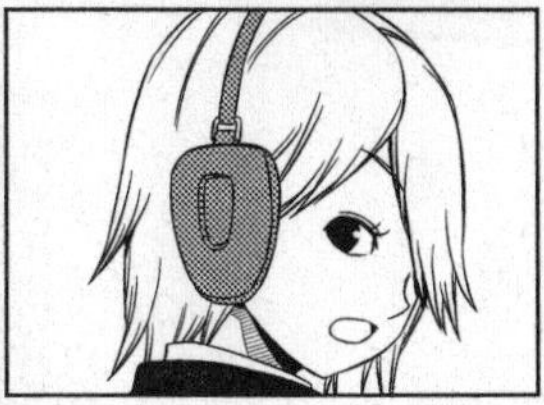

Mako Hitomi

Operator

■18 years old (high school student)
■Born Aug. 28
■Lupus, Blood type AB
■Height: 5′4″
■Likes: Crepes, horror movies

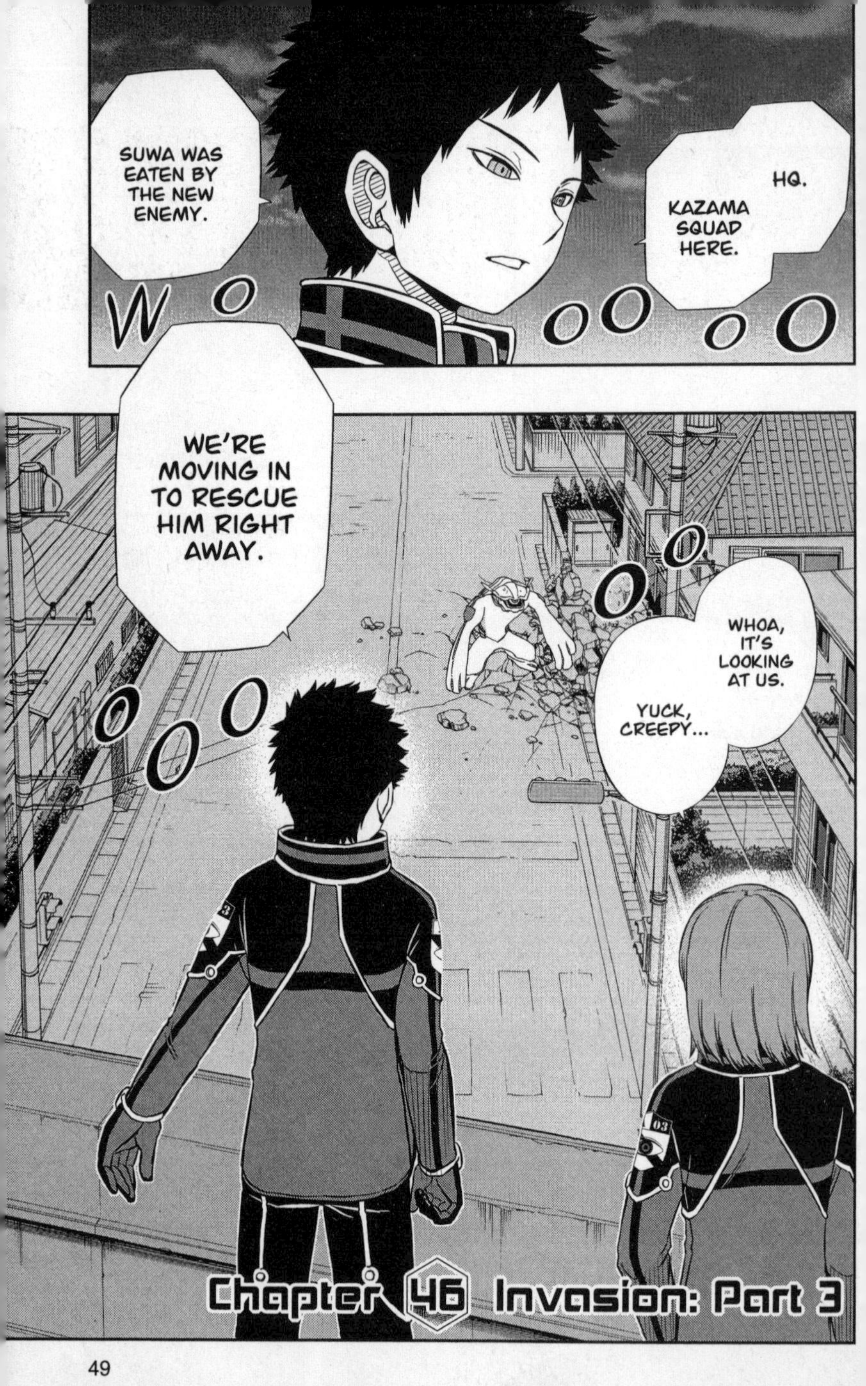
HQ.
KAZAMA SQUAD HERE.
SUWA WAS EATEN BY THE NEW ENEMY.
WOOOOOO
WE'RE MOVING IN TO RESCUE HIM RIGHT AWAY.
OOOOO
WHOA, IT'S LOOKING AT US.
YUCK, CREEPY...
OOO
Chapter 46 Invasion: Part 3

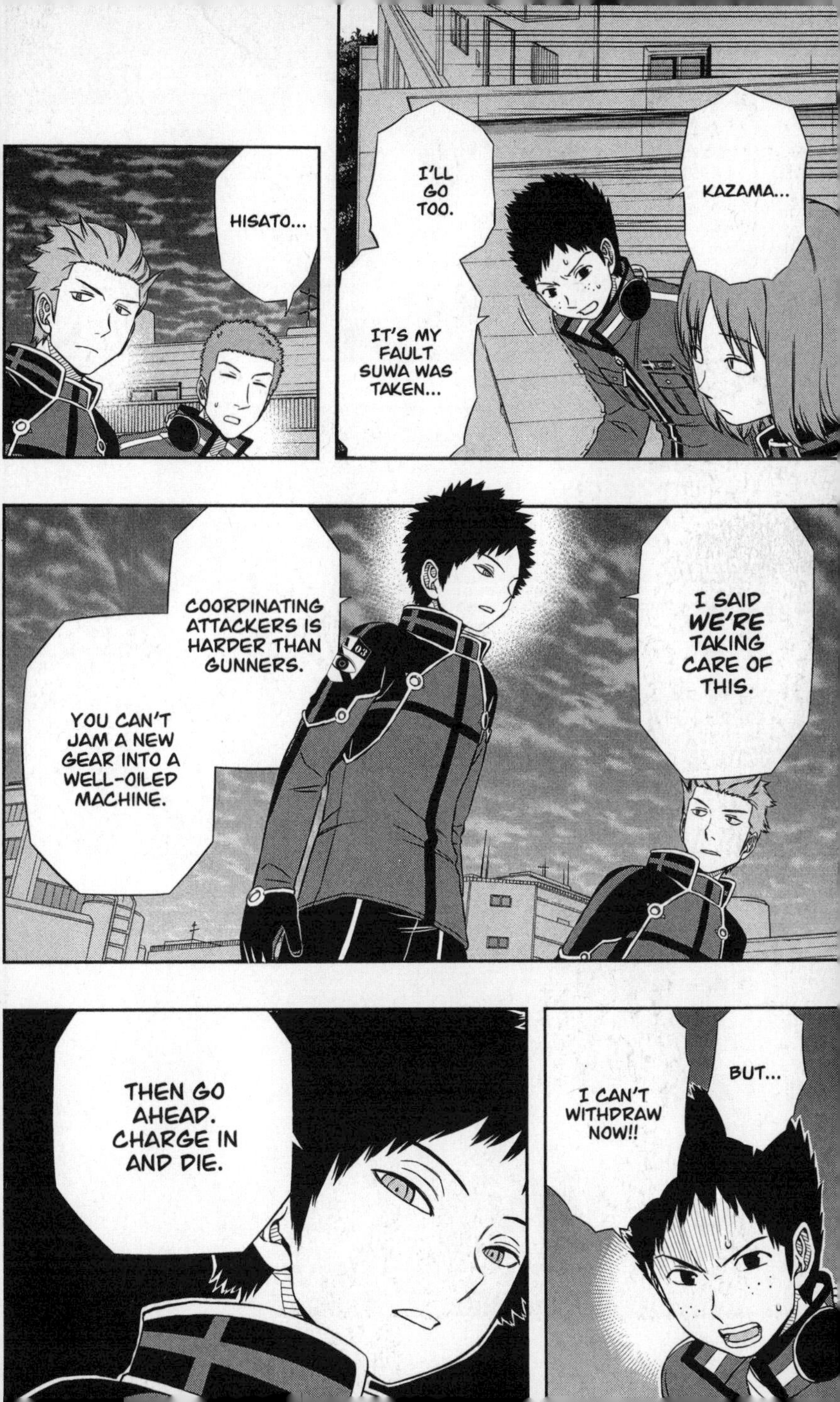
KAZAMA...
I'LL GO TOO.
IT'S MY FAULT SUWA WAS TAKEN...
HISATO...
I SAID WE'RE TAKING CARE OF THIS.
COORDINATING ATTACKERS IS HARDER THAN GUNNERS.
YOU CAN'T JAM A NEW GEAR INTO A WELL-OILED MACHINE.
BUT...
I CAN'T WITHDRAW NOW!!
THEN GO AHEAD. CHARGE IN AND DIE.

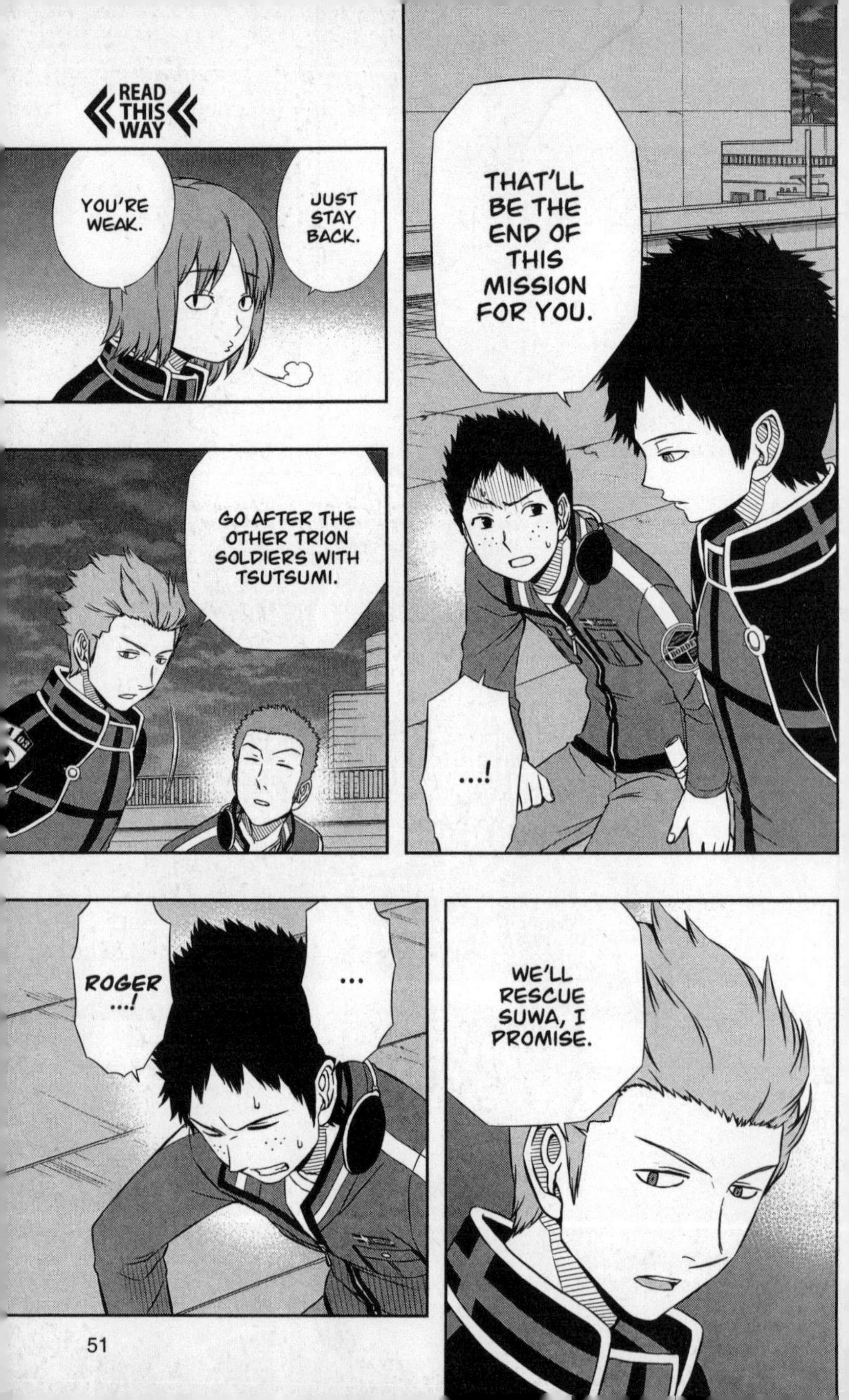
READ THIS WAY
THAT'LL BE THE END OF THIS MISSION FOR YOU.
...!
JUST STAY BACK.
YOU'RE WEAK.
GO AFTER THE OTHER TRION SOLDIERS WITH TSUTSUMI.
WE'LL RESCUE SUWA, I PROMISE.
...
ROGER ...!

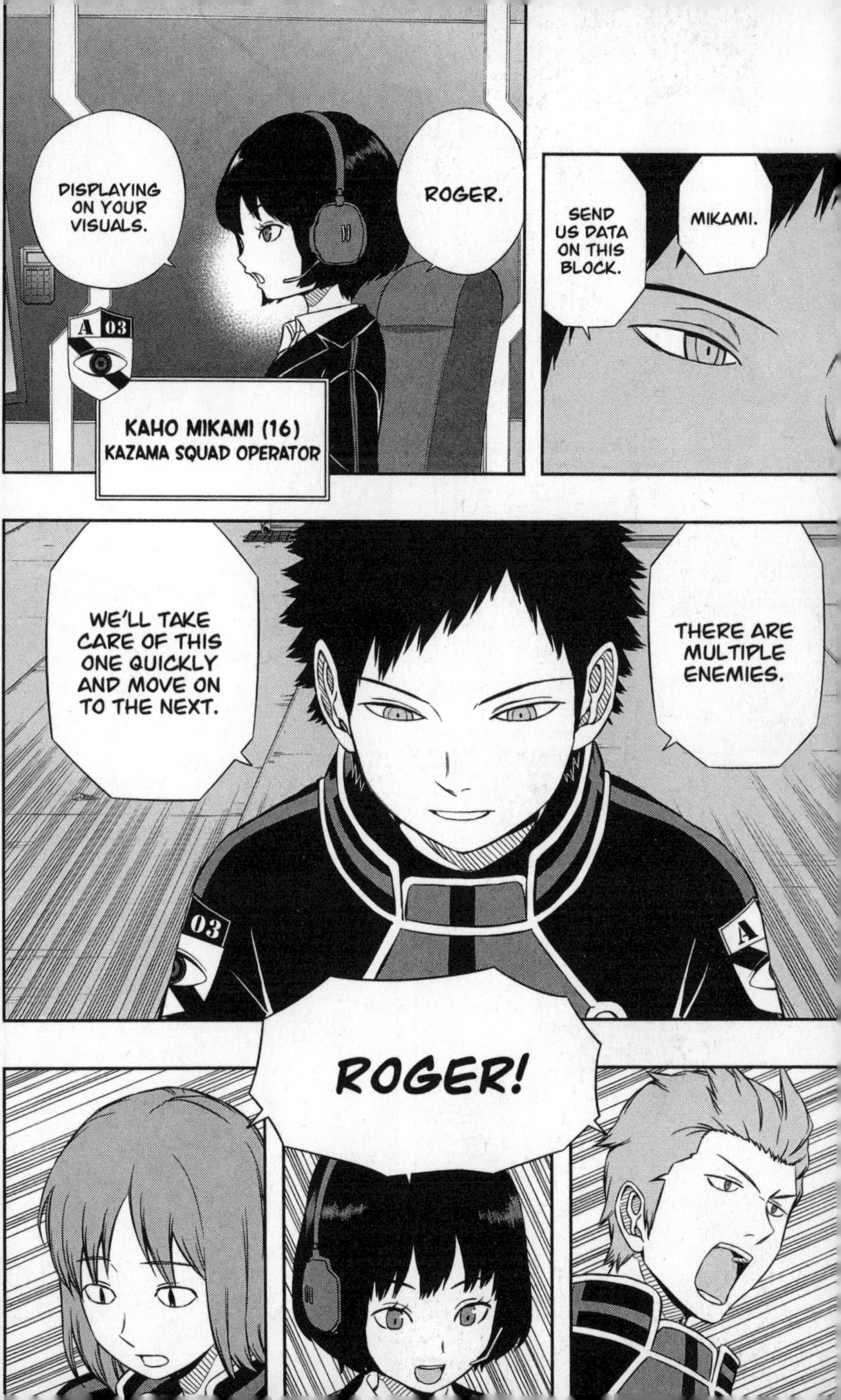
MIKAMI.
SEND US DATA ON THIS BLOCK.
ROGER.
DISPLAYING ON YOUR VISUALS.
KAHO MIKAMI (16)
KAZAMA SQUAD OPERATOR
THERE ARE MULTIPLE ENEMIES.
WE'LL TAKE CARE OF THIS ONE QUICKLY AND MOVE ON TO THE NEXT.
ROGER!

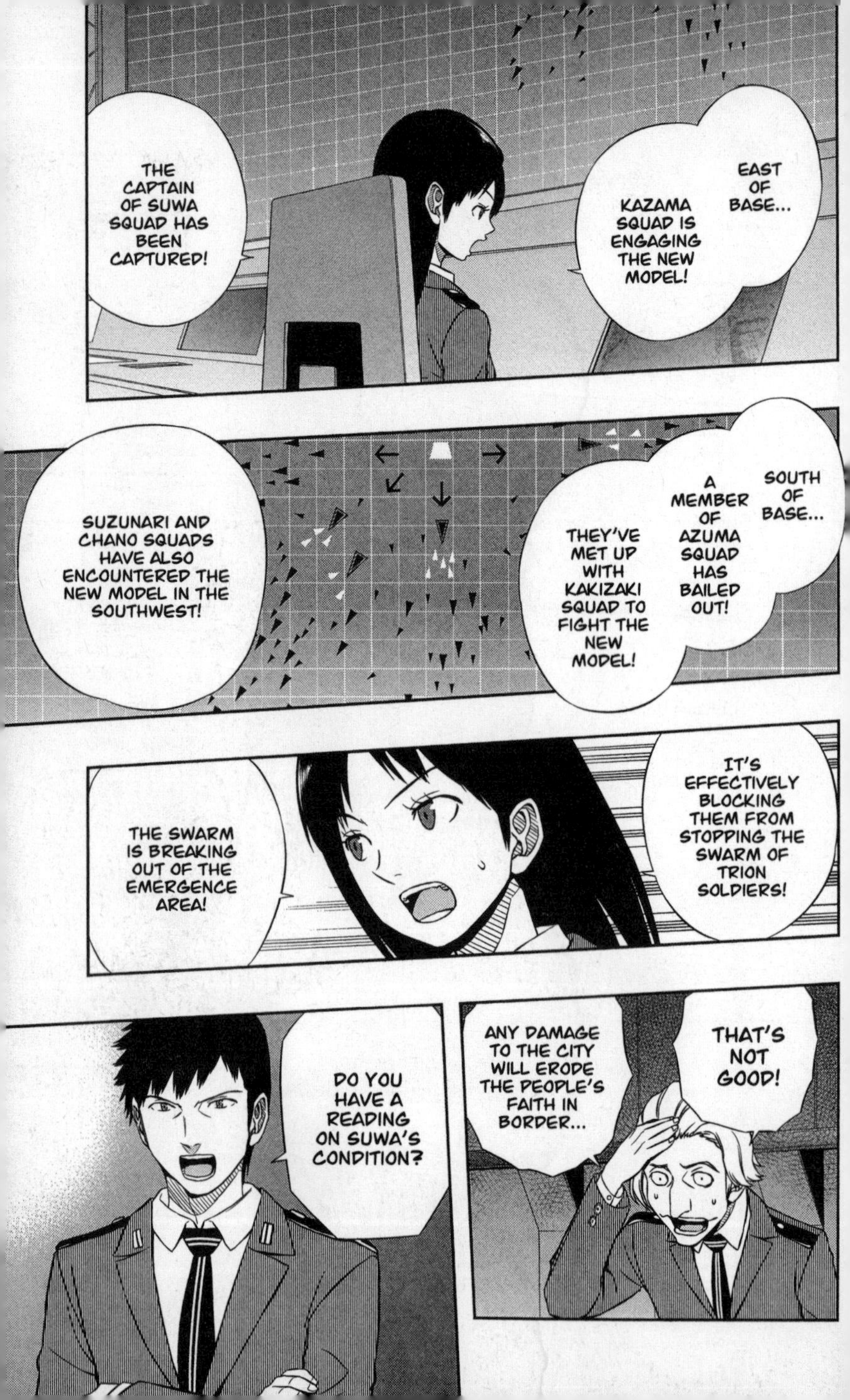
EAST OF BASE...
KAZAMA SQUAD IS ENGAGING THE NEW MODEL!
THE CAPTAIN OF SUWA SQUAD HAS BEEN CAPTURED!
SOUTH OF BASE...
A MEMBER OF AZUMA SQUAD HAS BAILED OUT!
THEY'VE MET UP WITH KAKIZAKI SQUAD TO FIGHT THE NEW MODEL!
SUZUNARI AND CHANO SQUADS HAVE ALSO ENCOUNTERED THE NEW MODEL IN THE SOUTHWEST!
IT'S EFFECTIVELY BLOCKING THEM FROM STOPPING THE SWARM OF TRION SOLDIERS!
THE SWARM IS BREAKING OUT OF THE EMERGENCE AREA!
THAT'S NOT GOOD!
ANY DAMAGE TO THE CITY WILL ERODE THE PEOPLE'S FAITH IN BORDER...
DO YOU HAVE A READING ON SUWA'S CONDITION?

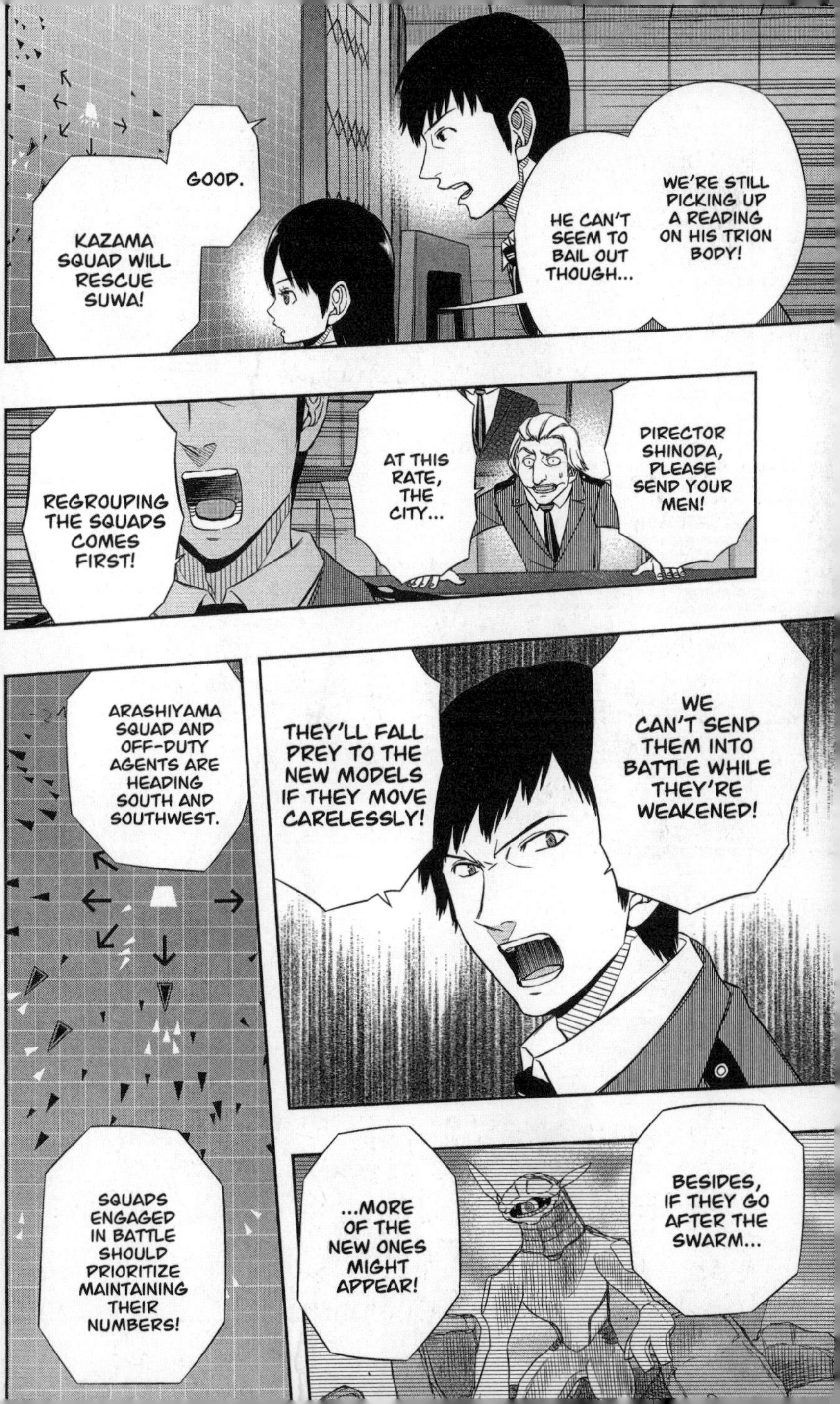
WE'RE STILL PICKING UP A READING ON HIS TRION BODY!
HE CAN'T SEEM TO BAIL OUT THOUGH...
GOOD.
KAZAMA SQUAD WILL RESCUE SUWA!
DIRECTOR SHINODA, PLEASE SEND YOUR MEN!
AT THIS RATE, THE CITY...
REGROUPING THE SQUADS COMES FIRST!
WE CAN'T SEND THEM INTO BATTLE WHILE THEY'RE WEAKENED!
THEY'LL FALL PREY TO THE NEW MODELS IF THEY MOVE CARELESSLY!
BESIDES, IF THEY GO AFTER THE SWARM...
...MORE OF THE NEW ONES MIGHT APPEAR!
ARASHIYAMA SQUAD AND OFF-DUTY AGENTS ARE HEADING SOUTH AND SOUTHWEST.
SQUADS ENGAGED IN BATTLE SHOULD PRIORITIZE MAINTAINING THEIR NUMBERS!

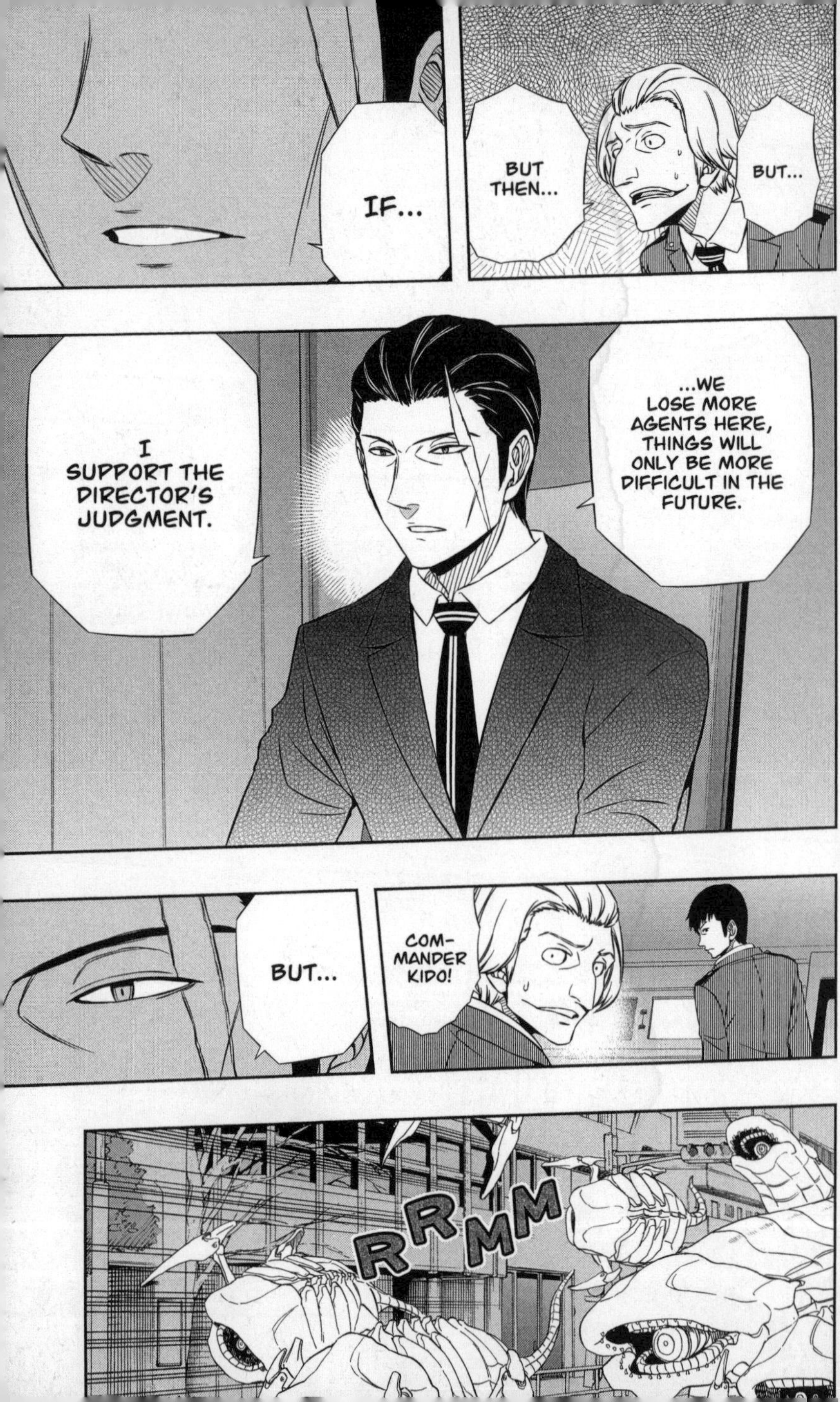
BUT...
BUT THEN...
IF...
...WE LOSE MORE AGENTS HERE, THINGS WILL ONLY BE MORE DIFFICULT IN THE FUTURE.
I SUPPORT THE DIRECTOR'S JUDGMENT.
COM-MANDER KIDO!
BUT...
RRMM

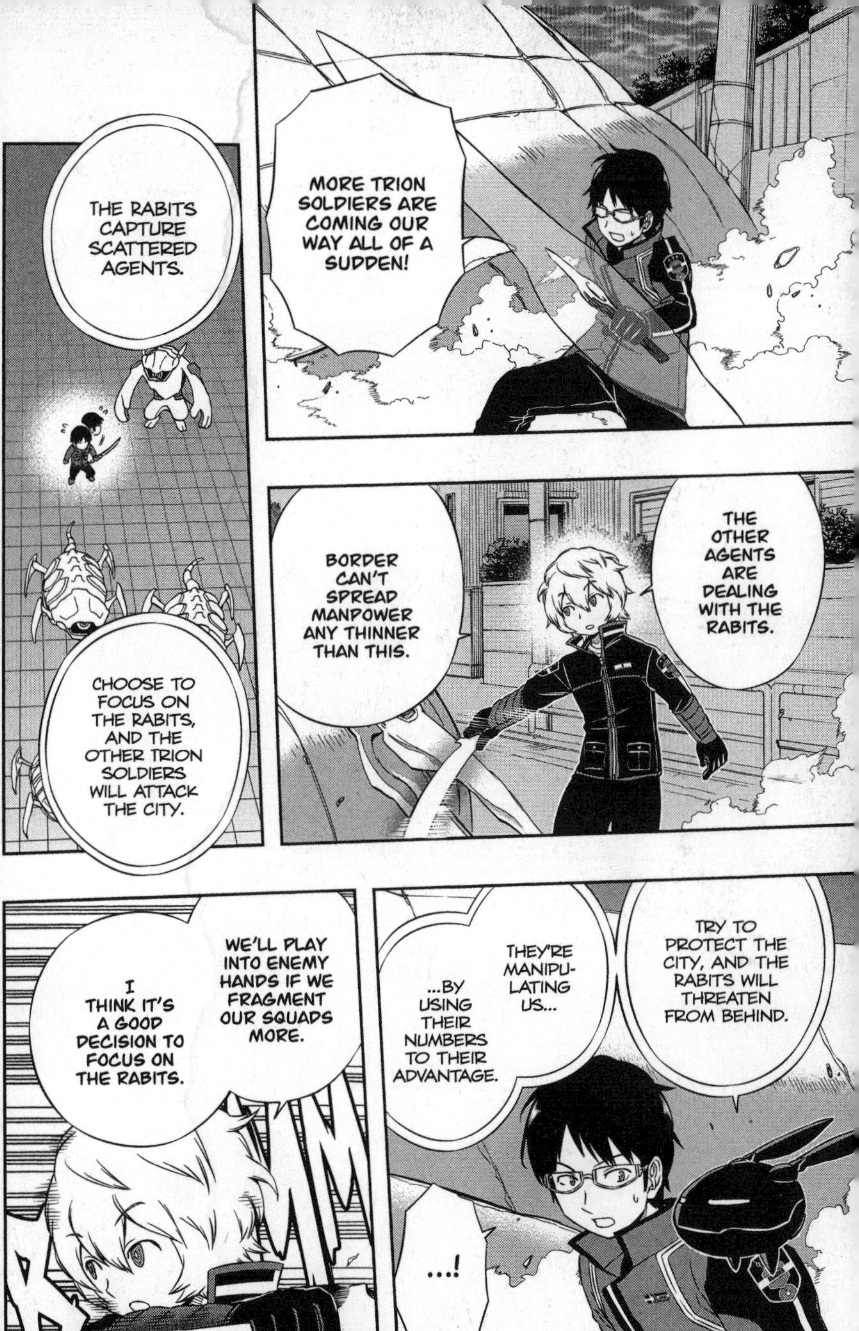
MORE TRION SOLDIERS ARE COMING OUR WAY ALL OF A SUDDEN!
THE OTHER AGENTS ARE DEALING WITH THE RABITS.
BORDER CAN'T SPREAD MANPOWER ANY THINNER THAN THIS.
THE RABITS CAPTURE SCATTERED AGENTS.
CHOOSE TO FOCUS ON THE RABITS, AND THE OTHER TRION SOLDIERS WILL ATTACK THE CITY.
TRY TO PROTECT THE CITY, AND THE RABITS WILL THREATEN FROM BEHIND.
THEY'RE MANIPU-LATING US...
...BY USING THEIR NUMBERS TO THEIR ADVANTAGE.
...!
WE'LL PLAY INTO ENEMY HANDS IF WE FRAGMENT OUR SQUADS MORE.
I THINK IT'S A GOOD DECISION TO FOCUS ON THE RABITS.

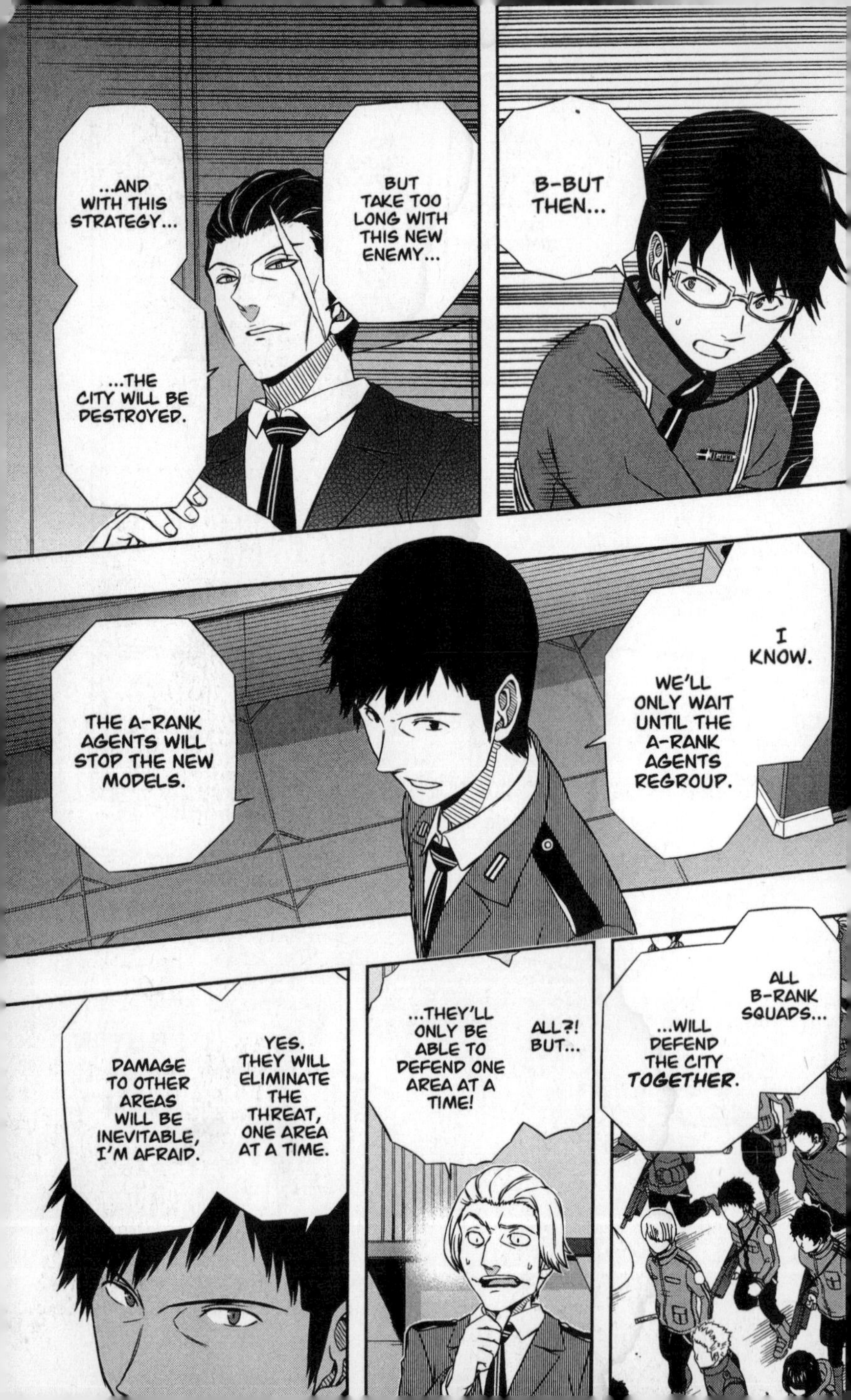
B-BUT THEN...
BUT TAKE TOO LONG WITH THIS NEW ENEMY...
...AND WITH THIS STRATEGY...
...THE CITY WILL BE DESTROYED.
I KNOW.
WE'LL ONLY WAIT UNTIL THE A-RANK AGENTS REGROUP.
THE A-RANK AGENTS WILL STOP THE NEW MODELS.
ALL B-RANK SQUADS...
...WILL DEFEND THE CITY TOGETHER.
ALL?! BUT...
...THEY'LL ONLY BE ABLE TO DEFEND ONE AREA AT A TIME!
YES. THEY WILL ELIMINATE THE THREAT, ONE AREA AT A TIME.
DAMAGE TO OTHER AREAS WILL BE INEVITABLE, I'M AFRAID.

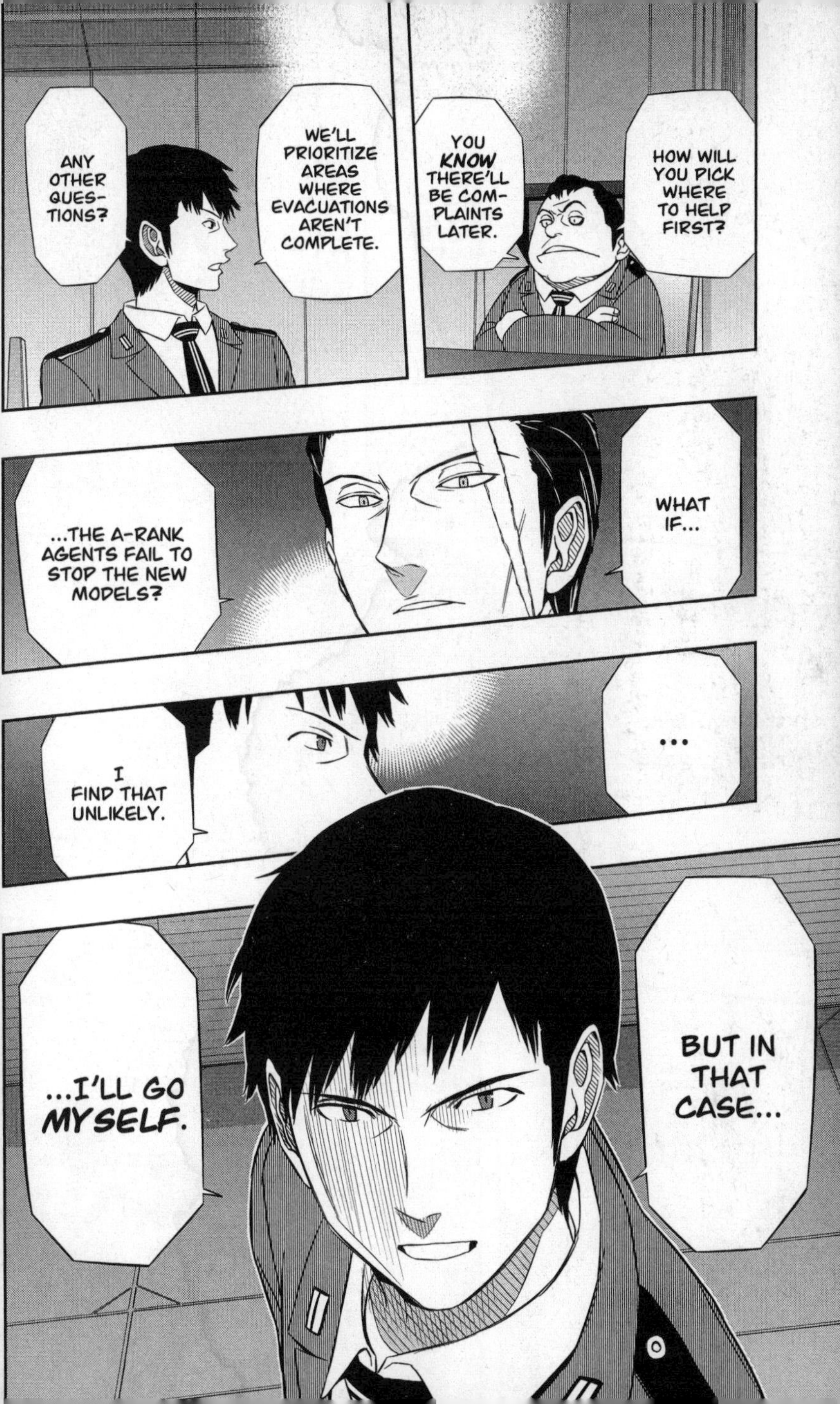
HOW WILL YOU PICK WHERE TO HELP FIRST?
YOU KNOW THERE'LL BE COMPLAINTS LATER.
WE'LL PRIORITIZE AREAS WHERE EVACUATIONS AREN'T COMPLETE.
ANY OTHER QUESTIONS?
WHAT IF...
...THE A-RANK AGENTS FAIL TO STOP THE NEW MODELS?
...
I FIND THAT UNLIKELY.
BUT IN THAT CASE...
...I'LL GO MYSELF.

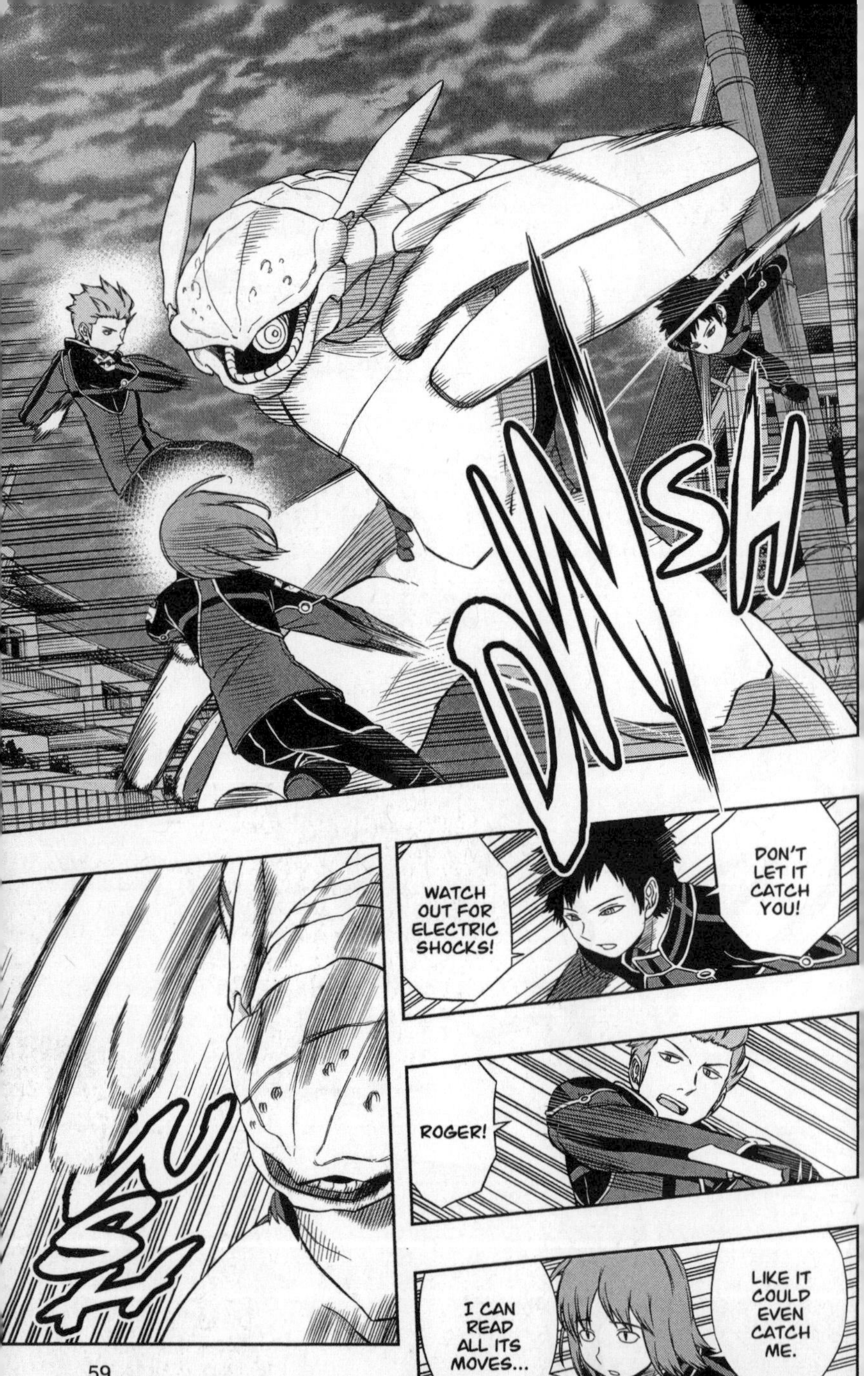
DWSH
DON'T LET IT CATCH YOU!
WATCH OUT FOR ELECTRIC SHOCKS!
ROGER!
LIKE IT COULD EVEN CATCH ME.
I CAN READ ALL ITS MOVES...
VWSH

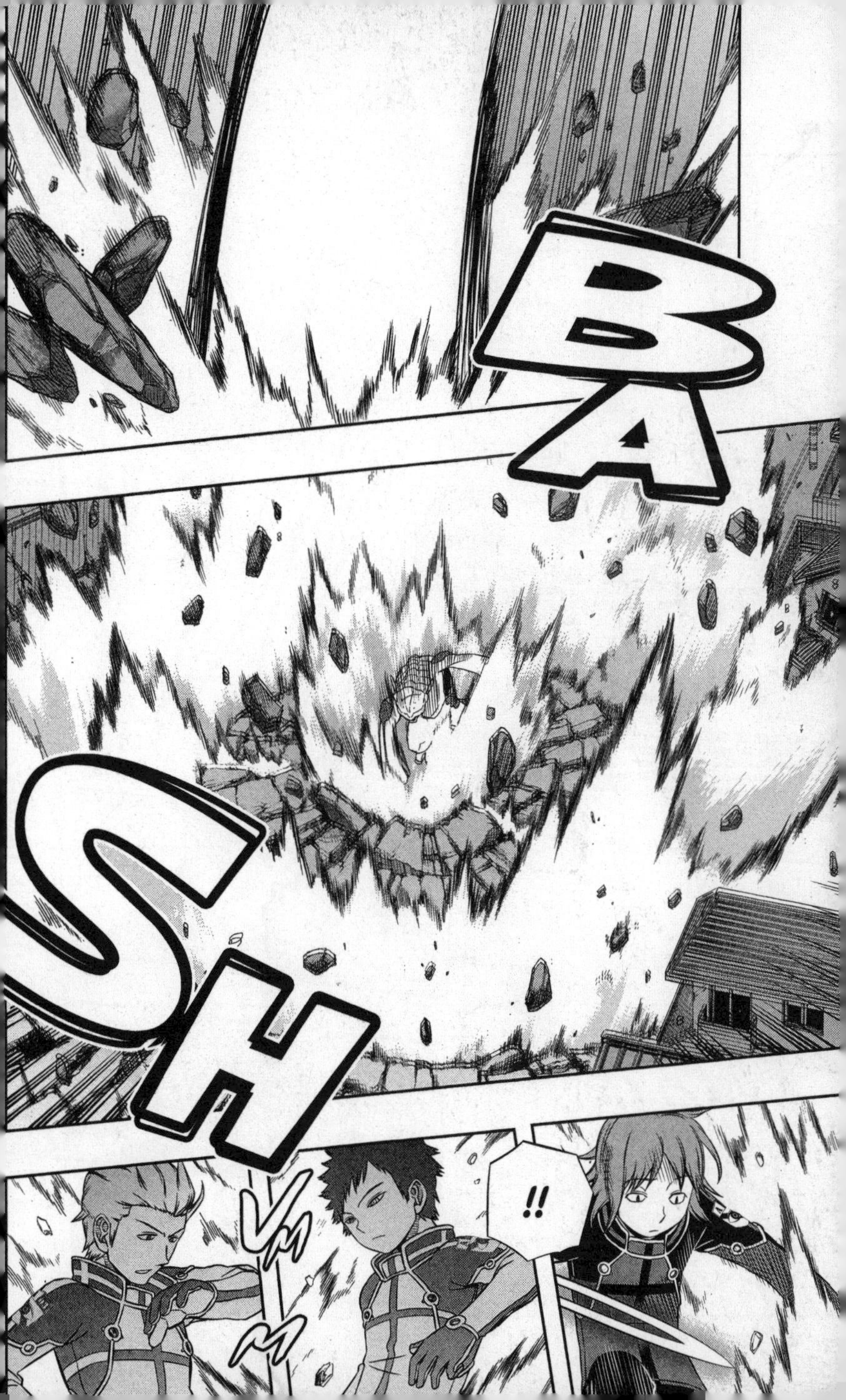
BASH
!!

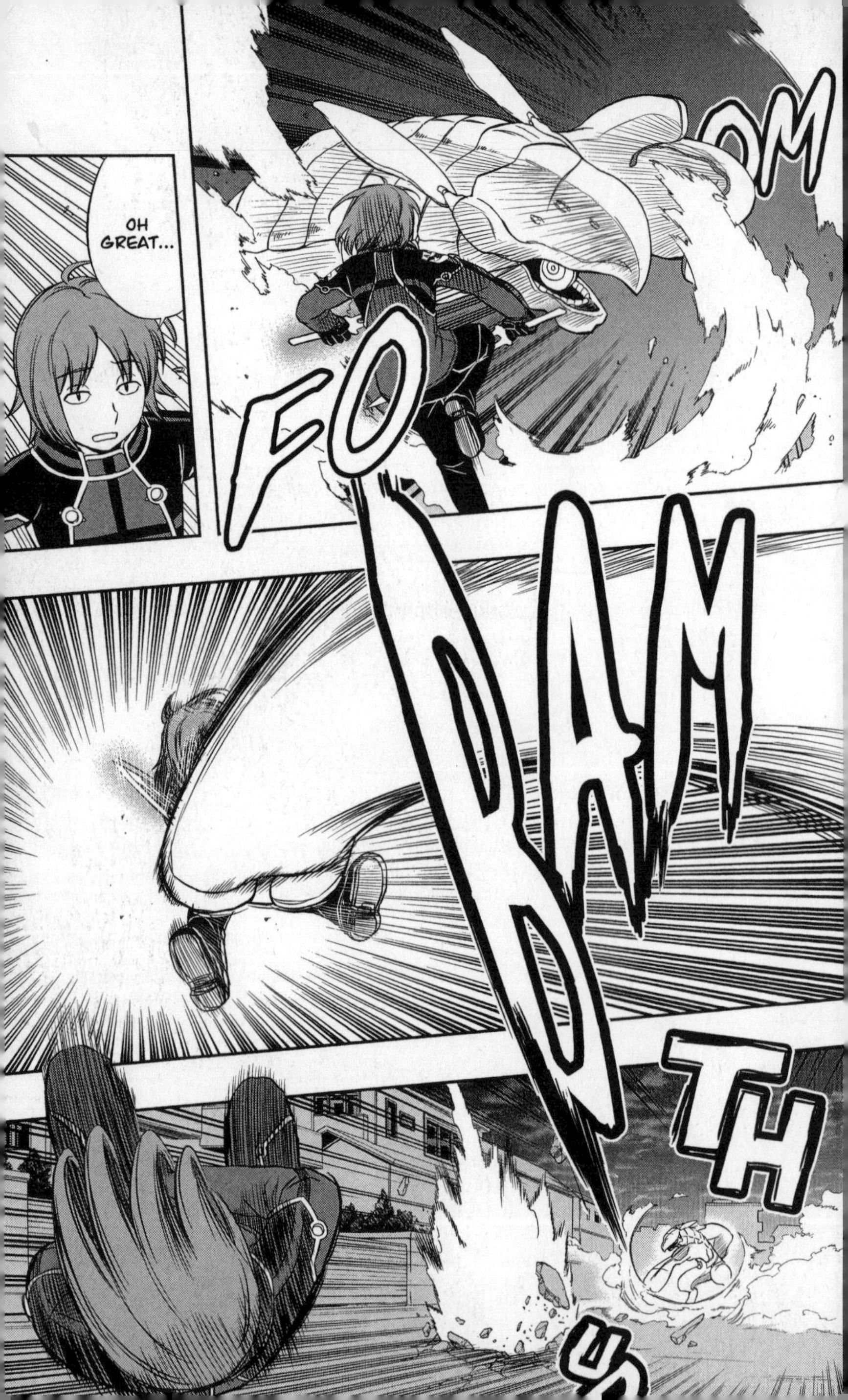
OM
FO
OH GREAT...
BAM
TH

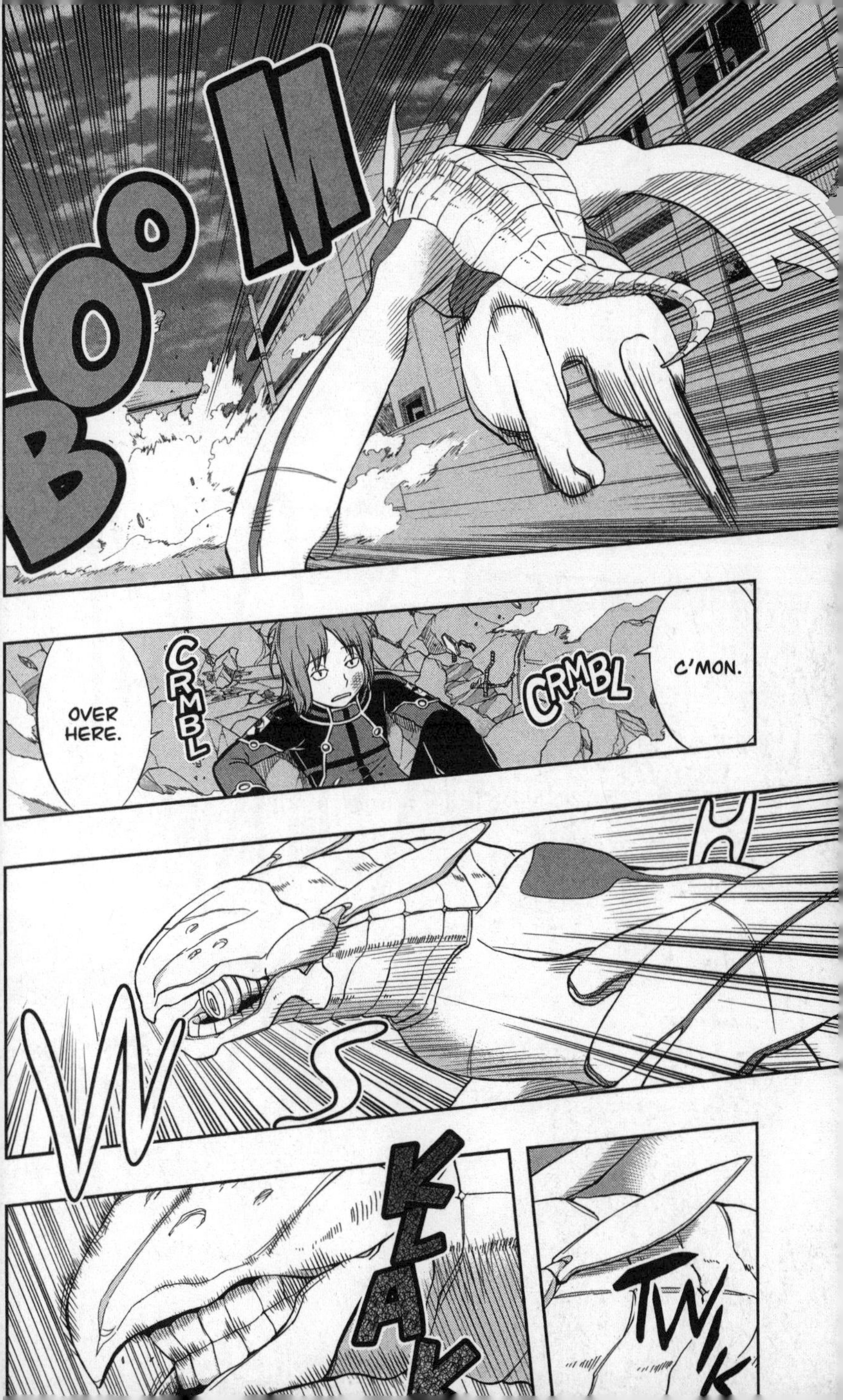
BOOM
C'MON.
CRMBL
CRMBL
OVER HERE.
H
WS
TWIK
KLAK

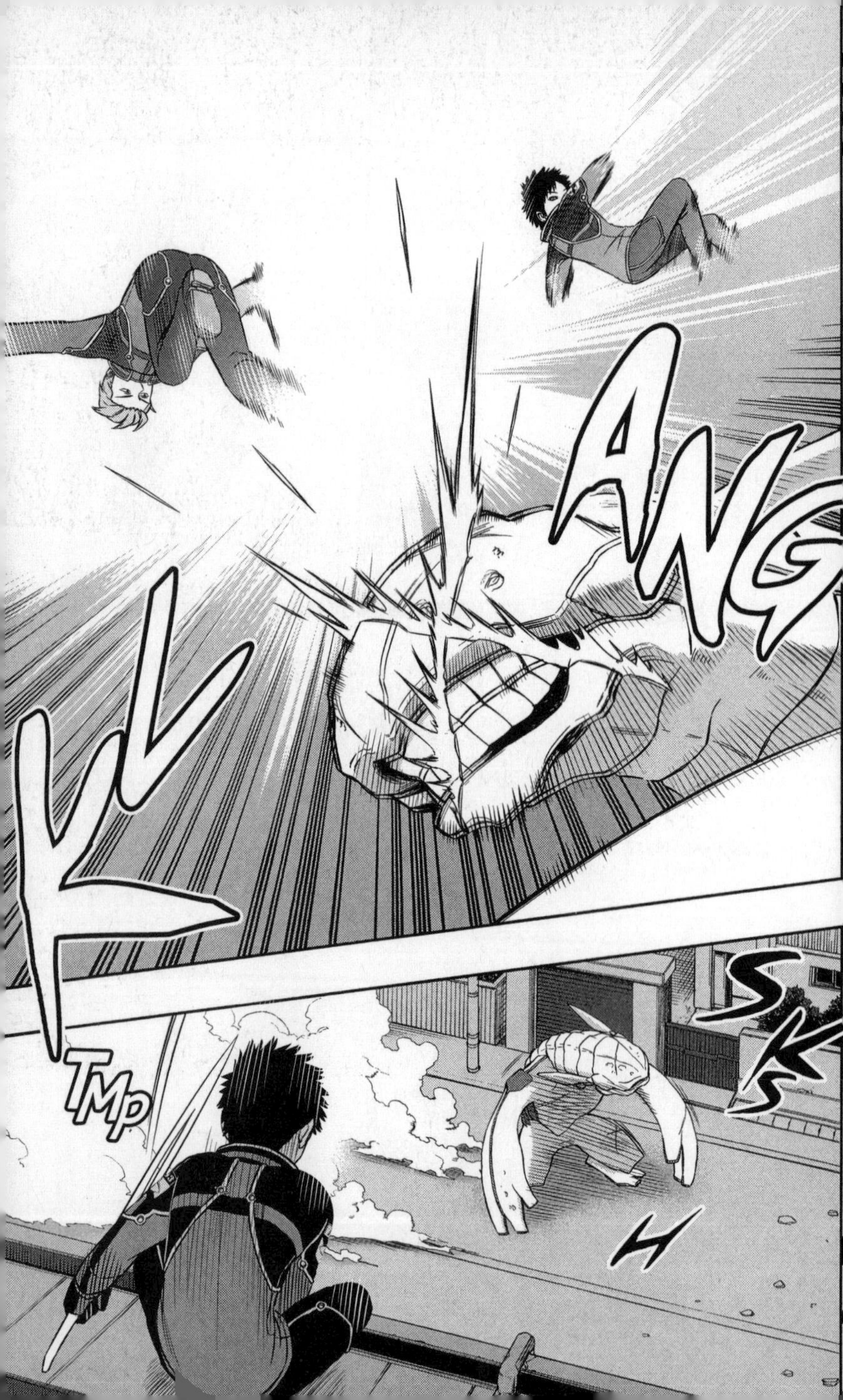
KLANG
SKS
H
TMp

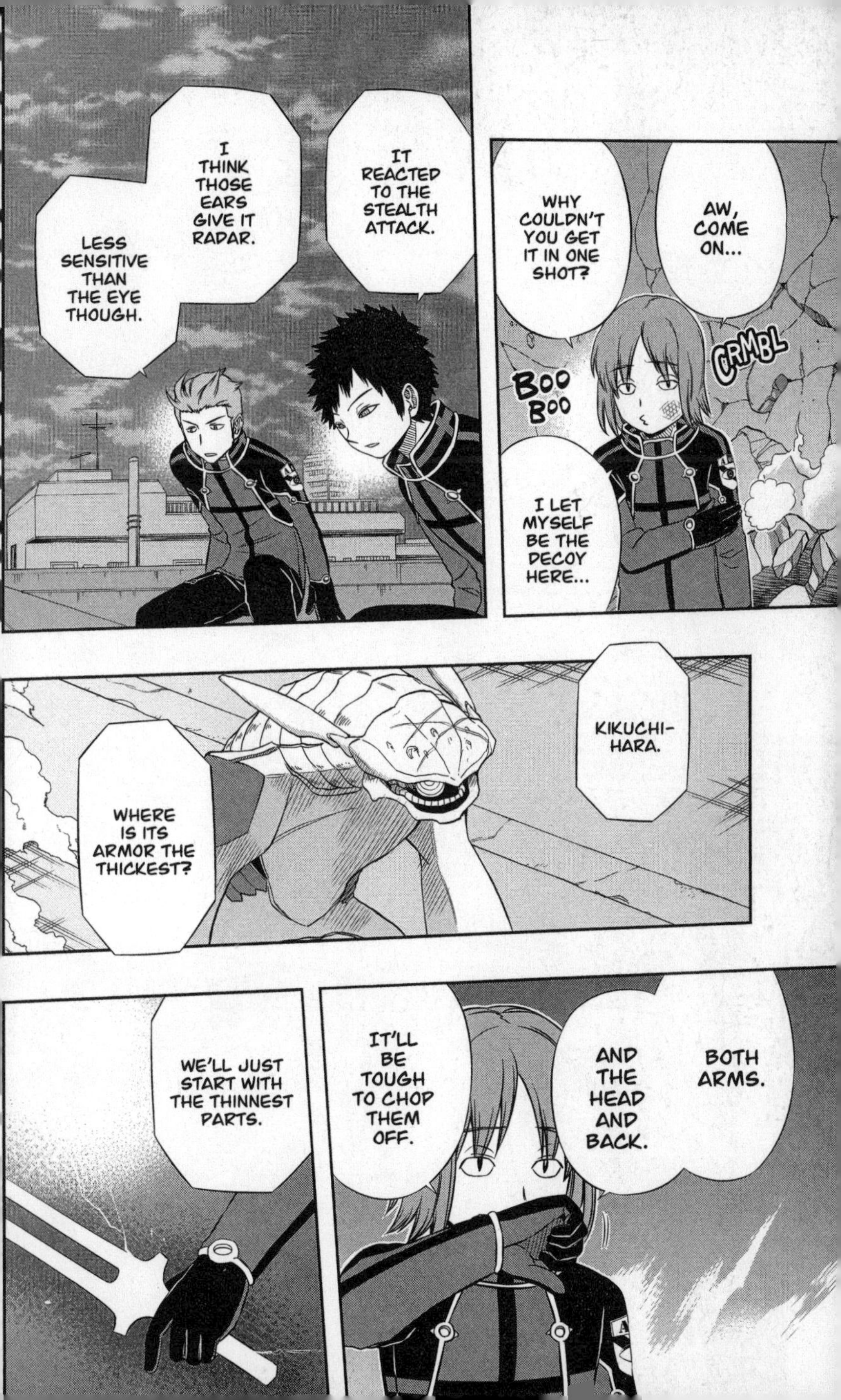
AW, COME ON...
WHY COULDN'T YOU GET IT IN ONE SHOT?
CRMBL
BOO BOO
I LET MYSELF BE THE DECOY HERE...
IT REACTED TO THE STEALTH ATTACK.
I THINK THOSE EARS GIVE IT RADAR.
LESS SENSITIVE THAN THE EYE THOUGH.
KIKUCHI-HARA.
WHERE IS ITS ARMOR THE THICKEST?
BOTH ARMS.
AND THE HEAD AND BACK.
IT'LL BE TOUGH TO CHOP THEM OFF.
WE'LL JUST START WITH THE THINNEST PARTS.

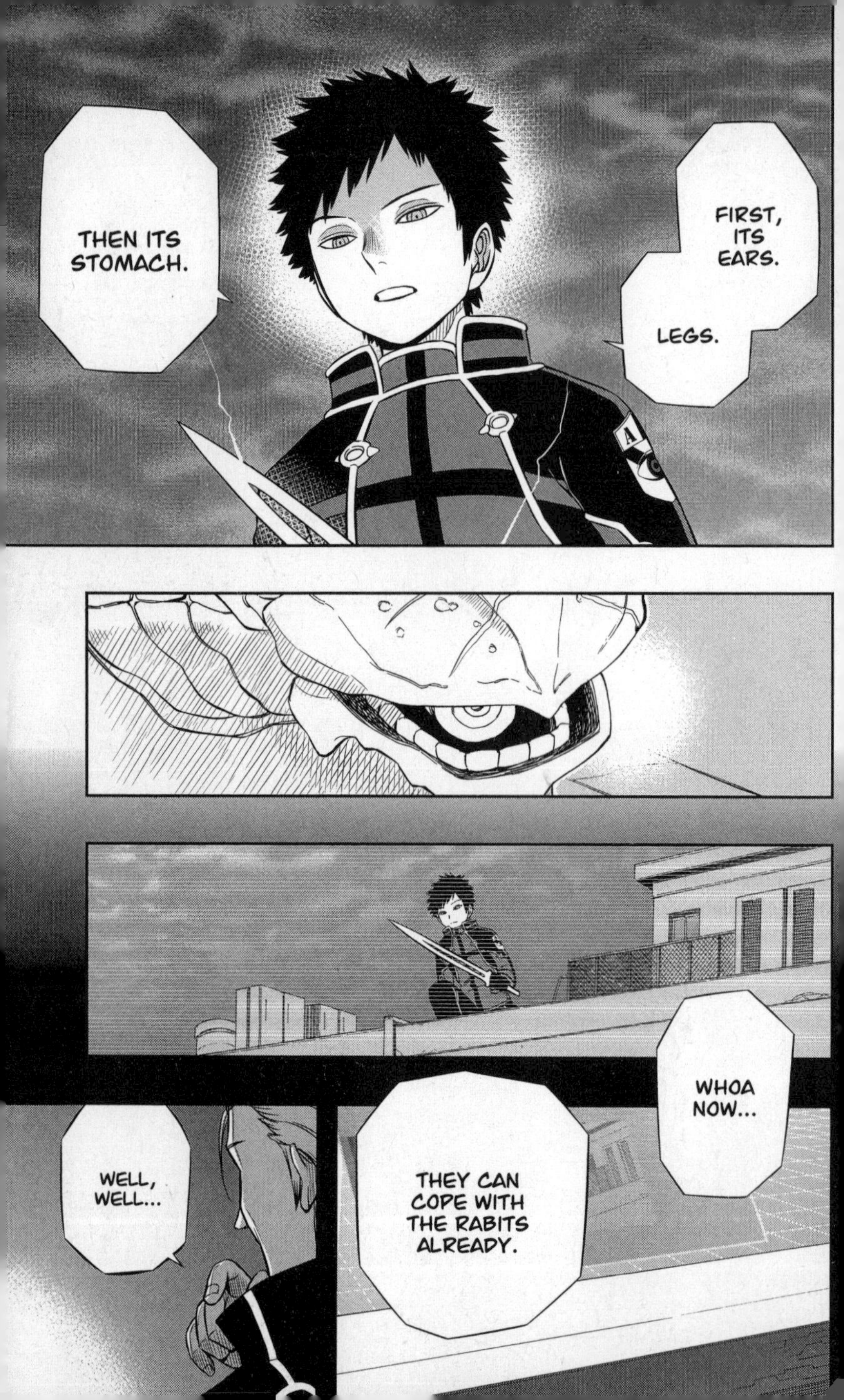
FIRST, ITS EARS.
LEGS.
THEN ITS STOMACH.
WHOA NOW...
THEY CAN COPE WITH THE RABITS ALREADY.
WELL, WELL...

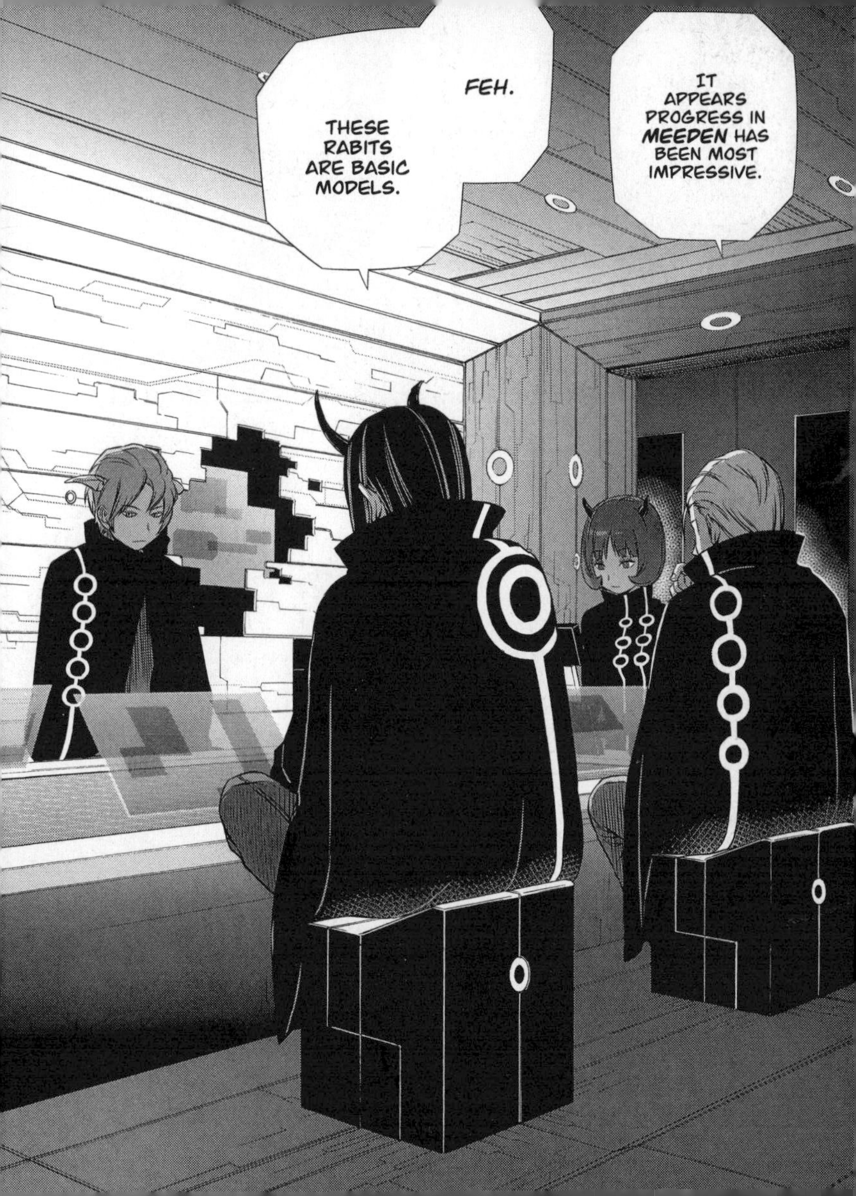
IT APPEARS PROGRESS IN MEEDEN HAS BEEN MOST IMPRESSIVE.
FEH.
THESE RABITS ARE BASIC MODELS.

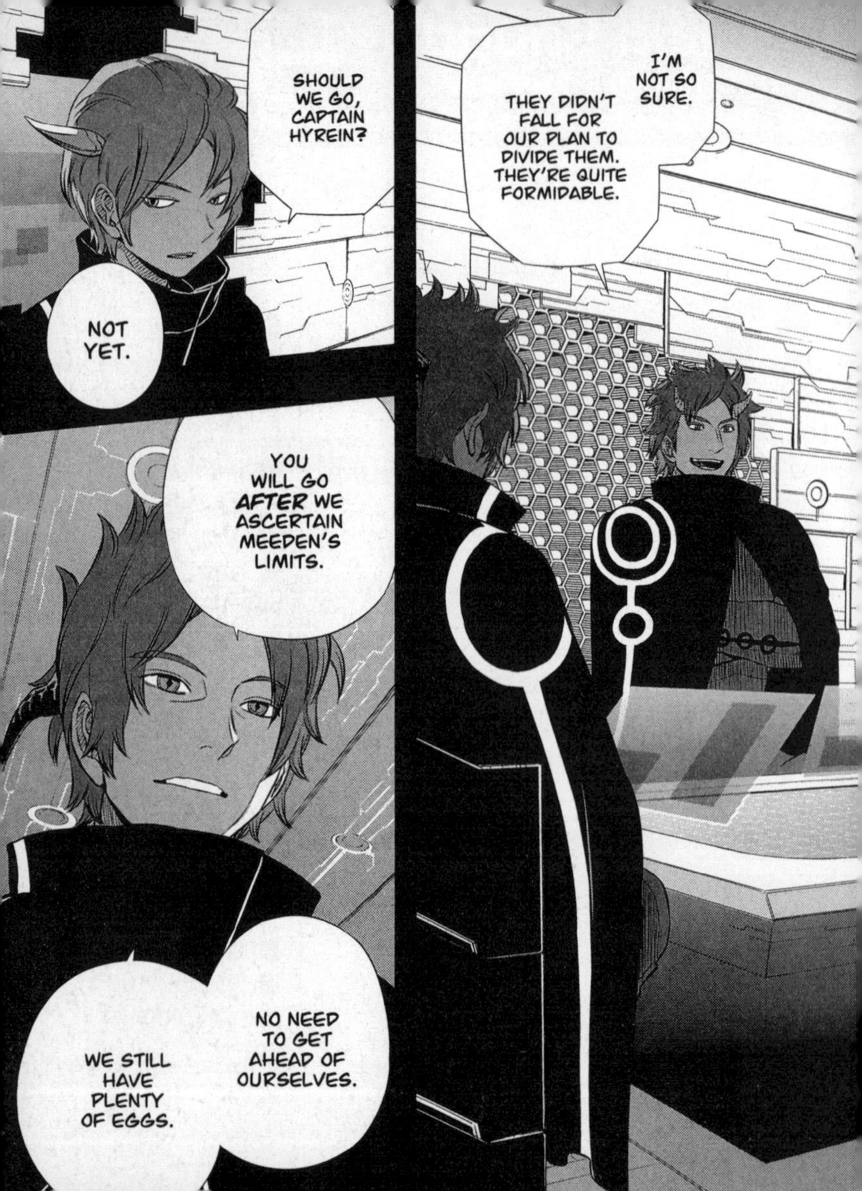
I'M NOT SO SURE.
THEY DIDN'T FALL FOR OUR PLAN TO DIVIDE THEM. THEY'RE QUITE FORMIDABLE.
SHOULD WE GO, CAPTAIN HYREIN?
NOT YET.
YOU WILL GO AFTER WE ASCERTAIN MEEDEN'S LIMITS.
NO NEED TO GET AHEAD OF OURSELVES.
WE STILL HAVE PLENTY OF EGGS.

Suwa Squad

Border HQ B-Rank #10

B-010

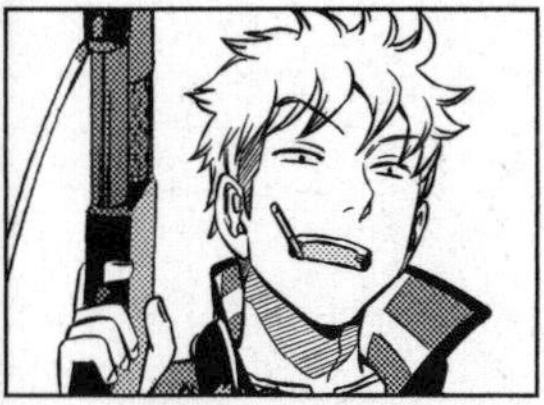

Kotaro Suwa
Captain, Gunner

■21 years old (college student)
■Born Aug. 1

■Aptenodytes, Blood type A
■Height: 5'10"
■Likes: Cigarettes, beer, meat, mahjong, detective novels

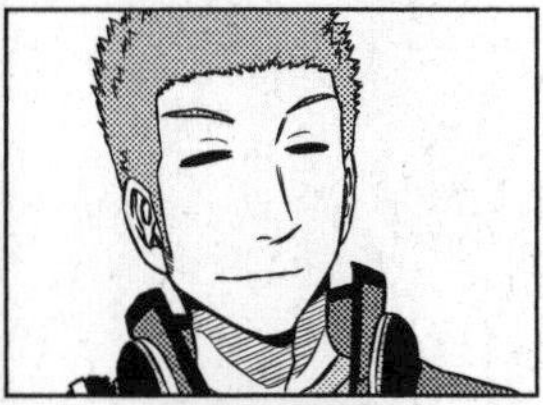

Daichi Tsutsumi
Gunner

■20 years old (college student)
■Born Oct. 11

■Luna Falcata, Blood type O
■Height: 5'11"
■Likes: Sake, octopus with wasabi, historical novels

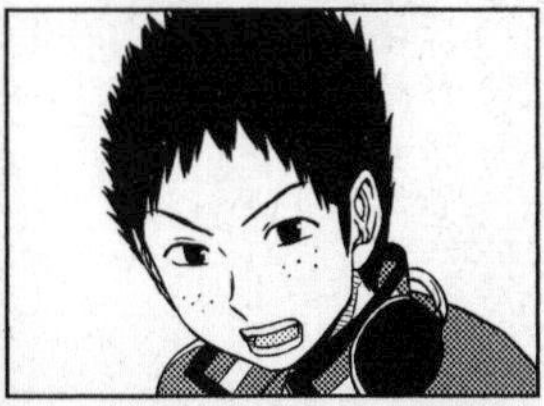

Hisato Sasamori
Attacker

■16 years old (high school student)
■Born Jan. 18

■Clavis, Blood type A
■Height: 5'7"
■Likes: Fried rice, croquettes, manga

Rui Kosano
Operator

■17 years old (high school student)
■Born July 3

■Gladius, Blood type A
■Height: 5'1"
■Likes: Fried udon, mahjong, foreign novels

Chapter 47 Invasion: Part 4

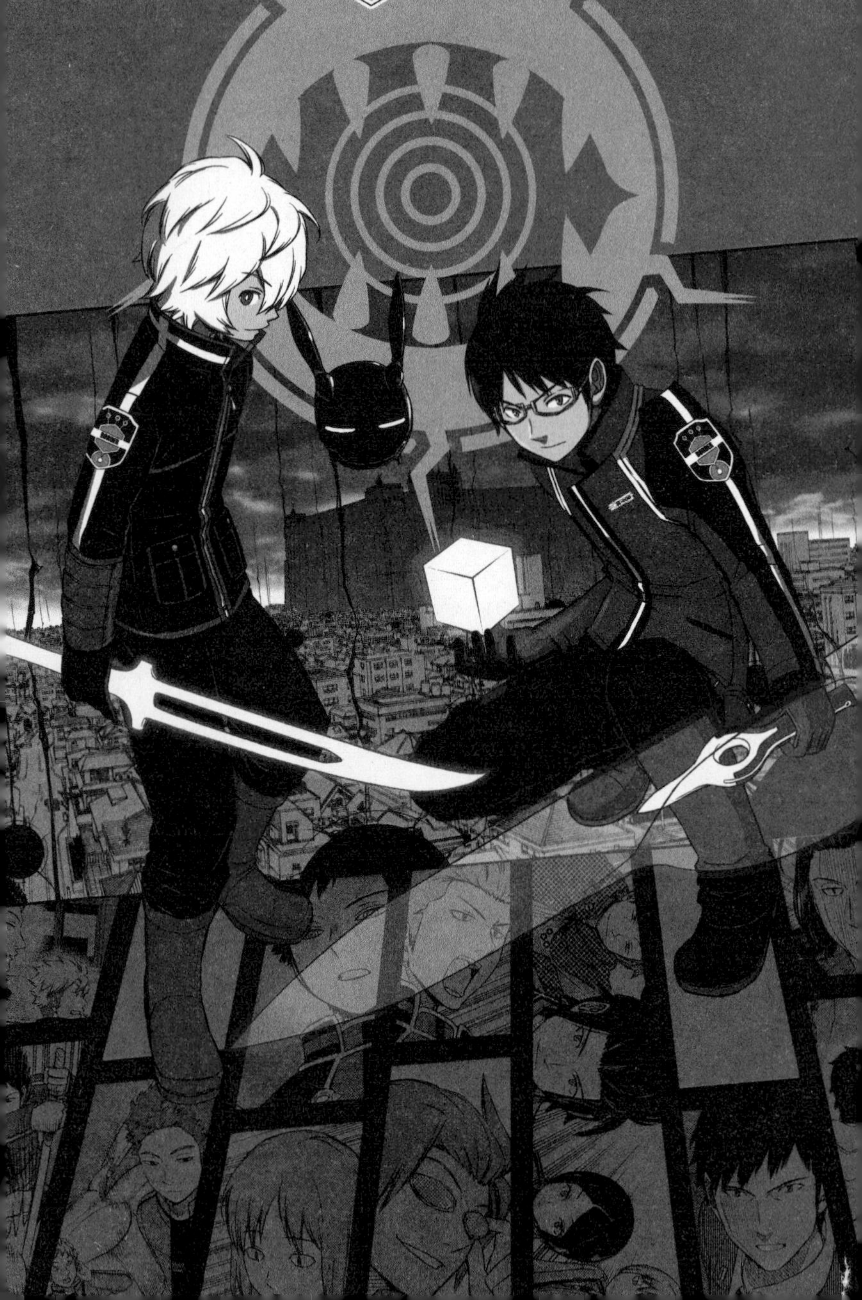

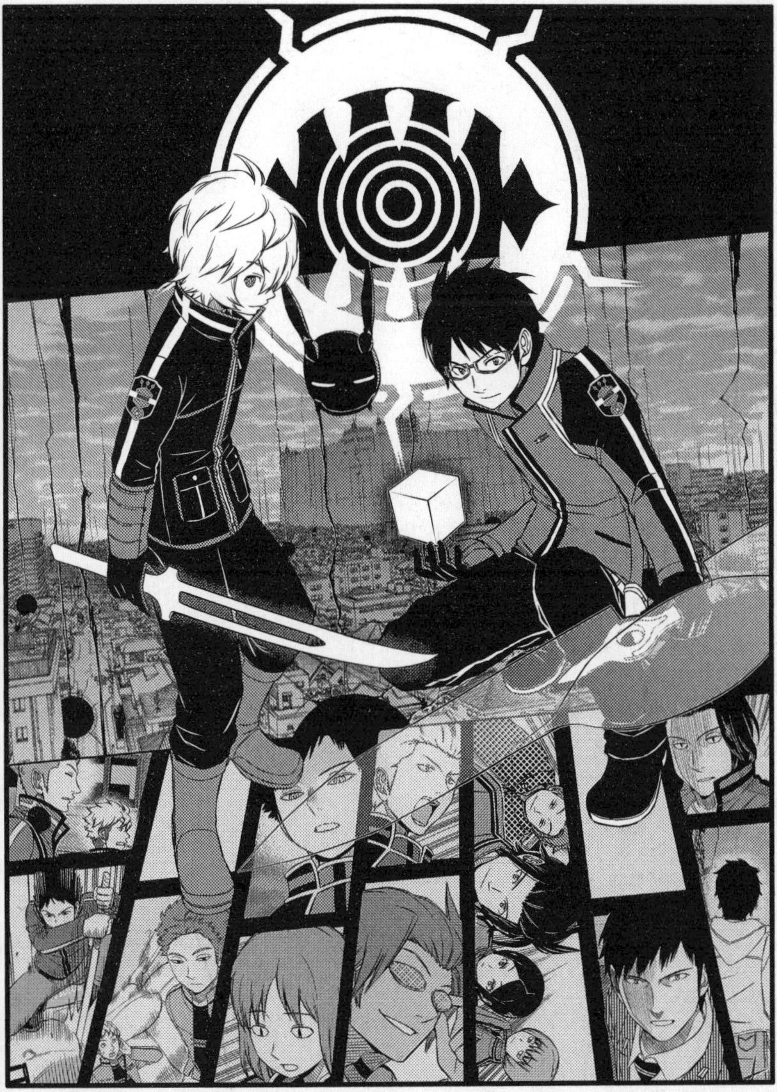

■ 2014 *Weekly Shonen Jump* issue 10, center color page (eighth one)
This was right after the hiatus for breaking my left hand. Is it my imagination or does Yuma look taller because I drew him while my hand was broken? I conserved effort by copying and pasting everything but Yuma and Osamu, but I like it more than many other color pages I've done.

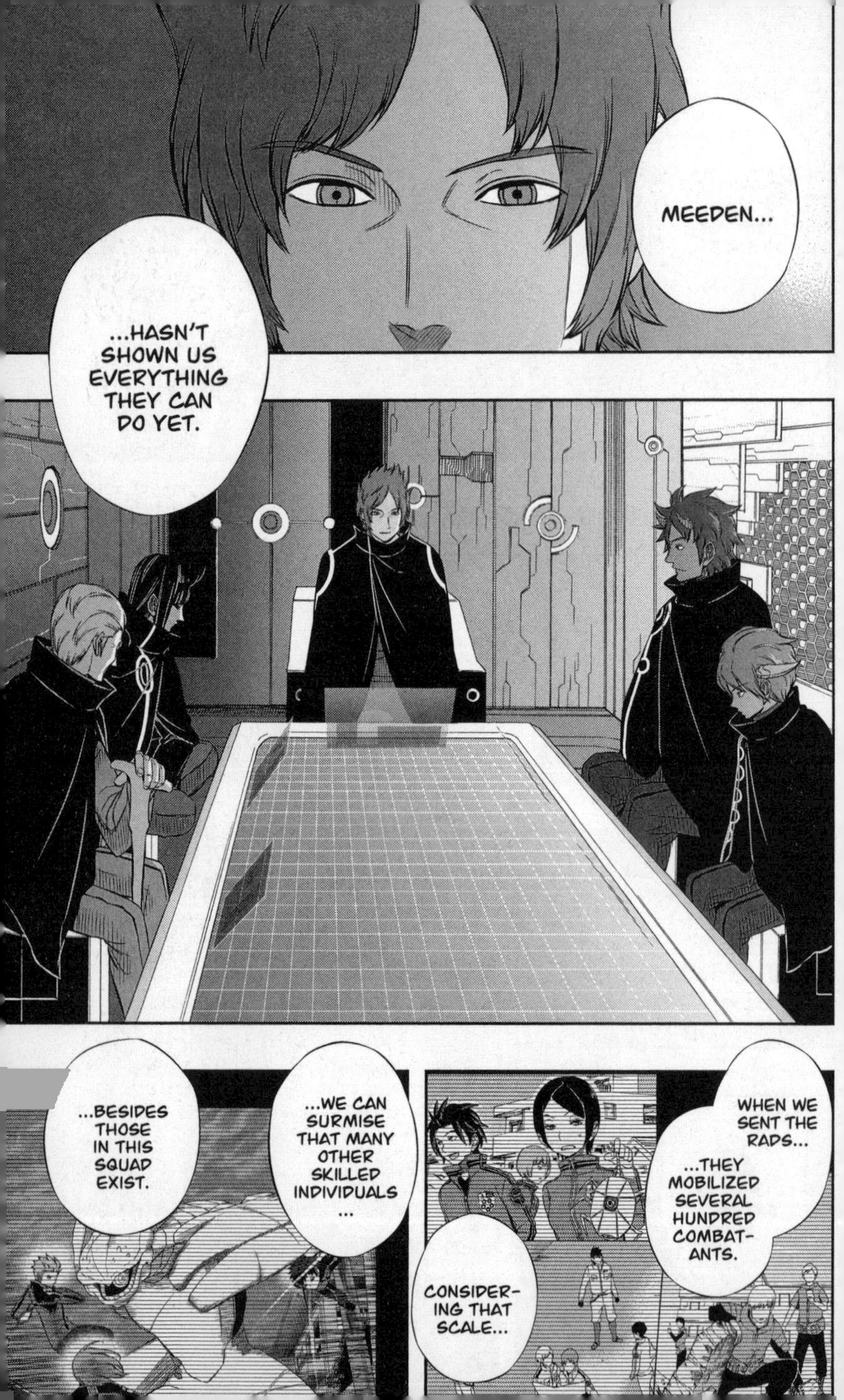

MEEDEN...
...HASN'T SHOWN US EVERYTHING THEY CAN DO YET.
WHEN WE SENT THE RADS...
...THEY MOBILIZED SEVERAL HUNDRED COMBAT-ANTS.
CONSIDER-ING THAT SCALE...
...WE CAN SURMISE THAT MANY OTHER SKILLED INDIVIDUALS ...
...BESIDES THOSE IN THIS SQUAD EXIST.

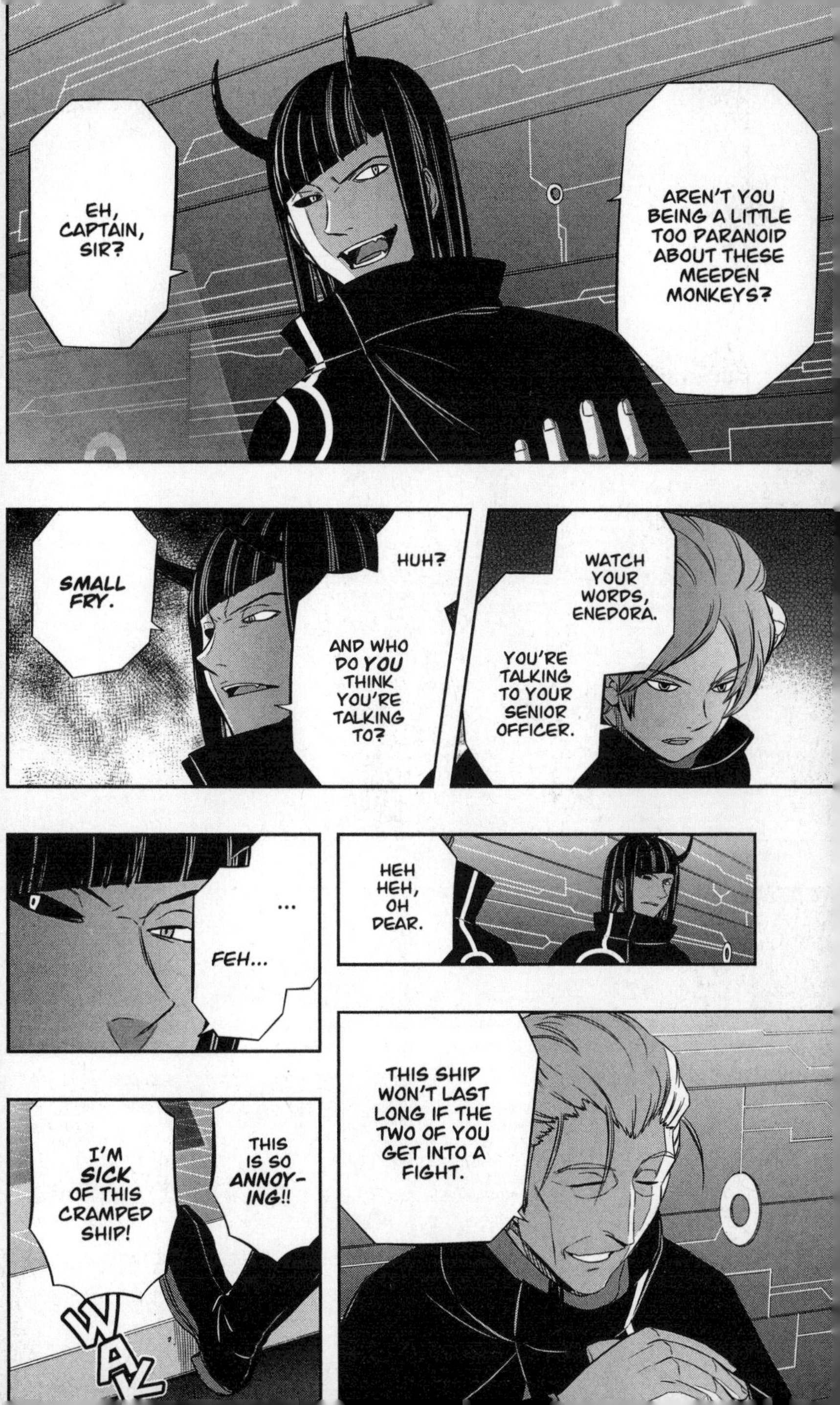
AREN'T YOU BEING A LITTLE TOO PARANOID ABOUT THESE MEEDEN MONKEYS?
EH, CAPTAIN, SIR?
WATCH YOUR WORDS, ENEDORA.
YOU'RE TALKING TO YOUR SENIOR OFFICER.
HUH?
AND WHO DO *YOU* THINK YOU'RE TALKING TO?
SMALL FRY.
HEH HEH, OH DEAR.
...
FEH...
THIS SHIP WON'T LAST LONG IF THE TWO OF YOU GET INTO A FIGHT.
THIS IS SO ANNOYING!!
I'M *SICK* OF THIS CRAMPED SHIP!
WAK

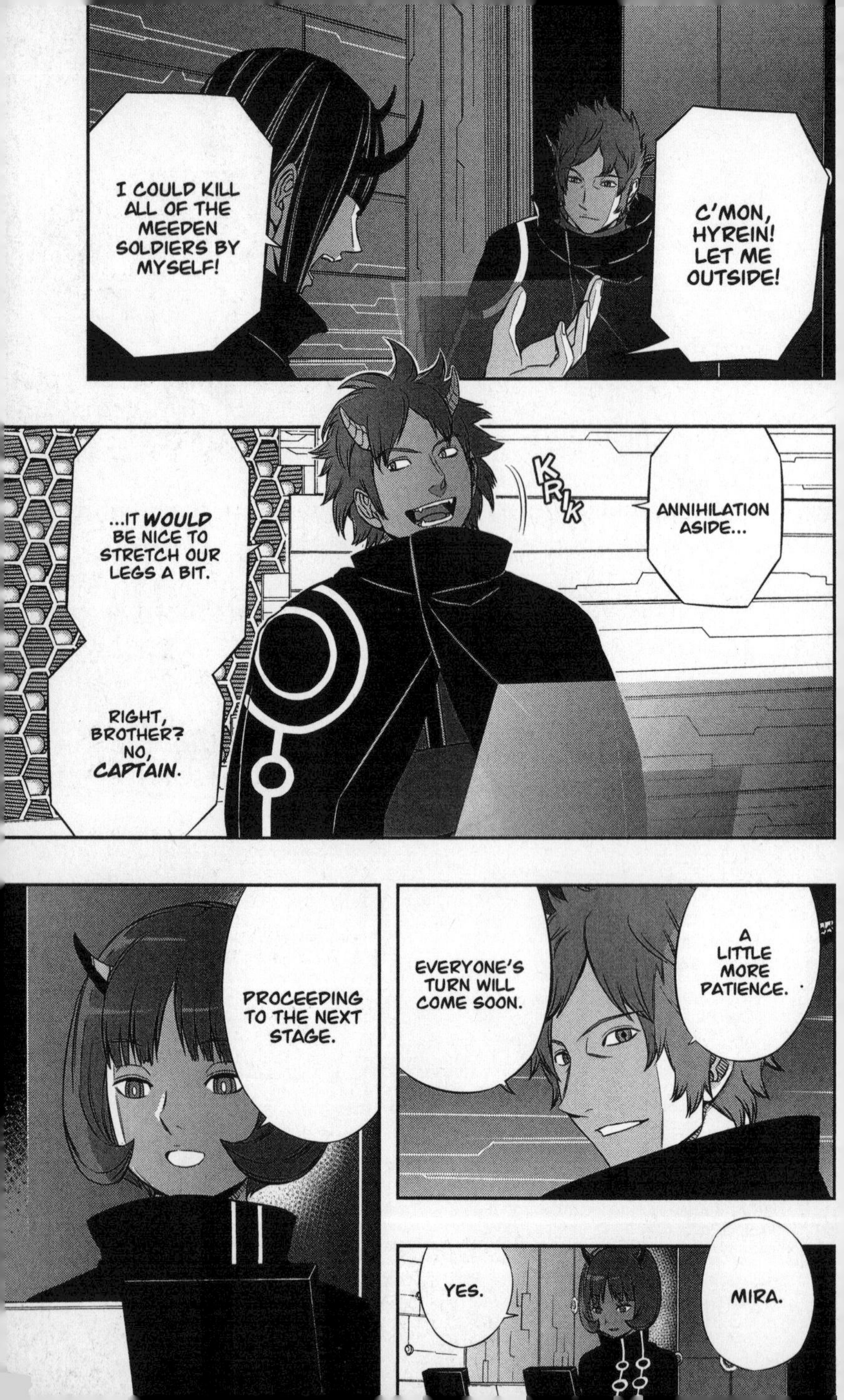
C'MON, HYREIN! LET ME OUTSIDE!
I COULD KILL ALL OF THE MEEDEN SOLDIERS BY MYSELF!
ANNIHILATION ASIDE...
KRIK
...IT **WOULD** BE NICE TO STRETCH OUR LEGS A BIT.
RIGHT, BROTHER? NO, **CAPTAIN**.
A LITTLE MORE PATIENCE.
EVERYONE'S TURN WILL COME SOON.
MIRA.
YES.
PROCEEDING TO THE NEXT STAGE.

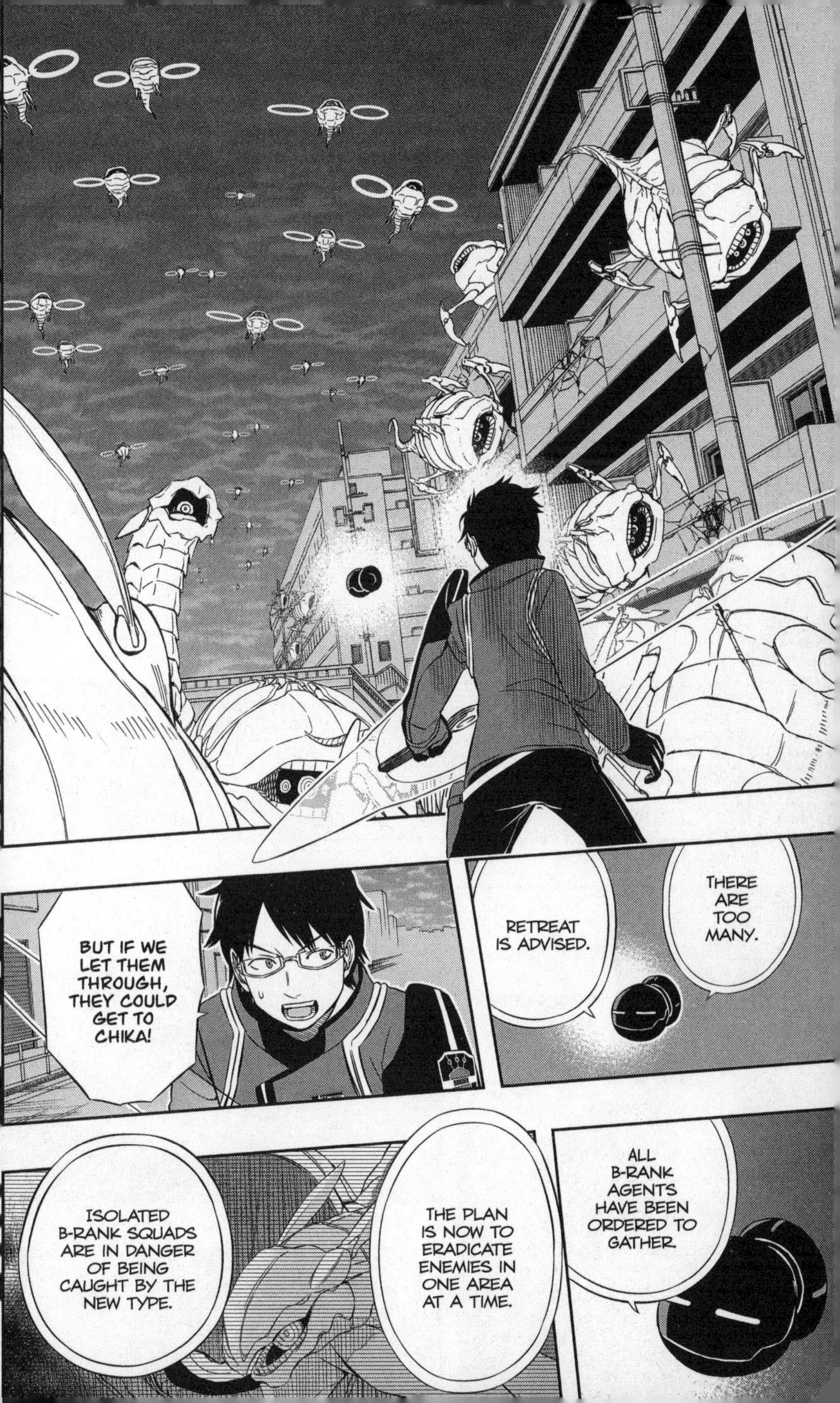
THERE ARE TOO MANY.
RETREAT IS ADVISED.
BUT IF WE LET THEM THROUGH, THEY COULD GET TO CHIKA!
ALL B-RANK AGENTS HAVE BEEN ORDERED TO GATHER.
THE PLAN IS NOW TO ERADICATE ENEMIES IN ONE AREA AT A TIME.
ISOLATED B-RANK SQUADS ARE IN DANGER OF BEING CAUGHT BY THE NEW TYPE.

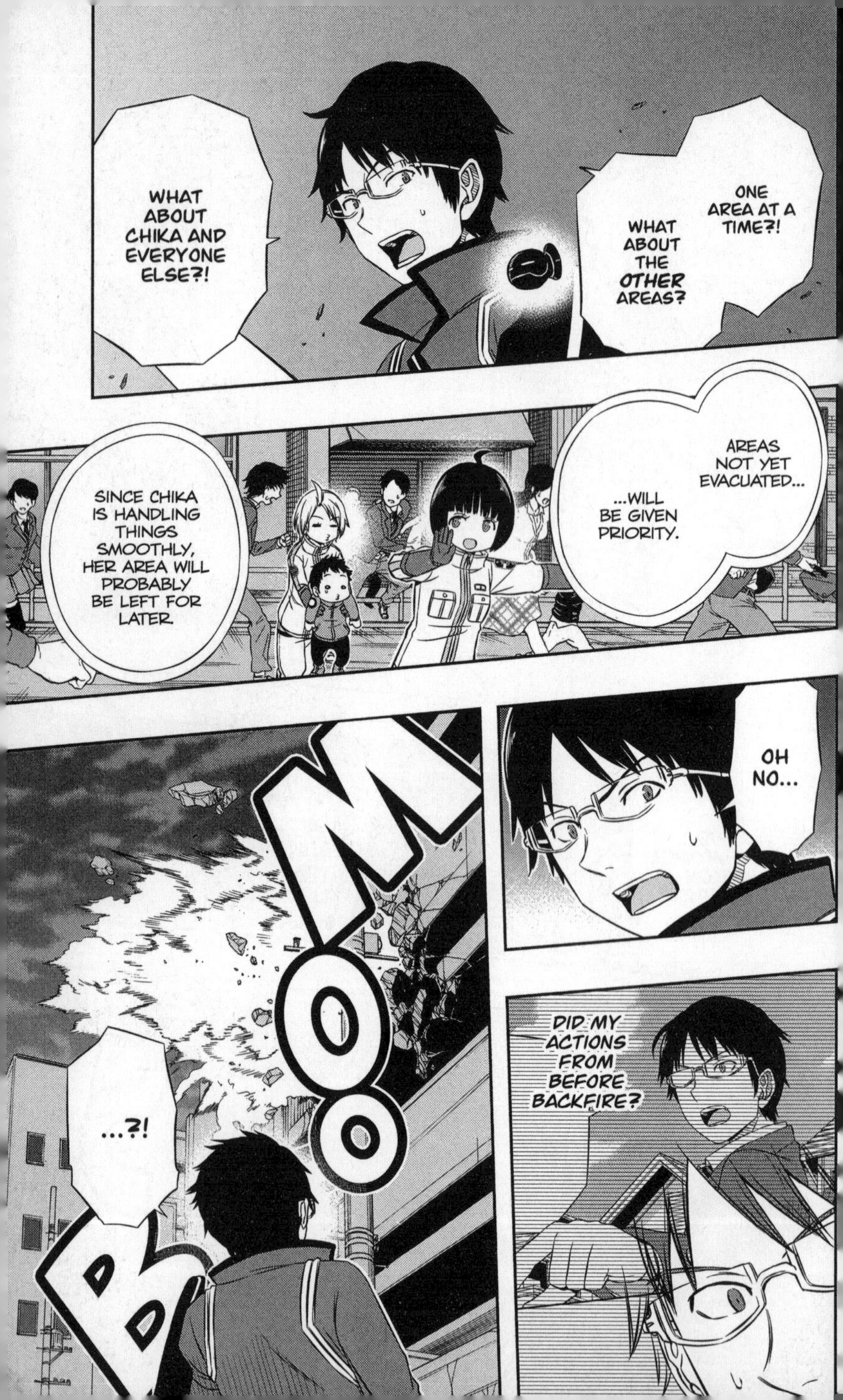
ONE AREA AT A TIME?!
WHAT ABOUT THE OTHER AREAS?
WHAT ABOUT CHIKA AND EVERYONE ELSE?!
AREAS NOT YET EVACUATED...
...WILL BE GIVEN PRIORITY.
SINCE CHIKA IS HANDLING THINGS SMOOTHLY, HER AREA WILL PROBABLY BE LEFT FOR LATER.
OH NO...
DID MY ACTIONS FROM BEFORE BACKFIRE?
BOOM
...?!

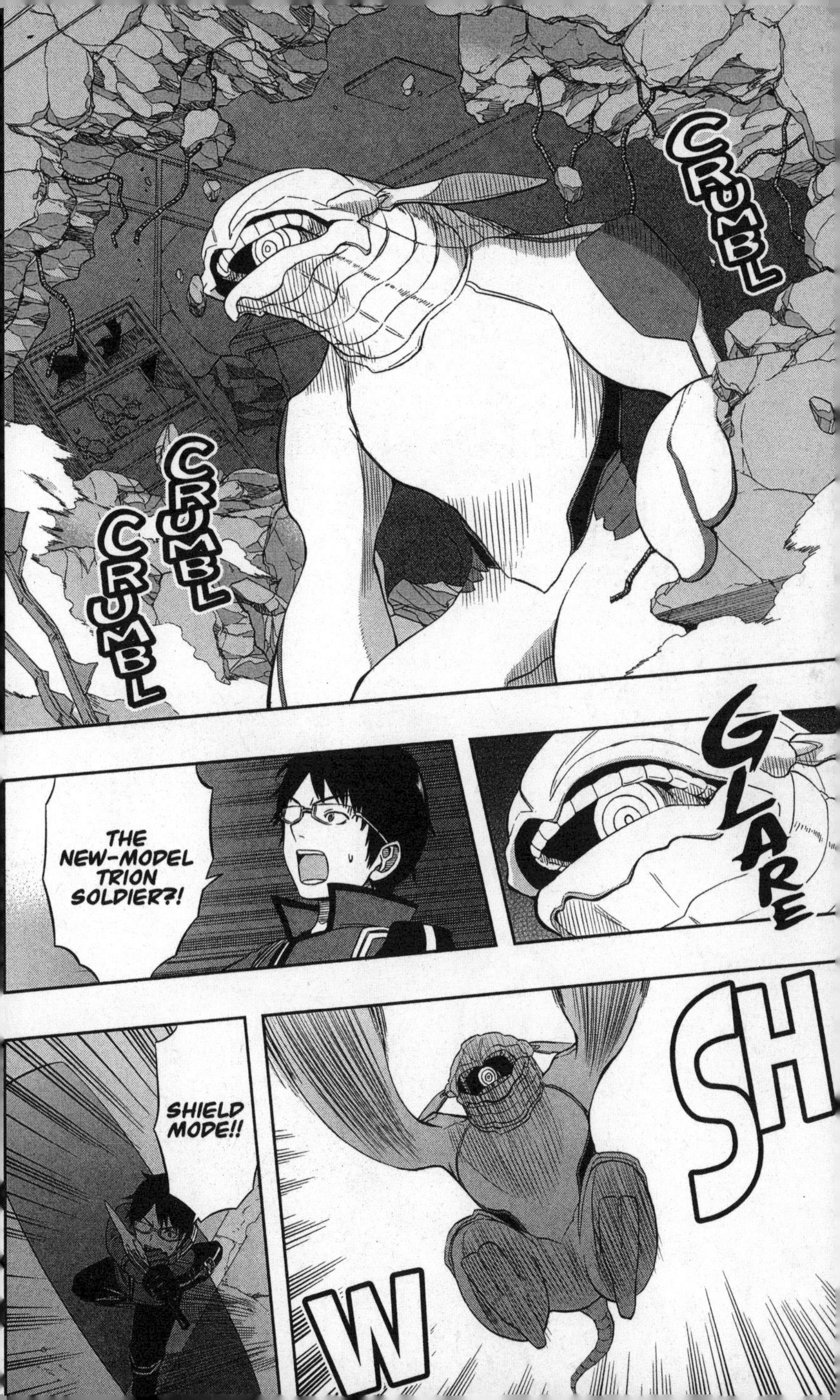
CRUMBL
CRUMBL
CRUMBL
GLARE
THE NEW-MODEL TRION SOLDIER?!
SH
W
SHIELD MODE!!

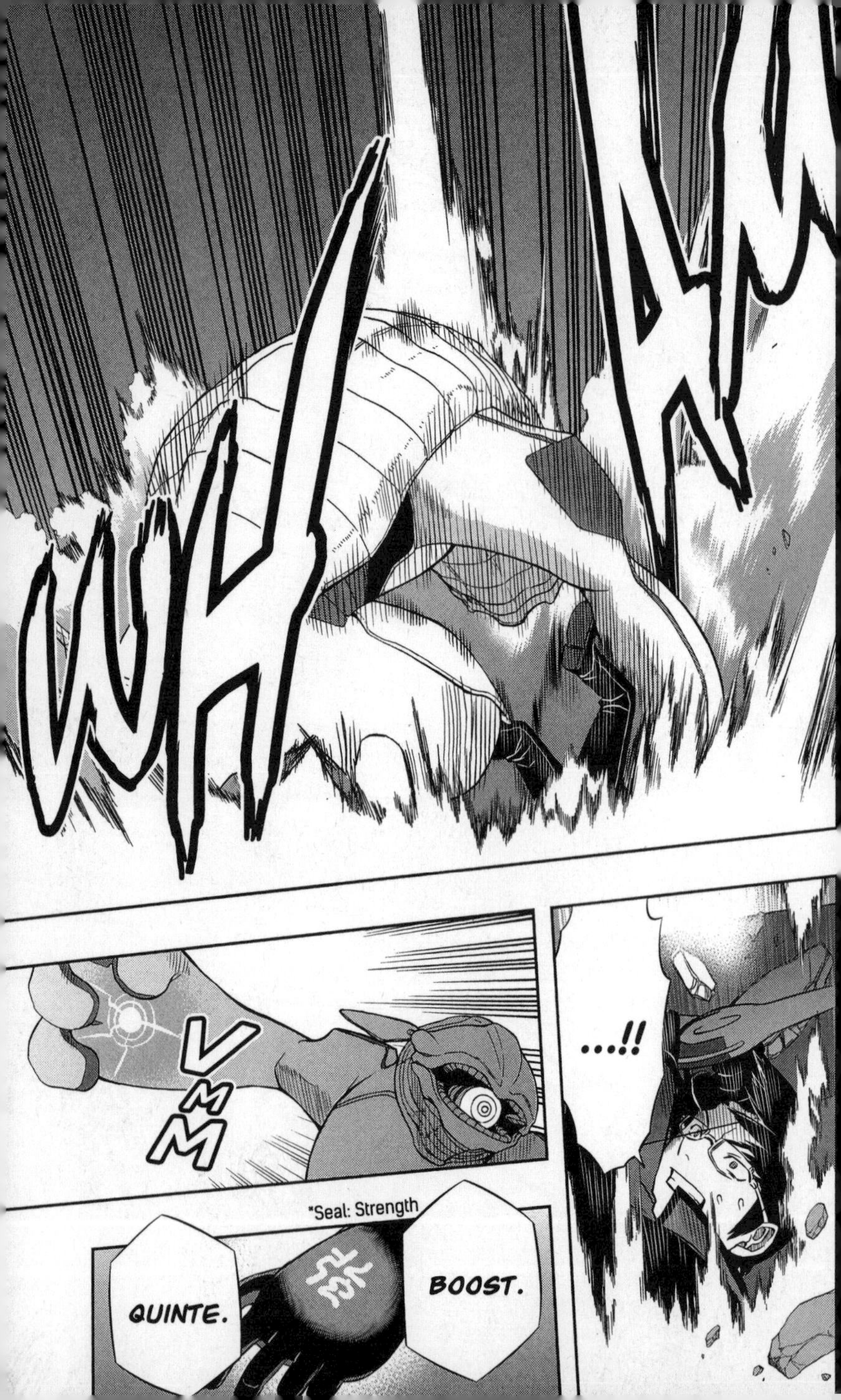
...!!
VMM
*Seal: Strength
BOOST.
QUINTE.

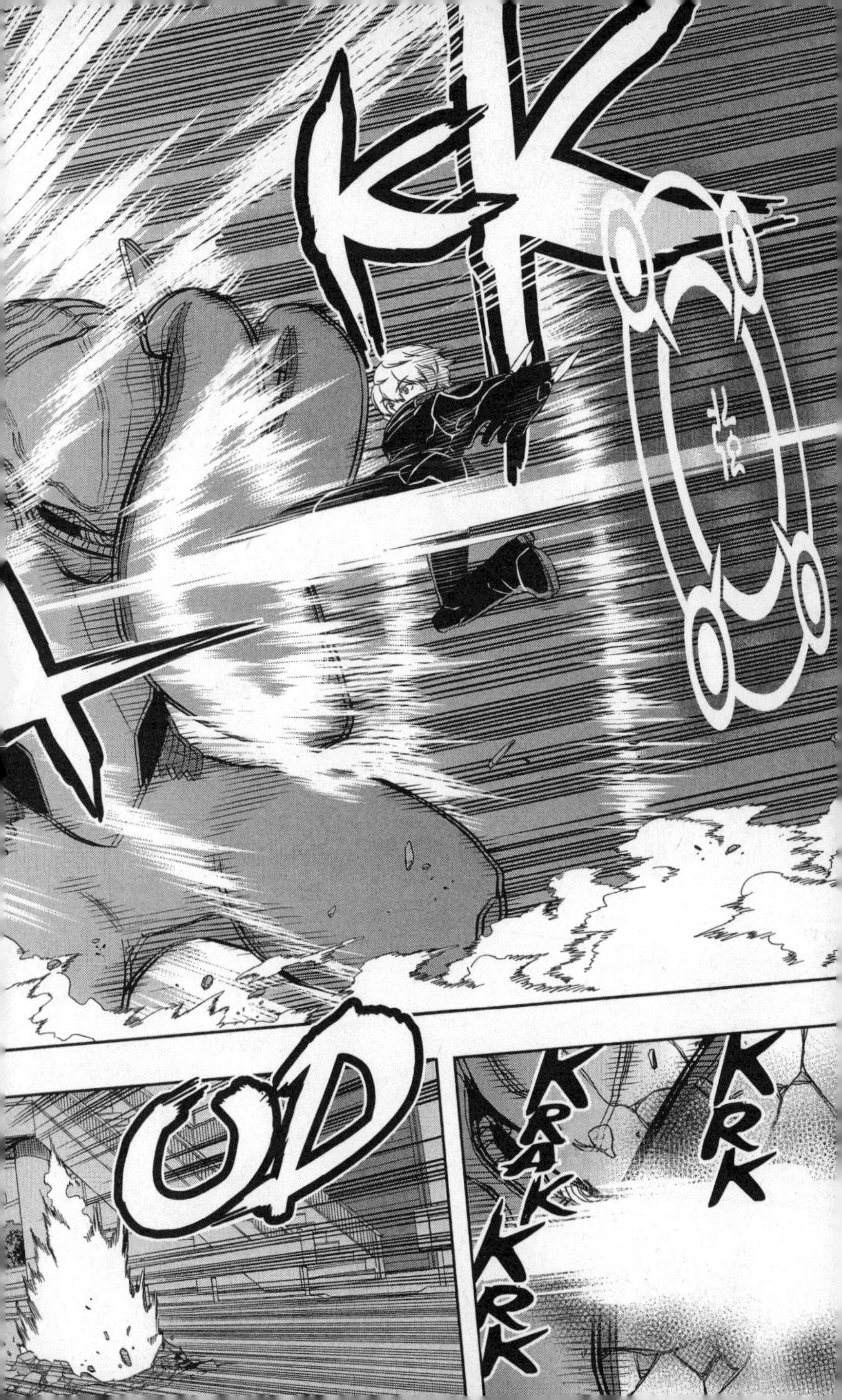

KRK
KRAK
KRK
OOD

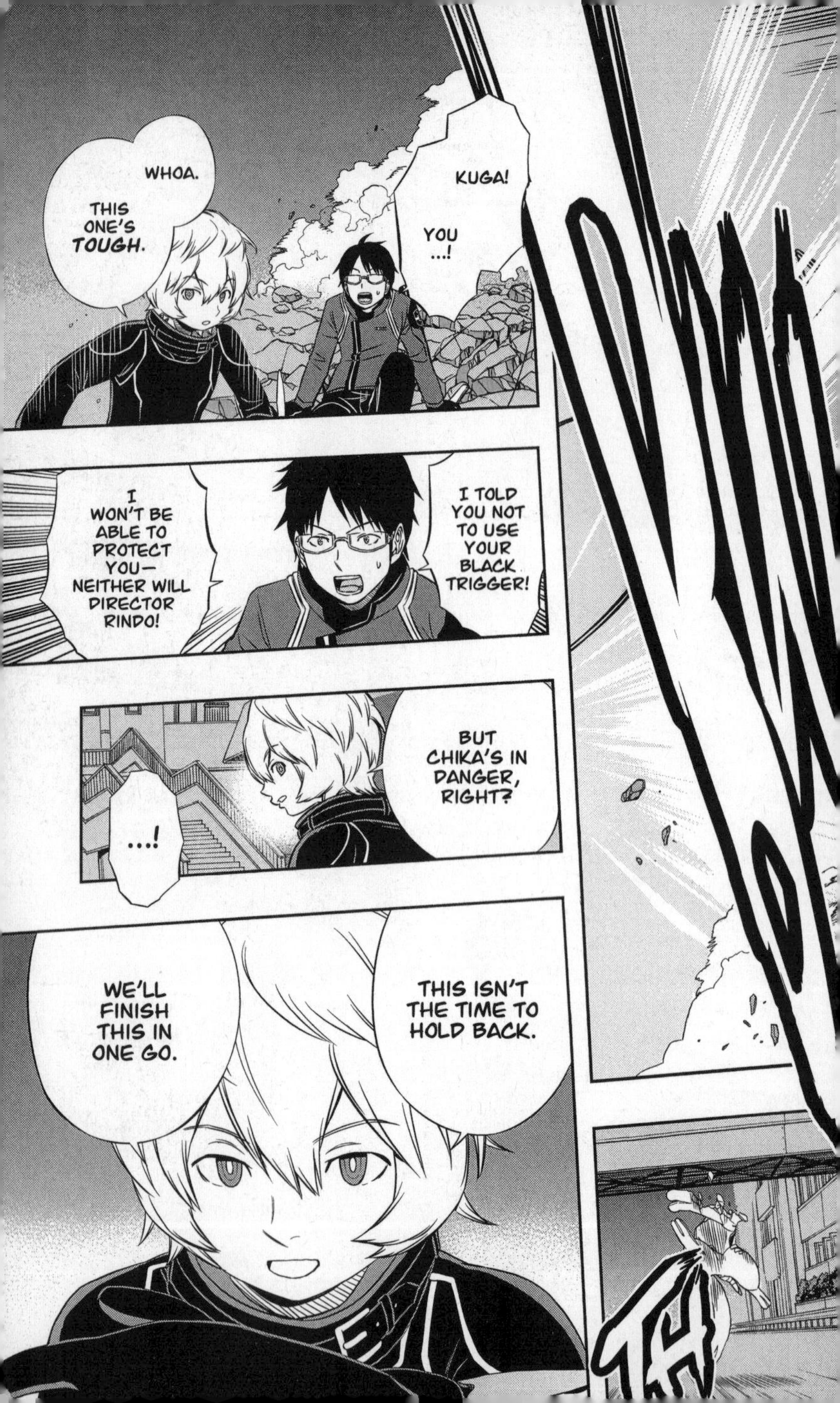
KUGA! YOU ...!
WHOA. THIS ONE'S TOUGH.
I TOLD YOU NOT TO USE YOUR BLACK TRIGGER!
I WON'T BE ABLE TO PROTECT YOU—NEITHER WILL DIRECTOR RINDO!
BUT CHIKA'S IN DANGER, RIGHT?
...!
THIS ISN'T THE TIME TO HOLD BACK.
WE'LL FINISH THIS IN ONE GO.

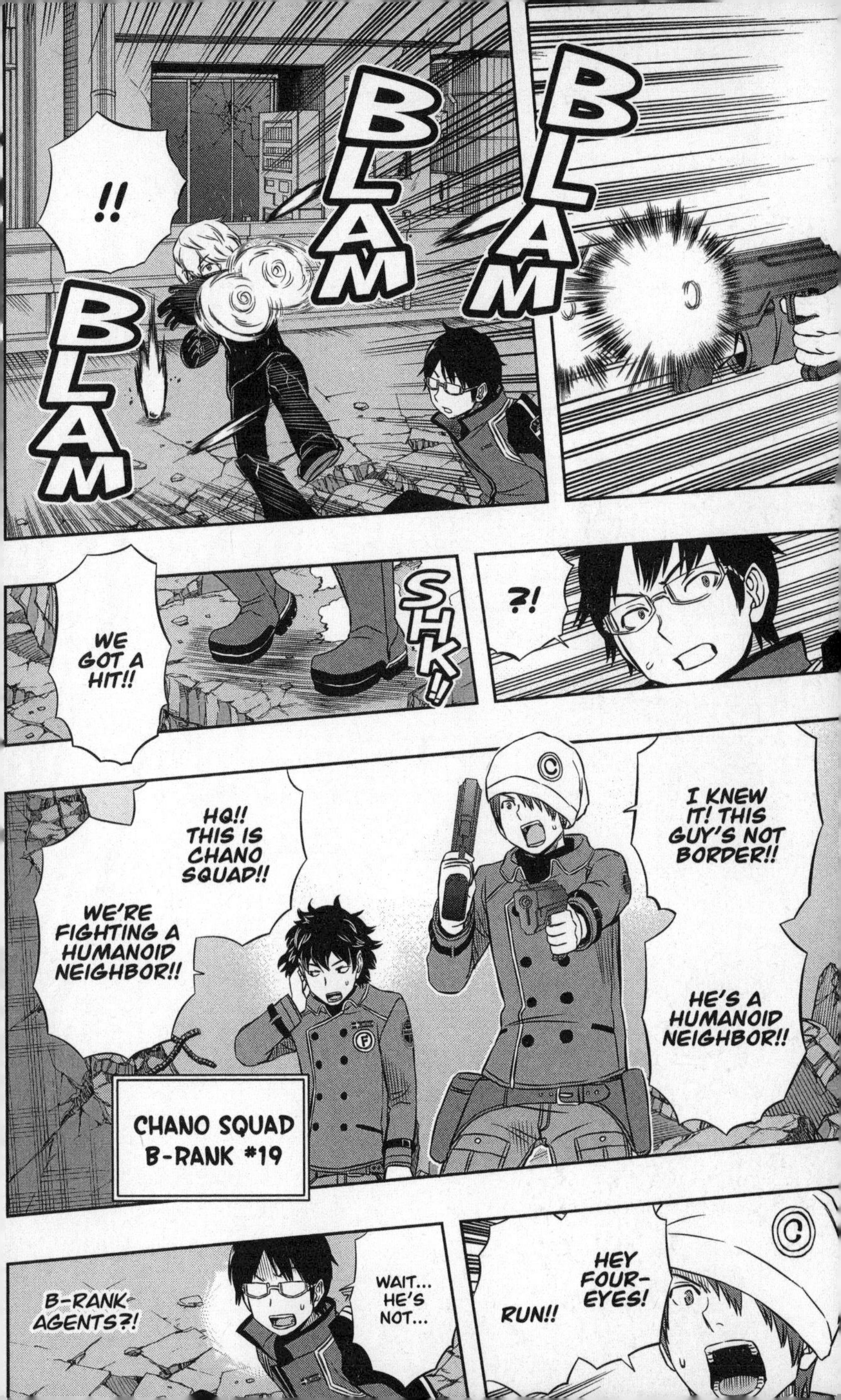
BLAM
BLAM
!!
BLAM
?!
SHK!!
WE GOT A HIT!!
I KNEW IT! THIS GUY'S NOT BORDER!!
HE'S A HUMANOID NEIGHBOR!!
HQ!! THIS IS CHANO SQUAD!!
WE'RE FIGHTING A HUMANOID NEIGHBOR!!
CHANO SQUAD
B-RANK #19
HEY FOUR-EYES!
RUN!!
WAIT... HE'S NOT...
B-RANK AGENTS?!

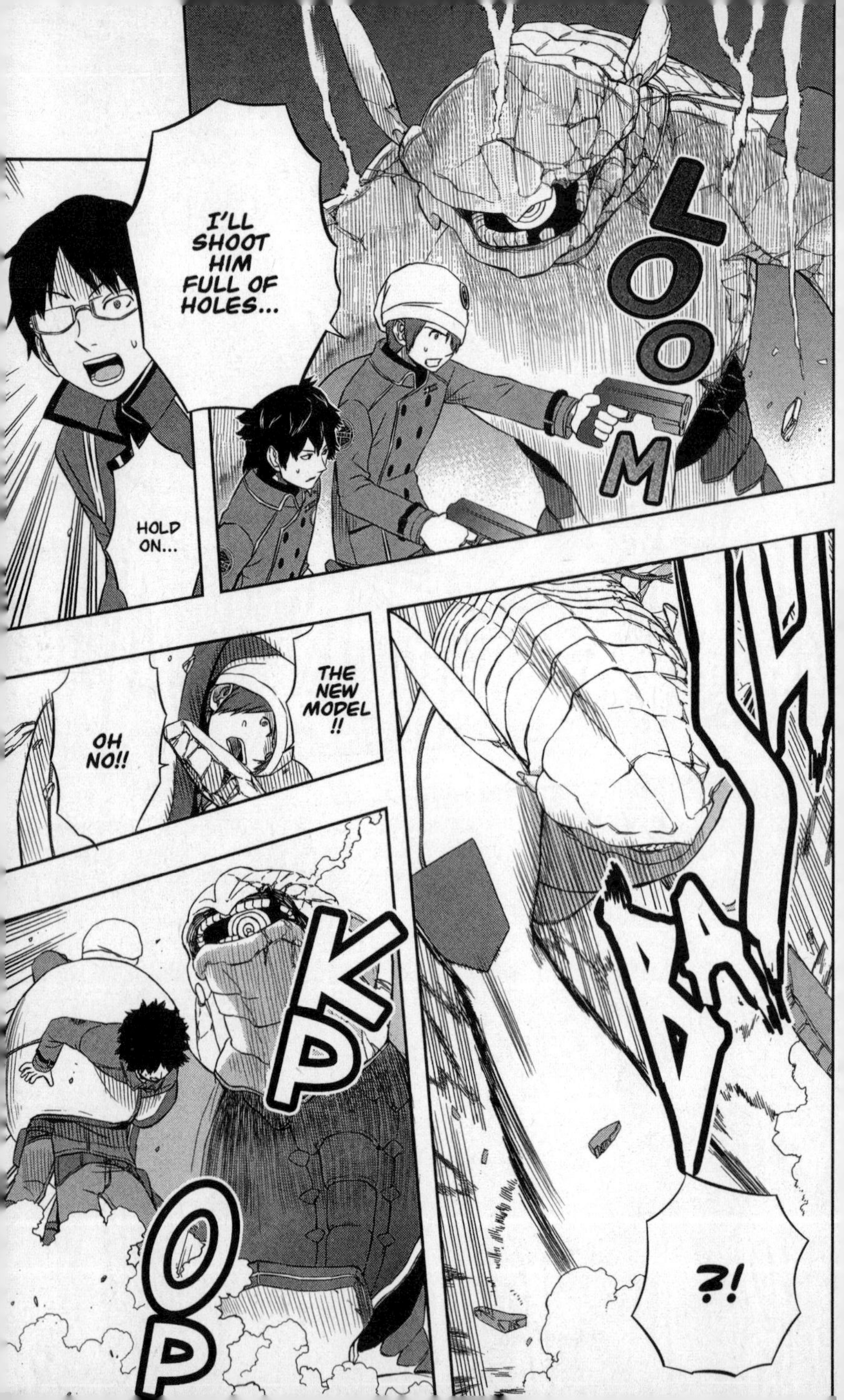
LOOOM
I'LL SHOOT HIM FULL OF HOLES...
HOLD ON...
?!
THE NEW MODEL!!
OH NO!!
KP
OP

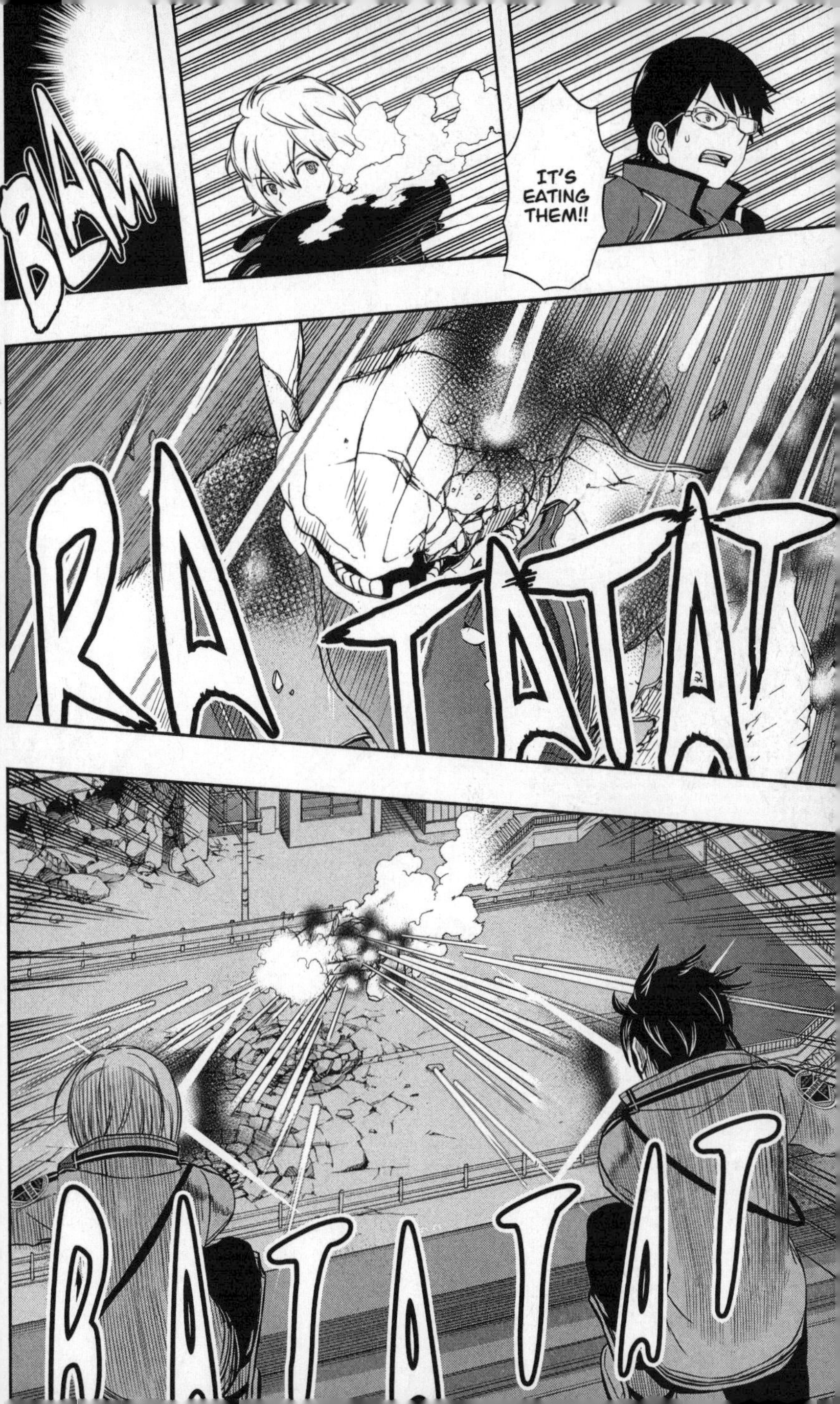
IT'S EATING THEM!!
BLAM
RATATAT
BRATATAT

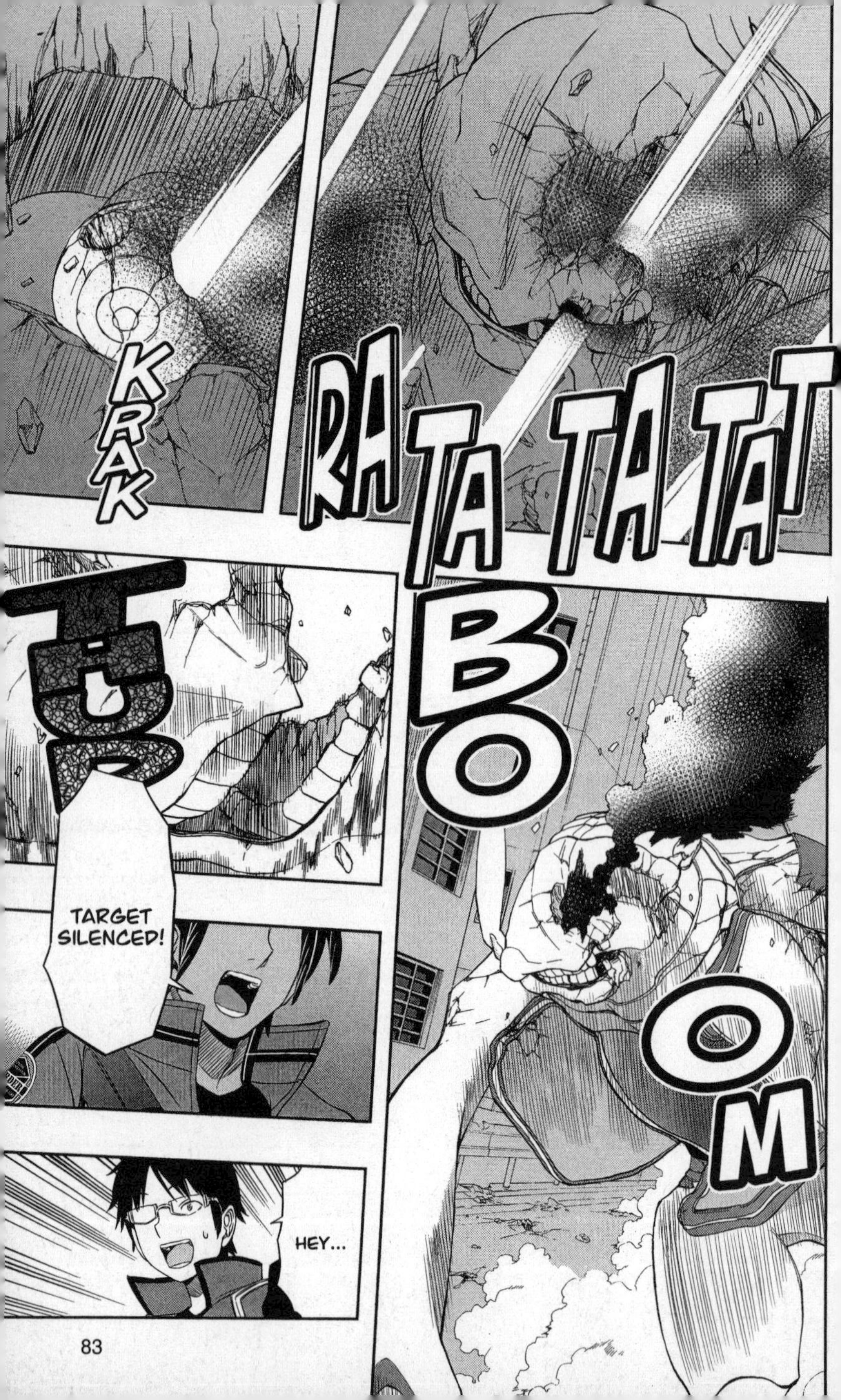
RA TA TA TAT
KRAK
BOOM
TARGET SILENCED!
HEY...

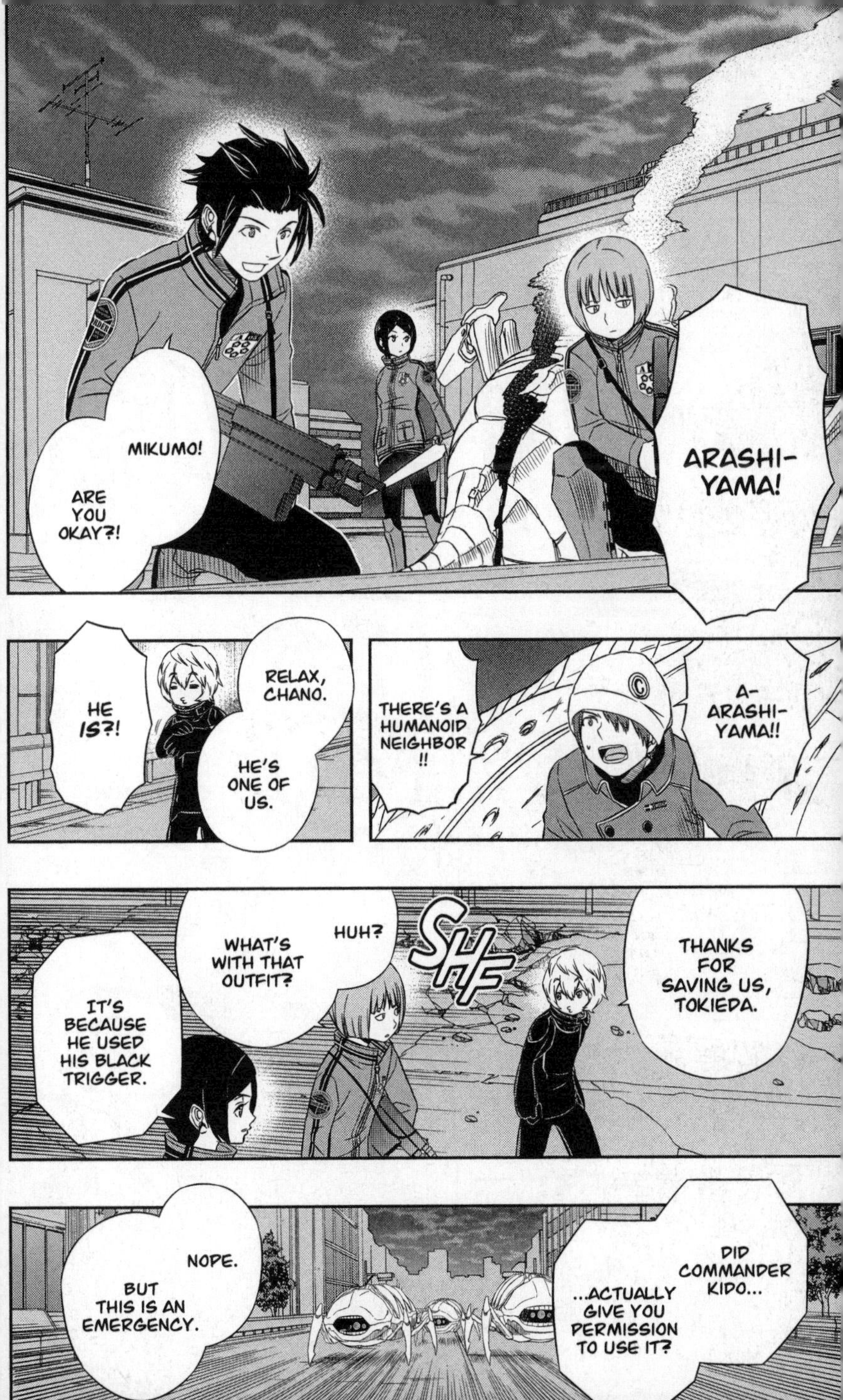
ARASHI-YAMA!
MIKUMO!
ARE YOU OKAY?!
A- ARASHI-YAMA!!
THERE'S A HUMANOID NEIGHBOR!!
RELAX, CHANO.
HE'S ONE OF US.
HE IS?!
THANKS FOR SAVING US, TOKIEDA.
SHF
HUH?
WHAT'S WITH THAT OUTFIT?
IT'S BECAUSE HE USED HIS BLACK TRIGGER.
DID COMMANDER KIDO...
...ACTUALLY GIVE YOU PERMISSION TO USE IT?
NOPE.
BUT THIS IS AN EMERGENCY.

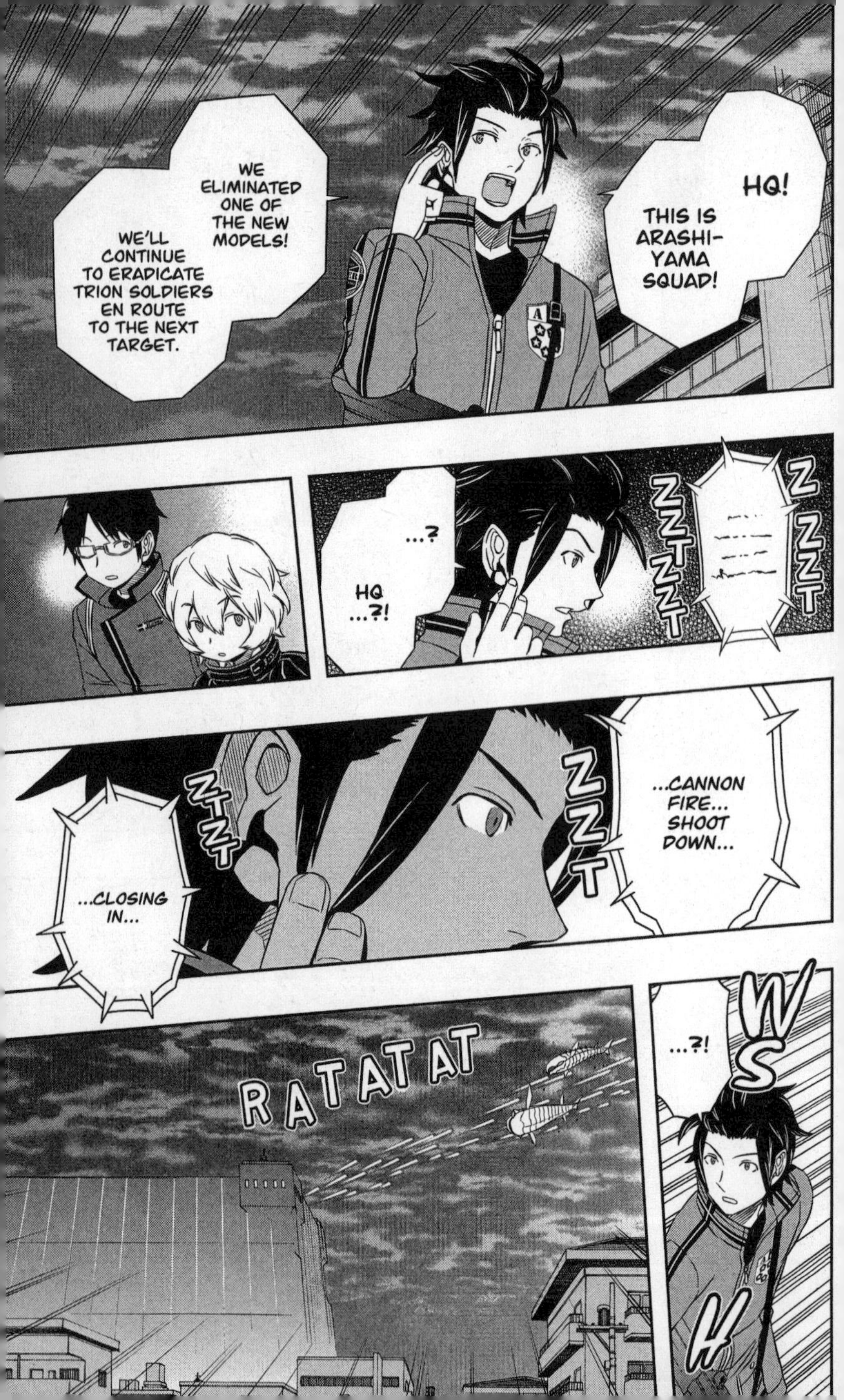
HQ!
THIS IS ARASHIYAMA SQUAD!
WE ELIMINATED ONE OF THE NEW MODELS!
WE'LL CONTINUE TO ERADICATE TRION SOLDIERS EN ROUTE TO THE NEXT TARGET.
ZZZT
ZZZT
...?
HQ ...?!
ZZZT
...CANNON FIRE... SHOOT DOWN...
ZZT
...CLOSING IN...
WSH
...?!
RATATAT

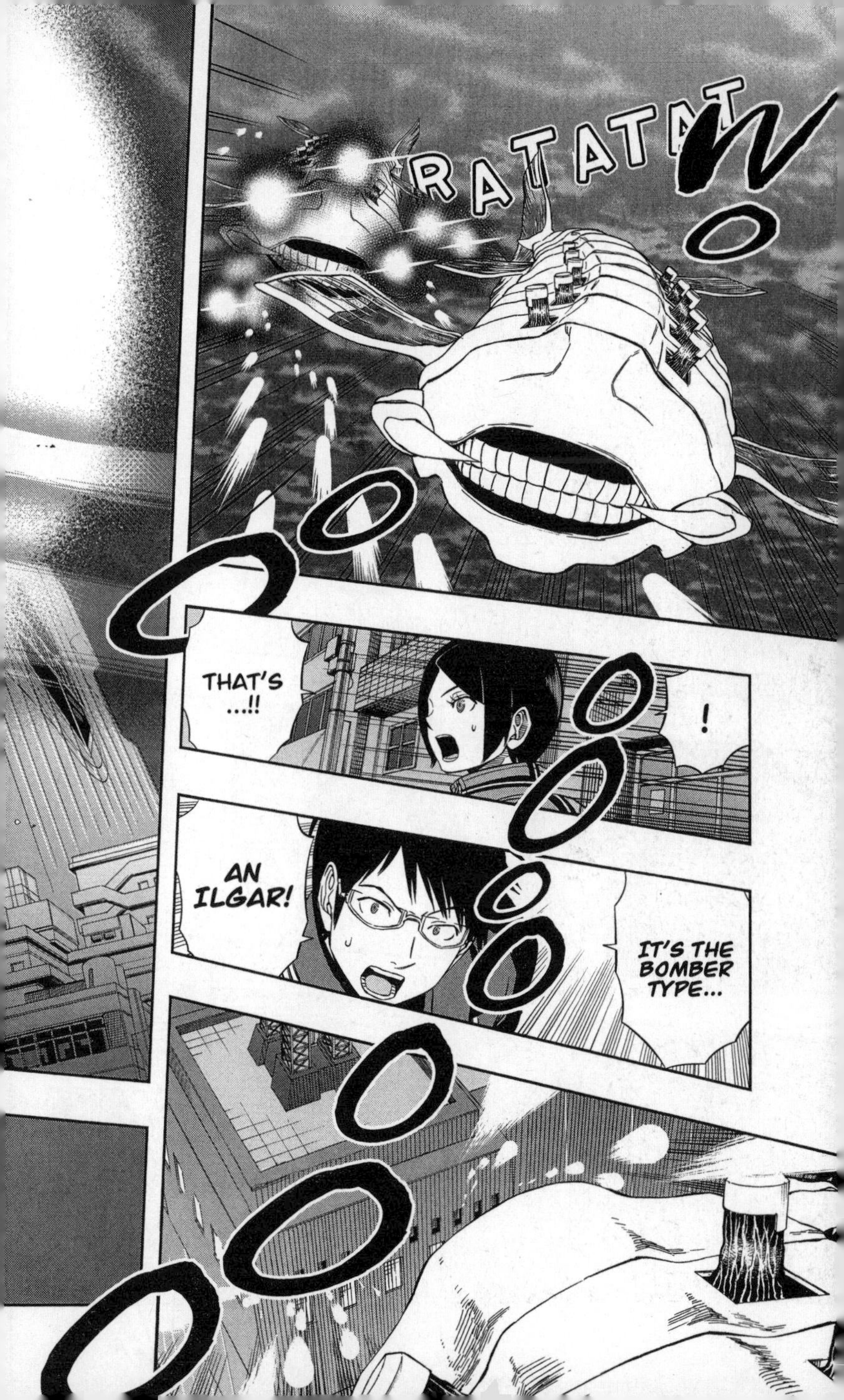
RATATATAT
VWOOOOOOOO
THAT'S ...!!
!
AN ILGAR!
IT'S THE BOMBER TYPE...

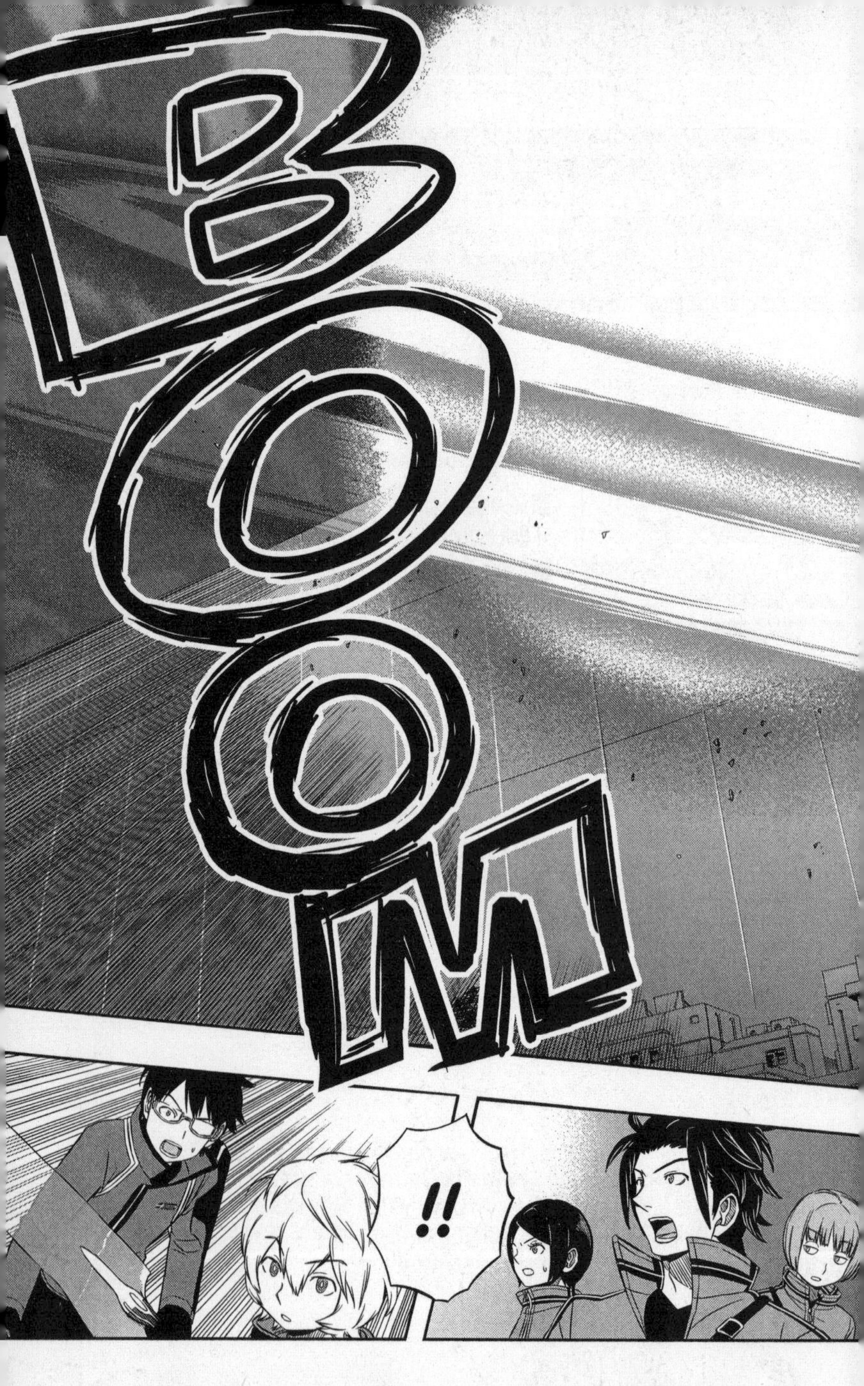
BOOM
!!

Chano Squad
Border HQ B-Rank #19

B-019

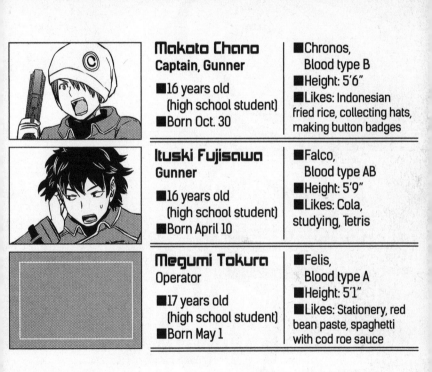

Makoto Chano
Captain, Gunner

■16 years old
  (high school student)
■Born Oct. 30

■Chronos,
  Blood type B
■Height: 5'6"
■Likes: Indonesian fried rice, collecting hats, making button badges

Ituski Fujisawa
Gunner

■16 years old
  (high school student)
■Born April 10

■Falco,
  Blood type AB
■Height: 5'9"
■Likes: Cola, studying, Tetris

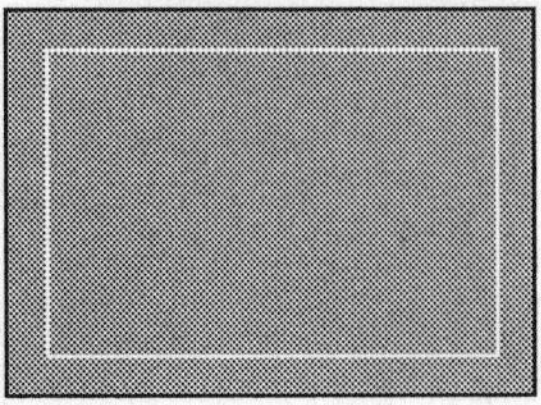

Megumi Tokura
Operator

■17 years old
  (high school student)
■Born May 1

■Felis,
  Blood type A
■Height: 5'1"
■Likes: Stationery, red bean paste, spaghetti with cod roe sauce

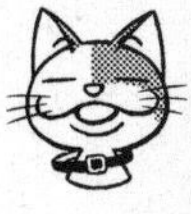

Netsuki formed this media-darling squad as a second Arashiyama Squad. There may or may not have been some allowances by Mr. Netsuki when they were promoted to B-Rank. They know nothing of this and are always serious and hardworking, so I hope they do well.

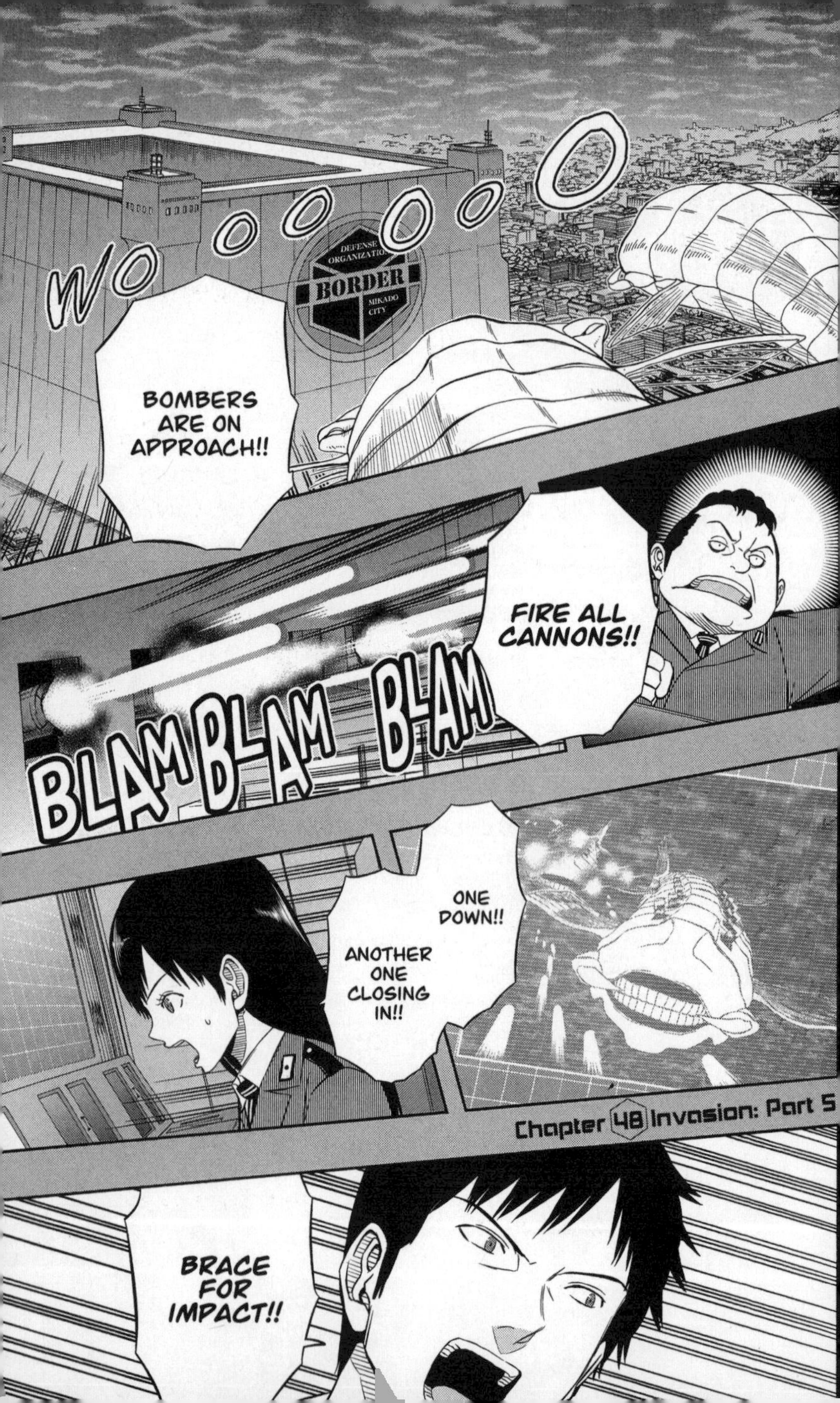

WOOOOOOO
DEFENSE ORGANIZATION
BORDER
MIKADO CITY
BOMBERS ARE ON APPROACH!!
FIRE ALL CANNONS!!
BLAM BLAM BLAM
ONE DOWN!!
ANOTHER ONE CLOSING IN!!
Chapter 48 Invasion: Part 5
BRACE FOR IMPACT!!

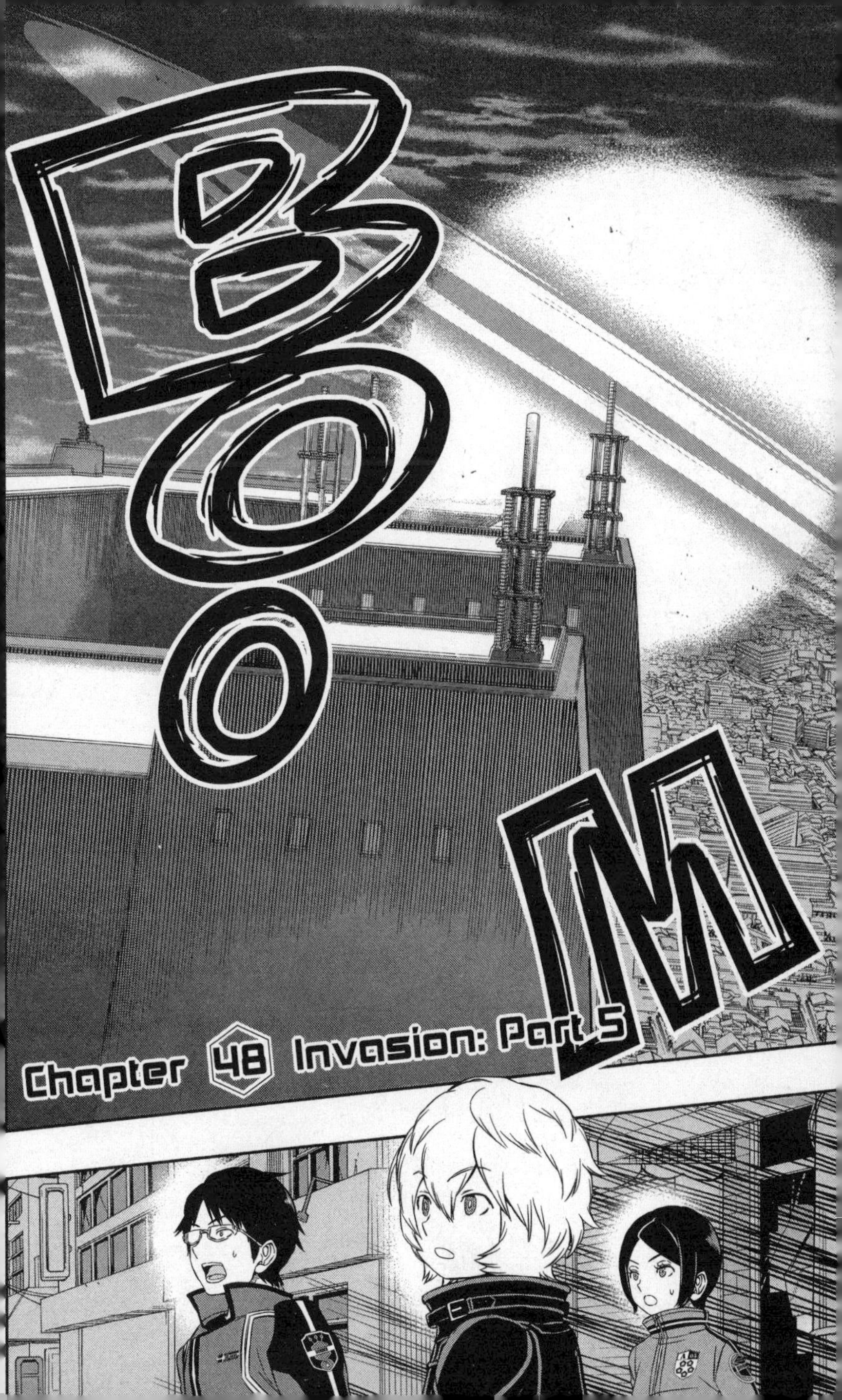
BOOM
Chapter 48 Invasion: Part 5

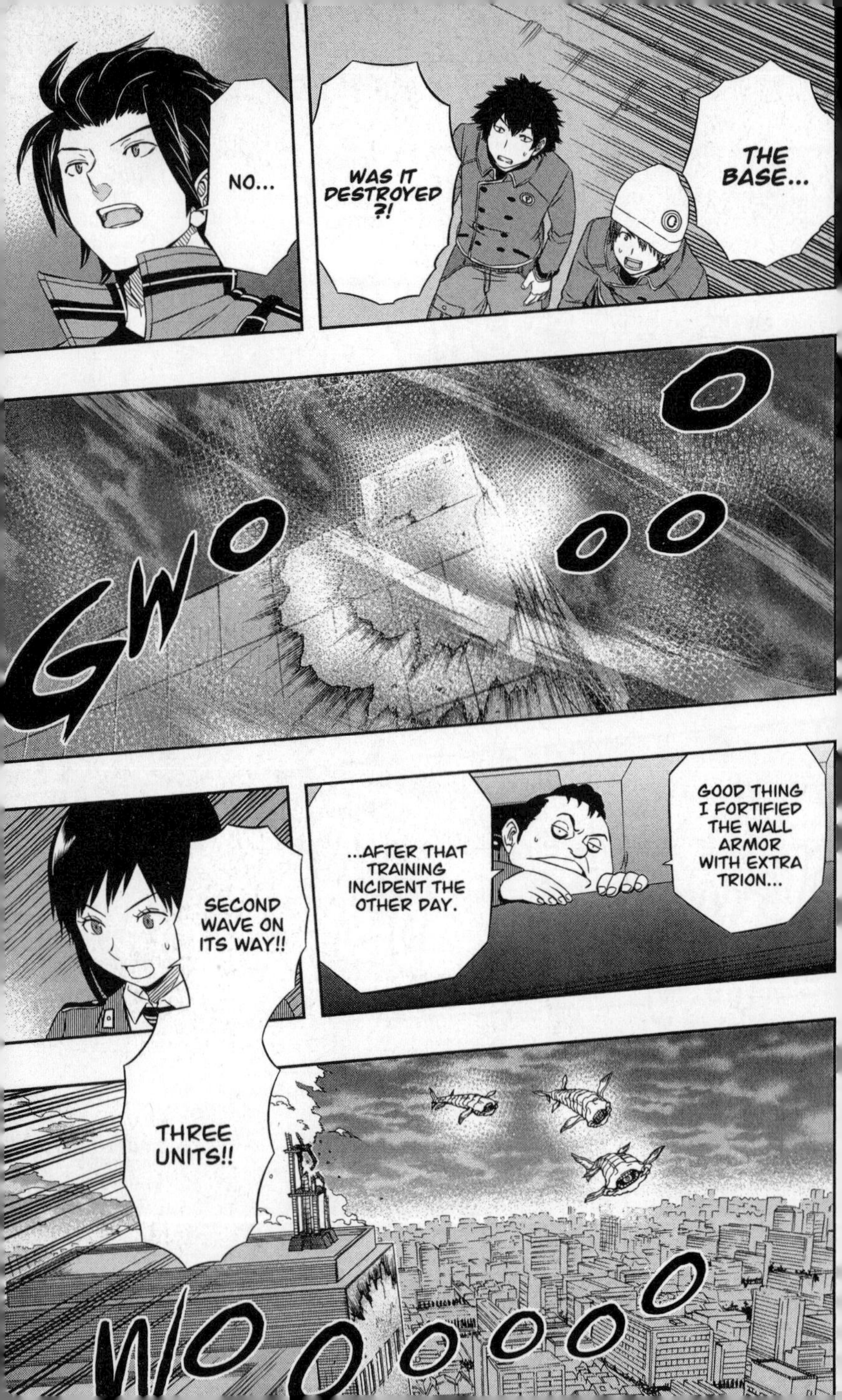
THE BASE...
WAS IT DESTROYED?!
NO...
GWOOOO
GOOD THING I FORTIFIED THE WALL ARMOR WITH EXTRA TRION...
...AFTER THAT TRAINING INCIDENT THE OTHER DAY.
SECOND WAVE ON ITS WAY!!
THREE UNITS!!
WOOOOOOO

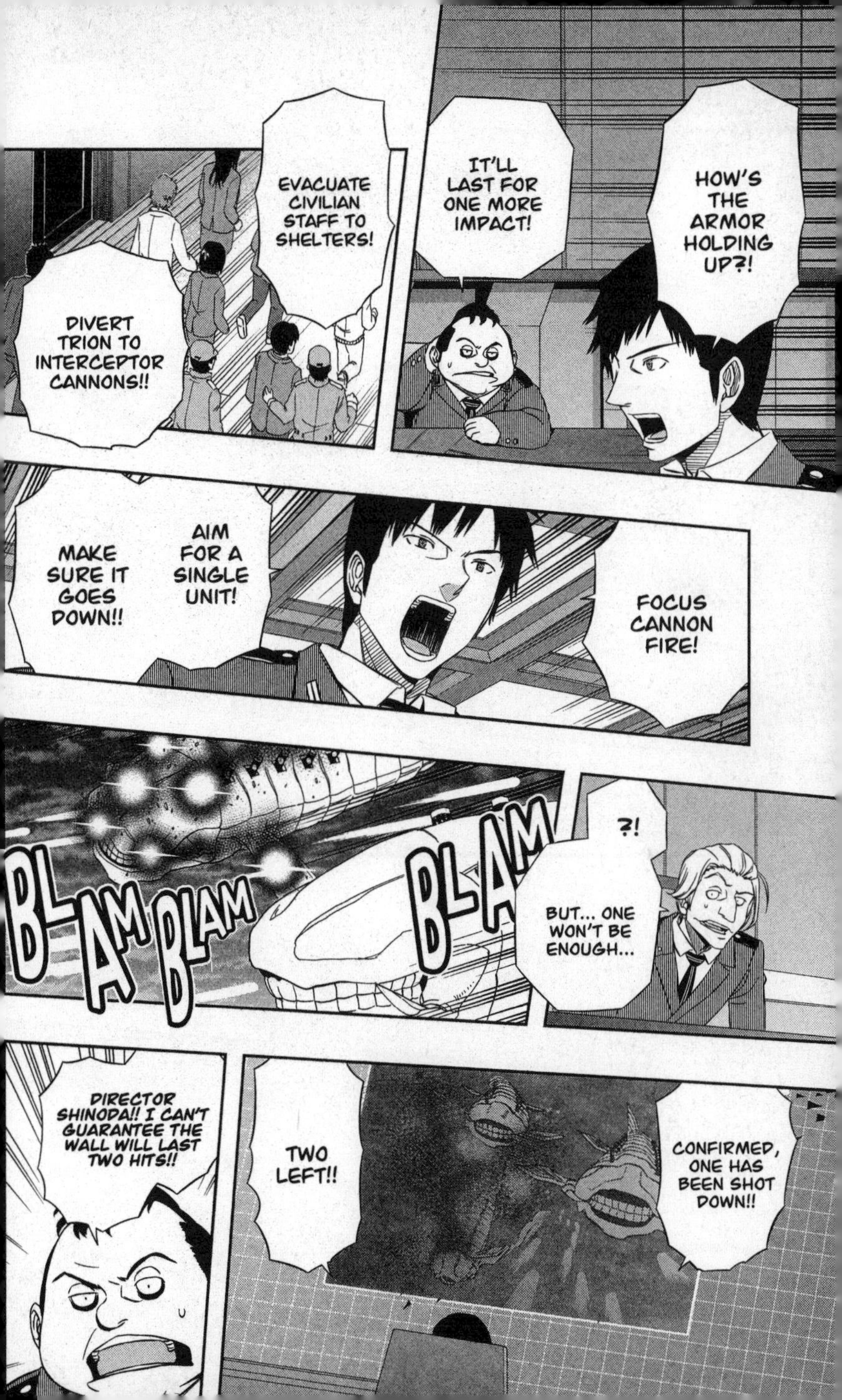
HOW'S THE ARMOR HOLDING UP?!
IT'LL LAST FOR ONE MORE IMPACT!
EVACUATE CIVILIAN STAFF TO SHELTERS!
DIVERT TRION TO INTERCEPTOR CANNONS!!
FOCUS CANNON FIRE!
AIM FOR A SINGLE UNIT!
MAKE SURE IT GOES DOWN!!
?!
BUT... ONE WON'T BE ENOUGH...
BLAM
BLAM
BLAM
CONFIRMED, ONE HAS BEEN SHOT DOWN!!
TWO LEFT!!
DIRECTOR SHINODA!! I CAN'T GUARANTEE THE WALL WILL LAST TWO HITS!!

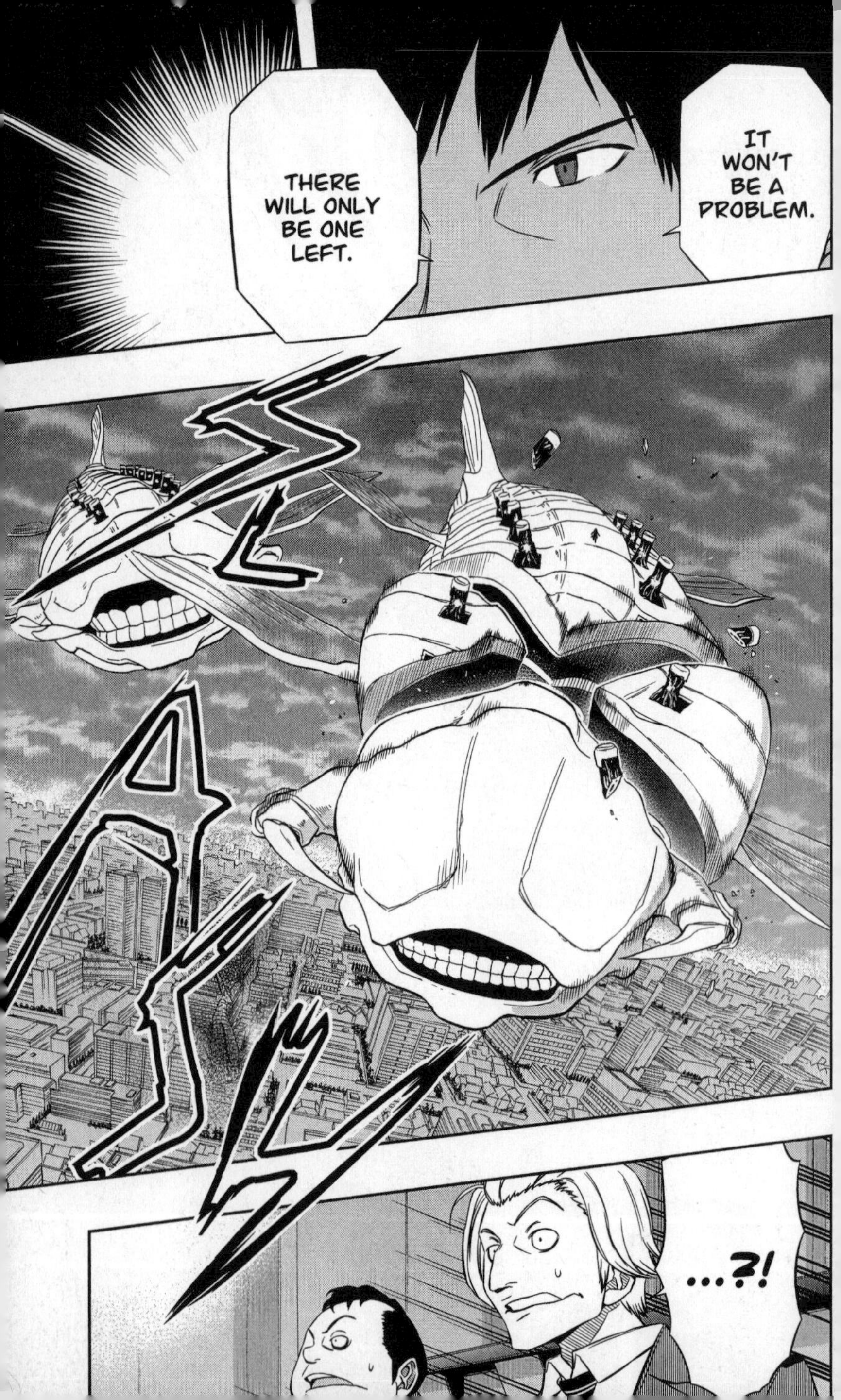
IT WON'T BE A PROBLEM.
THERE WILL ONLY BE ONE LEFT.
...?!

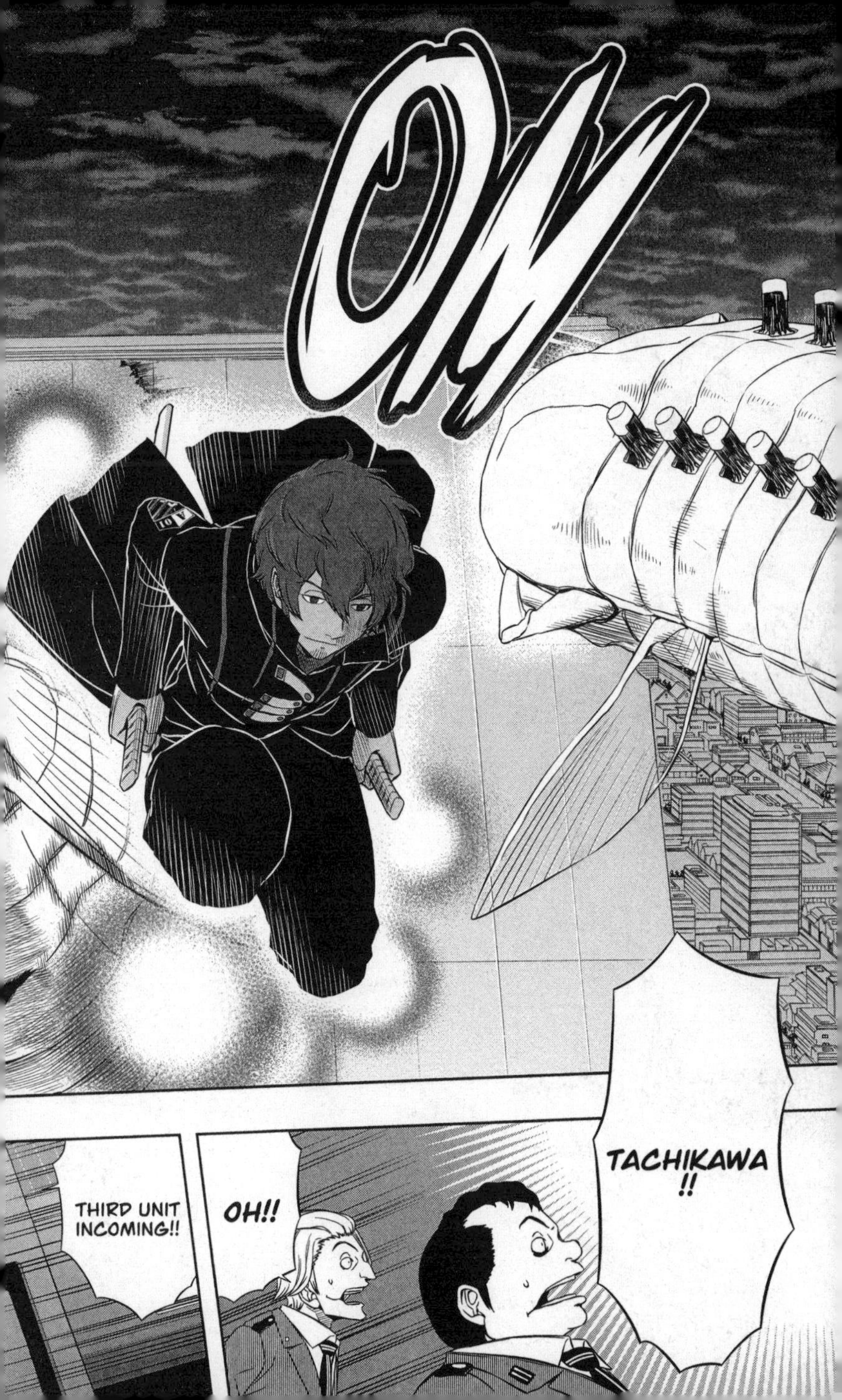
TACHIKAWA!!
OH!!
THIRD UNIT INCOMING!!

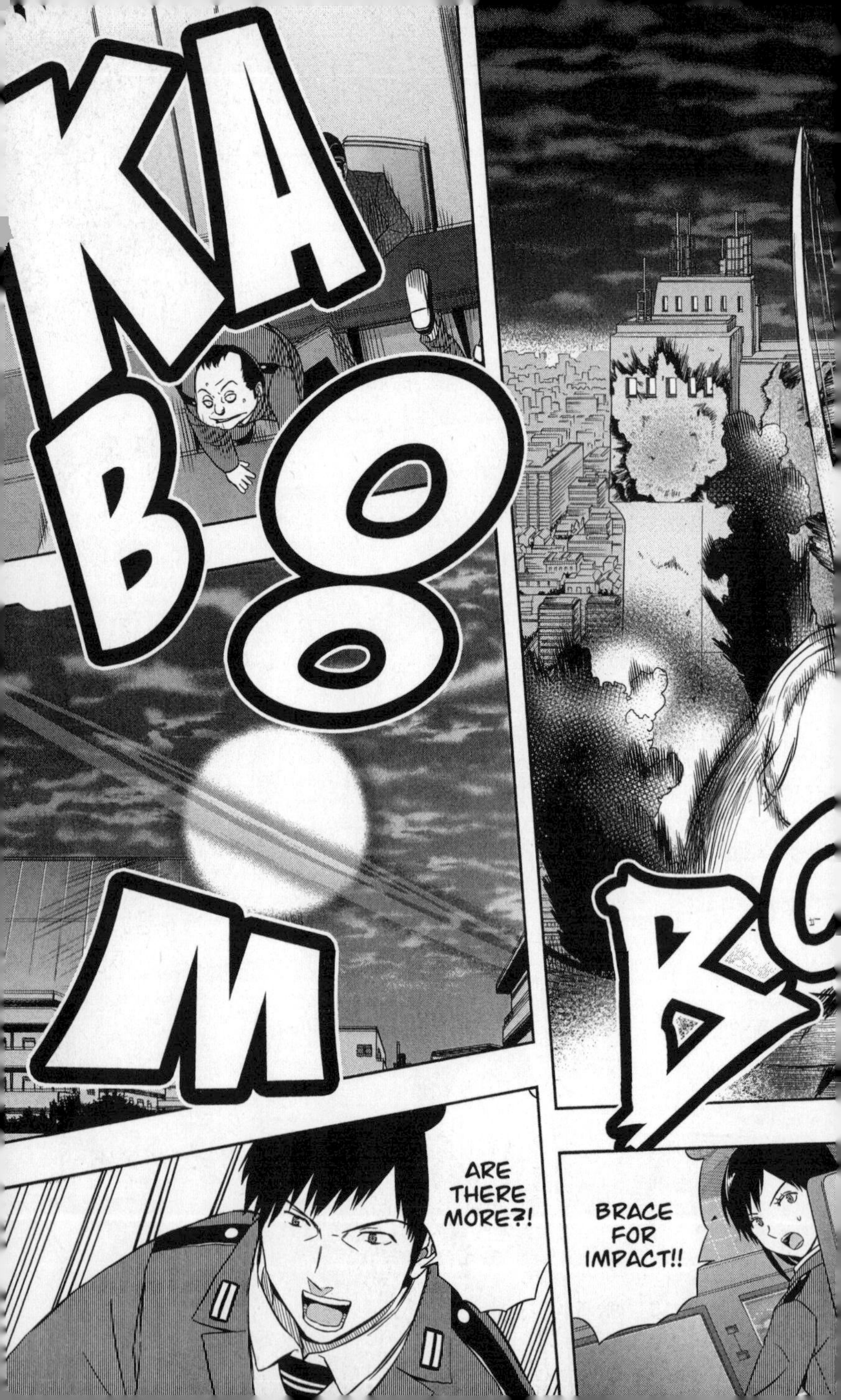
BO
KABOOM
BRACE FOR IMPACT!!
ARE THERE MORE?!

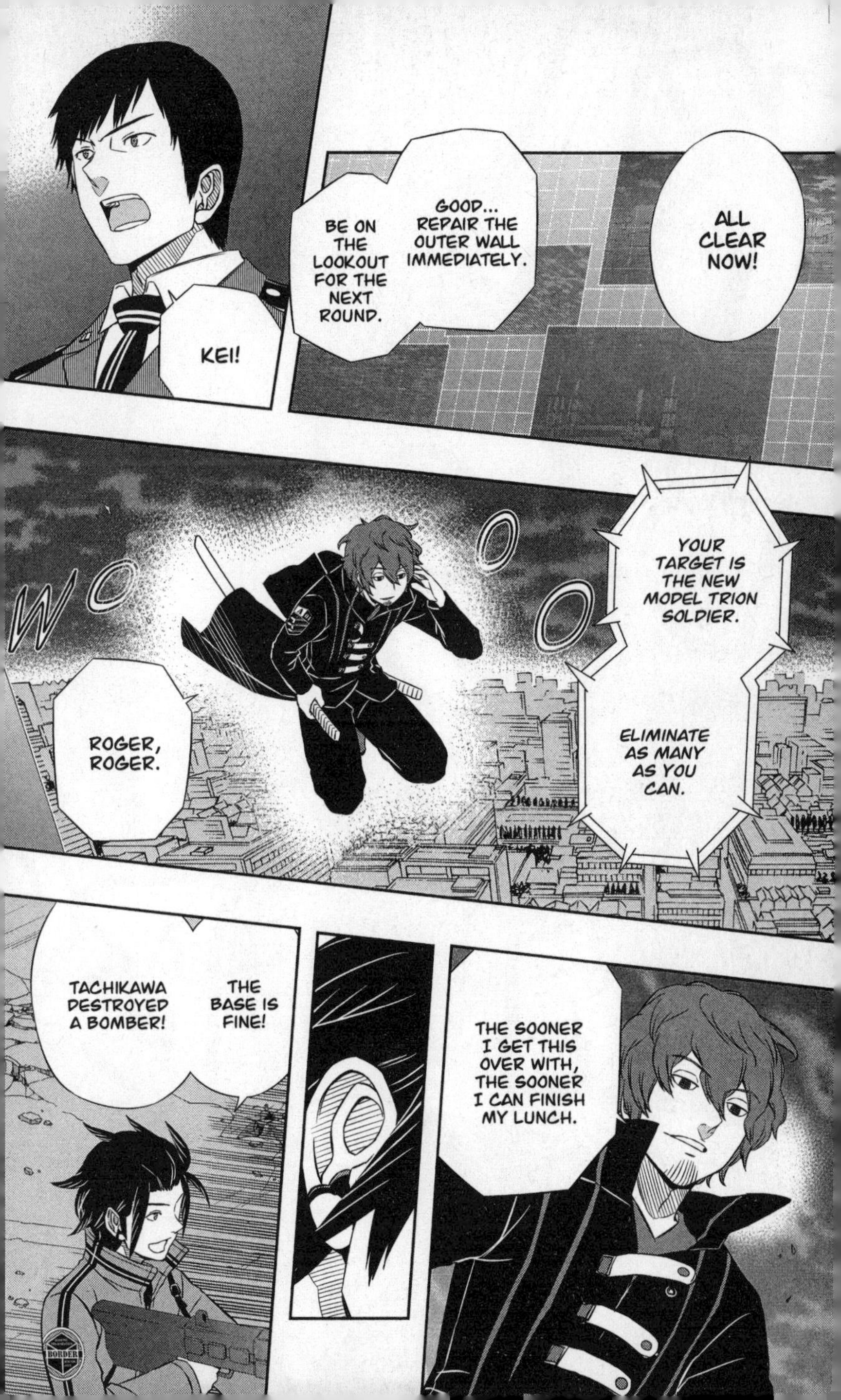
ALL CLEAR NOW!
GOOD... REPAIR THE OUTER WALL IMMEDIATELY.
BE ON THE LOOKOUT FOR THE NEXT ROUND.
KEI!
YOUR TARGET IS THE NEW MODEL TRION SOLDIER.
ELIMINATE AS MANY AS YOU CAN.
WOOOO
ROGER, ROGER.
THE SOONER I GET THIS OVER WITH, THE SOONER I CAN FINISH MY LUNCH.
THE BASE IS FINE!
TACHIKAWA DESTROYED A BOMBER!
BORDER

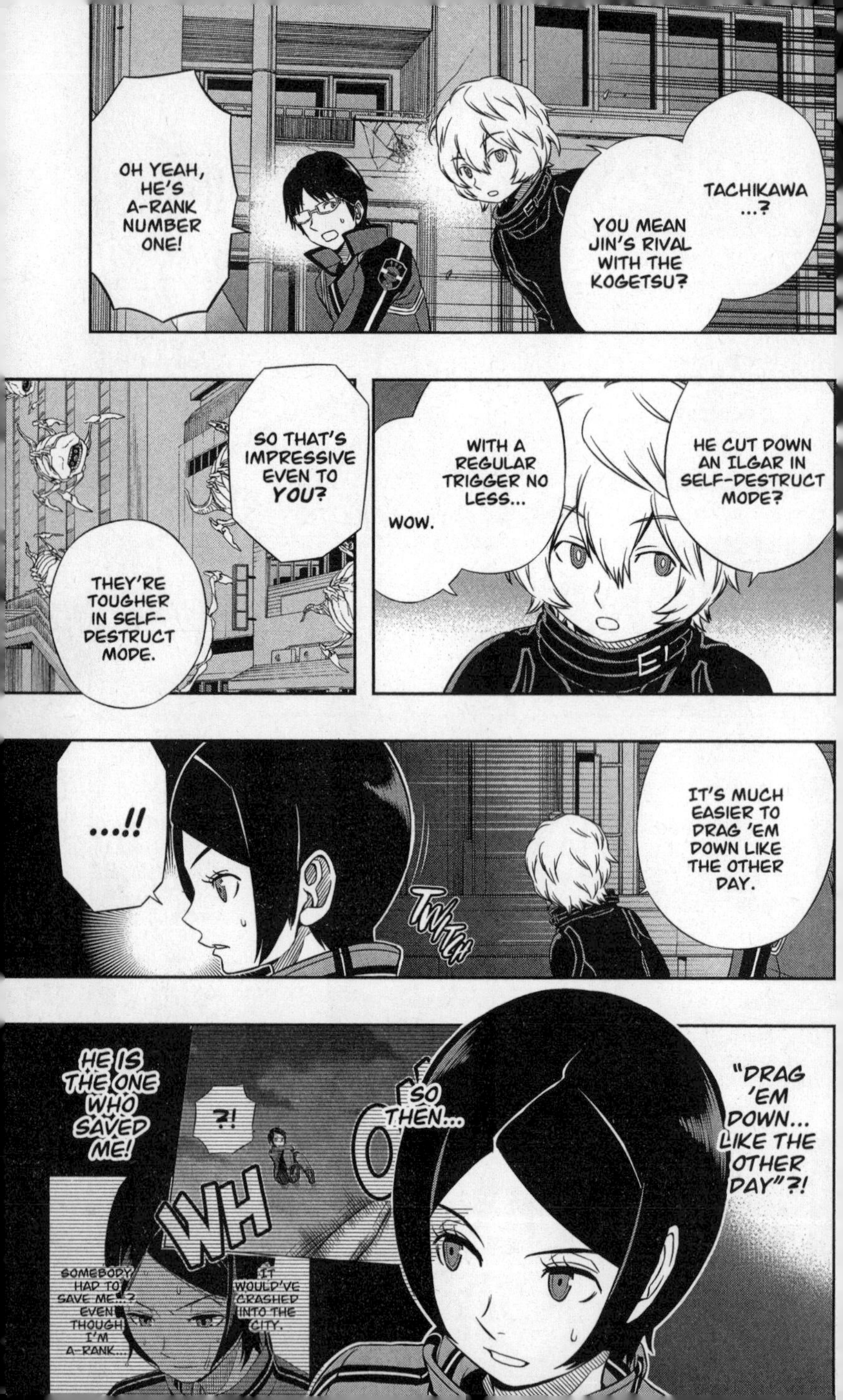
TACHIKAWA ...?
YOU MEAN JIN'S RIVAL WITH THE KOGETSU?
OH YEAH, HE'S A-RANK NUMBER ONE!
HE CUT DOWN AN ILGAR IN SELF-DESTRUCT MODE?
WITH A REGULAR TRIGGER NO LESS...
WOW.
SO THAT'S IMPRESSIVE EVEN TO *YOU*?
THEY'RE TOUGHER IN SELF-DESTRUCT MODE.
IT'S MUCH EASIER TO DRAG 'EM DOWN LIKE THE OTHER DAY.
TWITCH
...!!
"DRAG 'EM DOWN... LIKE THE OTHER DAY"?!
SO THEN...
?!
WH
HE IS THE ONE WHO SAVED ME!
IT WOULD'VE CRASHED INTO THE CITY.
SOMEBODY HAD TO SAVE ME...? EVEN THOUGH I'M A-RANK...

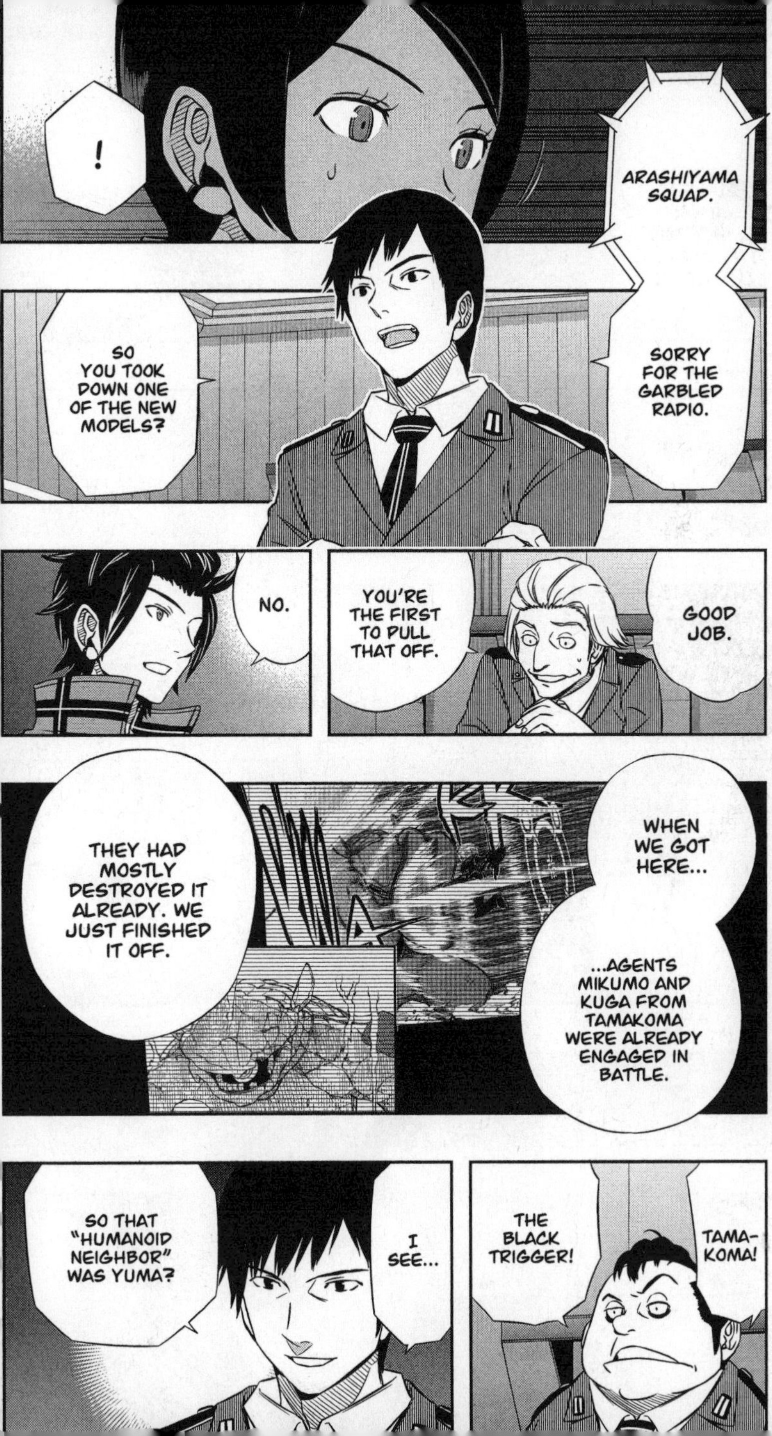
ARASHIYAMA SQUAD.
!
SORRY FOR THE GARBLED RADIO.
SO YOU TOOK DOWN ONE OF THE NEW MODELS?
GOOD JOB.
YOU'RE THE FIRST TO PULL THAT OFF.
NO.
WHEN WE GOT HERE...
...AGENTS MIKUMO AND KUGA FROM TAMAKOMA WERE ALREADY ENGAGED IN BATTLE.
THEY HAD MOSTLY DESTROYED IT ALREADY. WE JUST FINISHED IT OFF.
TAMA-KOMA!
THE BLACK TRIGGER!
I SEE...
SO THAT "HUMANOID NEIGHBOR" WAS YUMA?

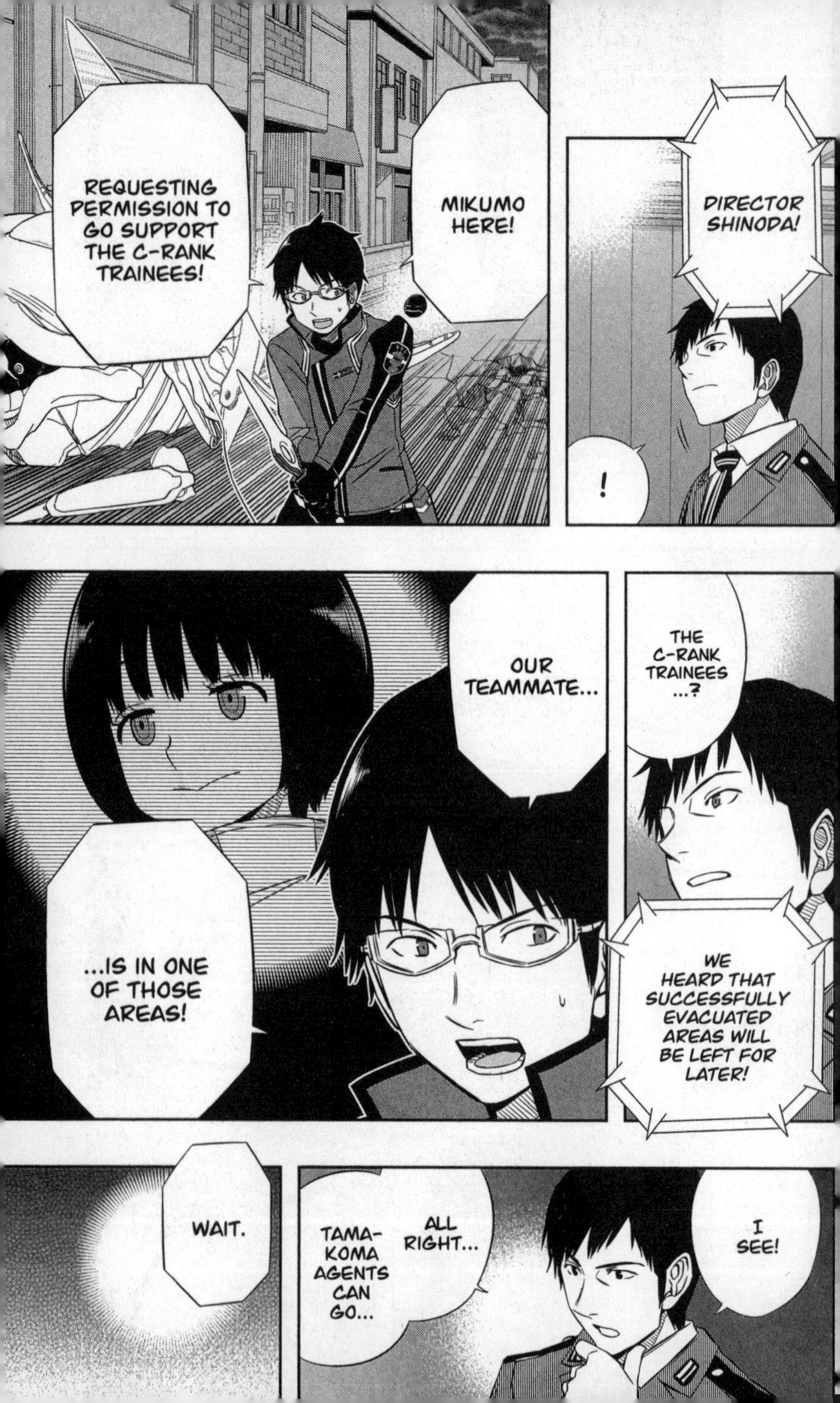
DIRECTOR SHINODA!
!
MIKUMO HERE!
REQUESTING PERMISSION TO GO SUPPORT THE C-RANK TRAINEES!
THE C-RANK TRAINEES ...?
WE HEARD THAT SUCCESSFULLY EVACUATED AREAS WILL BE LEFT FOR LATER!
OUR TEAMMATE...
...IS IN ONE OF THOSE AREAS!
I SEE!
ALL RIGHT...
TAMA-KOMA AGENTS CAN GO...
WAIT.

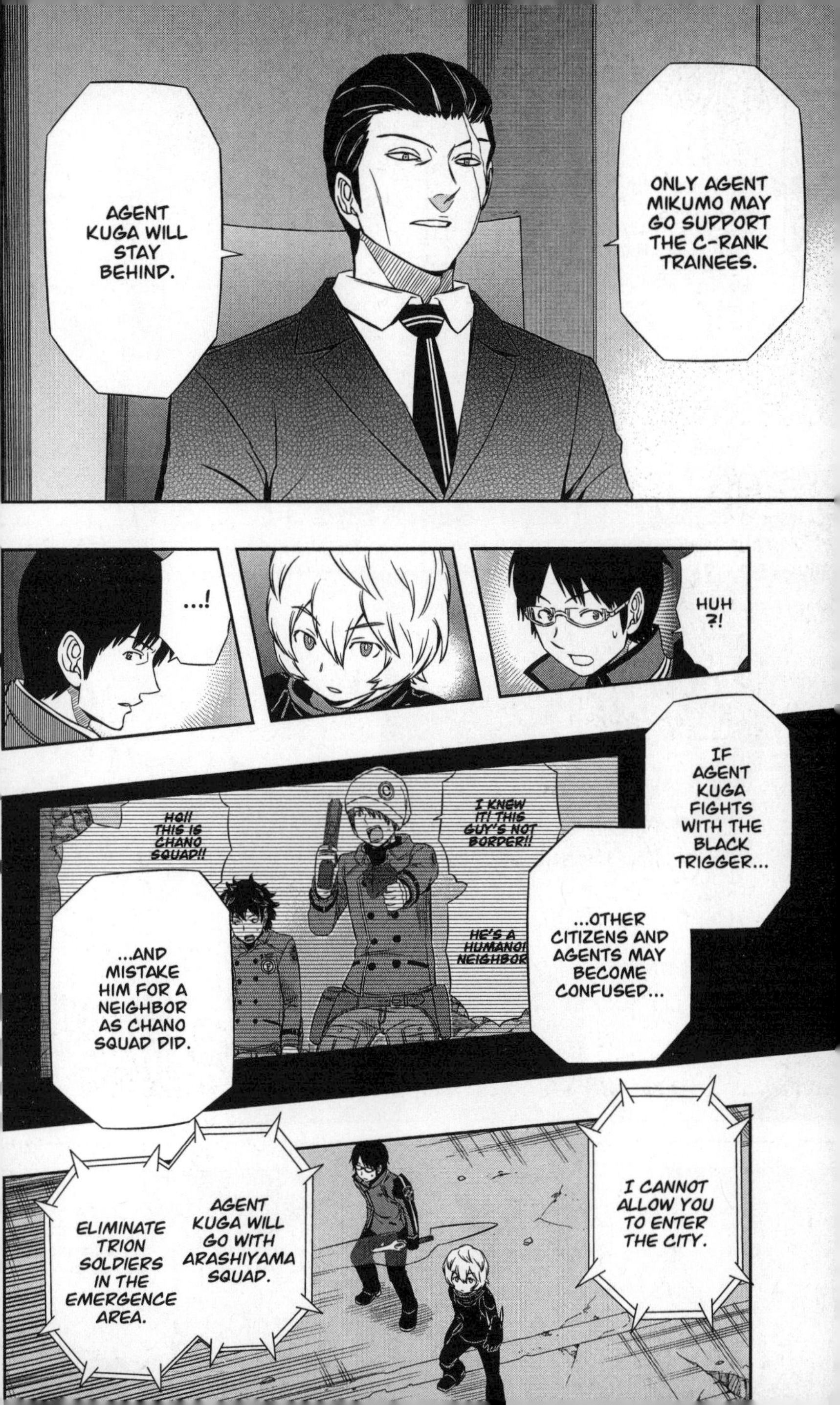
ONLY AGENT MIKUMO MAY GO SUPPORT THE C-RANK TRAINEES.
AGENT KUGA WILL STAY BEHIND.
HUH ?!
...!
IF AGENT KUGA FIGHTS WITH THE BLACK TRIGGER...
...OTHER CITIZENS AND AGENTS MAY BECOME CONFUSED...
I KNEW IT! THIS GUY'S NOT BORDER!!
HQ!! THIS IS CHANO SQUAD!!
HE'S A HUMANOI NEIGHBOR
...AND MISTAKE HIM FOR A NEIGHBOR AS CHANO SQUAD DID.
I CANNOT ALLOW YOU TO ENTER THE CITY.
AGENT KUGA WILL GO WITH ARASHIYAMA SQUAD.
ELIMINATE TRION SOLDIERS IN THE EMERGENCE AREA.

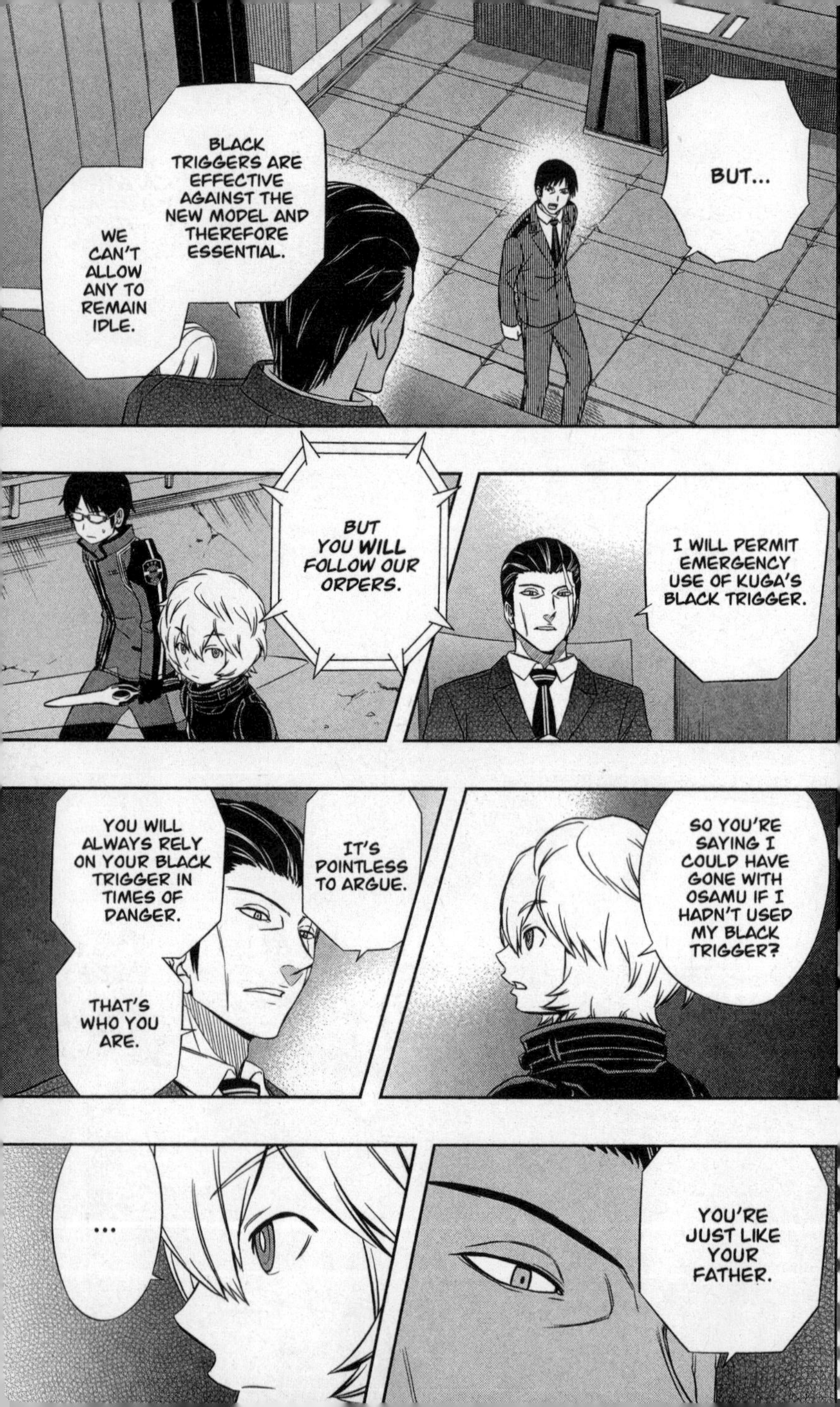
BUT...
BLACK TRIGGERS ARE EFFECTIVE AGAINST THE NEW MODEL AND THEREFORE ESSENTIAL.
WE CAN'T ALLOW ANY TO REMAIN IDLE.
I WILL PERMIT EMERGENCY USE OF KUGA'S BLACK TRIGGER.
BUT YOU **WILL** FOLLOW OUR ORDERS.
SO YOU'RE SAYING I COULD HAVE GONE WITH OSAMU IF I HADN'T USED MY BLACK TRIGGER?
IT'S POINTLESS TO ARGUE.
YOU WILL ALWAYS RELY ON YOUR BLACK TRIGGER IN TIMES OF DANGER.
THAT'S WHO YOU ARE.
YOU'RE JUST LIKE YOUR FATHER.
...

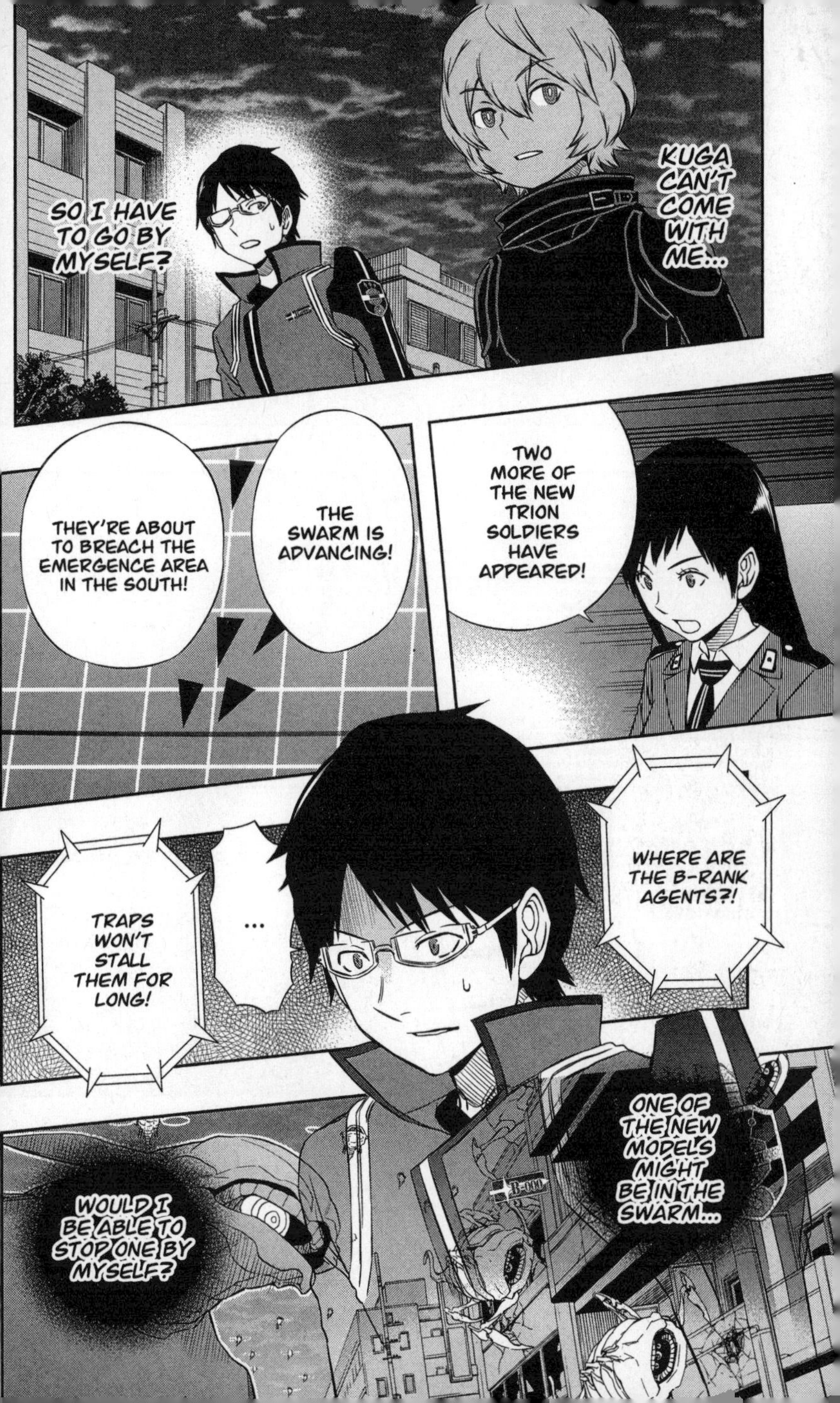

KUGA CAN'T COME WITH ME...
SO I HAVE TO GO BY MYSELF?
TWO MORE OF THE NEW TRION SOLDIERS HAVE APPEARED!
THE SWARM IS ADVANCING!
THEY'RE ABOUT TO BREACH THE EMERGENCE AREA IN THE SOUTH!
WHERE ARE THE B-RANK AGENTS?!
...
TRAPS WON'T STALL THEM FOR LONG!
ONE OF THE NEW MODELS MIGHT BE IN THE SWARM...
WOULD I BE ABLE TO STOP ONE BY MYSELF?

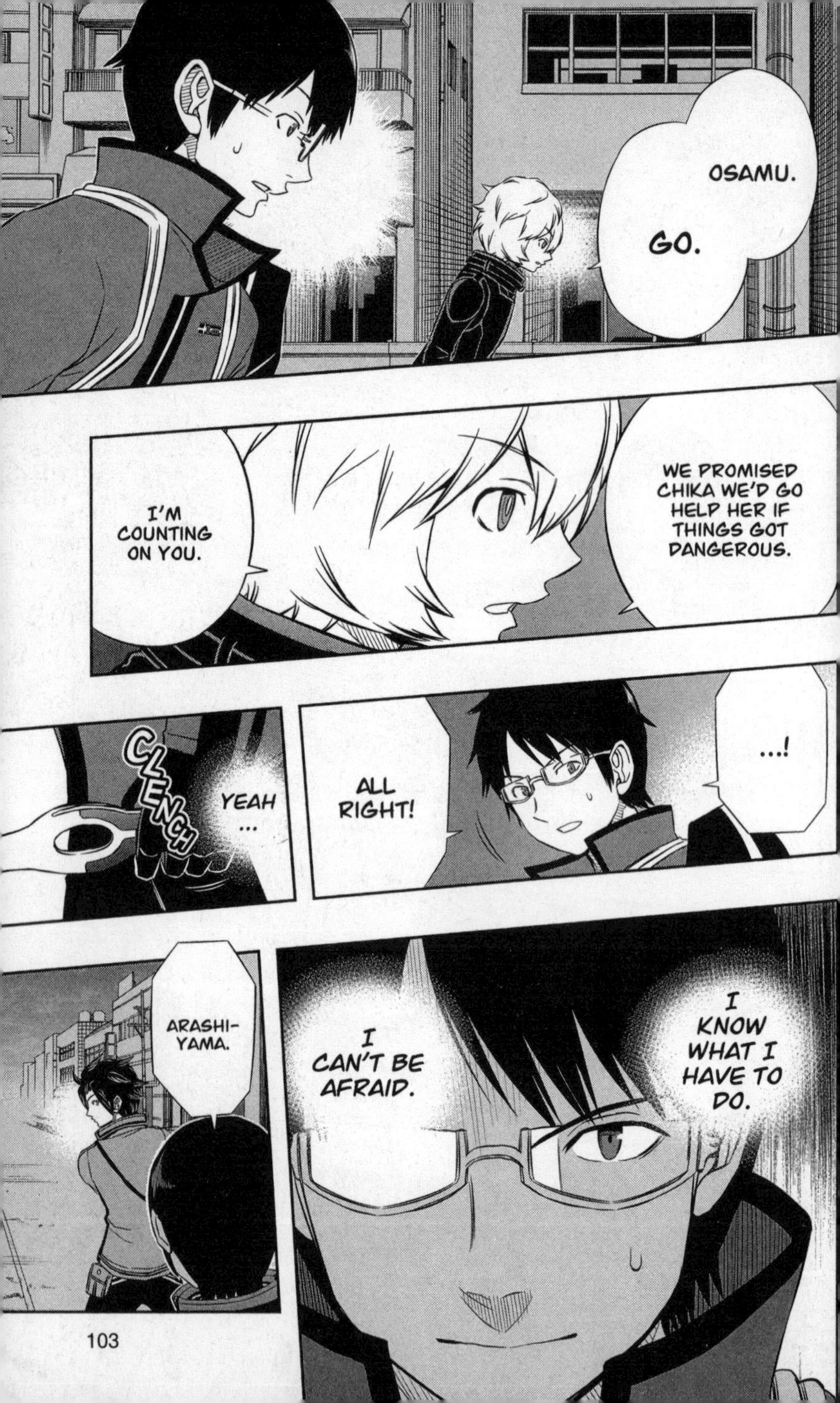
OSAMU.
GO.
WE PROMISED CHIKA WE'D GO HELP HER IF THINGS GOT DANGEROUS.
I'M COUNTING ON YOU.
...!
ALL RIGHT!
YEAH ...
CLENCH
I KNOW WHAT I HAVE TO DO.
I CAN'T BE AFRAID.
ARASHI-YAMA.

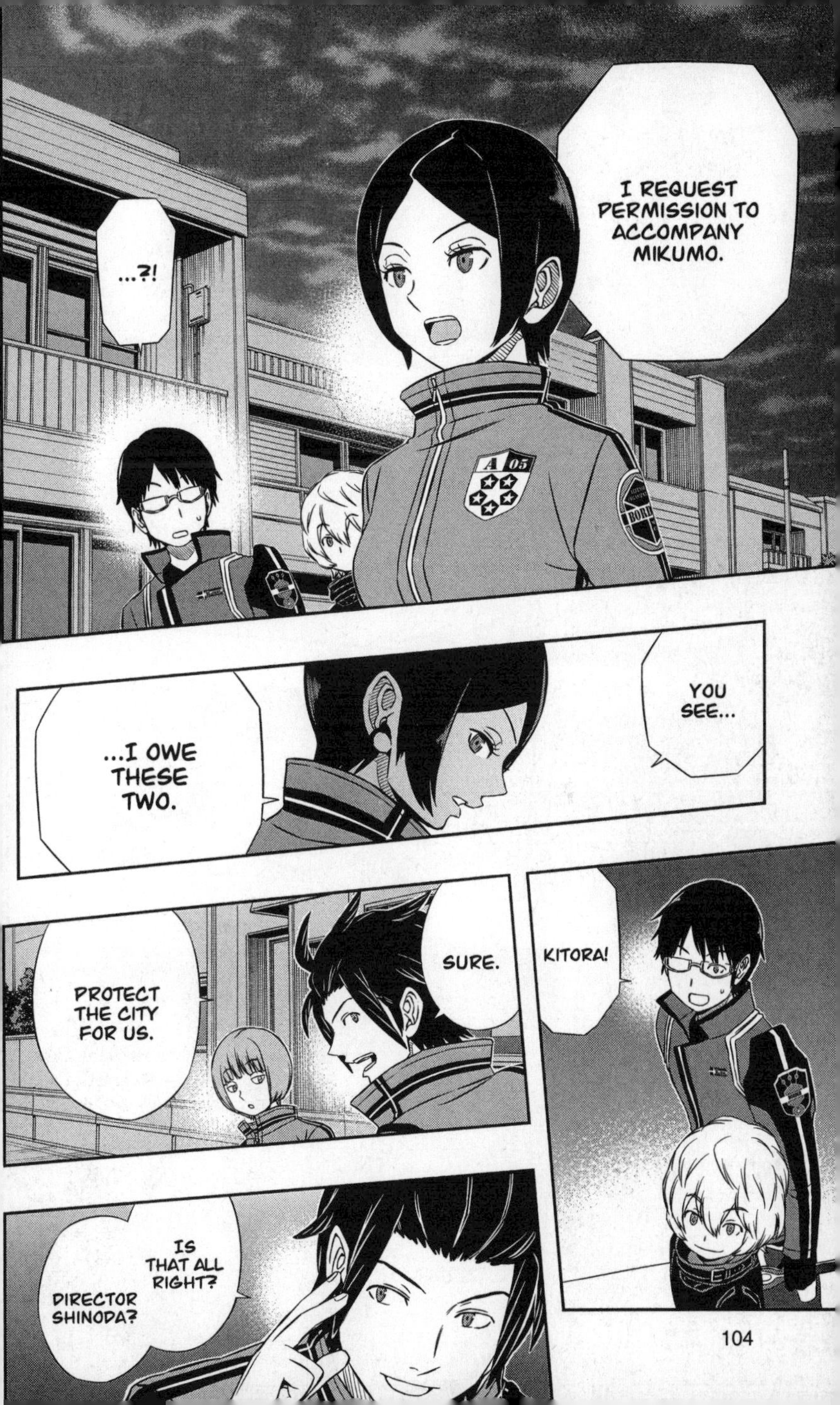
I REQUEST PERMISSION TO ACCOMPANY MIKUMO.
...?!
YOU SEE...
...I OWE THESE TWO.
KITORA!
SURE.
PROTECT THE CITY FOR US.
IS THAT ALL RIGHT?
DIRECTOR SHINODA?

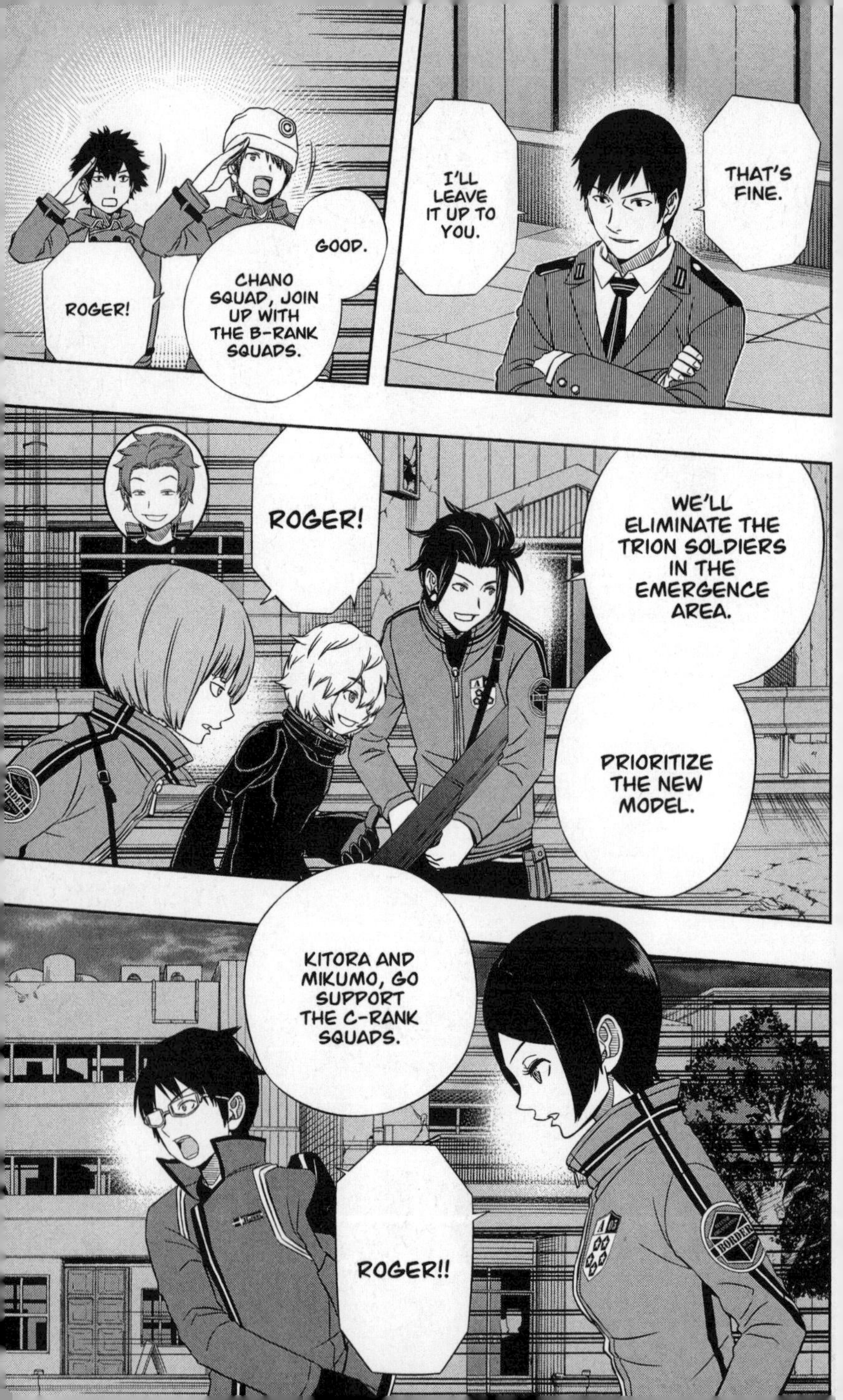
THAT'S FINE.
I'LL LEAVE IT UP TO YOU.
GOOD.
CHANO SQUAD, JOIN UP WITH THE B-RANK SQUADS.
ROGER!
WE'LL ELIMINATE THE TRION SOLDIERS IN THE EMERGENCE AREA.
PRIORITIZE THE NEW MODEL.
ROGER!
KITORA AND MIKUMO, GO SUPPORT THE C-RANK SQUADS.
ROGER!!

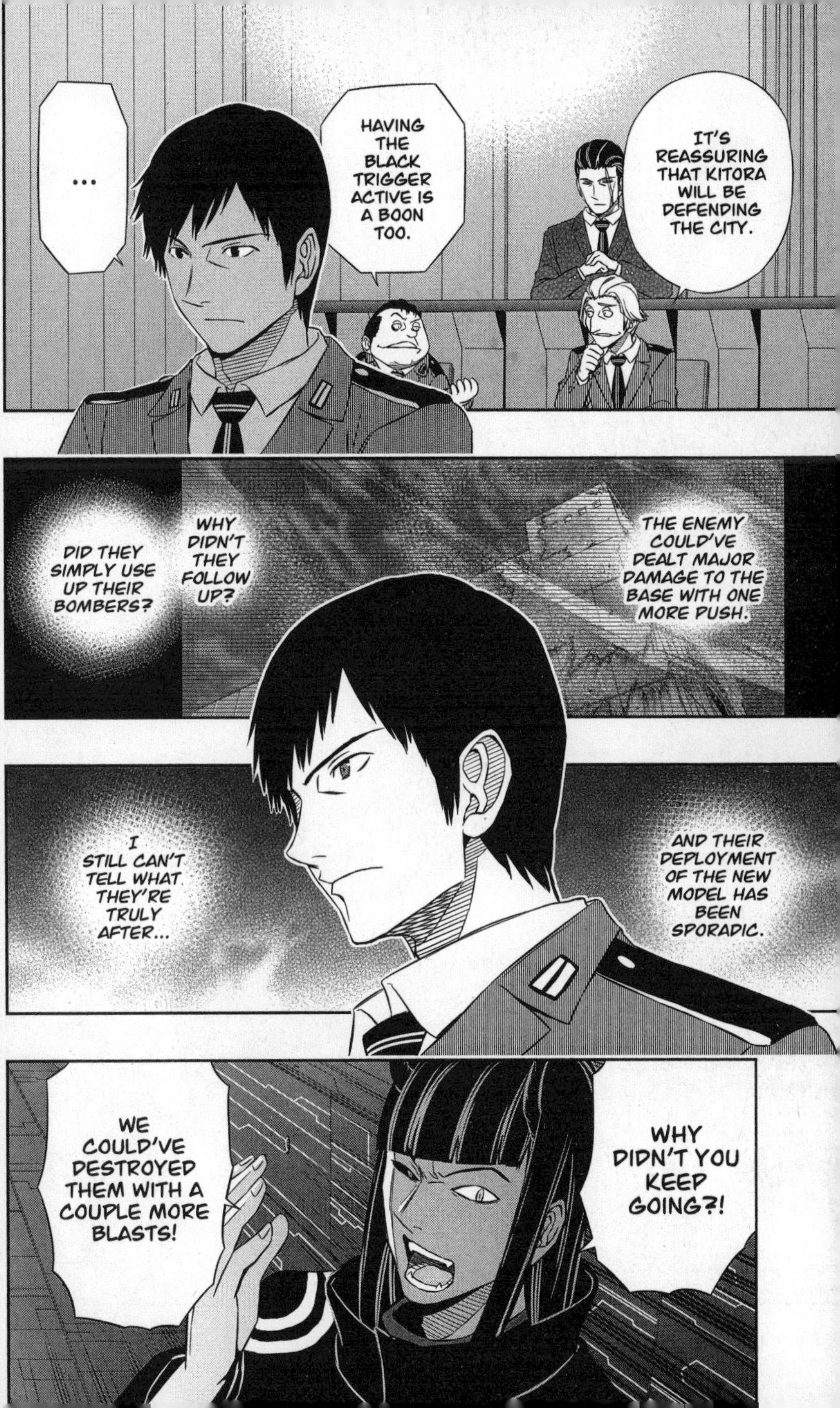

IT'S REASSURING THAT KITORA WILL BE DEFENDING THE CITY.
HAVING THE BLACK TRIGGER ACTIVE IS A BOON TOO.
...
THE ENEMY COULD'VE DEALT MAJOR DAMAGE TO THE BASE WITH ONE MORE PUSH.
WHY DIDN'T THEY FOLLOW UP?
DID THEY SIMPLY USE UP THEIR BOMBERS?
AND THEIR DEPLOYMENT OF THE NEW MODEL HAS BEEN SPORADIC.
I STILL CAN'T TELL WHAT THEY'RE TRULY AFTER...
WHY DIDN'T YOU KEEP GOING?!
WE COULD'VE DESTROYED THEM WITH A COUPLE MORE BLASTS!

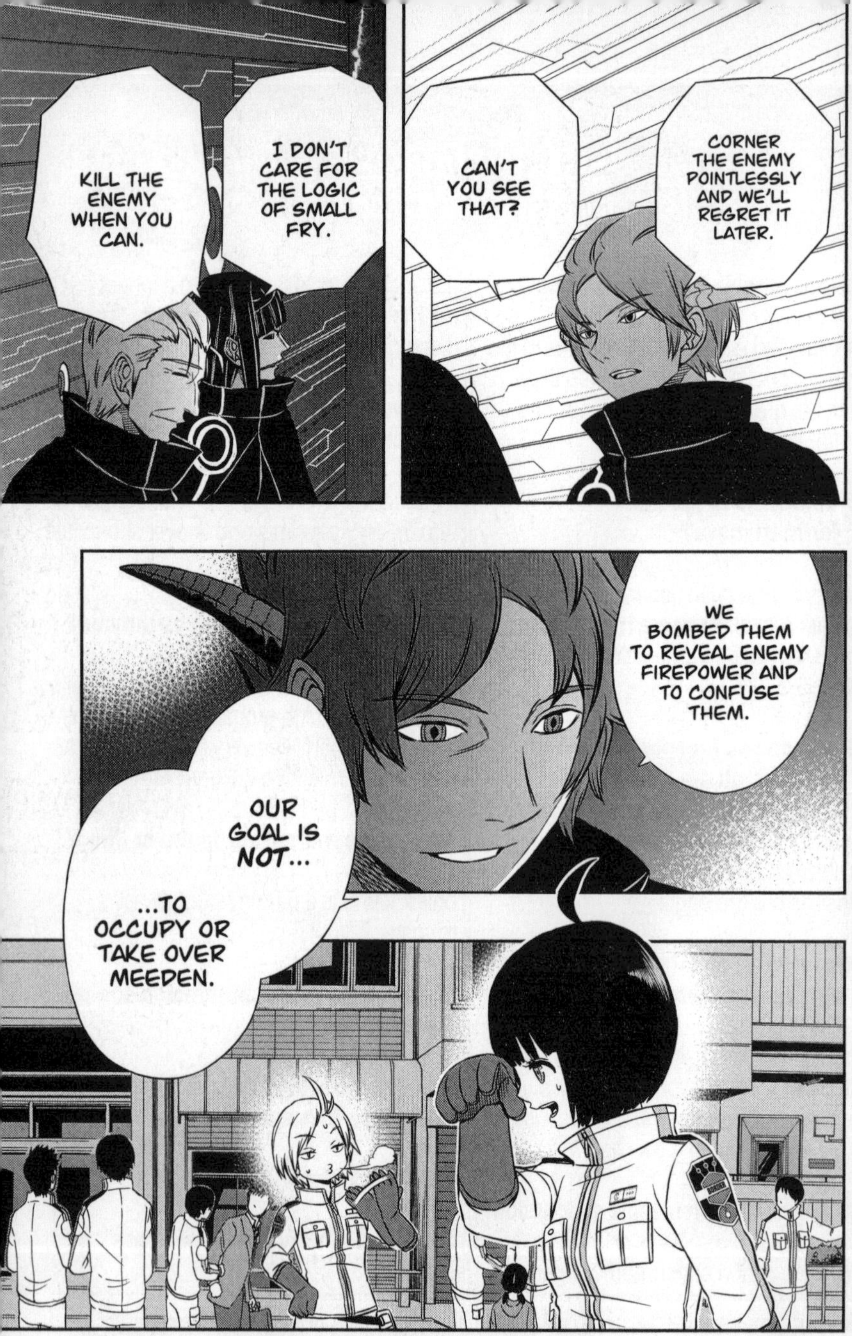
CORNER THE ENEMY POINTLESSLY AND WE'LL REGRET IT LATER.
CAN'T YOU SEE THAT?
I DON'T CARE FOR THE LOGIC OF SMALL FRY.
KILL THE ENEMY WHEN YOU CAN.
WE BOMBED THEM TO REVEAL ENEMY FIREPOWER AND TO CONFUSE THEM.
OUR GOAL IS NOT...
...TO OCCUPY OR TAKE OVER MEEDEN.

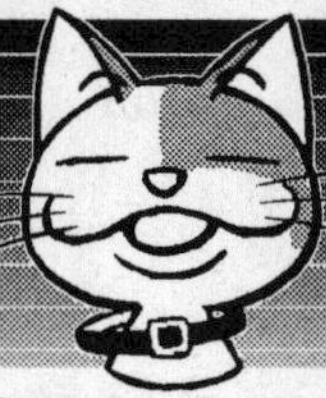

Q&A: Part 3

Some important stuff is revealed here.

Does Arashiyama have parents?

es. His dad is an office worker and his nom works part-time. He also lives vith his grandmother, a brother and ister, and one dog.

What kind of job does Torimaru have?

elivering the newspaper, grocery ashier, waiter. There are rumors that nore female customers come in on his hift days.

How do you feel about Osamu sweating all the time?

samu breaking into a cold sweat like ketchup on omelet rice (his lasses are the eggs).

Is there an age limit to applying to Border?

here isn't a strict age limit as long as ou have Trion, but you're more likely to e hired the younger you are because he Trion gland can grow more.

Can you teleport in rapid succession?

istance = Trion consumed. Longer distances (over 300m) require a longer resting interval of several seconds. Short distances (2-3m) require 0.5 seconds or so.

■Is World Trigger abbreviated to "WorTri" or just "Trigger"?

My editor calls it "Trigger." My manager calls it "WorTri." My assistants and I never abbreviate it and call it "World Trigger."

■How far into the future can Jin see?

He can see several years into a future that's pretty certain (high probability of actualization). But he can't see very far into uncertain futures that might be tinkered with.

■Who has more Trion, Izumi or Chika?

Chika. Izumi is a prodigy, but Chika is a monster.

■Was Raijin-maru purchased at a pet store?

Director Rindo brought him from somewhere. It's a mystery.

■Why is Kazama so short?

"Big power in a small package." That's Kazama.

I sometimes answer questions I get in fan mail on my official Twitter feed. Make my editor appy by following me on Twitter. **World Trigger official Twitter account: @W_Trigger_off**

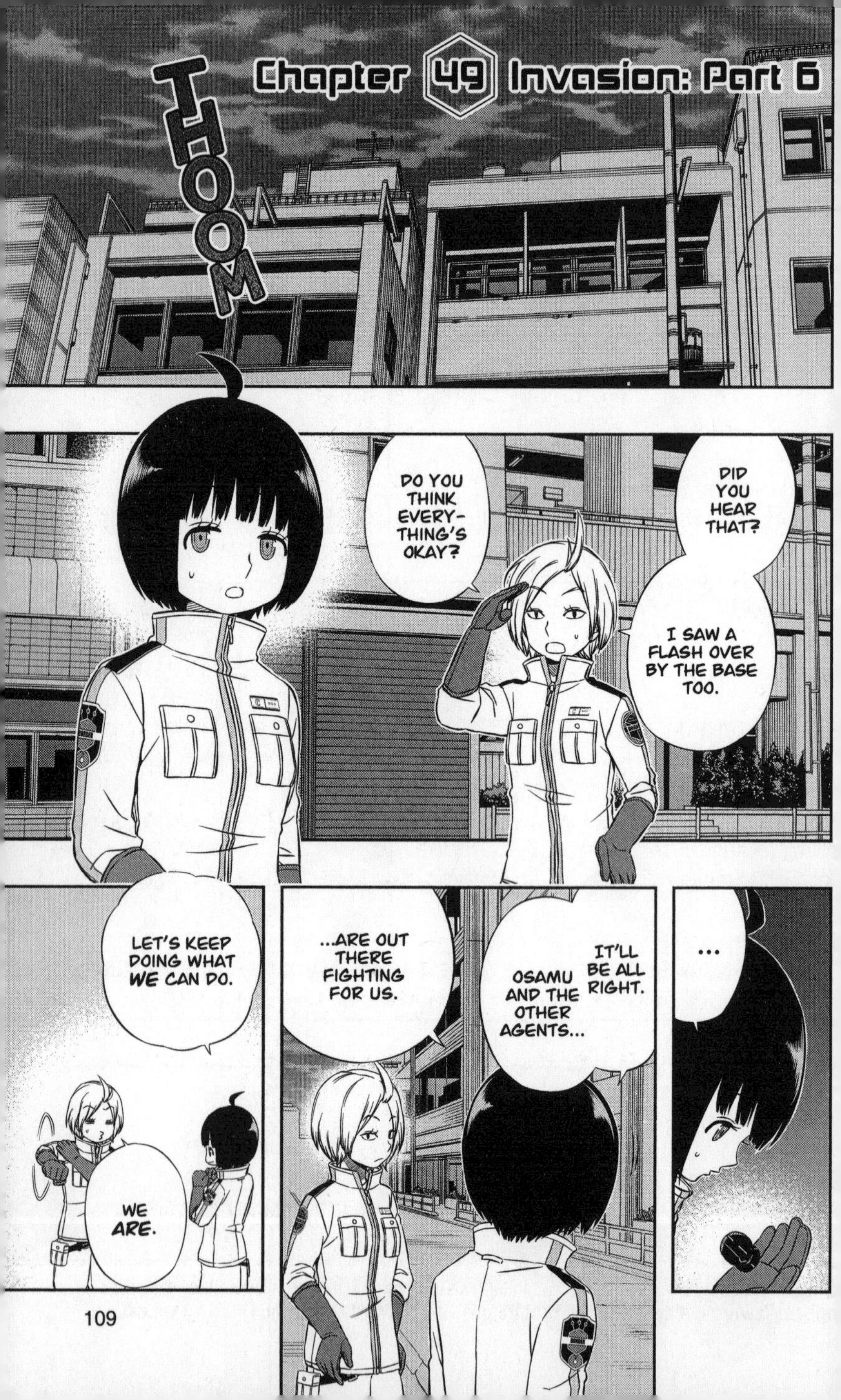
Chapter 49 Invasion: Part 6
THOOM
DID YOU HEAR THAT?
I SAW A FLASH OVER BY THE BASE TOO.
DO YOU THINK EVERY-THING'S OKAY?
...
IT'LL BE ALL RIGHT.
OSAMU AND THE OTHER AGENTS...
...ARE OUT THERE FIGHTING FOR US.
LET'S KEEP DOING WHAT WE CAN DO.
WE ARE.

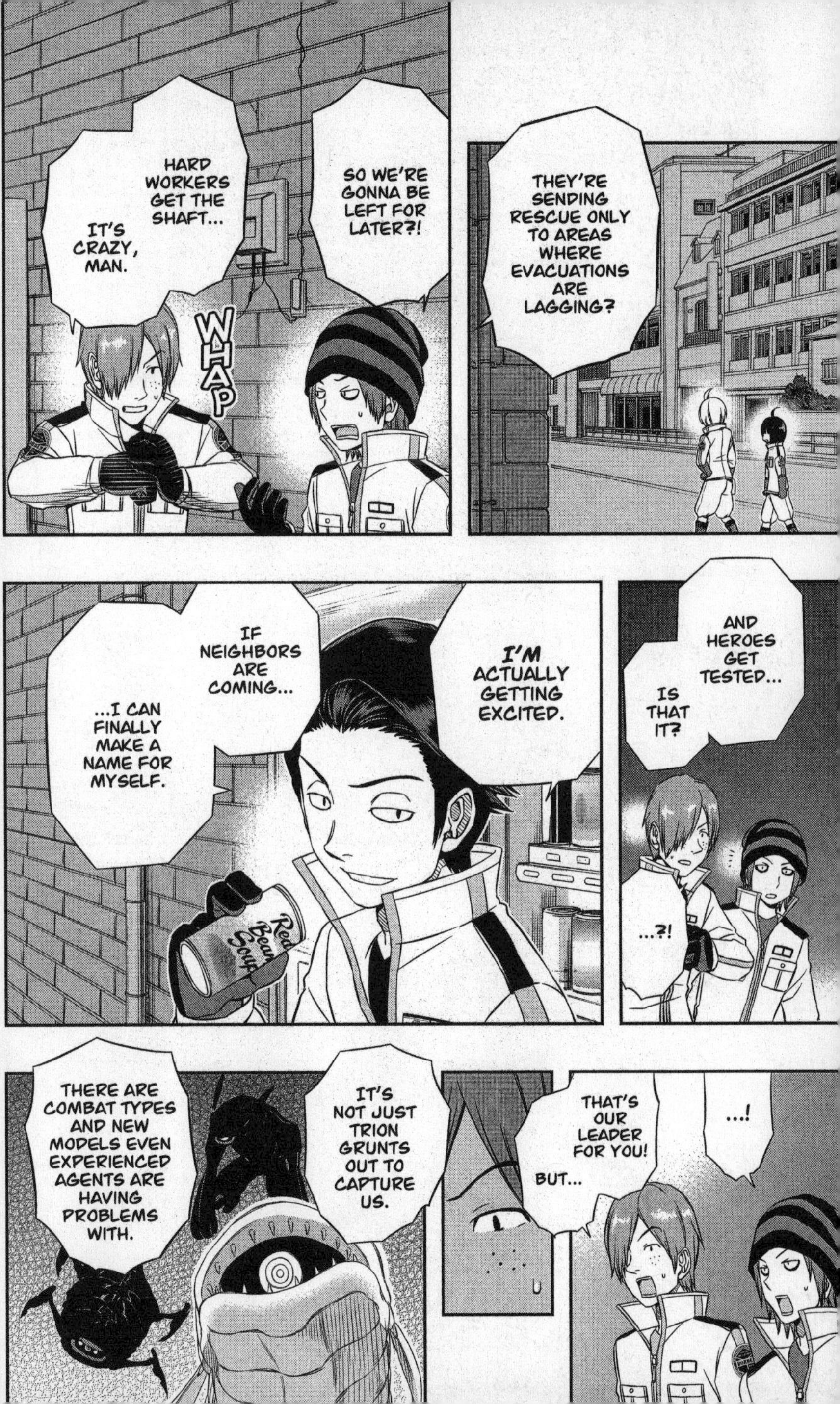
THEY'RE SENDING RESCUE ONLY TO AREAS WHERE EVACUATIONS ARE LAGGING?
SO WE'RE GONNA BE LEFT FOR LATER?!
HARD WORKERS GET THE SHAFT...
IT'S CRAZY, MAN.
WHAP
AND HEROES GET TESTED...
IS THAT IT?
...?!
I'M ACTUALLY GETTING EXCITED.
IF NEIGHBORS ARE COMING...
...I CAN FINALLY MAKE A NAME FOR MYSELF.
Red Bean Soup
...!
THAT'S OUR LEADER FOR YOU!
BUT...
IT'S NOT JUST TRION GRUNTS OUT TO CAPTURE US.
THERE ARE COMBAT TYPES AND NEW MODELS EVEN EXPERIENCED AGENTS ARE HAVING PROBLEMS WITH.

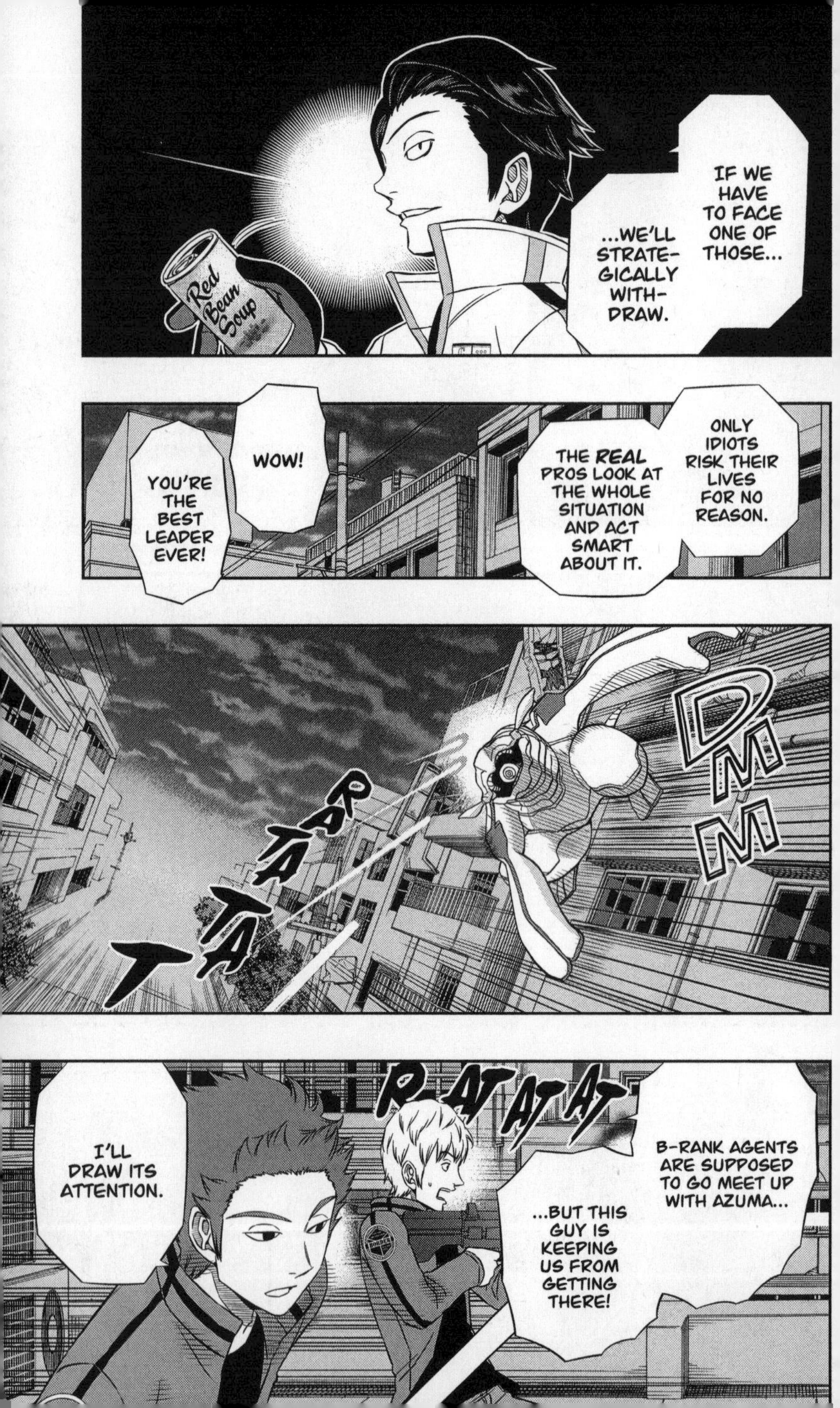
IF WE HAVE TO FACE ONE OF THOSE...
...WE'LL STRATE-GICALLY WITH-DRAW.
ONLY IDIOTS RISK THEIR LIVES FOR NO REASON.
THE **REAL** PROS LOOK AT THE WHOLE SITUATION AND ACT SMART ABOUT IT.
WOW!
YOU'RE THE BEST LEADER EVER!
DMM
RATATAT
RATATATAT
B-RANK AGENTS ARE SUPPOSED TO GO MEET UP WITH AZUMA...
...BUT THIS GUY IS KEEPING US FROM GETTING THERE!
I'LL DRAW ITS ATTENTION.

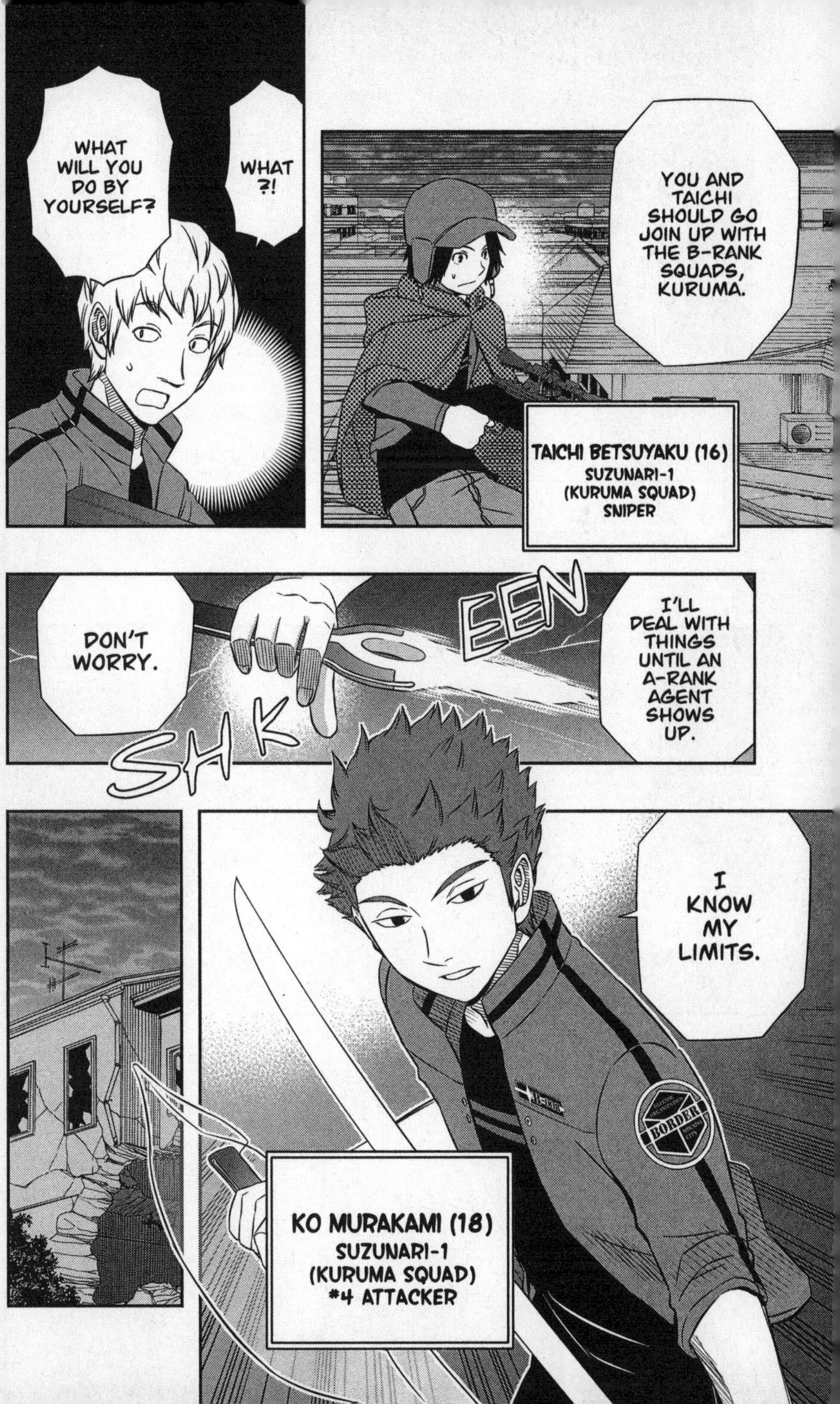
YOU AND TAICHI SHOULD GO JOIN UP WITH THE B-RANK SQUADS, KURUMA.
TAICHI BETSUYAKU (16) SUZUNARI-1 (KURUMA SQUAD) SNIPER
WHAT ?!
WHAT WILL YOU DO BY YOURSELF?
I'LL DEAL WITH THINGS UNTIL AN A-RANK AGENT SHOWS UP.
EEN
DON'T WORRY.
SHK
I KNOW MY LIMITS.
KO MURAKAMI (18) SUZUNARI-1 (KURUMA SQUAD) #4 ATTACKER

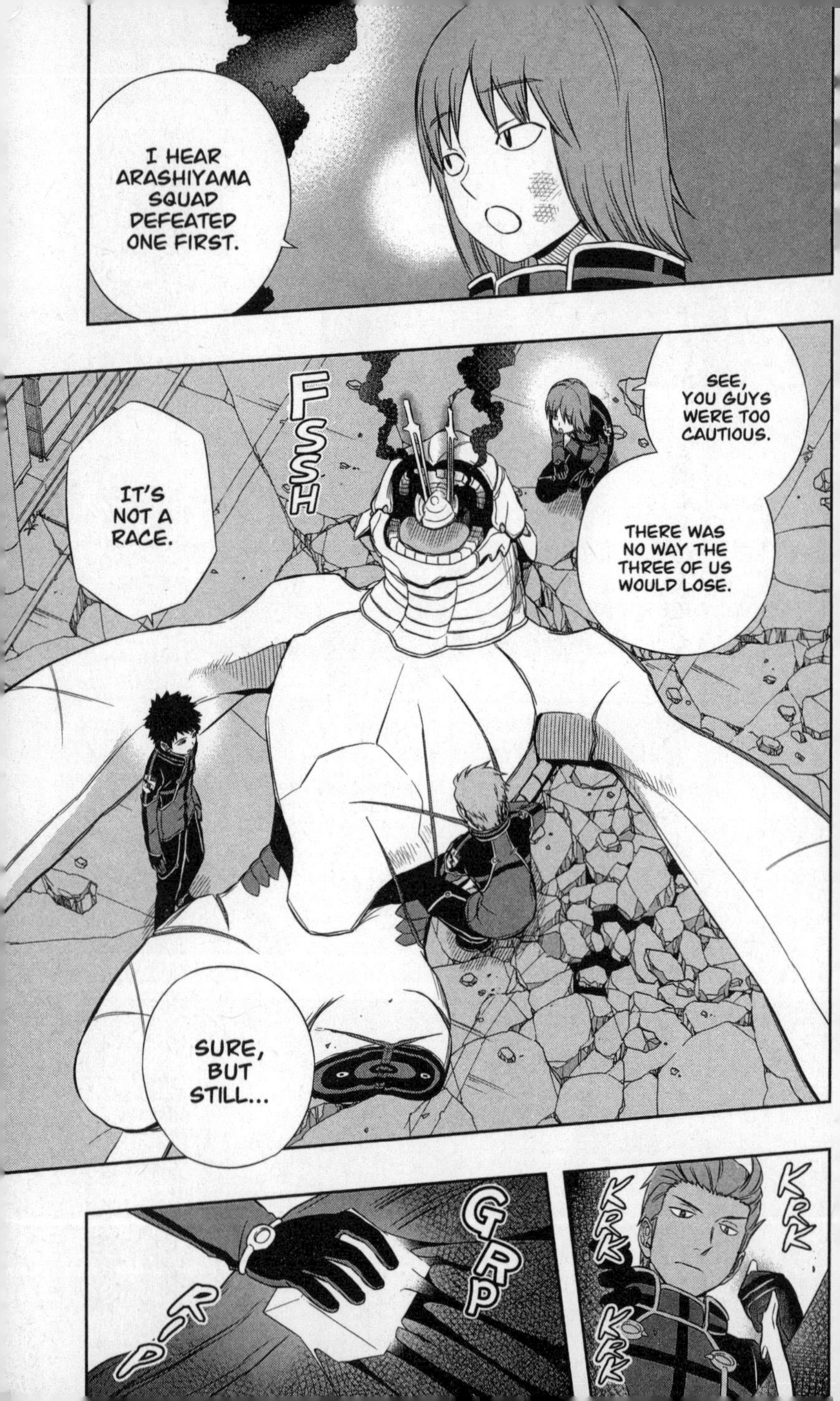

I HEAR ARASHIYAMA SQUAD DEFEATED ONE FIRST.
SEE, YOU GUYS WERE TOO CAUTIOUS.
THERE WAS NO WAY THE THREE OF US WOULD LOSE.
FSSH
IT'S NOT A RACE.
SURE, BUT STILL...
KRK KRK
KRK KRK
GRP
R-I-P

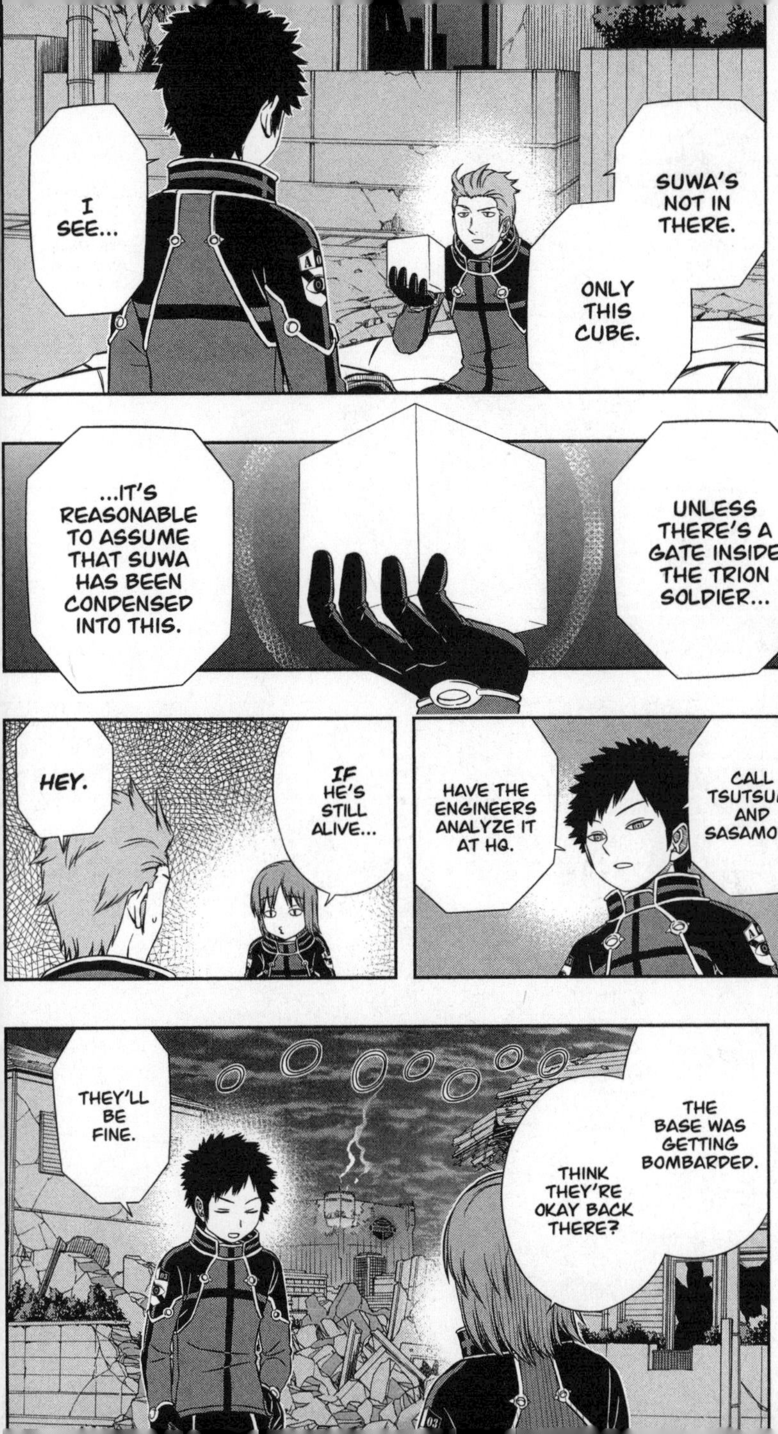
SUWA'S NOT IN THERE.
ONLY THIS CUBE.
I SEE...
UNLESS THERE'S A GATE INSIDE THE TRION SOLDIER...
...IT'S REASONABLE TO ASSUME THAT SUWA HAS BEEN CONDENSED INTO THIS.
CALL TSUTSUMI AND SASAMORI.
HAVE THE ENGINEERS ANALYZE IT AT HQ.
IF HE'S STILL ALIVE...
HEY.
THE BASE WAS GETTING BOMBARDED.
THINK THEY'RE OKAY BACK THERE?
THEY'LL BE FINE.

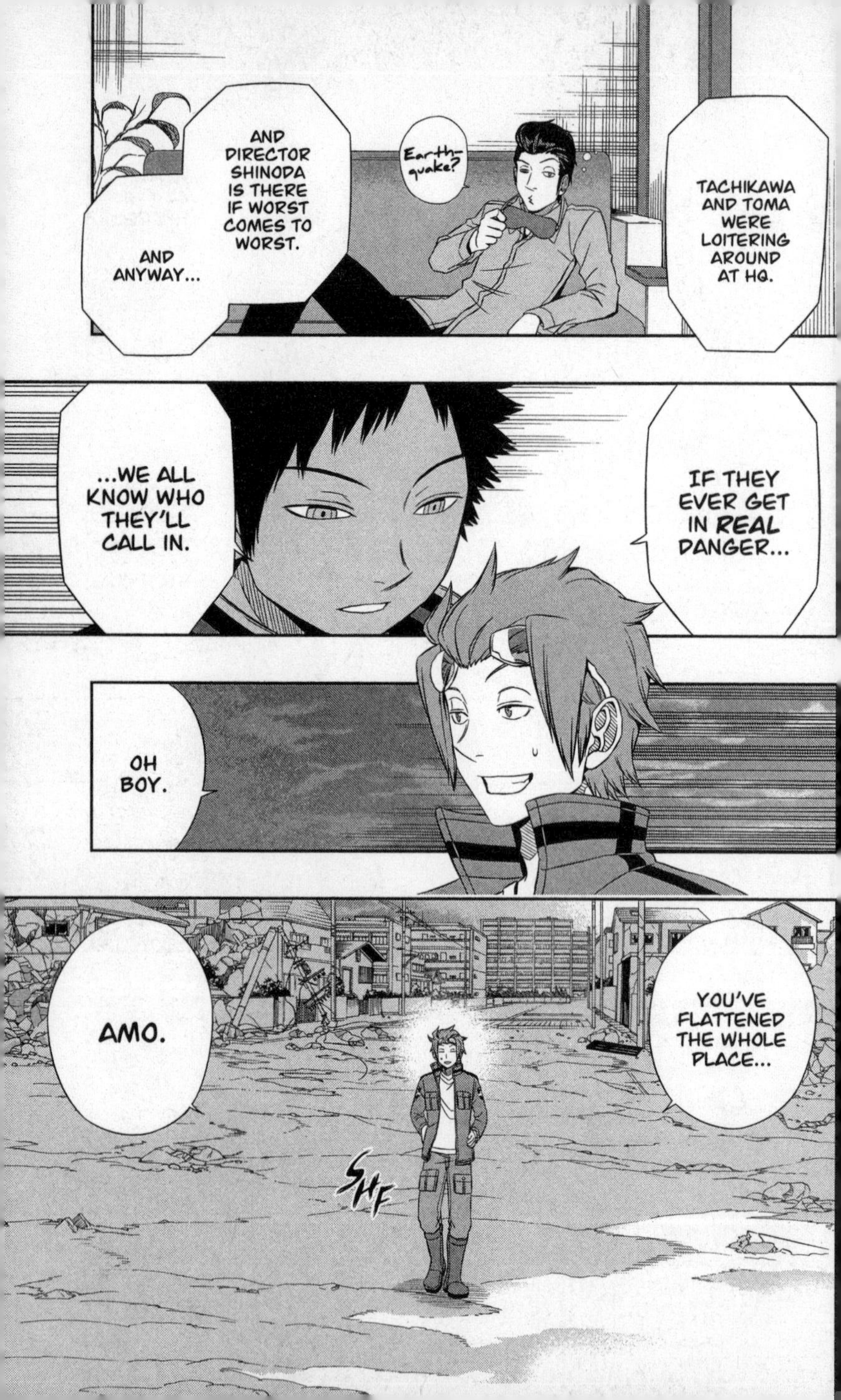
TACHIKAWA AND TOMA WERE LOITERING AROUND AT HQ.
Earth-quake?
AND DIRECTOR SHINODA IS THERE IF WORST COMES TO WORST.
AND ANYWAY...
IF THEY EVER GET IN REAL DANGER...
...WE ALL KNOW WHO THEY'LL CALL IN.
OH BOY.
YOU'VE FLATTENED THE WHOLE PLACE...
AMO.
SHF

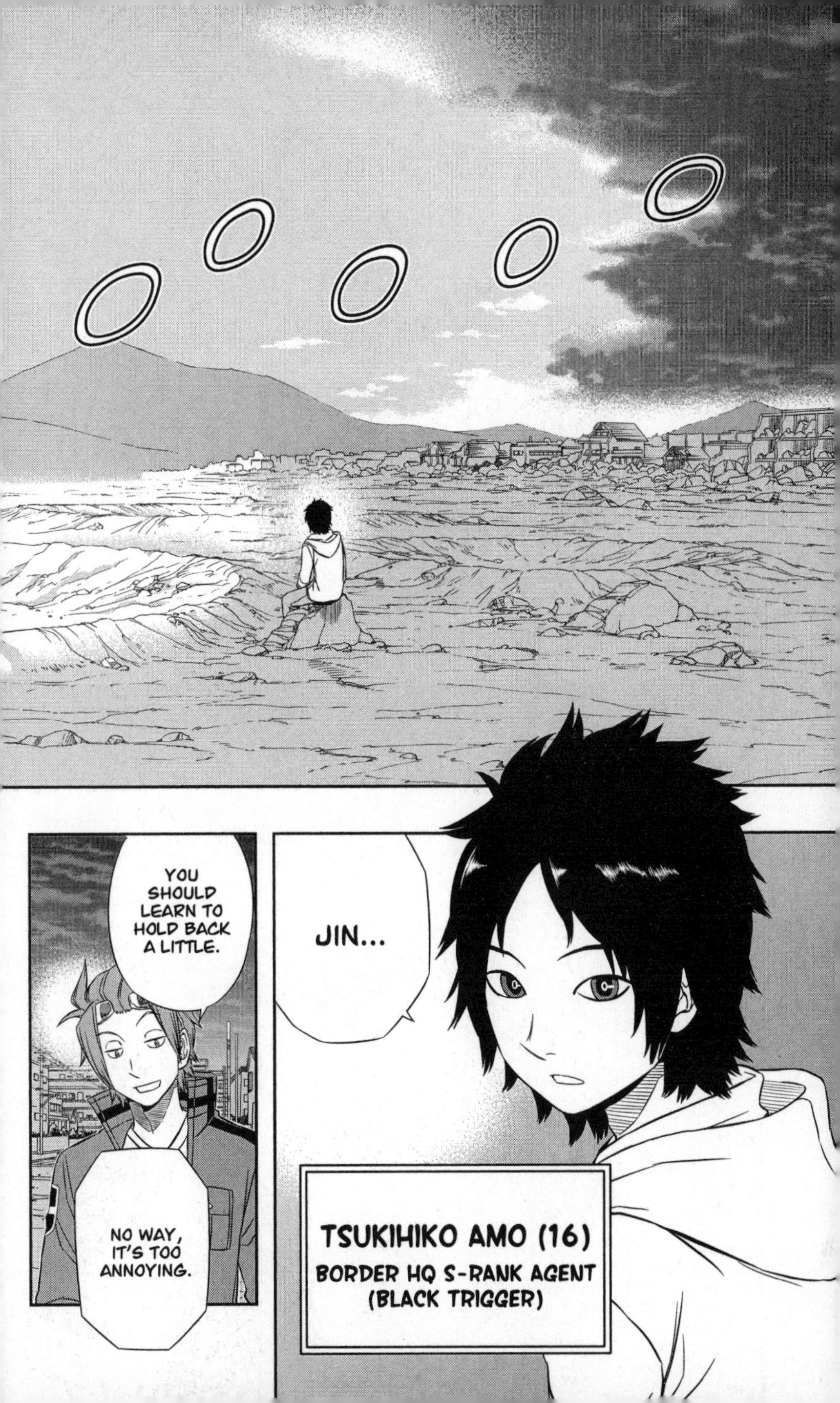
JIN...
TSUKIHIKO AMO (16)
BORDER HQ S-RANK AGENT
(BLACK TRIGGER)
YOU SHOULD LEARN TO HOLD BACK A LITTLE.
NO WAY, IT'S TOO ANNOYING.

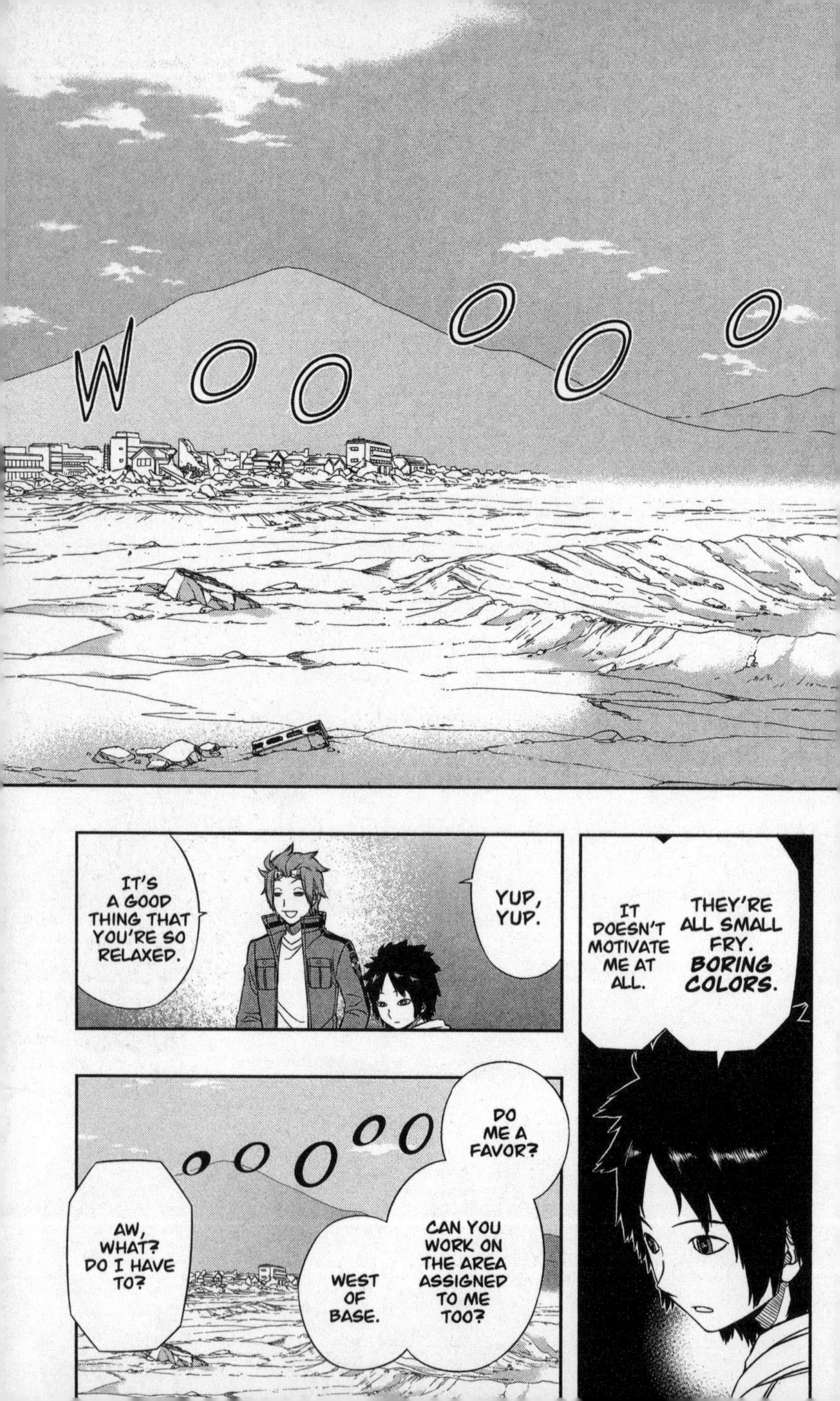
WOOOOOOO
YUP, YUP.
IT'S A GOOD THING THAT YOU'RE SO RELAXED.
THEY'RE ALL SMALL FRY. BORING COLORS.
IT DOESN'T MOTIVATE ME AT ALL.
OOOOO
DO ME A FAVOR?
CAN YOU WORK ON THE AREA ASSIGNED TO ME TOO?
WEST OF BASE.
AW, WHAT? DO I HAVE TO?

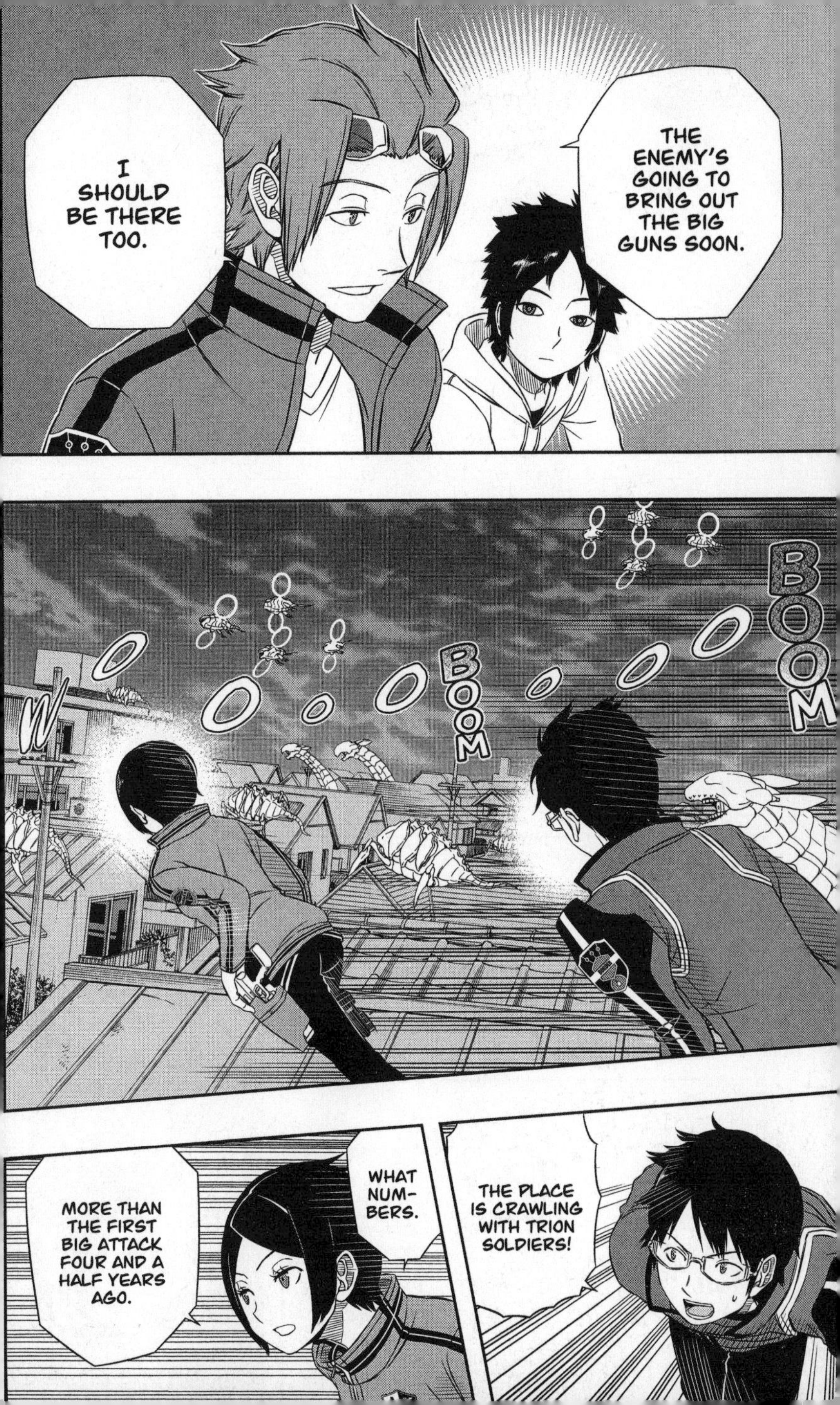
THE ENEMY'S GOING TO BRING OUT THE BIG GUNS SOON.
I SHOULD BE THERE TOO.
BOOM
BOOM
THE PLACE IS CRAWLING WITH TRION SOLDIERS!
WHAT NUM-BERS.
MORE THAN THE FIRST BIG ATTACK FOUR AND A HALF YEARS AGO.

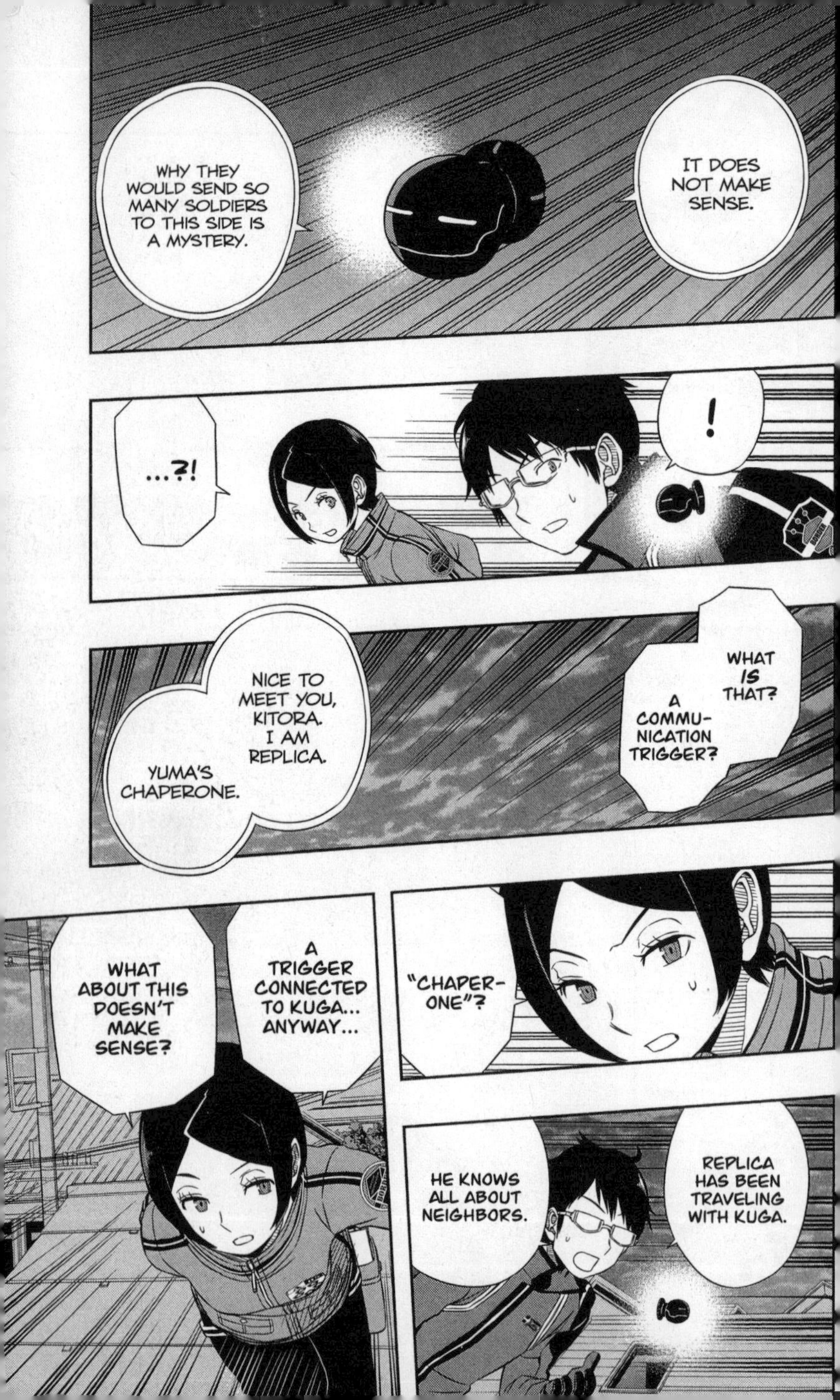
IT DOES NOT MAKE SENSE.
WHY THEY WOULD SEND SO MANY SOLDIERS TO THIS SIDE IS A MYSTERY.
!
...?!
WHAT IS THAT?
A COMMUNICATION TRIGGER?
NICE TO MEET YOU, KITORA. I AM REPLICA.
YUMA'S CHAPERONE.
"CHAPERONE"?
REPLICA HAS BEEN TRAVELING WITH KUGA.
HE KNOWS ALL ABOUT NEIGHBORS.
A TRIGGER CONNECTED TO KUGA... ANYWAY...
WHAT ABOUT THIS DOESN'T MAKE SENSE?

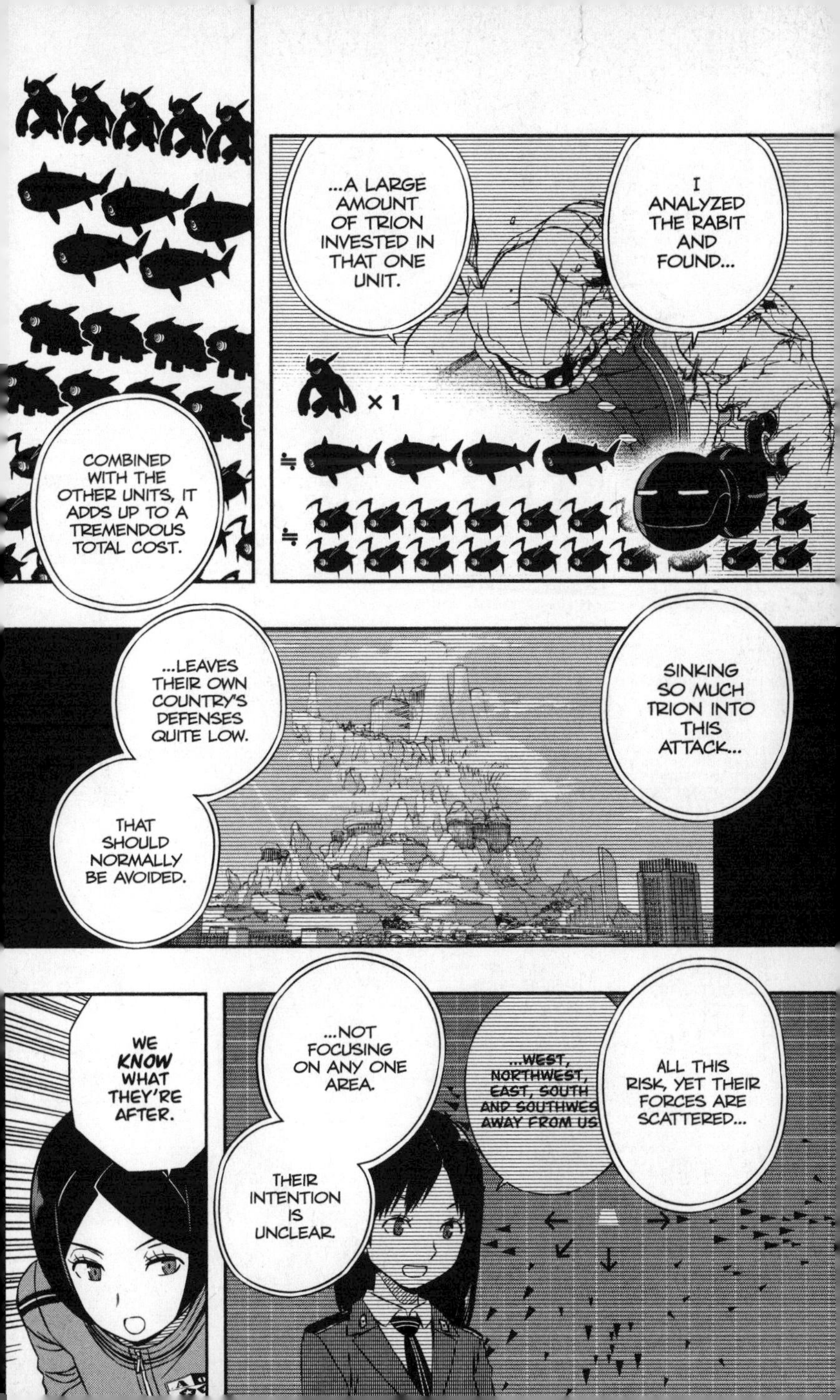
I ANALYZED THE RABIT AND FOUND...
...A LARGE AMOUNT OF TRION INVESTED IN THAT ONE UNIT.
× 1
COMBINED WITH THE OTHER UNITS, IT ADDS UP TO A TREMENDOUS TOTAL COST.
SINKING SO MUCH TRION INTO THIS ATTACK...
...LEAVES THEIR OWN COUNTRY'S DEFENSES QUITE LOW.
THAT SHOULD NORMALLY BE AVOIDED.
ALL THIS RISK, YET THEIR FORCES ARE SCATTERED...
...WEST, NORTHWEST, EAST, SOUTH AND SOUTHWES AWAY FROM US
...NOT FOCUSING ON ANY ONE AREA.
THEIR INTENTION IS UNCLEAR.
WE *KNOW* WHAT THEY'RE AFTER.

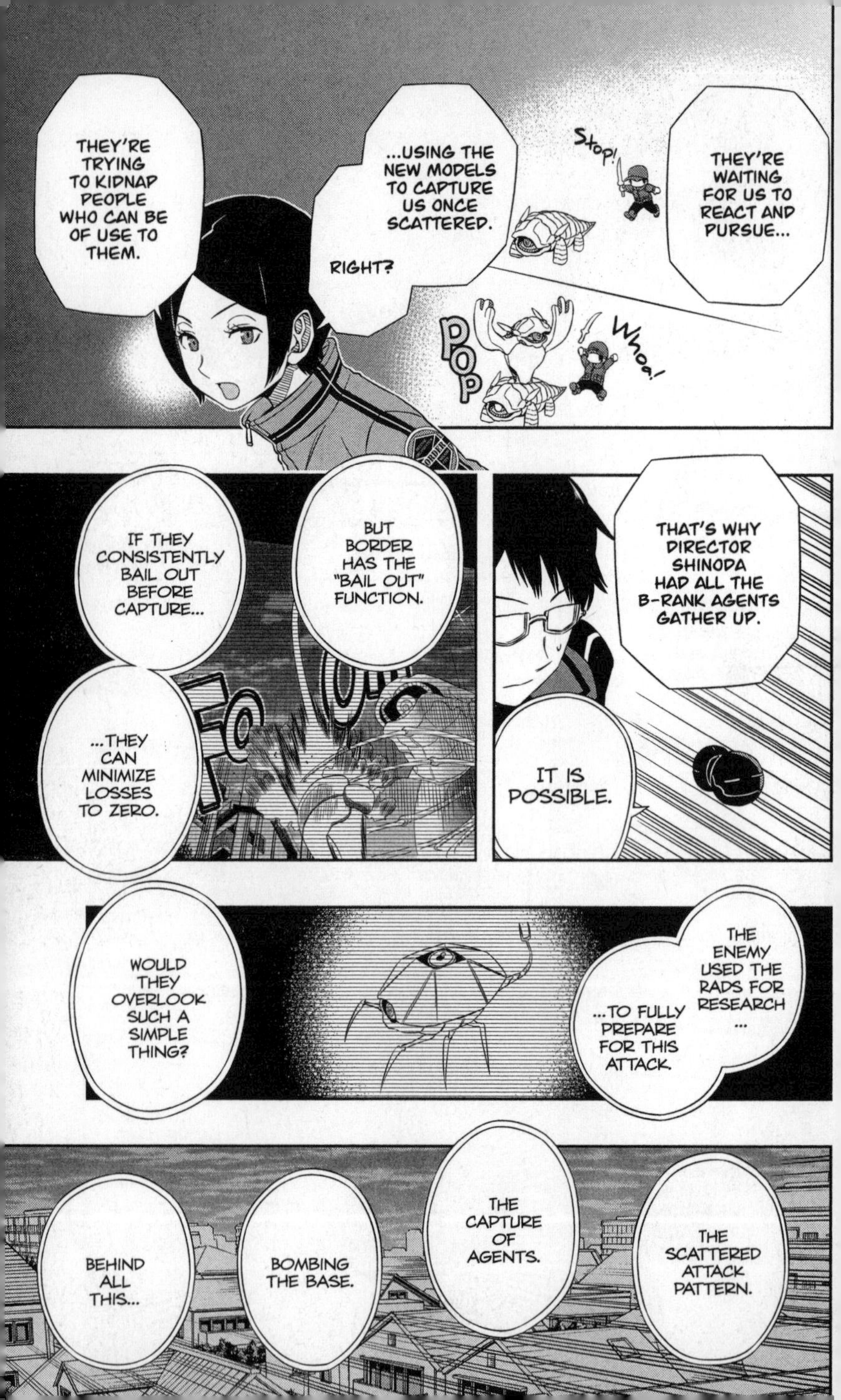
THEY'RE WAITING FOR US TO REACT AND PURSUE...
Stop!
...USING THE NEW MODELS TO CAPTURE US ONCE SCATTERED.
RIGHT?
Whoa!
POP
THEY'RE TRYING TO KIDNAP PEOPLE WHO CAN BE OF USE TO THEM.
THAT'S WHY DIRECTOR SHINODA HAD ALL THE B-RANK AGENTS GATHER UP.
IT IS POSSIBLE.
BUT BORDER HAS THE "BAIL OUT" FUNCTION.
IF THEY CONSISTENTLY BAIL OUT BEFORE CAPTURE...
...THEY CAN MINIMIZE LOSSES TO ZERO.
THE ENEMY USED THE RADS FOR RESEARCH ...
...TO FULLY PREPARE FOR THIS ATTACK.
WOULD THEY OVERLOOK SUCH A SIMPLE THING?
THE SCATTERED ATTACK PATTERN.
THE CAPTURE OF AGENTS.
BOMBING THE BASE.
BEHIND ALL THIS...

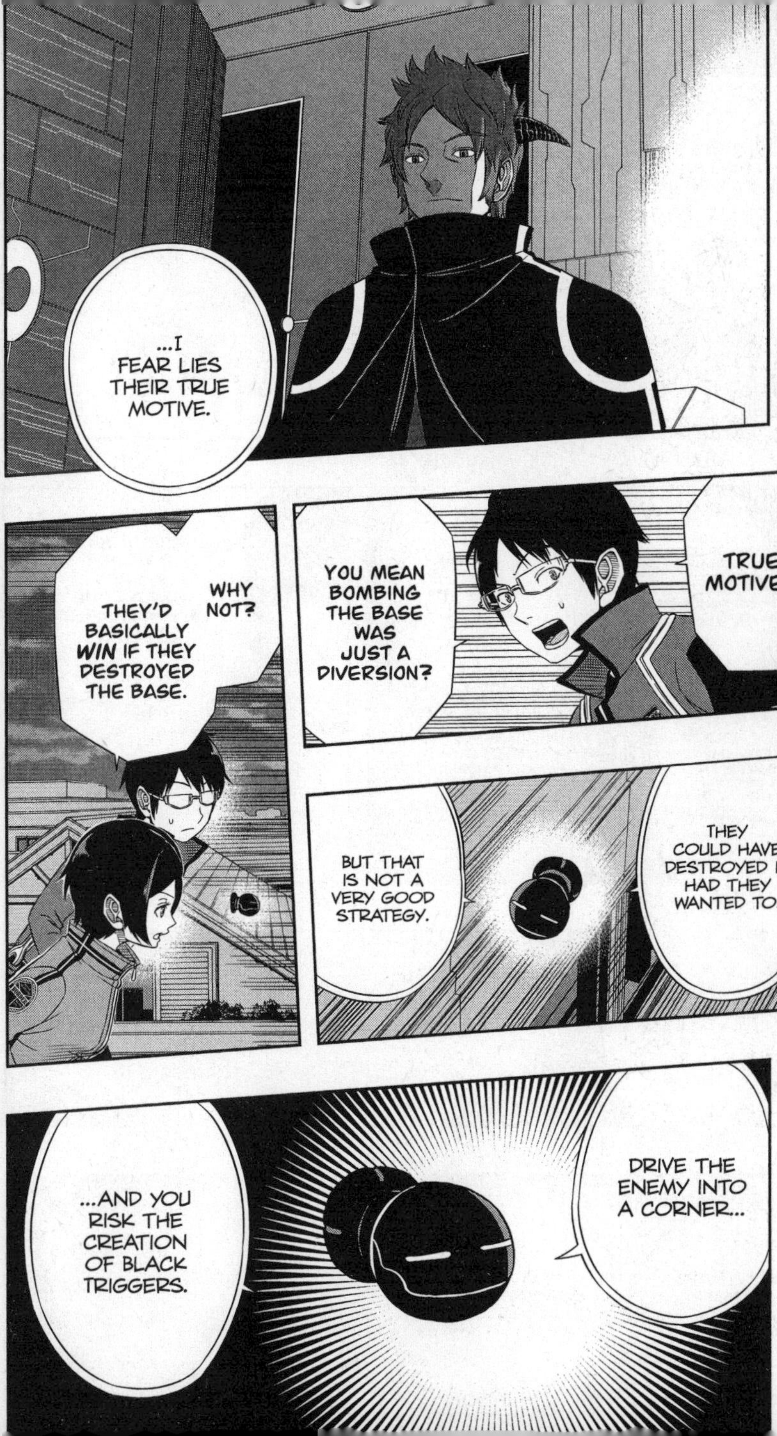

...I FEAR LIES THEIR TRUE MOTIVE.
TRUE MOTIVE?
YOU MEAN BOMBING THE BASE WAS JUST A DIVERSION?
THEY COULD HAVE DESTROYED IT HAD THEY WANTED TO.
BUT THAT IS NOT A VERY GOOD STRATEGY.
WHY NOT?
THEY'D BASICALLY *WIN* IF THEY DESTROYED THE BASE.
DRIVE THE ENEMY INTO A CORNER...
...AND YOU RISK THE CREATION OF BLACK TRIGGERS.

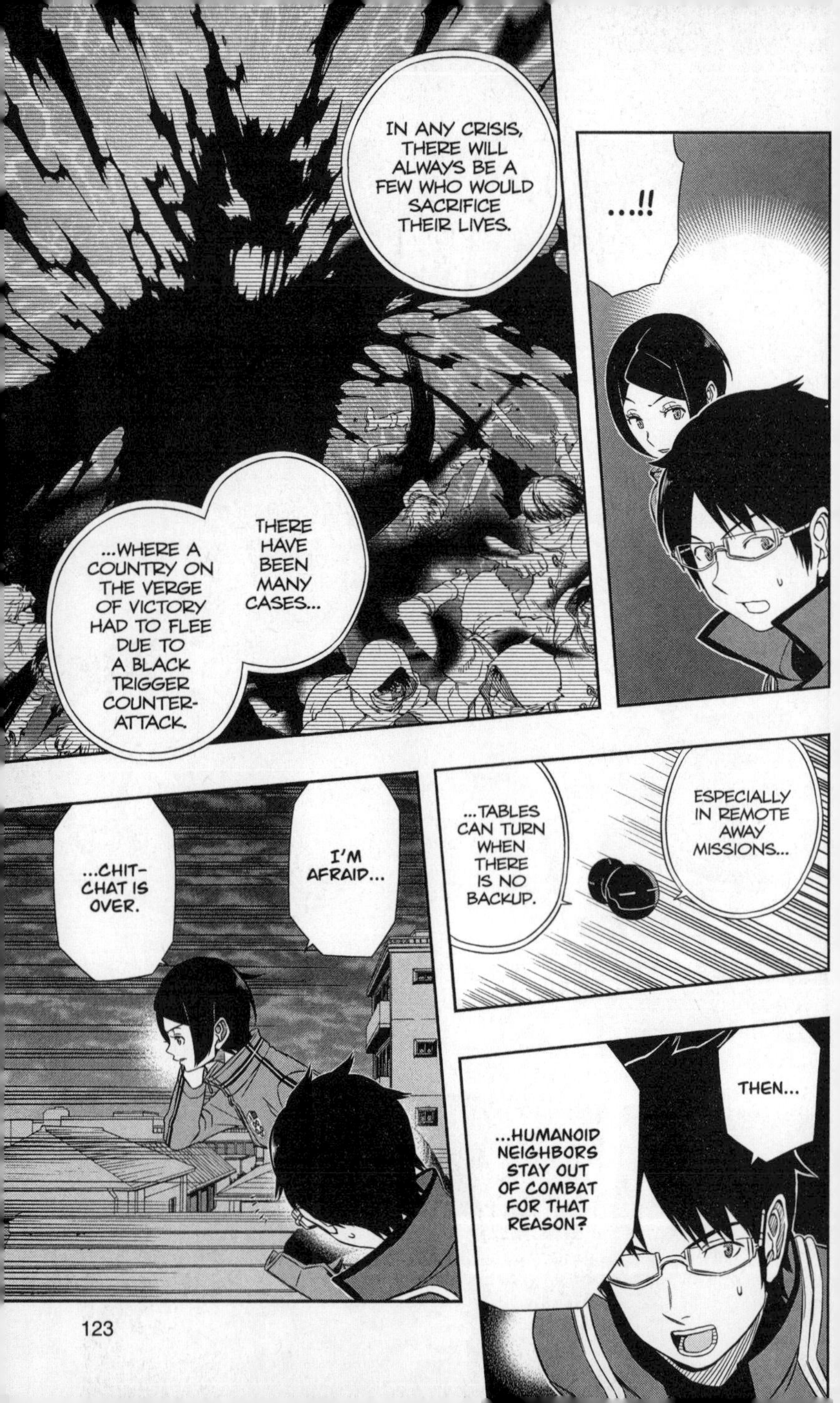

...!!
IN ANY CRISIS, THERE WILL ALWAYS BE A FEW WHO WOULD SACRIFICE THEIR LIVES.
THERE HAVE BEEN MANY CASES...
...WHERE A COUNTRY ON THE VERGE OF VICTORY HAD TO FLEE DUE TO A BLACK TRIGGER COUNTER-ATTACK.
ESPECIALLY IN REMOTE AWAY MISSIONS...
...TABLES CAN TURN WHEN THERE IS NO BACKUP.
THEN...
...HUMANOID NEIGHBORS STAY OUT OF COMBAT FOR THAT REASON?
I'M AFRAID...
...CHIT-CHAT IS OVER.

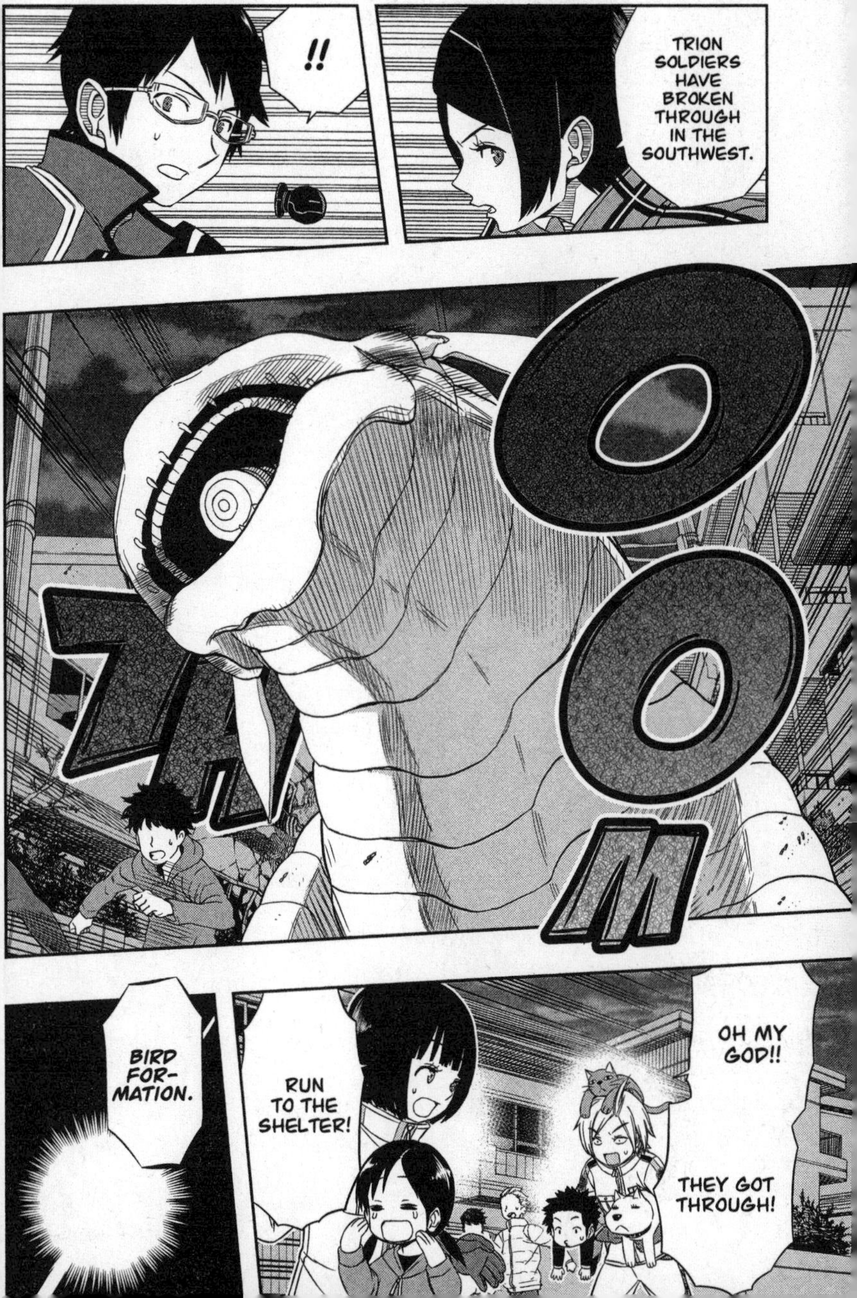
TRION SOLDIERS HAVE BROKEN THROUGH IN THE SOUTHWEST.
!!
OH MY GOD!!
RUN TO THE SHELTER!
THEY GOT THROUGH!
BIRD FOR-MATION.

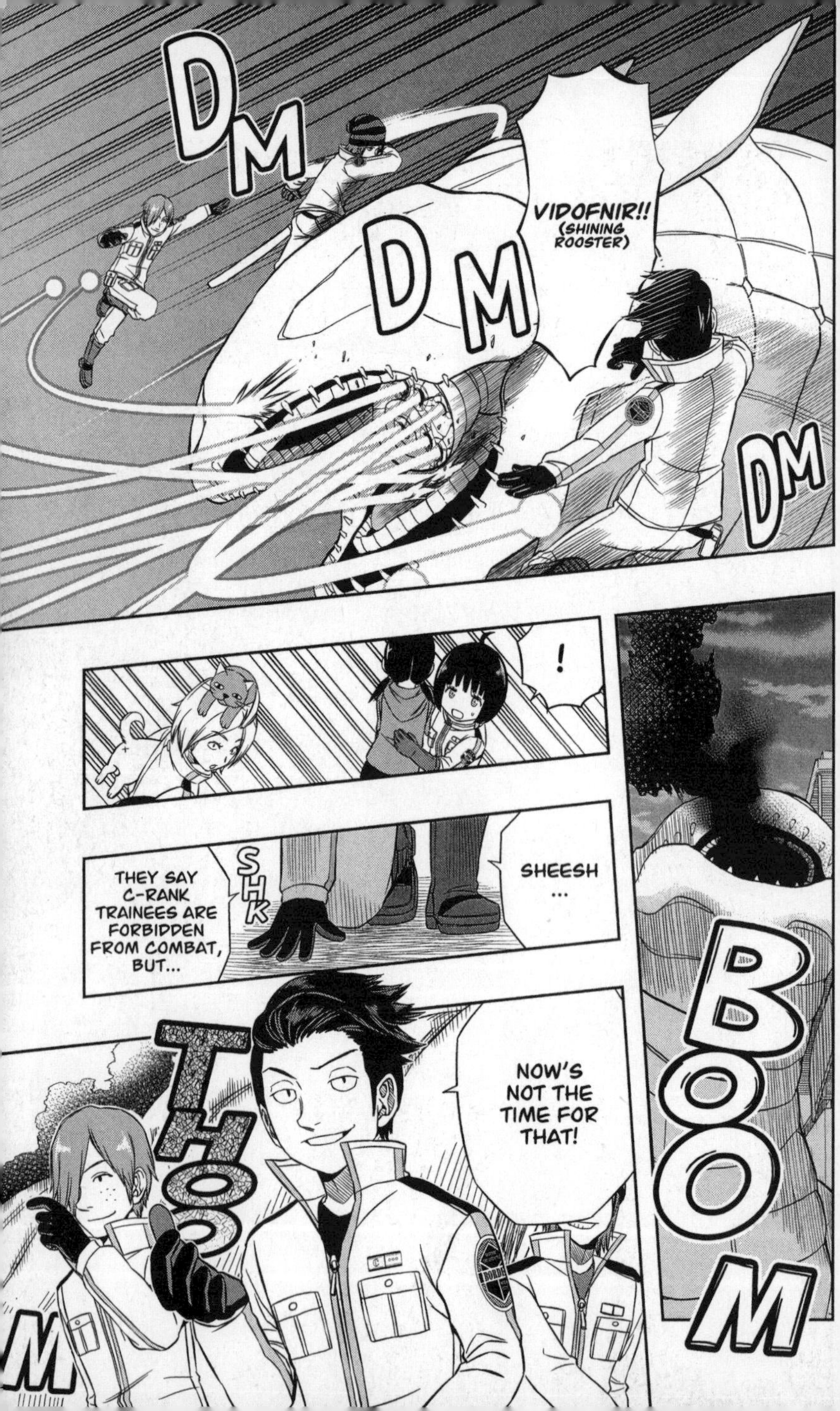
VIDOFNIR!! (SHINING ROOSTER)
DM
DM
DM
BOOM
!
SHEESH ...
SHK
THEY SAY C-RANK TRAINEES ARE FORBIDDEN FROM COMBAT, BUT...
NOW'S NOT THE TIME FOR THAT!
THOOM

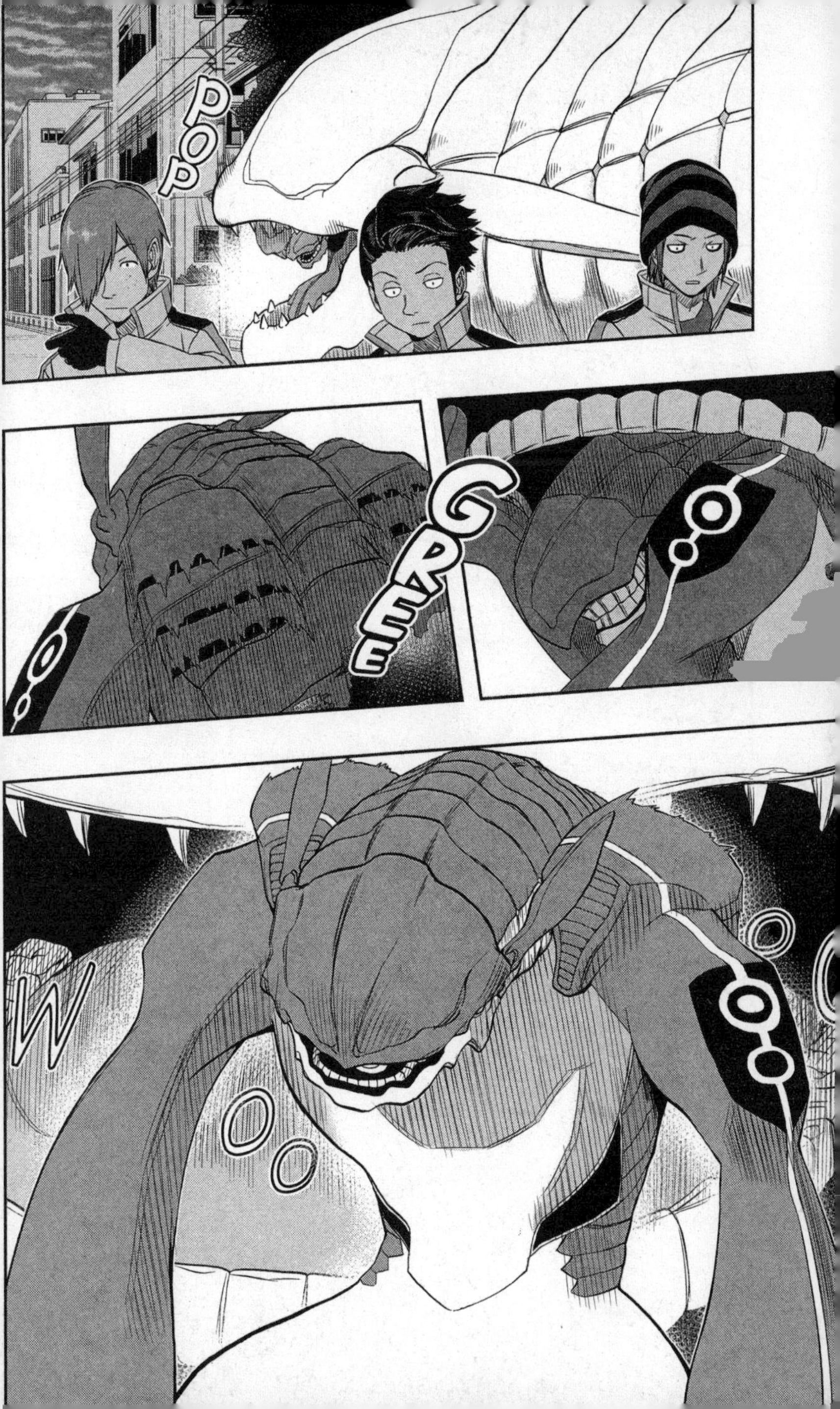
POP
GREE
WOOOO

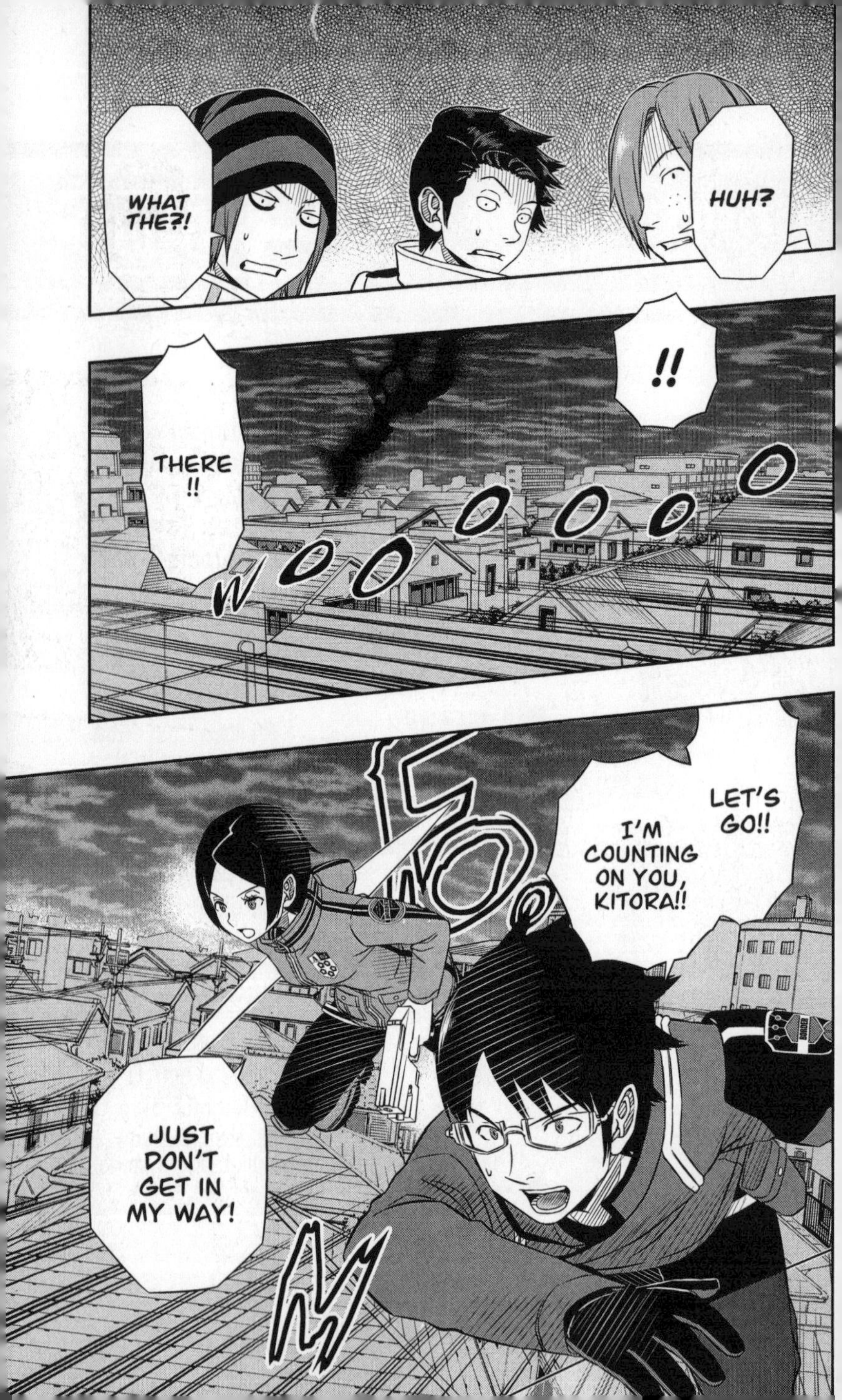
HUH?
WHAT THE?!
!!
THERE !!
WOOOOOO
LET'S GO!!
I'M COUNTING ON YOU, KITORA!!
JUST DON'T GET IN MY WAY!

Kuruma Squad

Border HQ B-Rank #8

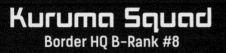

B-008

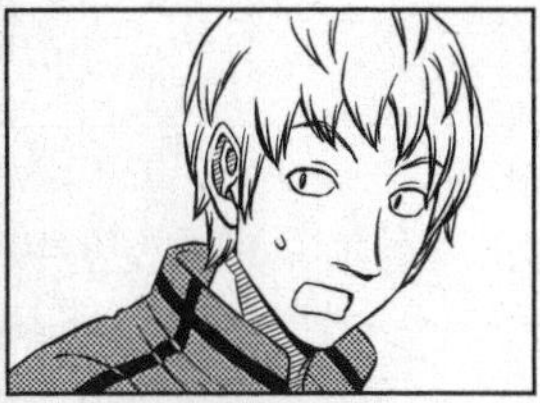

Tatsuya Kuruma
Captain, Gunner

■19 years old (college student)
■Born Feb. 18

■Amphibious, Blood type A
■Height: 5'9"
■Likes: Fish tanks, macaroni au gratin

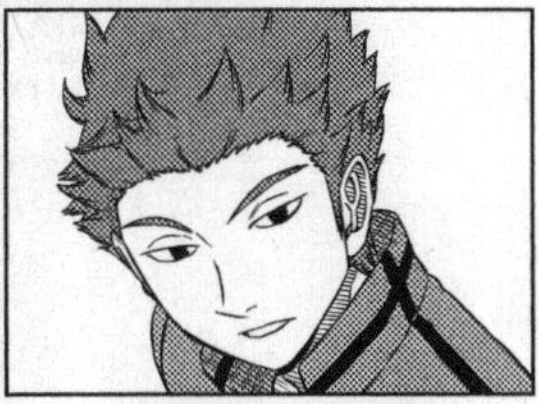

Ko Murakami
Attacker

■18 years old (high school student)
■Born June 15

■Lepus, Blood type B
■Height: 5'8"
■Likes: Cold soba noodles, white rice, training

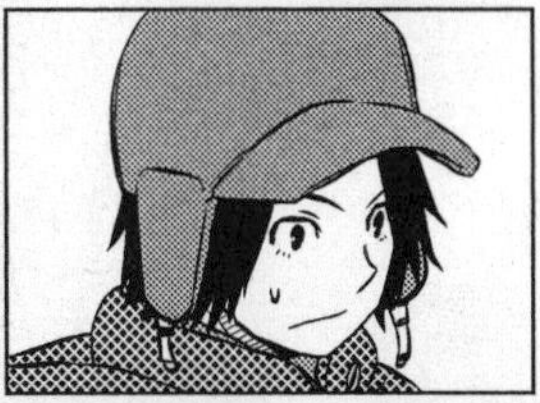

Taichi Betsuyaku
Sniper

■16 years old (high school student)
■Born Nov. 27

■Cetacea, Blood type B
■Height: 5'6"
■Likes: Spaghetti Napolitano, tomatoes, building dioramas

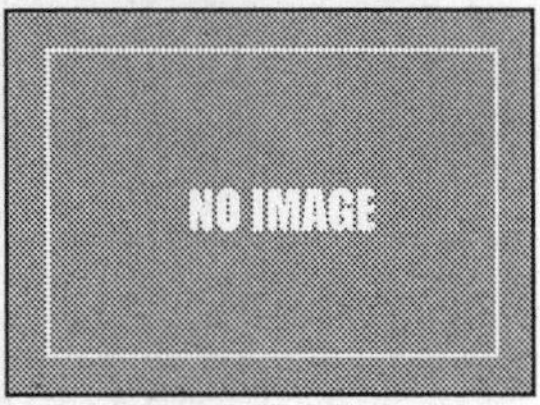
NO IMAGE

Yuka Kon
Operator

■18 years old (high school student)
■Born Sept. 1

■Lupus, Blood type O
■Height: 5'3"
■Likes: Cooking, calligraphy, matcha green tea

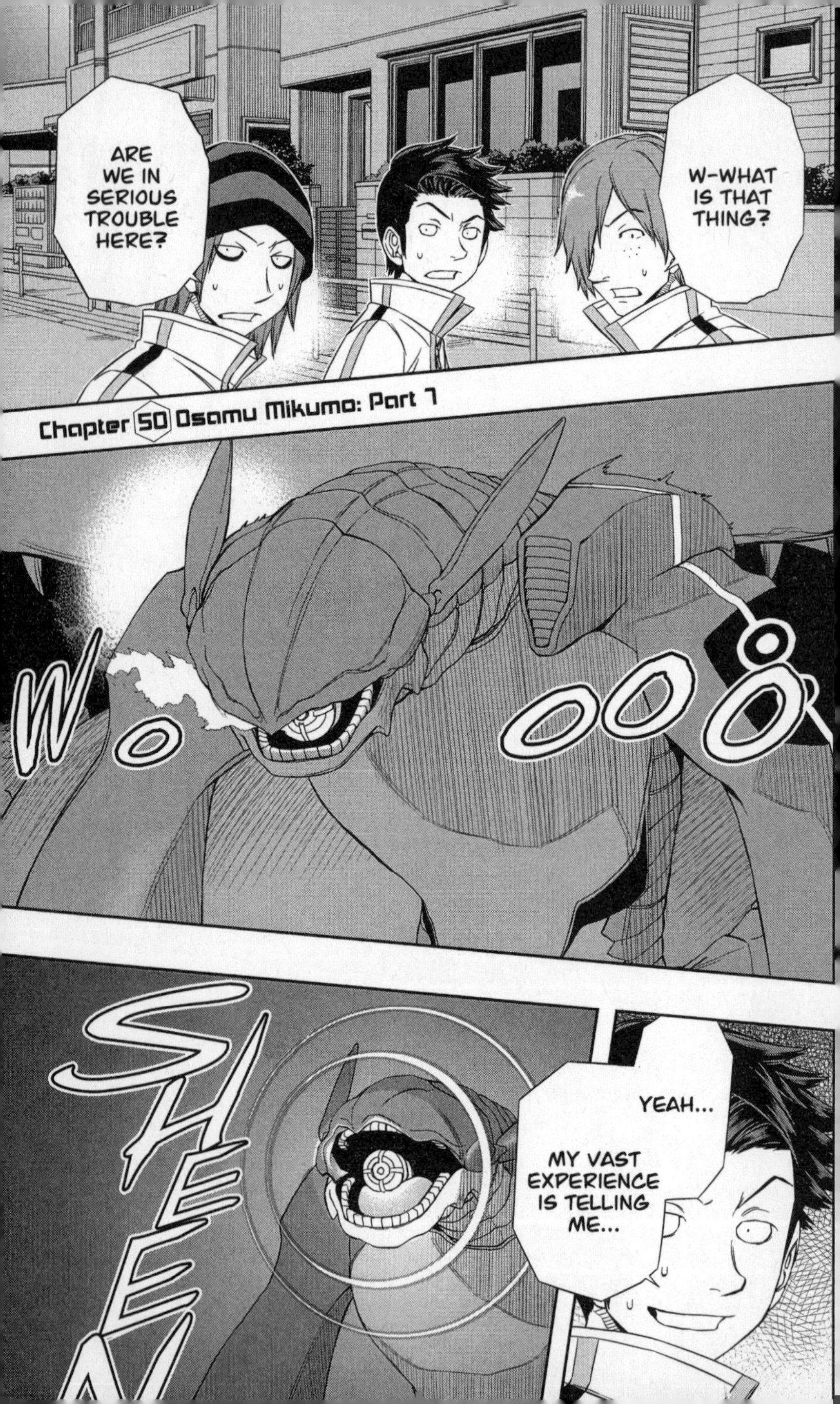

W-WHAT IS THAT THING?
ARE WE IN SERIOUS TROUBLE HERE?
Chapter 50 Osamu Mikumo: Part 7
WOOOO
YEAH... MY VAST EXPERIENCE IS TELLING ME...
SHEE

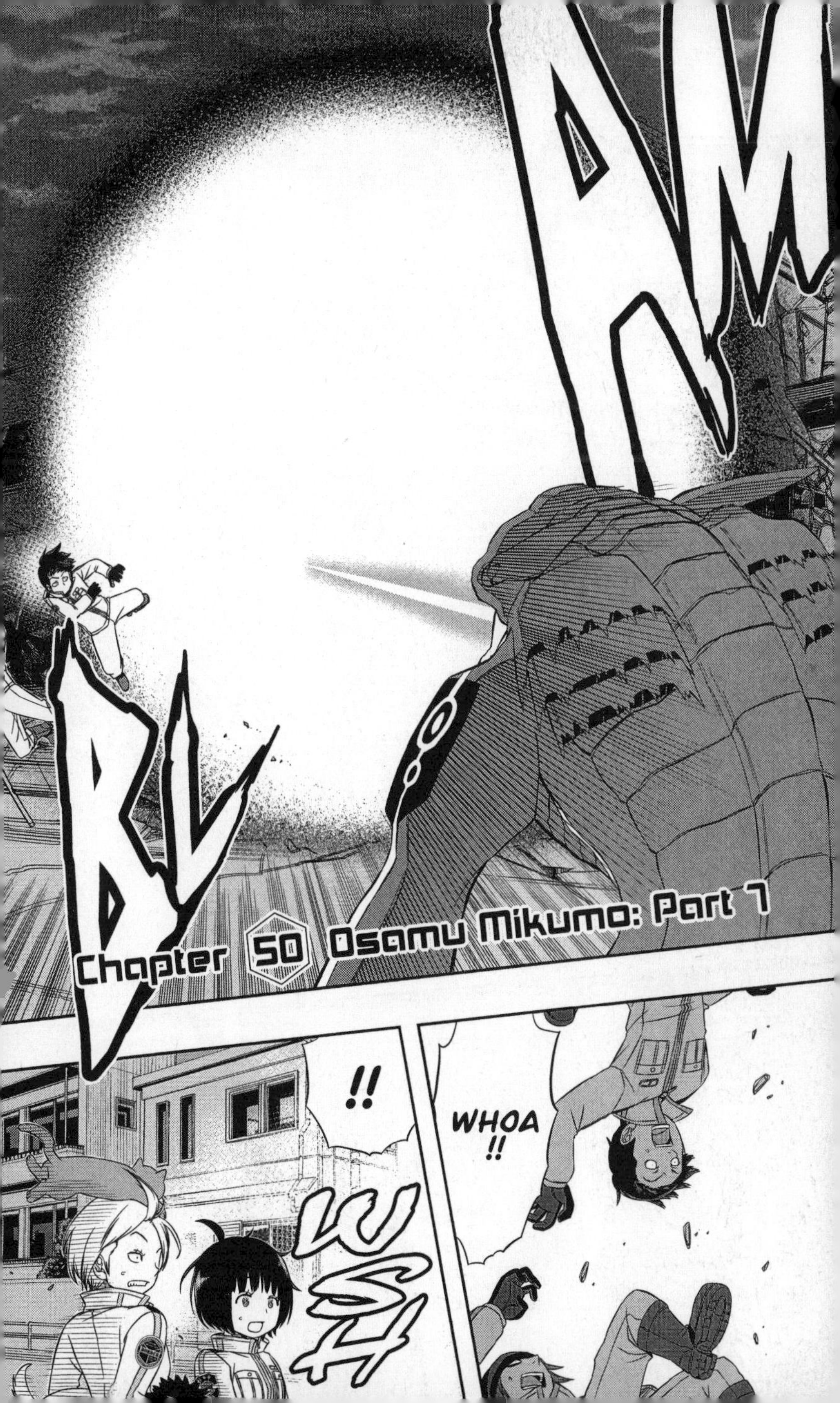
Chapter 50 Osamu Mikumo: Part 7
WHOA !!
!!
WUSH

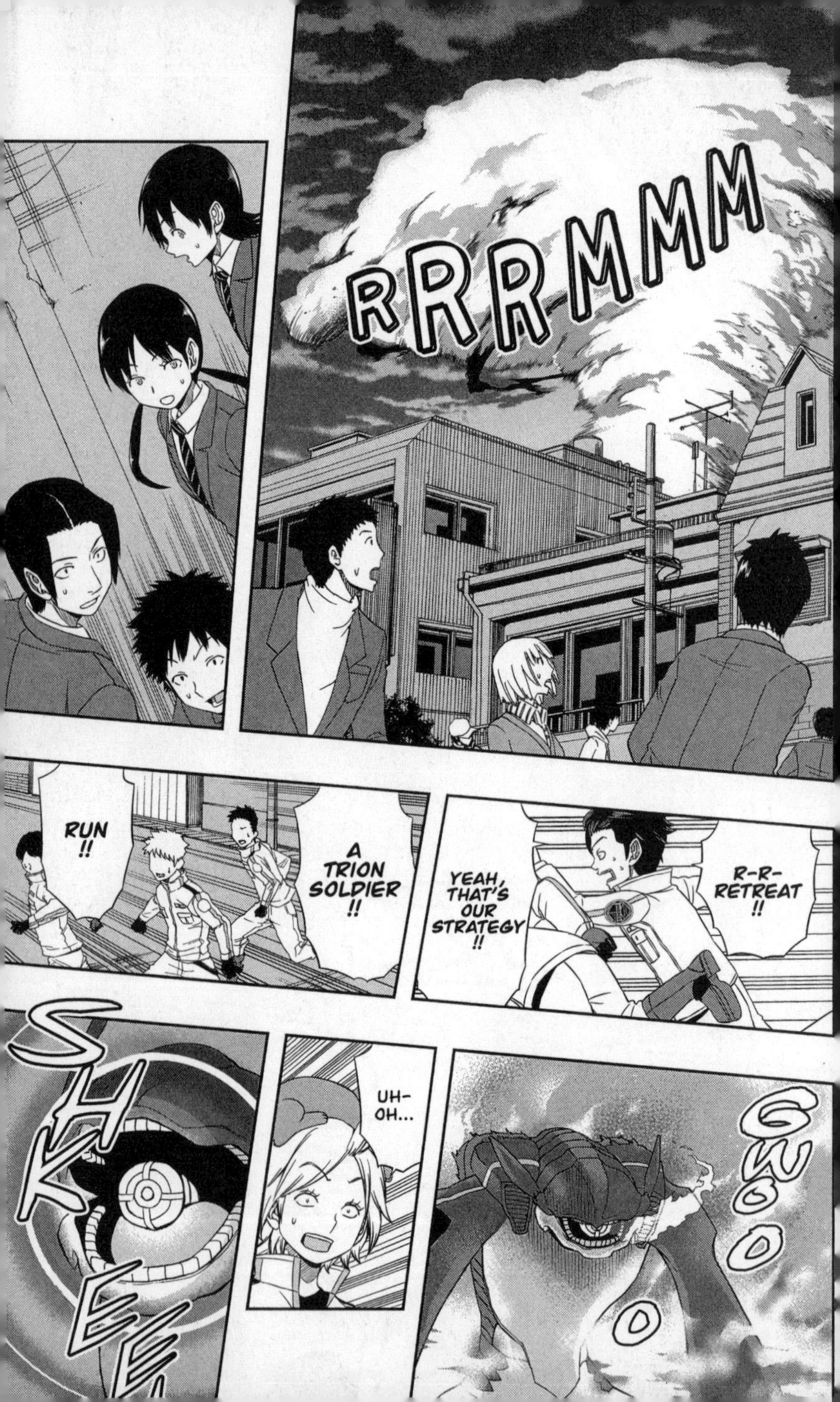
RRRMMMM
R-R-RETREAT!!
YEAH, THAT'S OUR STRATEGY!!
A TRION SOLDIER!!
RUN!!
GWOOO
UH-OH...
SHKEE

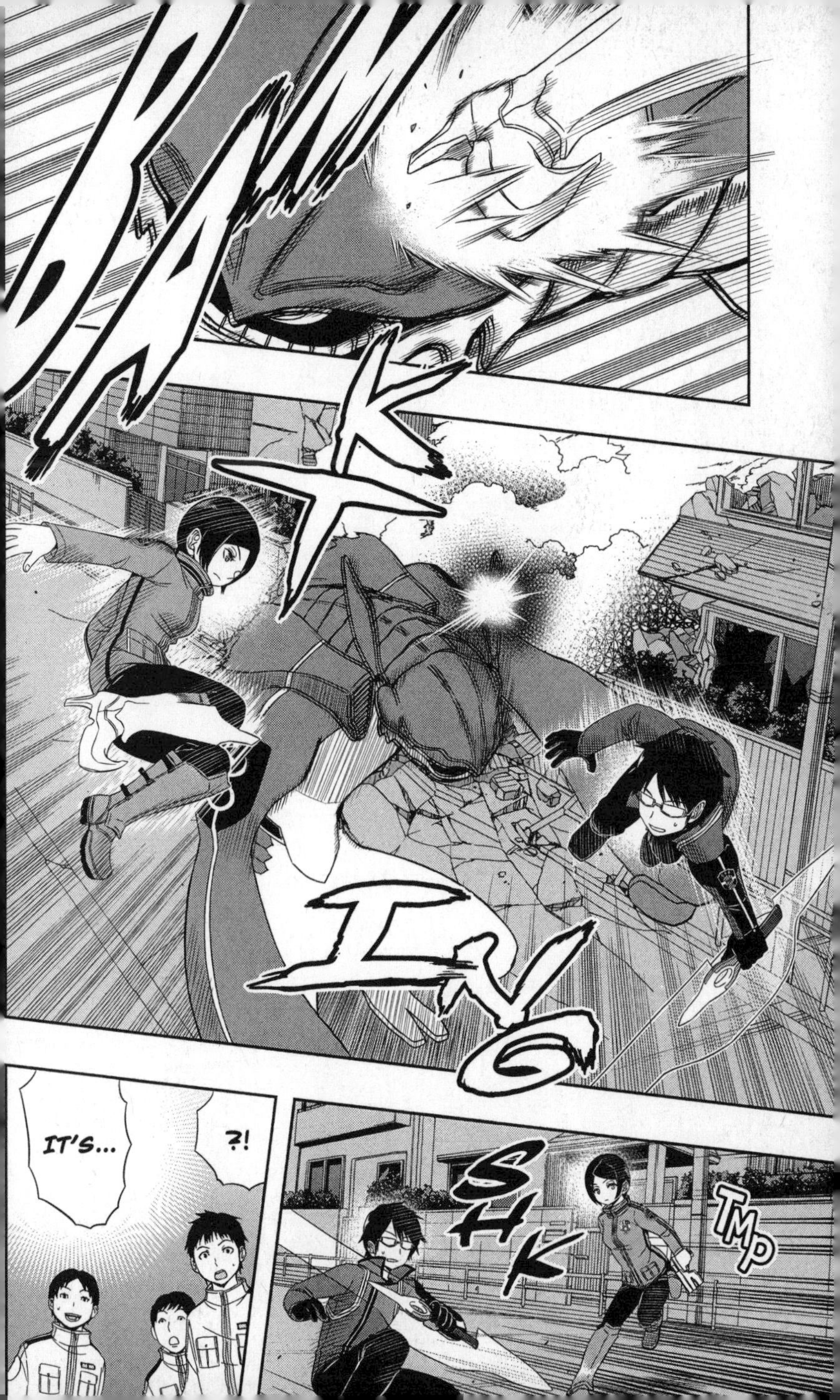

SHK
TMP
?!
IT'S...

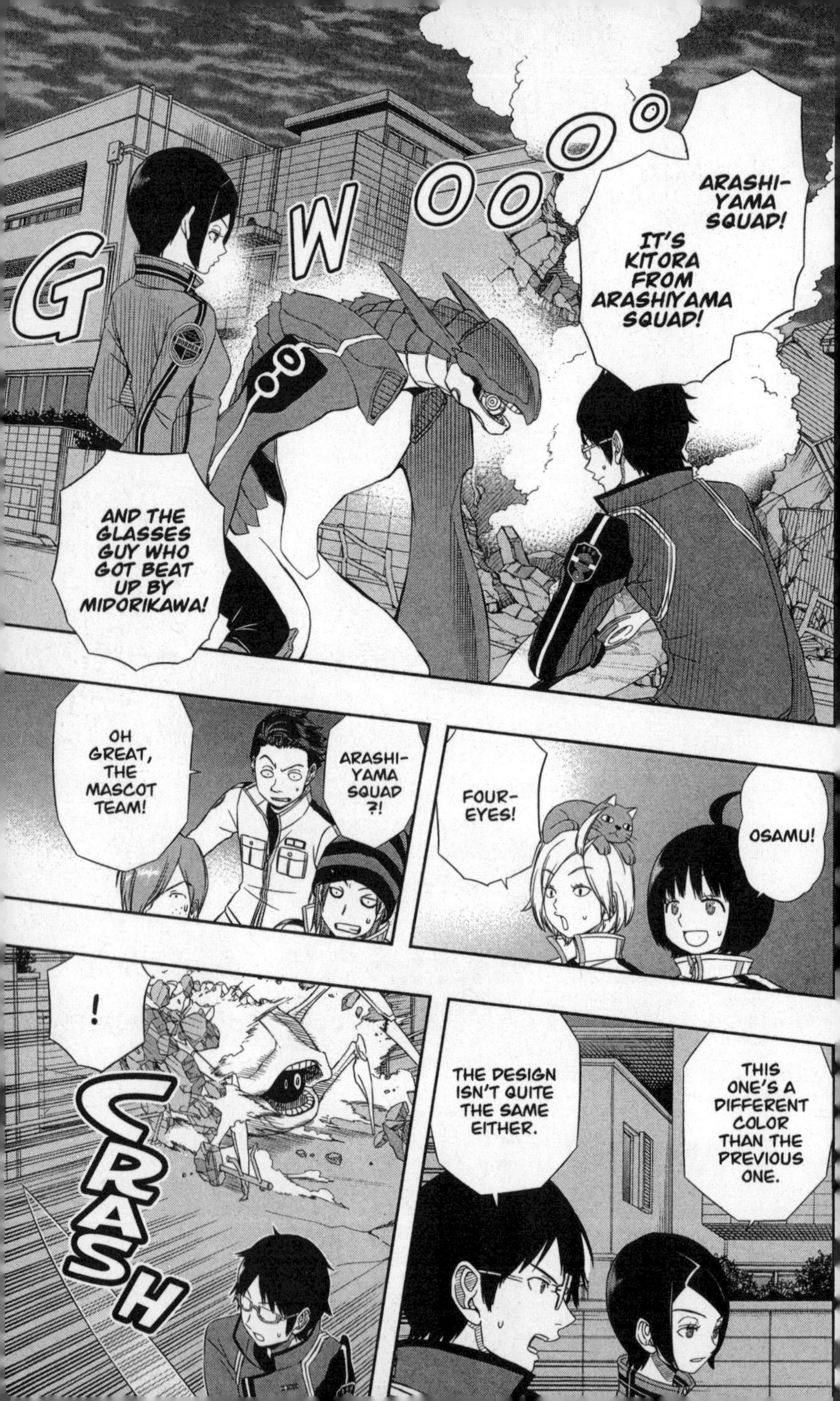
ARASHI-YAMA SQUAD!
IT'S KITORA FROM ARASHIYAMA SQUAD!
GWOOOO
AND THE GLASSES GUY WHO GOT BEAT UP BY MIDORIKAWA!
OSAMU!
FOUR-EYES!
ARASHI-YAMA SQUAD?!
OH GREAT, THE MASCOT TEAM!
THIS ONE'S A DIFFERENT COLOR THAN THE PREVIOUS ONE.
THE DESIGN ISN'T QUITE THE SAME EITHER.
!
CRASH

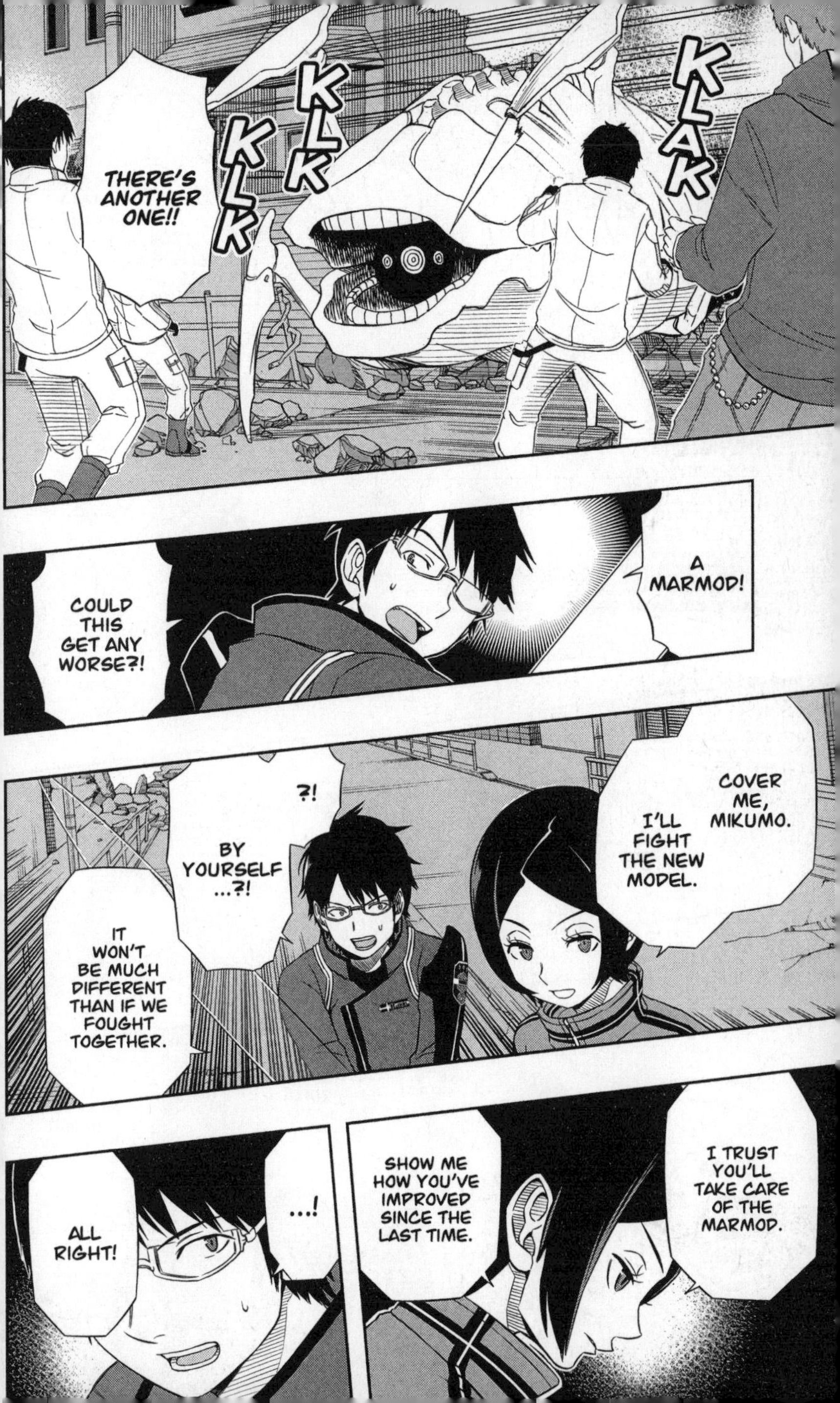
KLAK
KLK
KLK
THERE'S ANOTHER ONE!!
A MARMOD!
COULD THIS GET ANY WORSE?!
COVER ME, MIKUMO.
I'LL FIGHT THE NEW MODEL.
?!
BY YOURSELF ...?!
IT WON'T BE MUCH DIFFERENT THAN IF WE FOUGHT TOGETHER.
I TRUST YOU'LL TAKE CARE OF THE MARMOD.
SHOW ME HOW YOU'VE IMPROVED SINCE THE LAST TIME.
...!
ALL RIGHT!

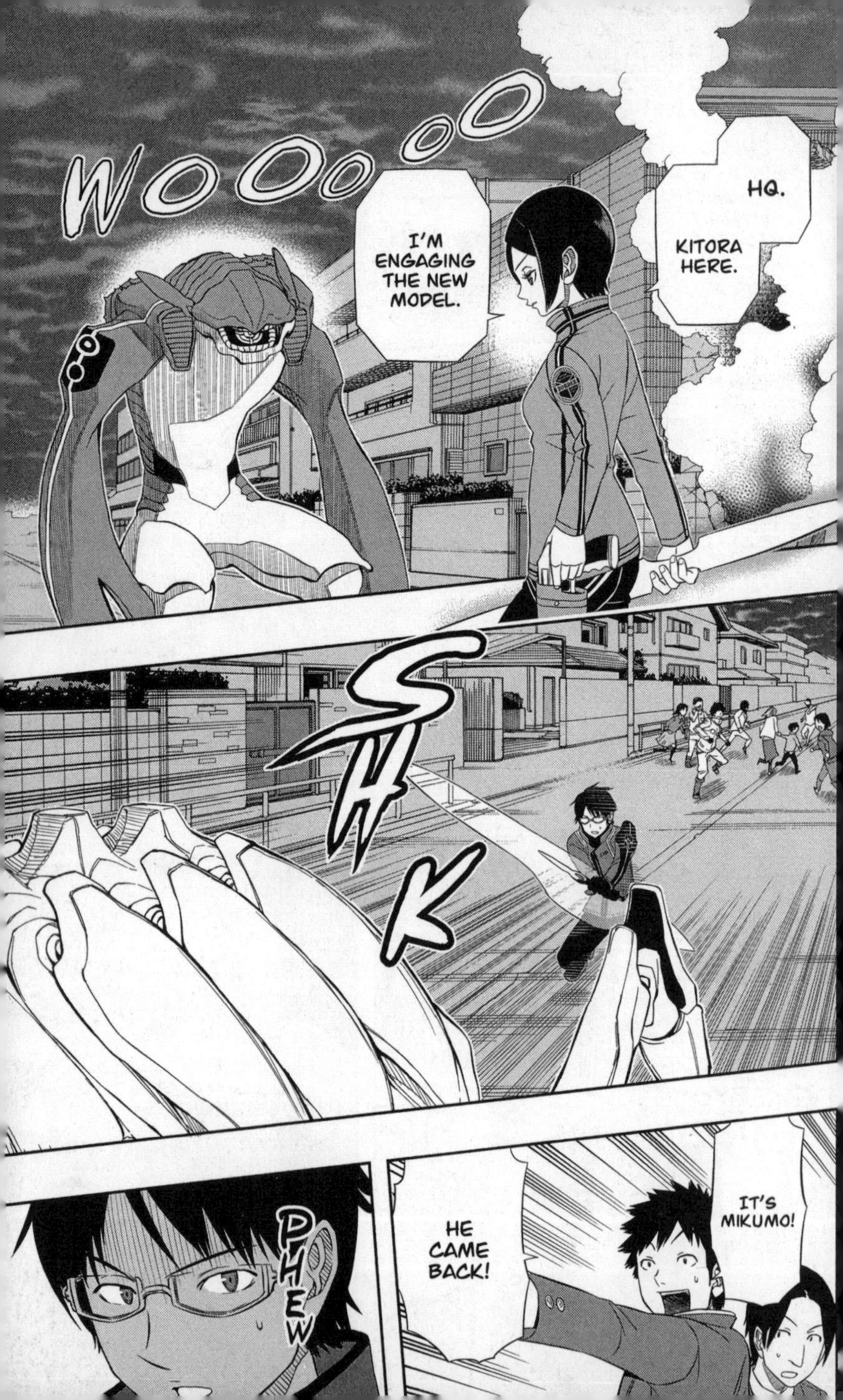
HQ.
KITORA HERE.
I'M ENGAGING THE NEW MODEL.
WOOOOoO
SHK
IT'S MIKUMO!
HE CAME BACK!
PHEW

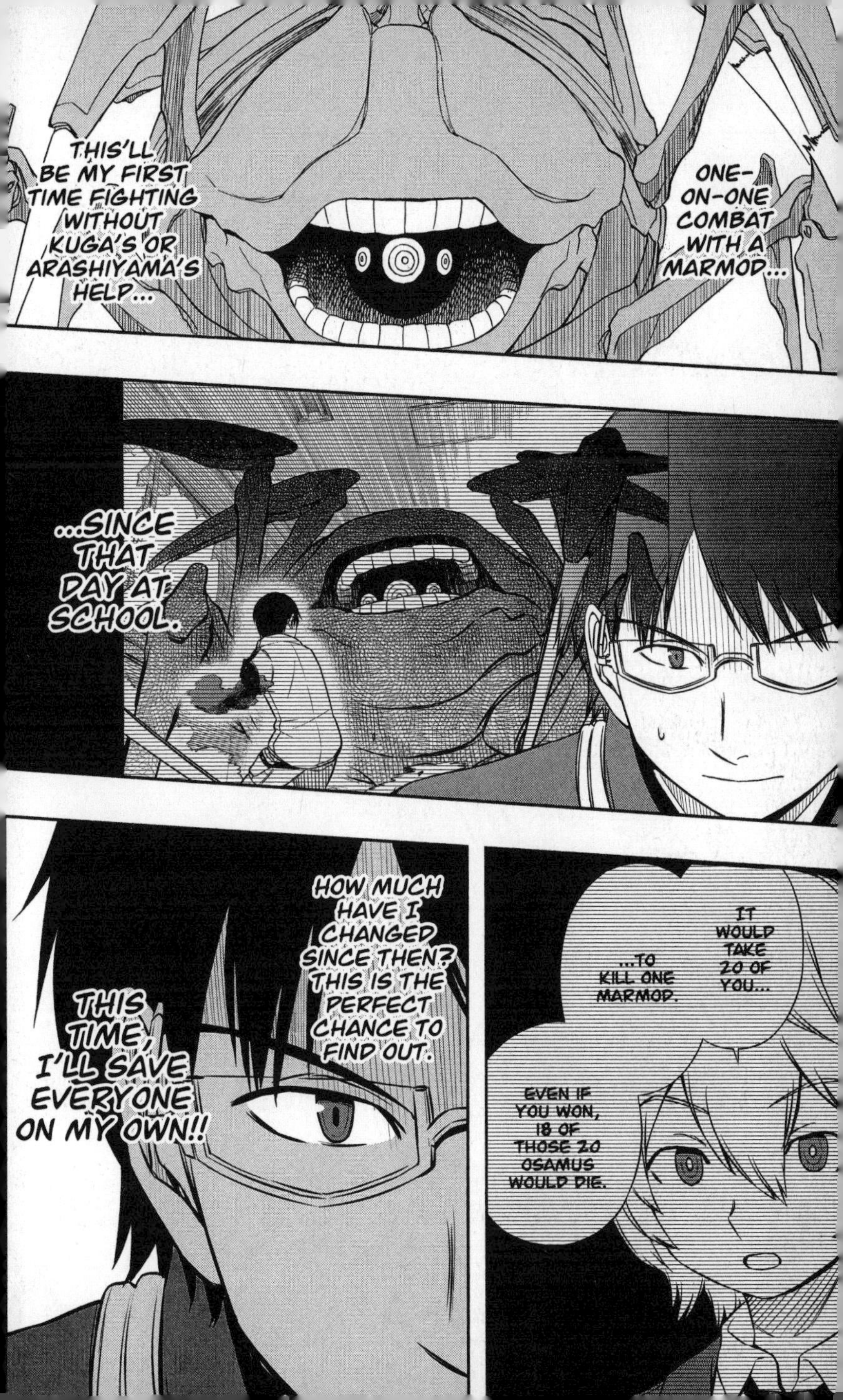
ONE-ON-ONE COMBAT WITH A MARMOD...
THIS'LL BE MY FIRST TIME FIGHTING WITHOUT KUGA'S OR ARASHIYAMA'S HELP...
...SINCE THAT DAY AT SCHOOL.
IT WOULD TAKE 20 OF YOU...
...TO KILL ONE MARMOD.
EVEN IF YOU WON, 18 OF THOSE 20 OSAMUS WOULD DIE.
HOW MUCH HAVE I CHANGED SINCE THEN? THIS IS THE PERFECT CHANCE TO FIND OUT.
THIS TIME, I'LL SAVE EVERYONE ON MY OWN!!

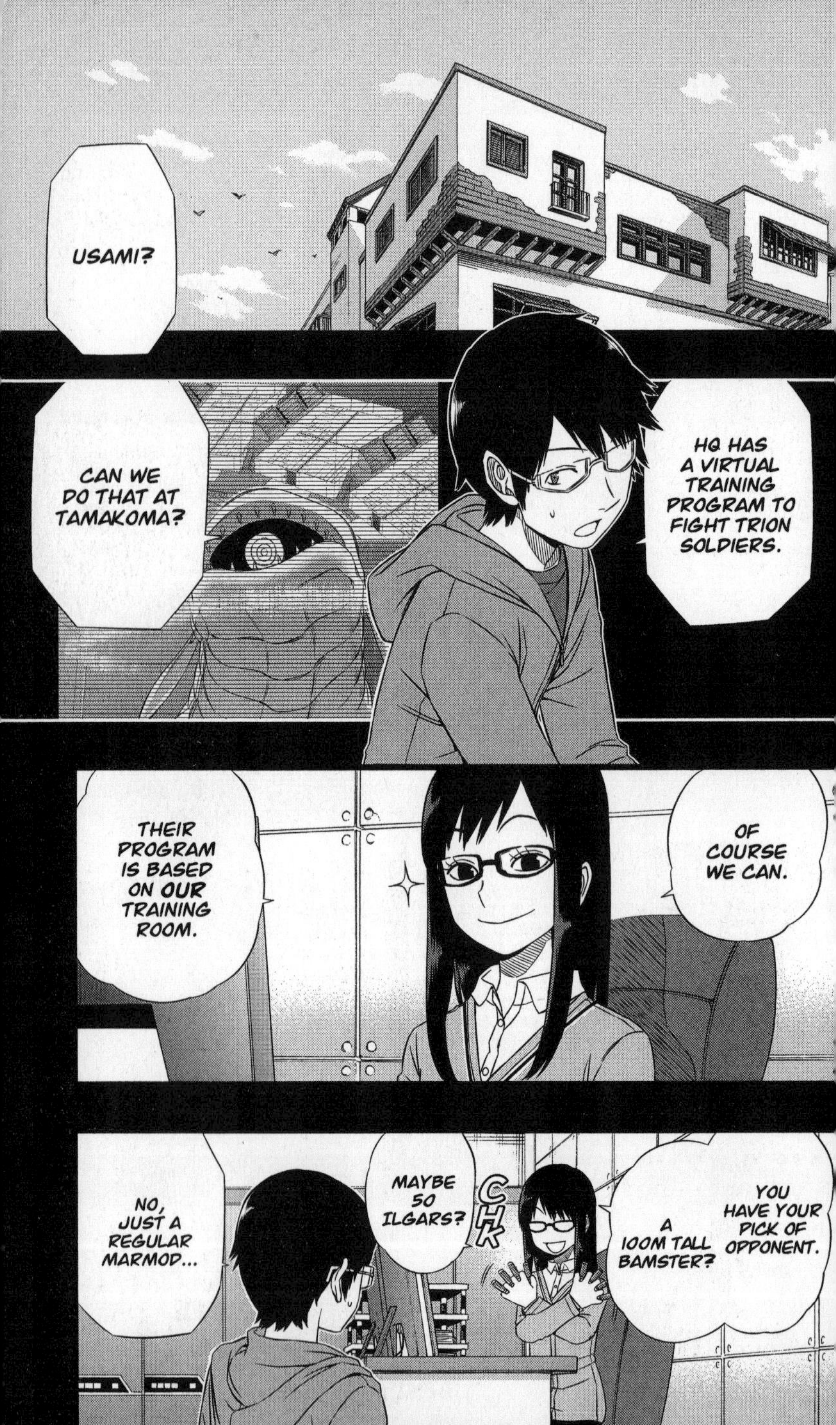
USAMI?
HQ HAS A VIRTUAL TRAINING PROGRAM TO FIGHT TRION SOLDIERS.
CAN WE DO THAT AT TAMAKOMA?
OF COURSE WE CAN.
THEIR PROGRAM IS BASED ON OUR TRAINING ROOM.
YOU HAVE YOUR PICK OF OPPONENT.
A 100M TALL BAMSTER?
CHK
MAYBE 50 ILGARS?
NO, JUST A REGULAR MARMOD...

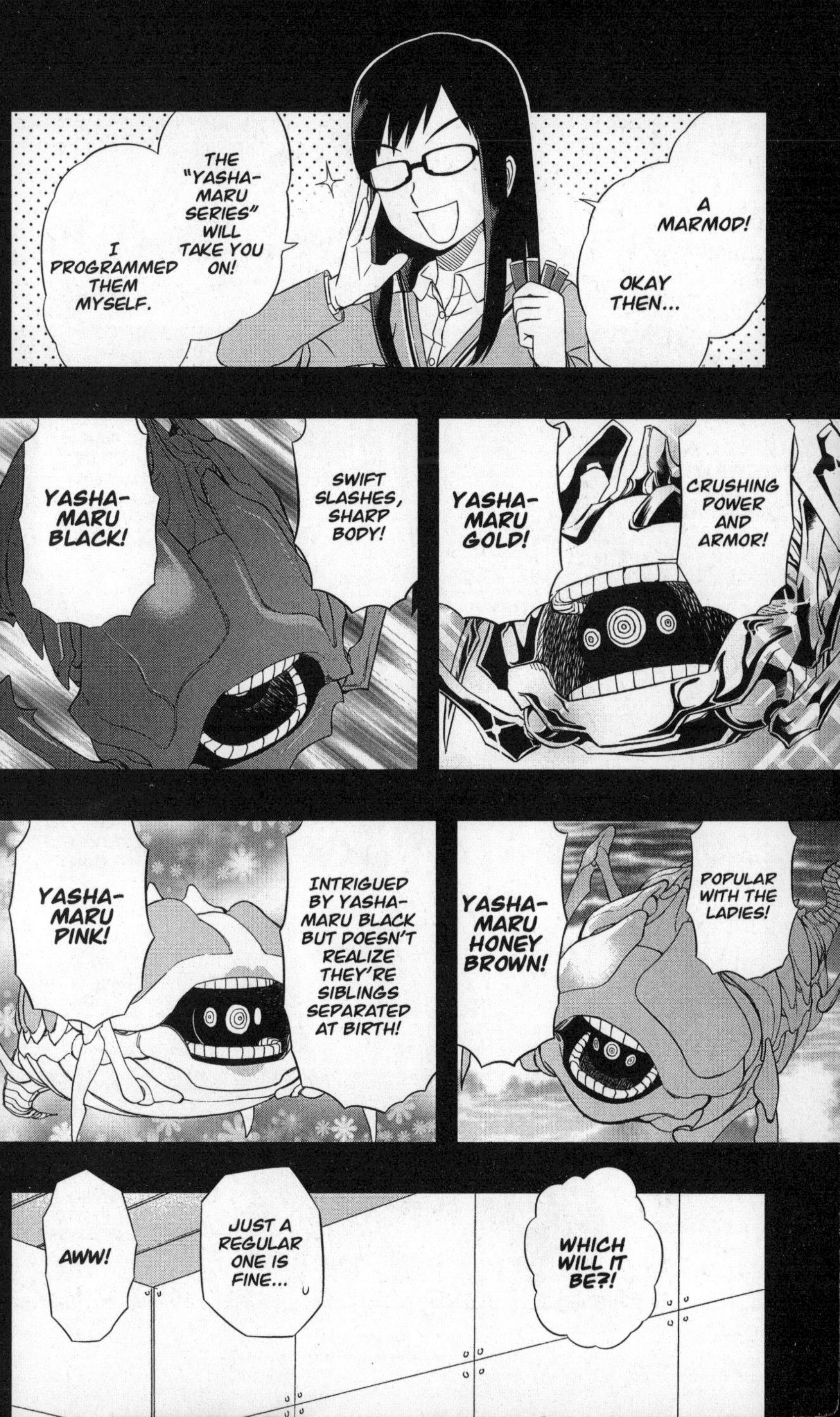
A MARMOD!
OKAY THEN...
THE "YASHA-MARU SERIES" WILL TAKE YOU ON!
I PROGRAMMED THEM MYSELF.
CRUSHING POWER AND ARMOR!
YASHA-MARU GOLD!
SWIFT SLASHES, SHARP BODY!
YASHA-MARU BLACK!
POPULAR WITH THE LADIES!
YASHA-MARU HONEY BROWN!
INTRIGUED BY YASHA-MARU BLACK BUT DOESN'T REALIZE THEY'RE SIBLINGS SEPARATED AT BIRTH!
YASHA-MARU PINK!
WHICH WILL IT BE?!
JUST A REGULAR ONE IS FINE...
AWW!

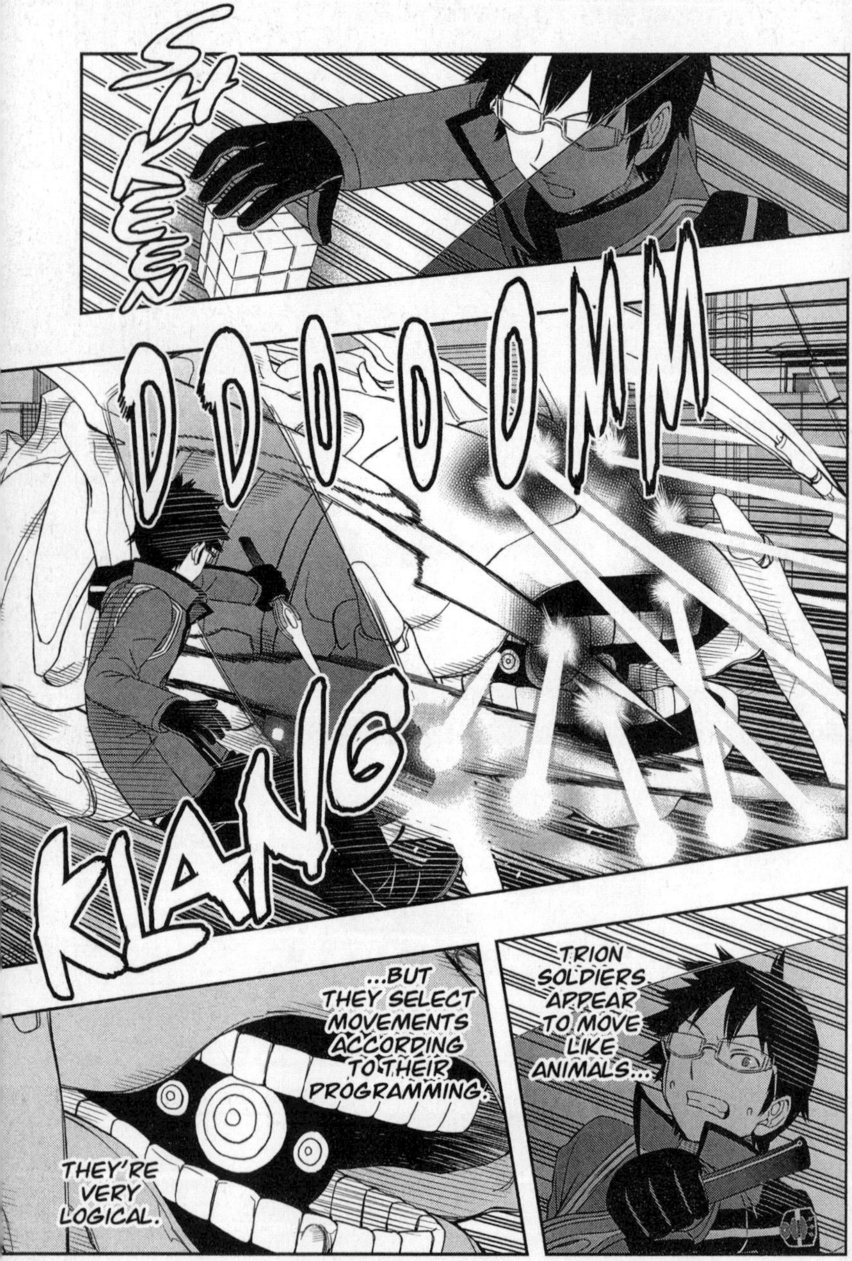
SHKEEN
DDDOOMM
KLANG
TRION SOLDIERS APPEAR TO MOVE LIKE ANIMALS...
...BUT THEY SELECT MOVEMENTS ACCORDING TO THEIR PROGRAMMING.
THEY'RE VERY LOGICAL.

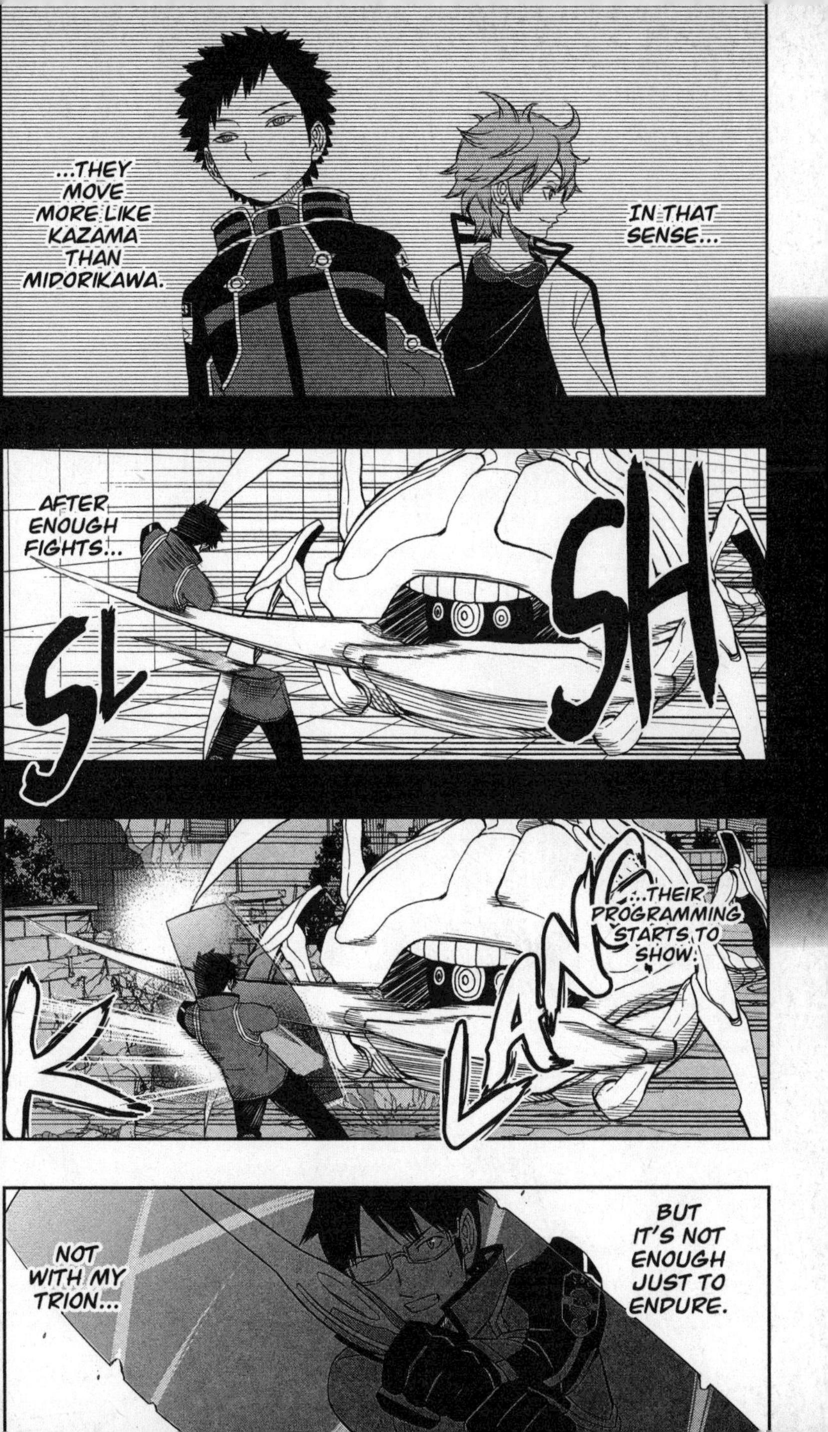
IN THAT SENSE...
...THEY MOVE MORE LIKE KAZAMA THAN MIDORIKAWA.
AFTER ENOUGH FIGHTS...
SLSH
...THEIR PROGRAMMING STARTS TO SHOW.
KLANG
BUT IT'S NOT ENOUGH JUST TO ENDURE.
NOT WITH MY TRION...

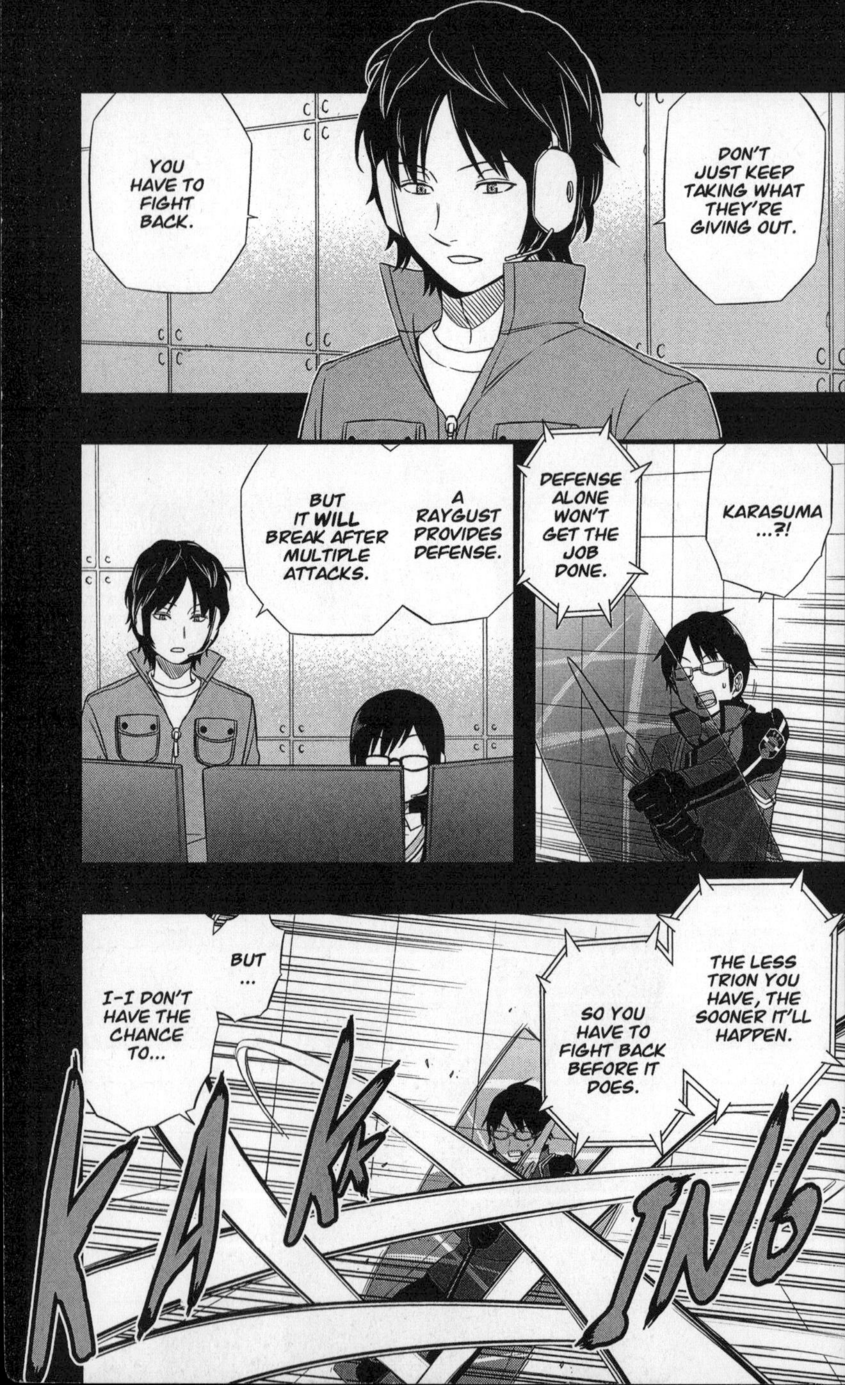
DON'T JUST KEEP TAKING WHAT THEY'RE GIVING OUT.
YOU HAVE TO FIGHT BACK.
KARASUMA ...?!
DEFENSE ALONE WON'T GET THE JOB DONE.
A RAYGUST PROVIDES DEFENSE.
BUT IT WILL BREAK AFTER MULTIPLE ATTACKS.
THE LESS TRION YOU HAVE, THE SOONER IT'LL HAPPEN.
SO YOU HAVE TO FIGHT BACK BEFORE IT DOES.
BUT ...
I-I DON'T HAVE THE CHANCE TO...
KAKKING

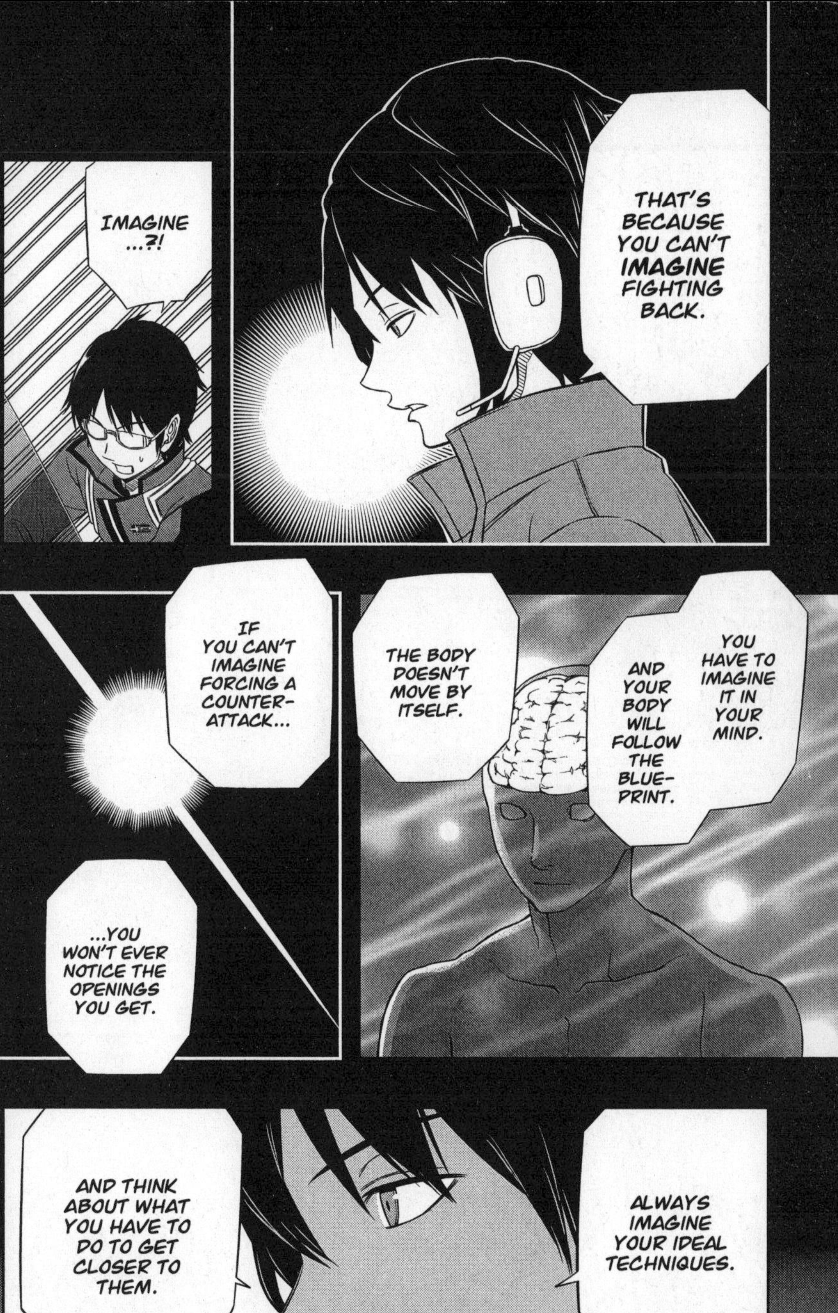
THAT'S BECAUSE YOU CAN'T IMAGINE FIGHTING BACK.
IMAGINE ...?!
YOU HAVE TO IMAGINE IT IN YOUR MIND.
AND YOUR BODY WILL FOLLOW THE BLUE-PRINT.
THE BODY DOESN'T MOVE BY ITSELF.
IF YOU CAN'T IMAGINE FORCING A COUNTER-ATTACK...
...YOU WON'T EVER NOTICE THE OPENINGS YOU GET.
ALWAYS IMAGINE YOUR IDEAL TECHNIQUES.
AND THINK ABOUT WHAT YOU HAVE TO DO TO GET CLOSER TO THEM.

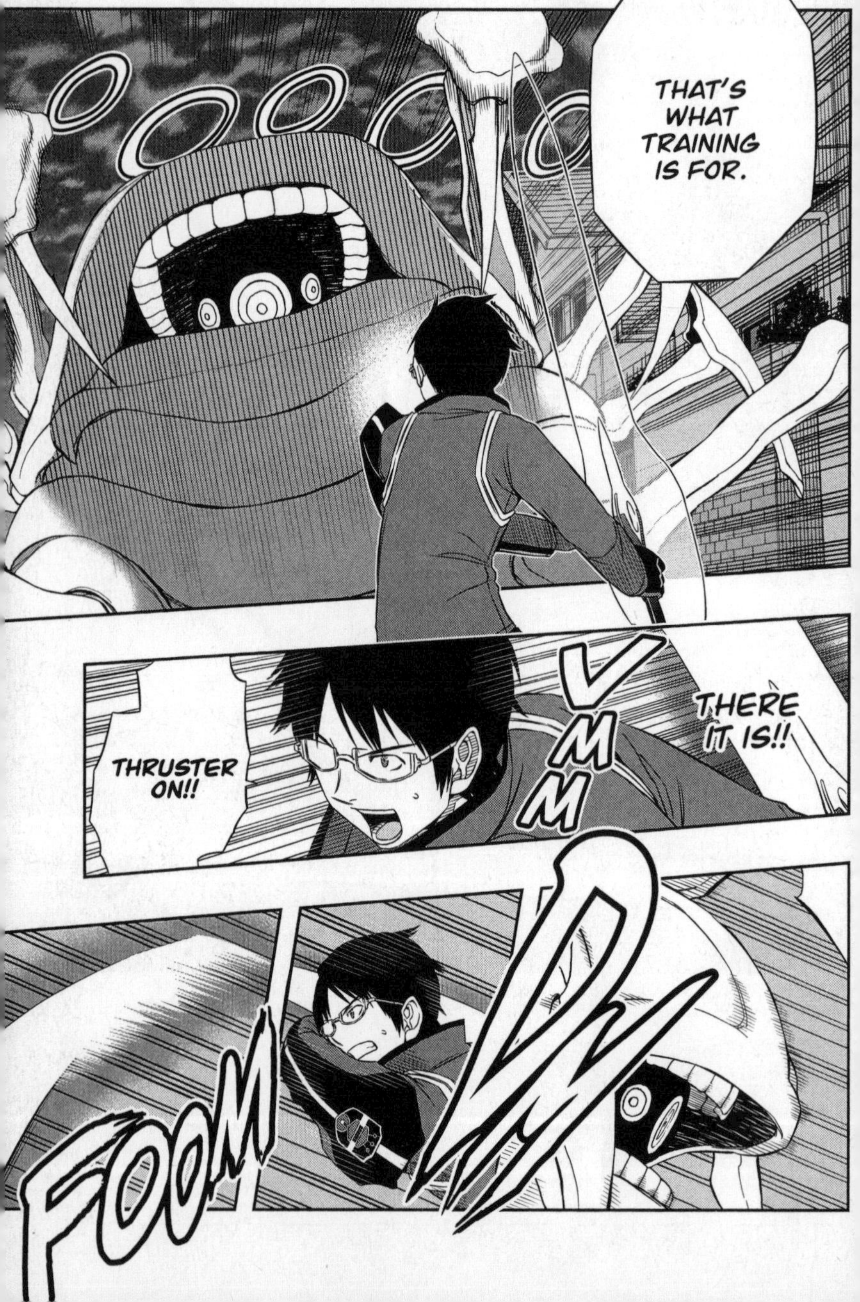
THAT'S WHAT TRAINING IS FOR.
THERE IT IS!!
VMM
THRUSTER ON!!
VOOM
FOOM

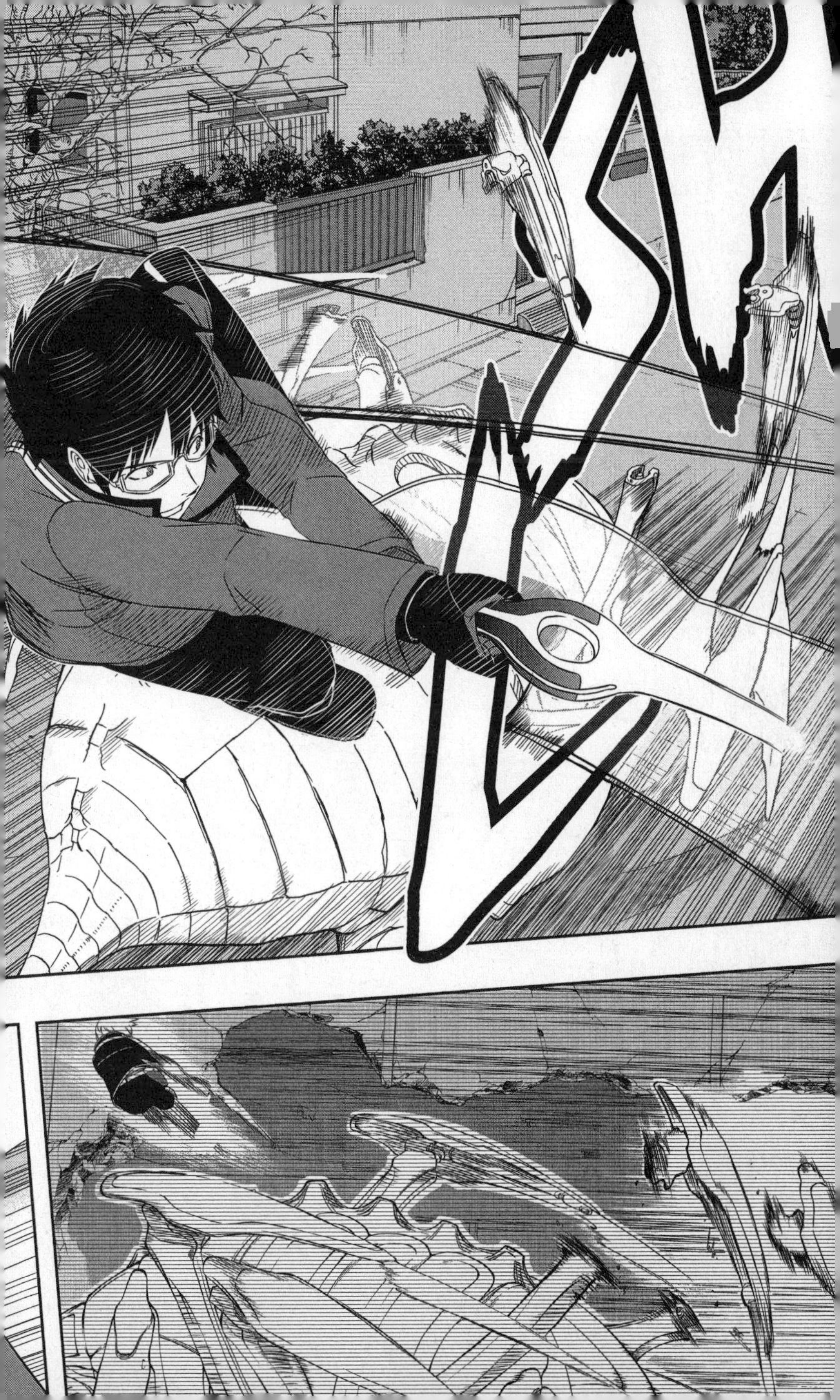

READ THIS WAY

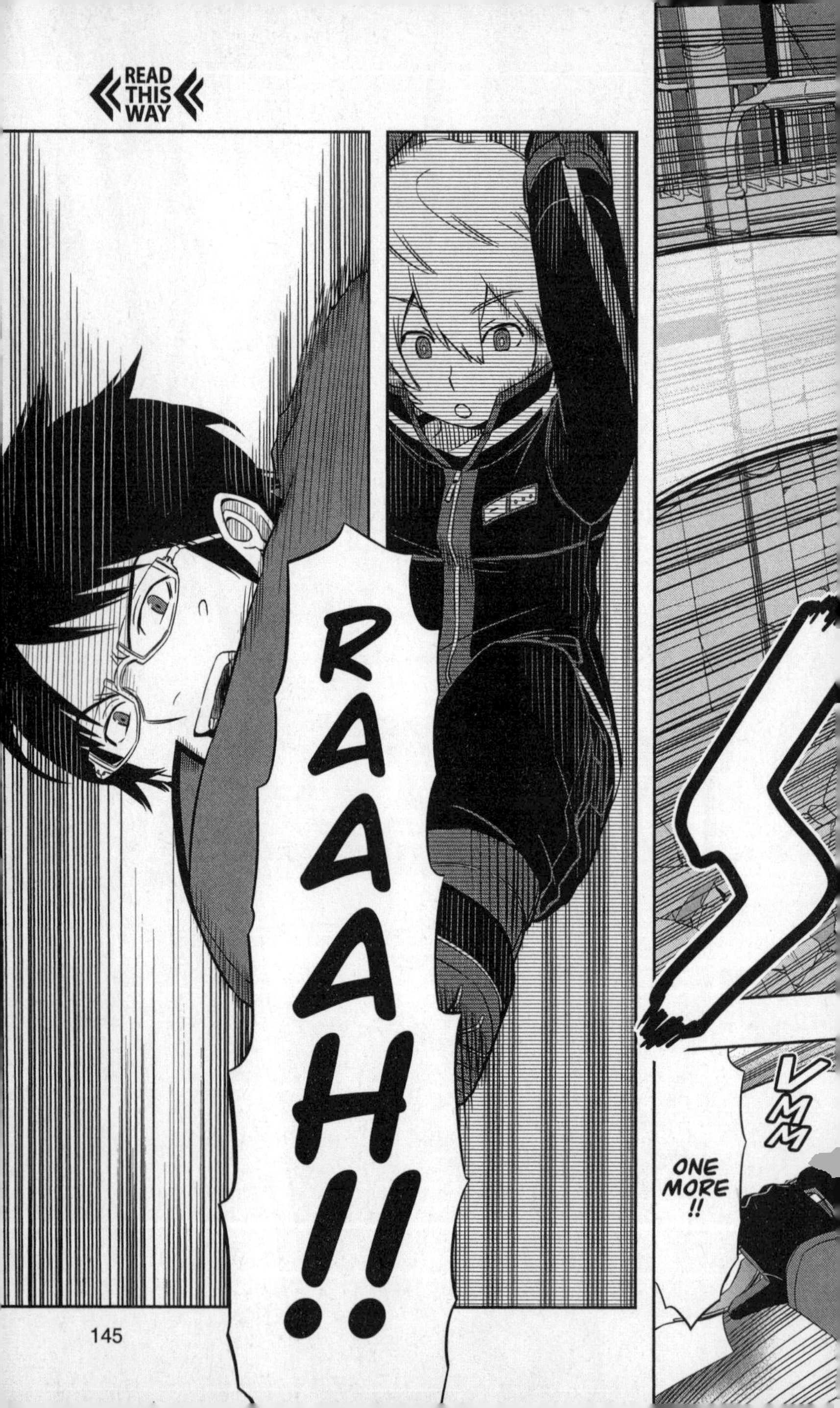
VMM
ONE MORE!!
RAAAH!!

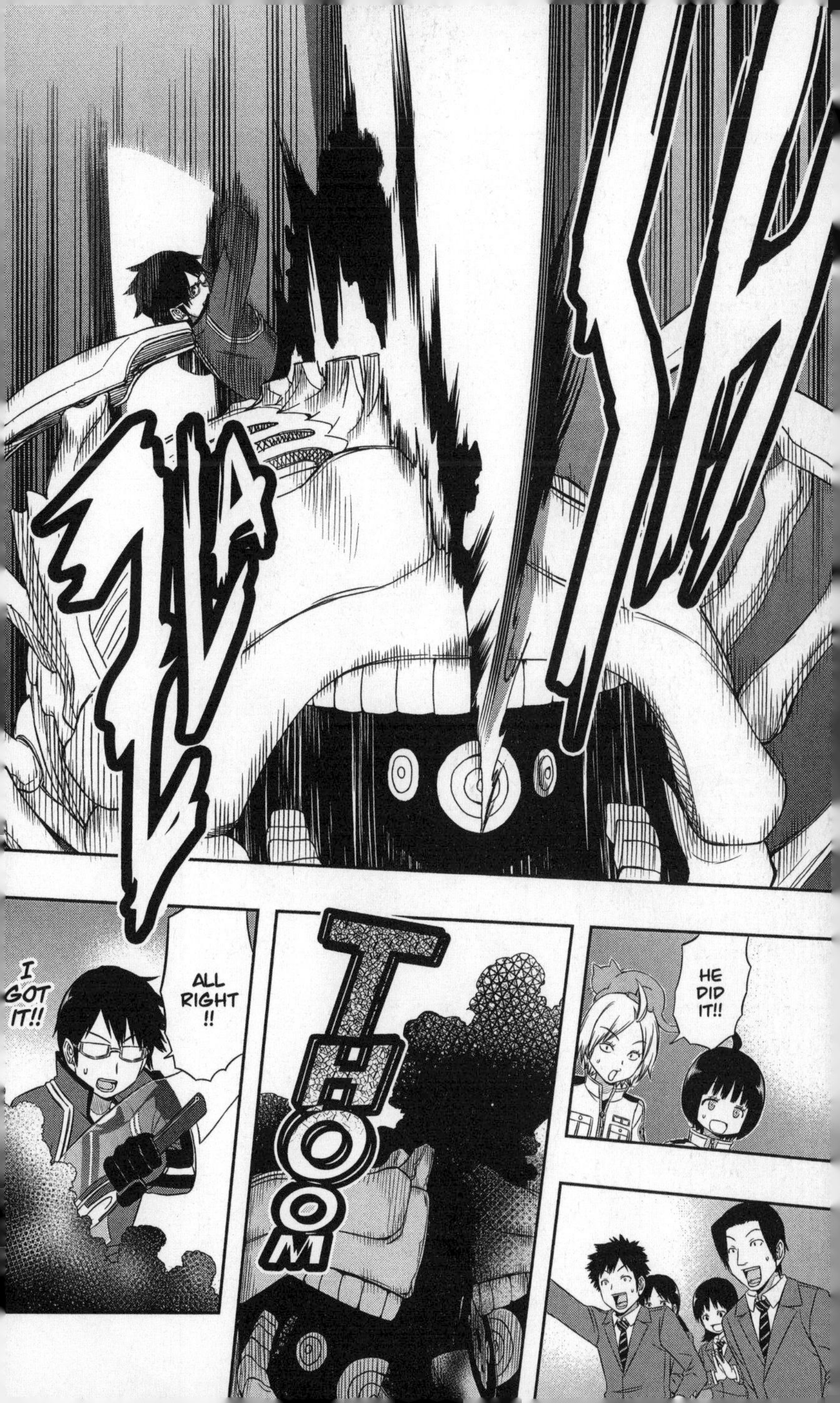
HE DID IT!!
THOOOOM
ALL RIGHT!!
I GOT IT!!

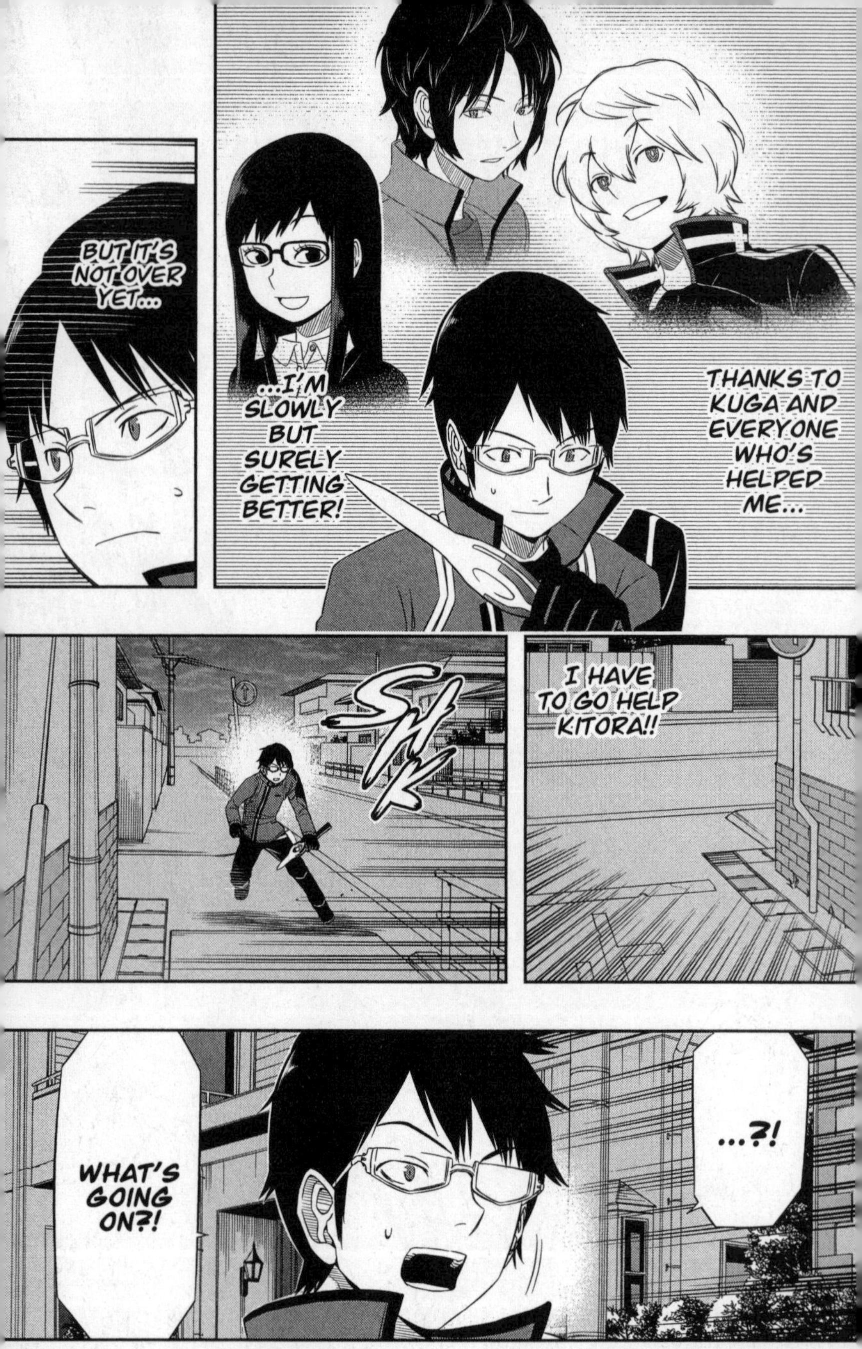
THANKS TO KUGA AND EVERYONE WHO'S HELPED ME...
...I'M SLOWLY BUT SURELY GETTING BETTER!
BUT IT'S NOT OVER YET...
I HAVE TO GO HELP KITORA!!
SHK
...?!
WHAT'S GOING ON?!

Rejected Storyboard

I've improved...or not.

Chapter 4 Reject (continued)

More of the rejected chapter 4 storyboards. Yuma brings down one of the Ilgars and Jin shows up to destroy the other one. Tachikawa inherited the visuals in this volume. I drew this and it occurred to me that it makes Ilgars look really soft, so then I came up with the self-destruct mode. I can learn from my mistakes.

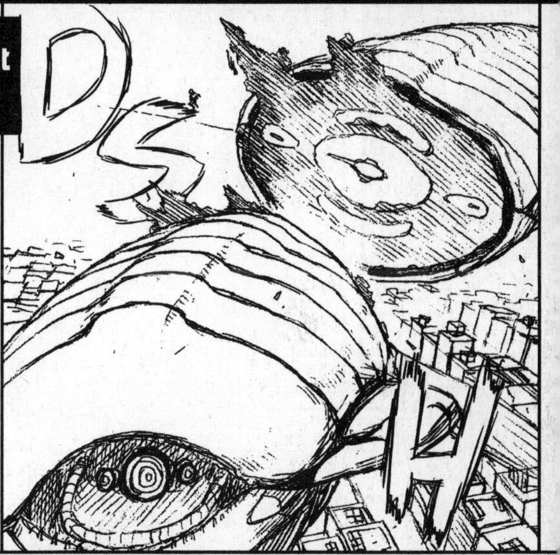

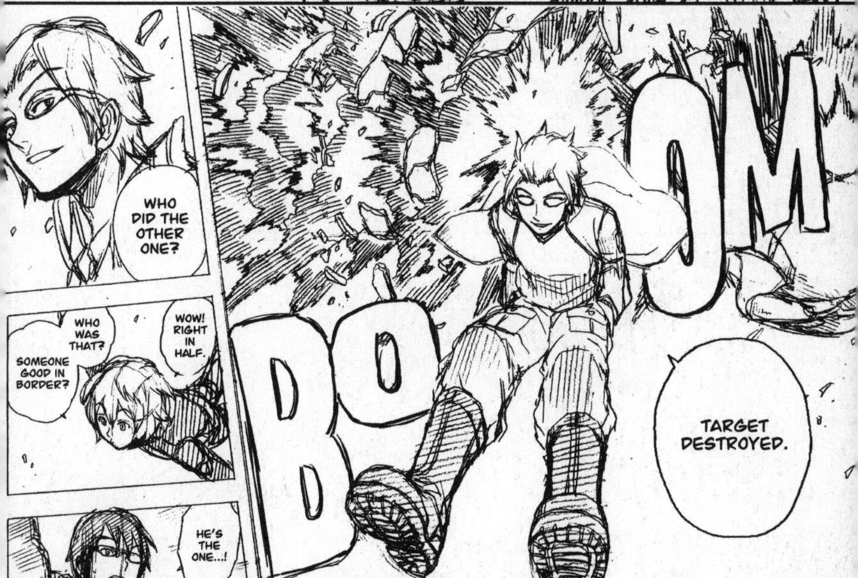
BOOM
TARGET DESTROYED.
WHO DID THE OTHER ONE?
WOW! RIGHT IN HALF.
WHO WAS THAT?
SOMEONE GOOD IN BORDER?
HE'S THE ONE...!

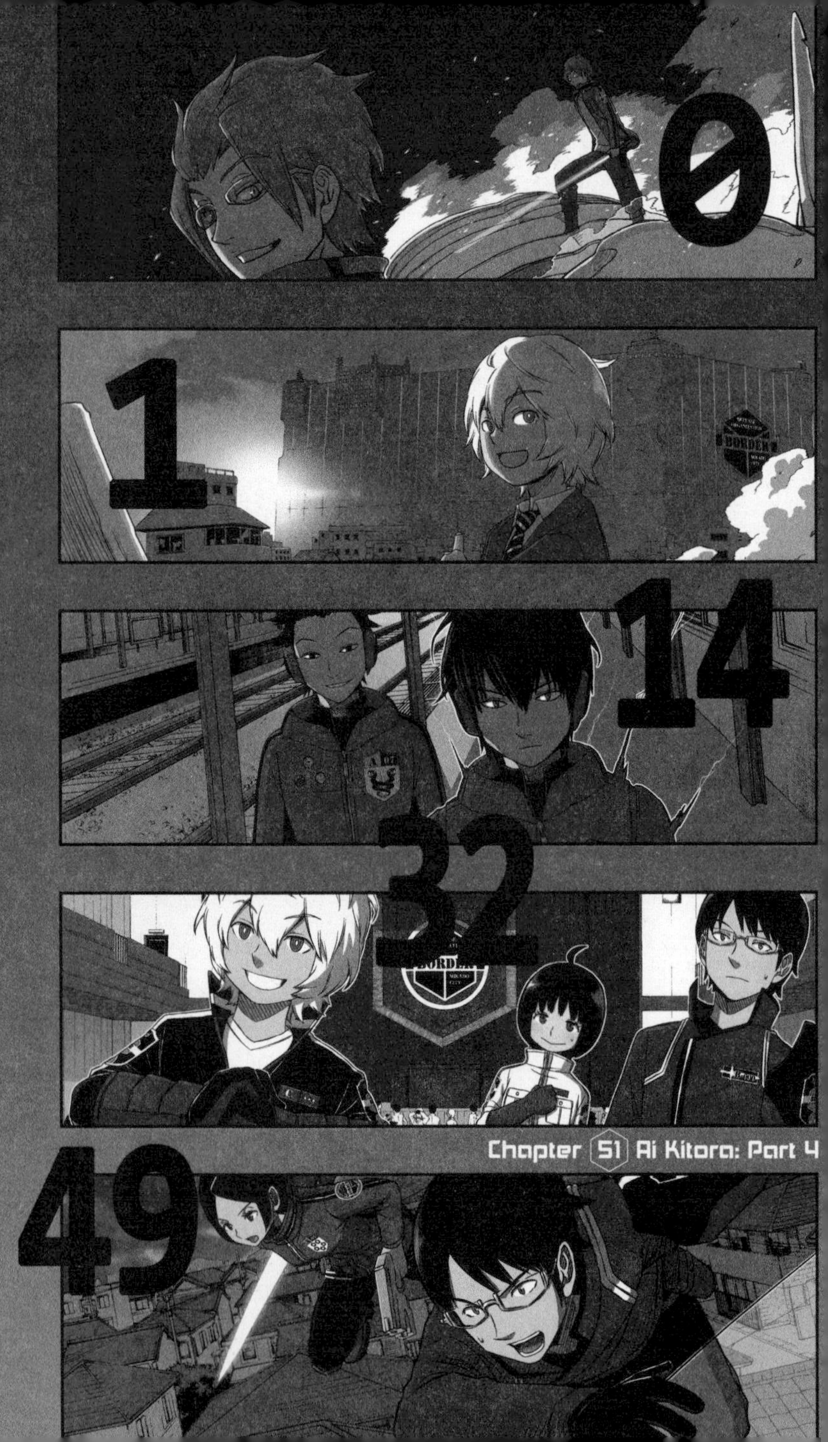
0
1
14
32
Chapter 51 Ai Kitora: Part 4
49

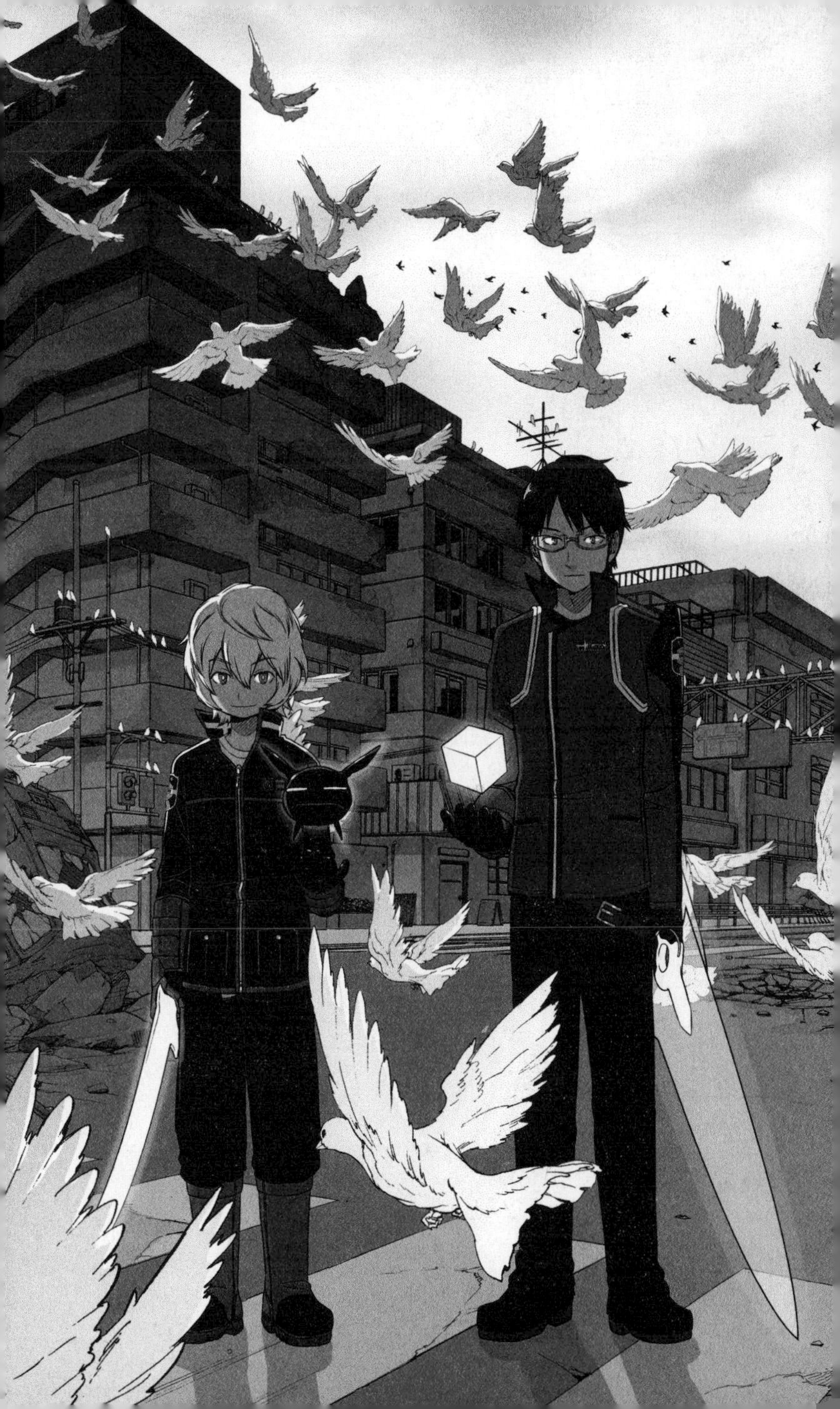

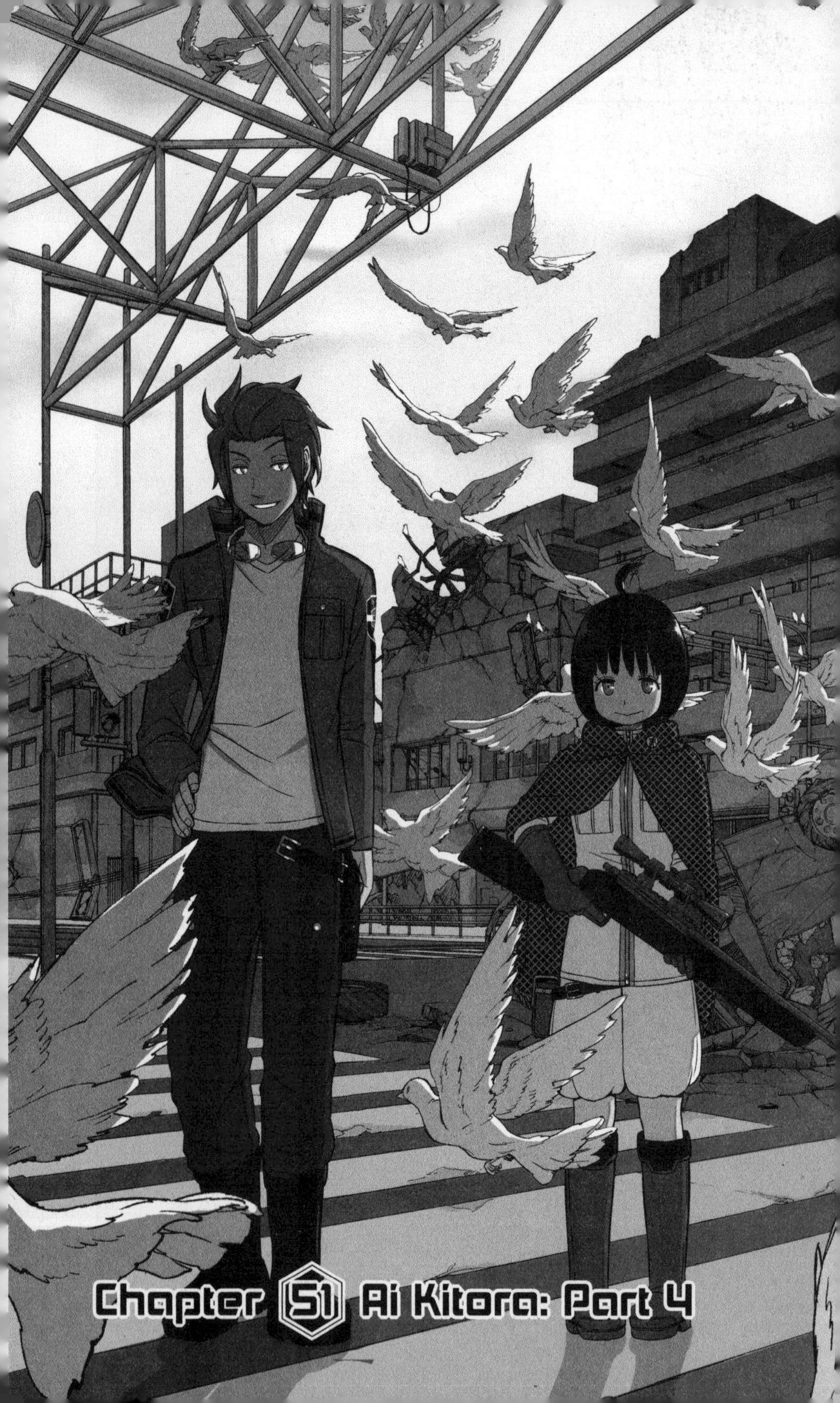
Chapter 51 Ai Kitora: Part 4

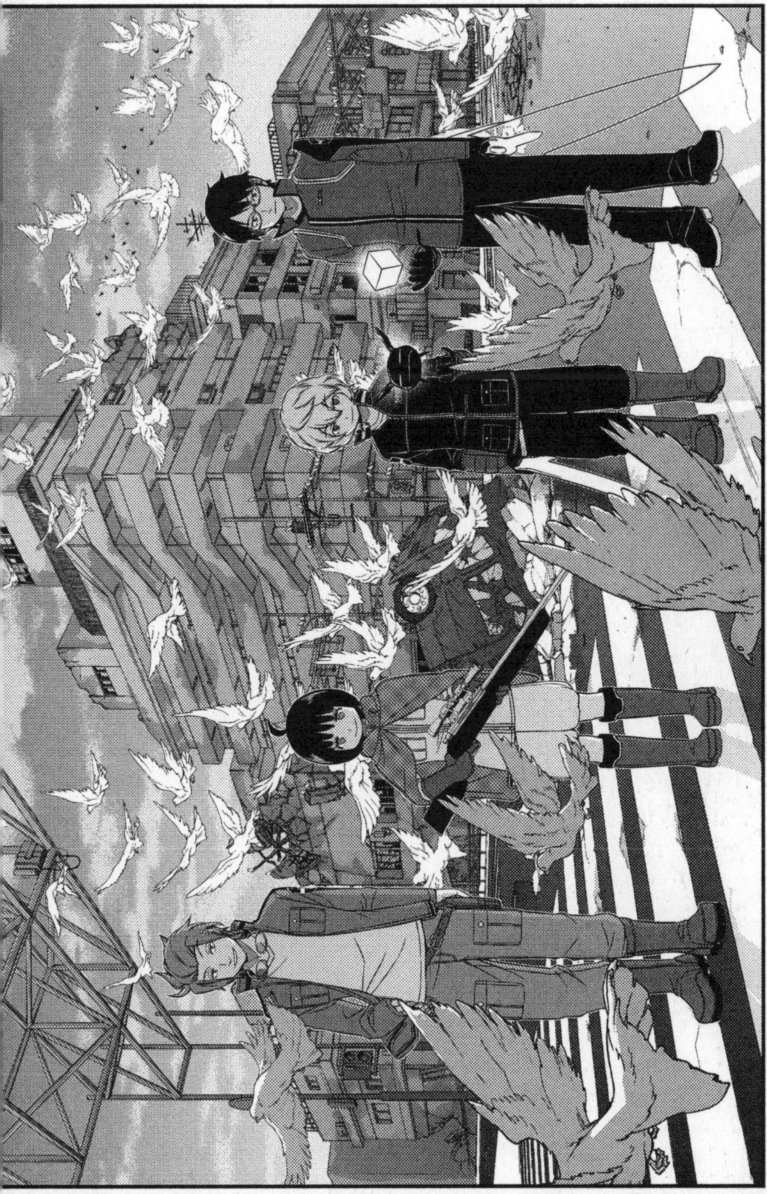

2014 *Weekly Shonen Jump* issue 15, initial color page [second one]

The color page that ran in the front of the magazine to commemorate *World Trigger*'s first anniversary. I wanted it to match the composition of chapter 1. Thanks to all my readers for their support. I hope I'll be able to do another one like this for the second anniversary.

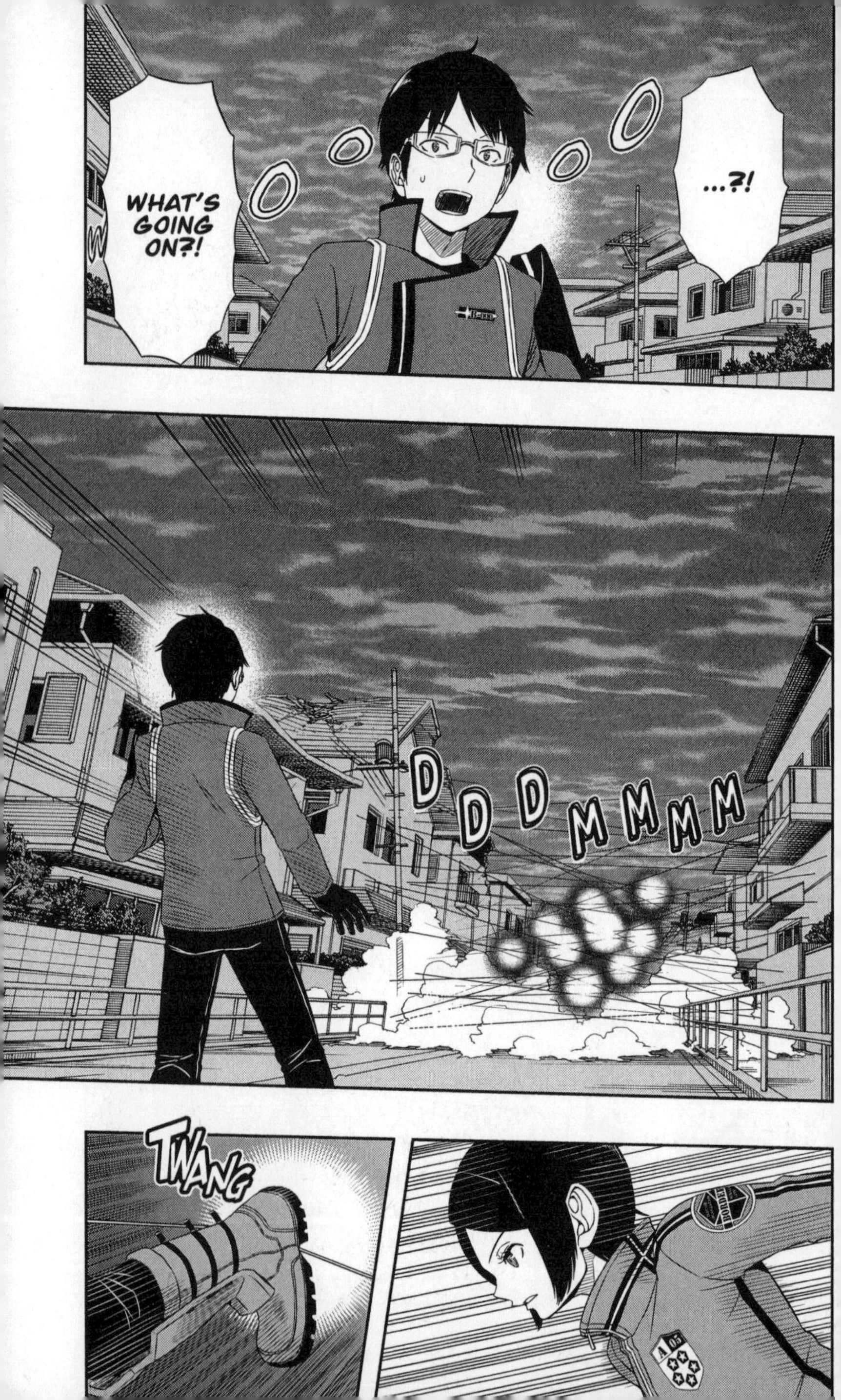
...?!
WHAT'S GOING ON?!
DDDMMMM
TWANG

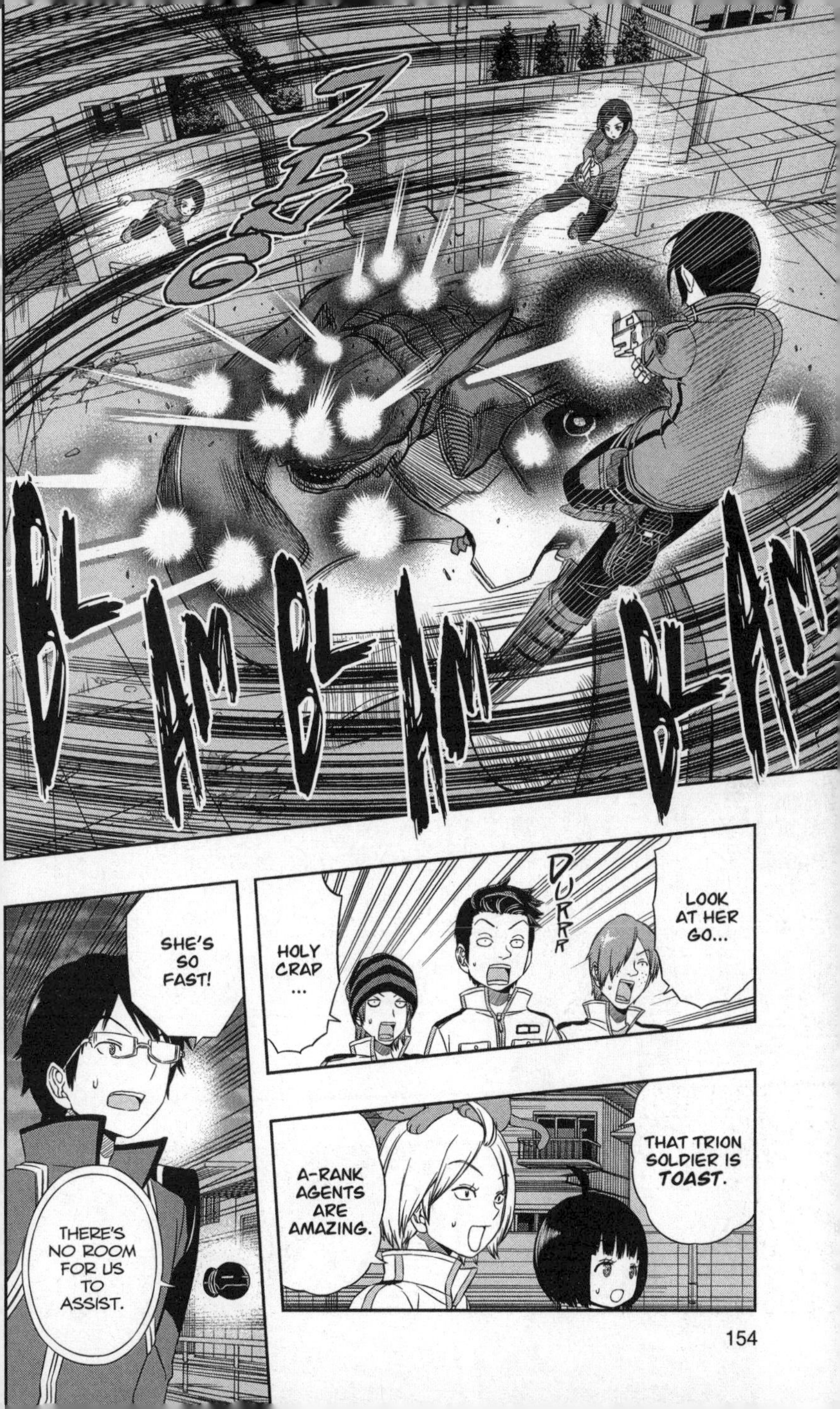
ZING
BLAM BLAM BLAM
DURRR
LOOK AT HER GO...
HOLY CRAP ...
THAT TRION SOLDIER IS TOAST.
A-RANK AGENTS ARE AMAZING.
SHE'S SO FAST!
THERE'S NO ROOM FOR US TO ASSIST.

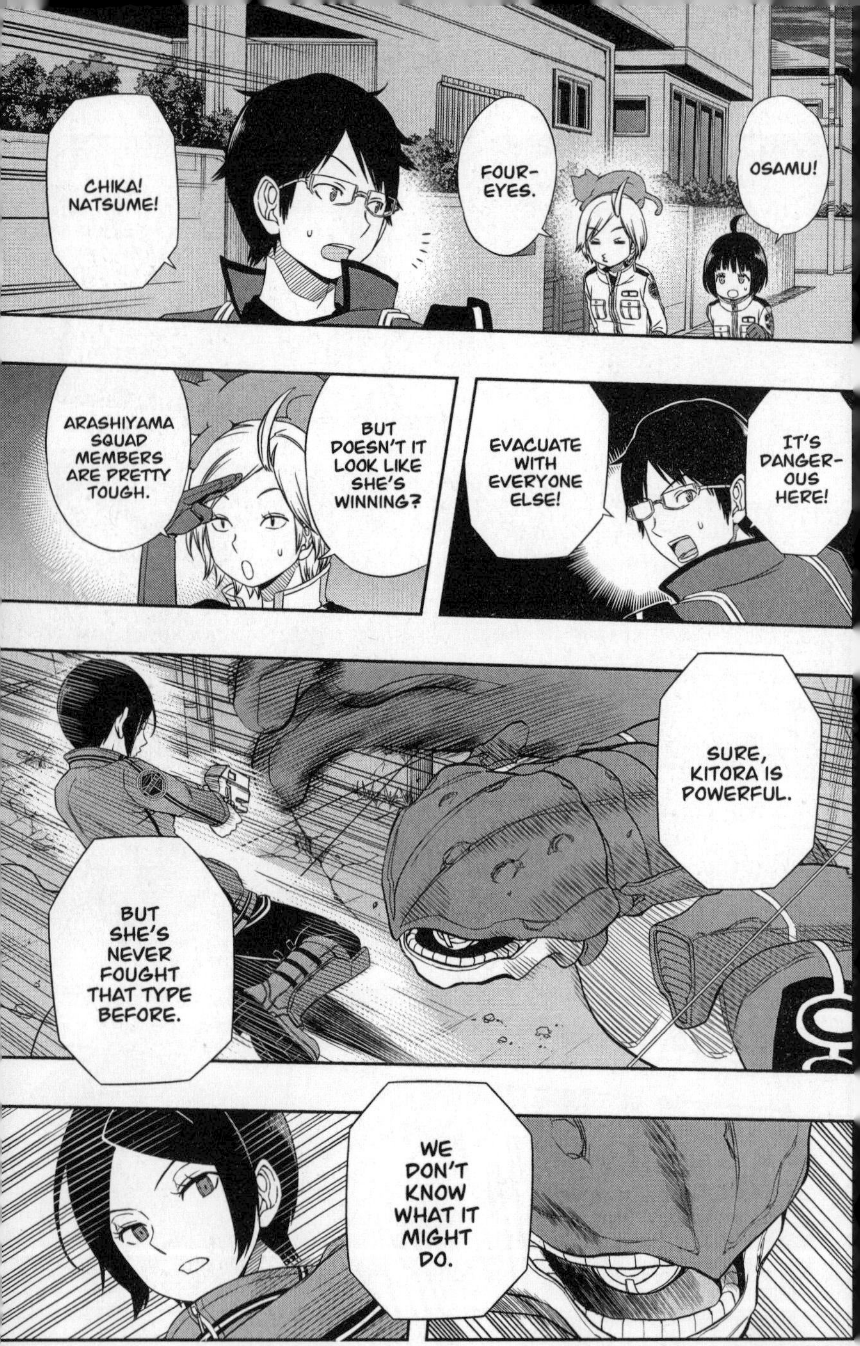
OSAMU!
FOUR-EYES.
CHIKA! NATSUME!
IT'S DANGEROUS HERE!
EVACUATE WITH EVERYONE ELSE!
BUT DOESN'T IT LOOK LIKE SHE'S WINNING?
ARASHIYAMA SQUAD MEMBERS ARE PRETTY TOUGH.
SURE, KITORA IS POWERFUL.
BUT SHE'S NEVER FOUGHT THAT TYPE BEFORE.
WE DON'T KNOW WHAT IT MIGHT DO.

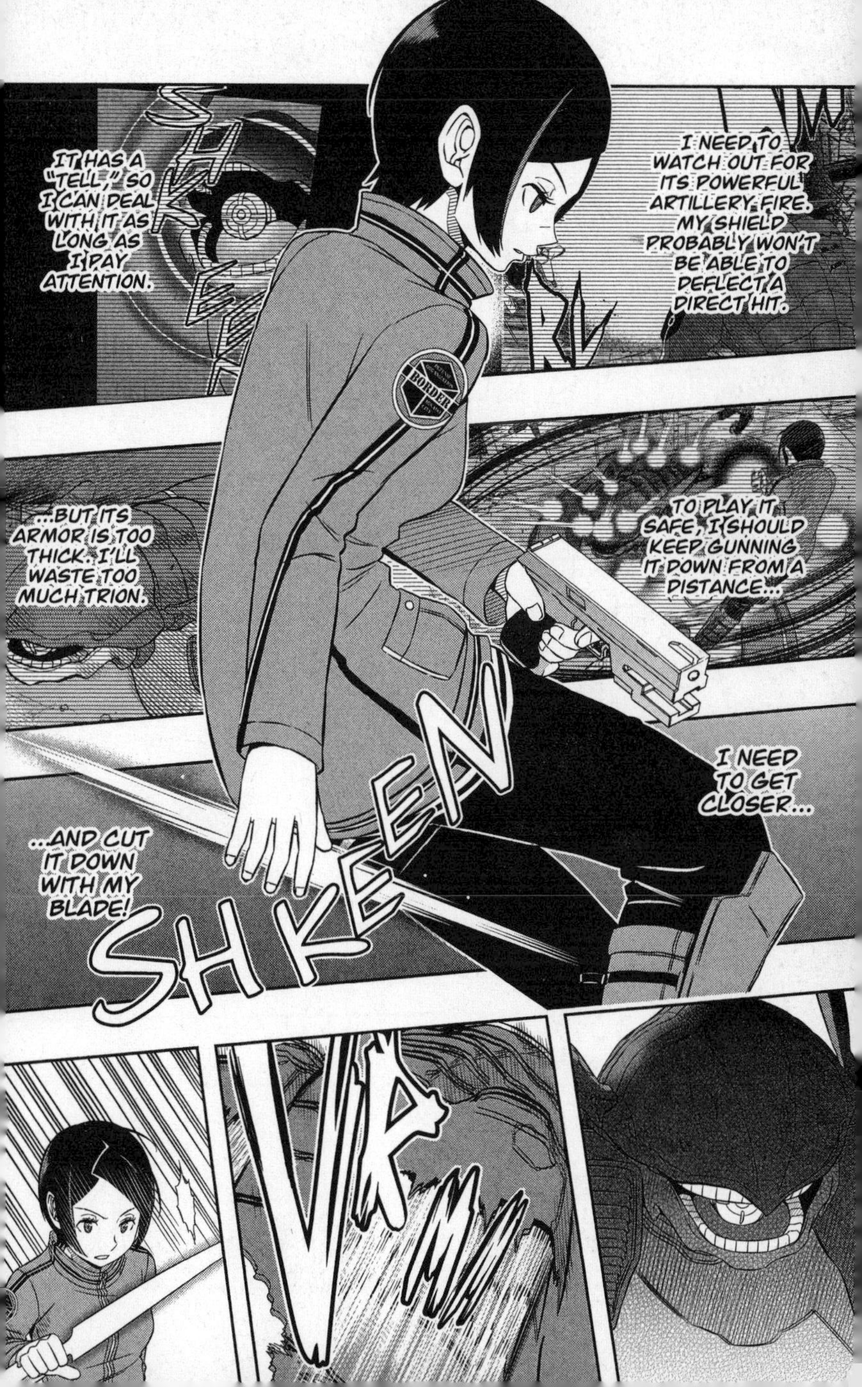
I NEED TO WATCH OUT FOR ITS POWERFUL ARTILLERY FIRE. MY SHIELD PROBABLY WON'T BE ABLE TO DEFLECT A DIRECT HIT.
IT HAS A "TELL," SO I CAN DEAL WITH IT AS LONG AS I PAY ATTENTION.
TO PLAY IT SAFE, I SHOULD KEEP GUNNING IT DOWN FROM A DISTANCE...
...BUT ITS ARMOR IS TOO THICK. I'LL WASTE TOO MUCH TRION.
I NEED TO GET CLOSER...
...AND CUT IT DOWN WITH MY BLADE!
SHKEEN

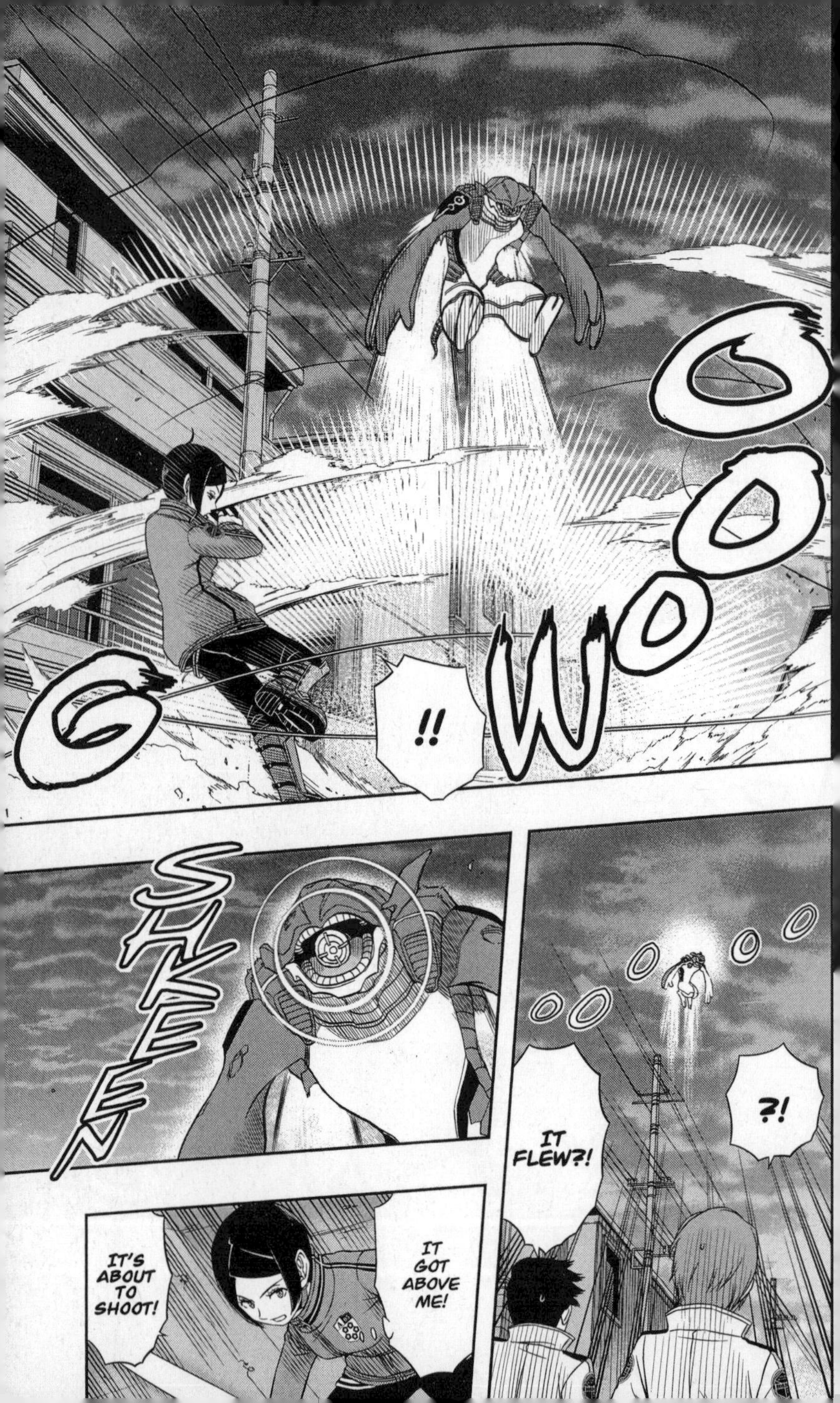
GWOOOO
!!
?!
IT FLEW?!
SHKEEN
IT GOT ABOVE ME!
IT'S ABOUT TO SHOOT!

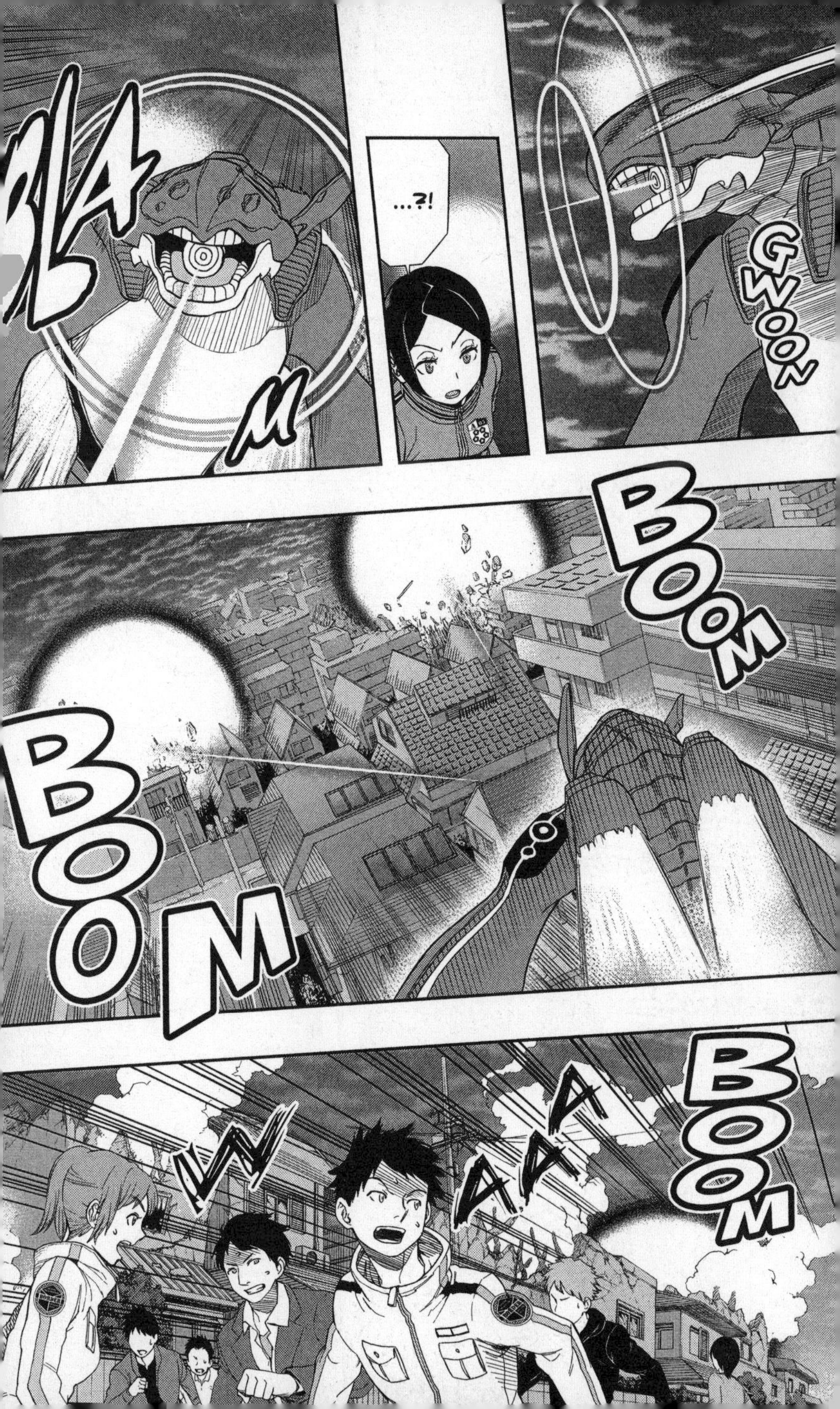
GWOON
...?!
BOOM
BOOM
BOOM
WAAA

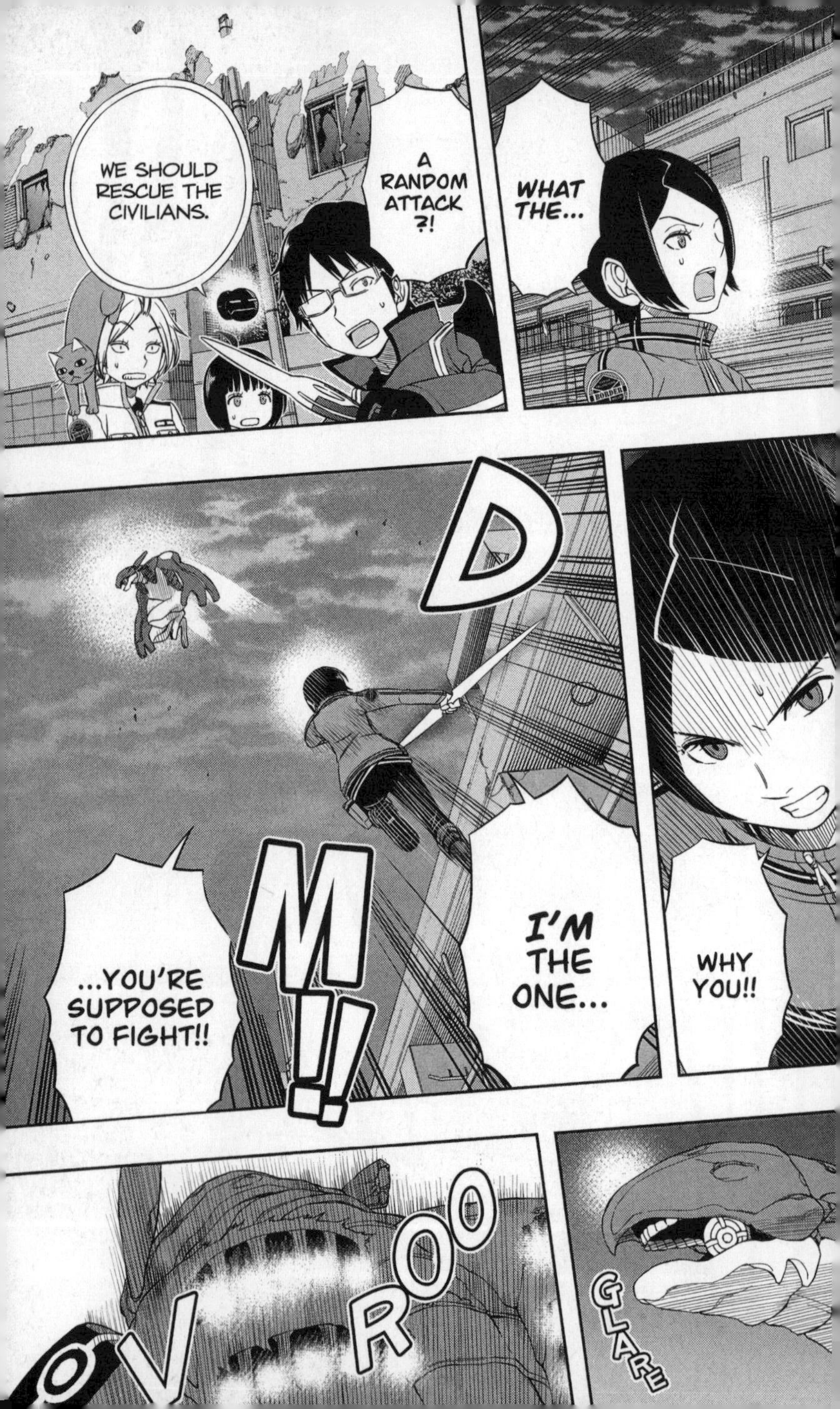
WHAT THE...
A RANDOM ATTACK ?!
WE SHOULD RESCUE THE CIVILIANS.
WHY YOU!!
I'M THE ONE...
D
M!!
...YOU'RE SUPPOSED TO FIGHT!!
GLARE
OVROO

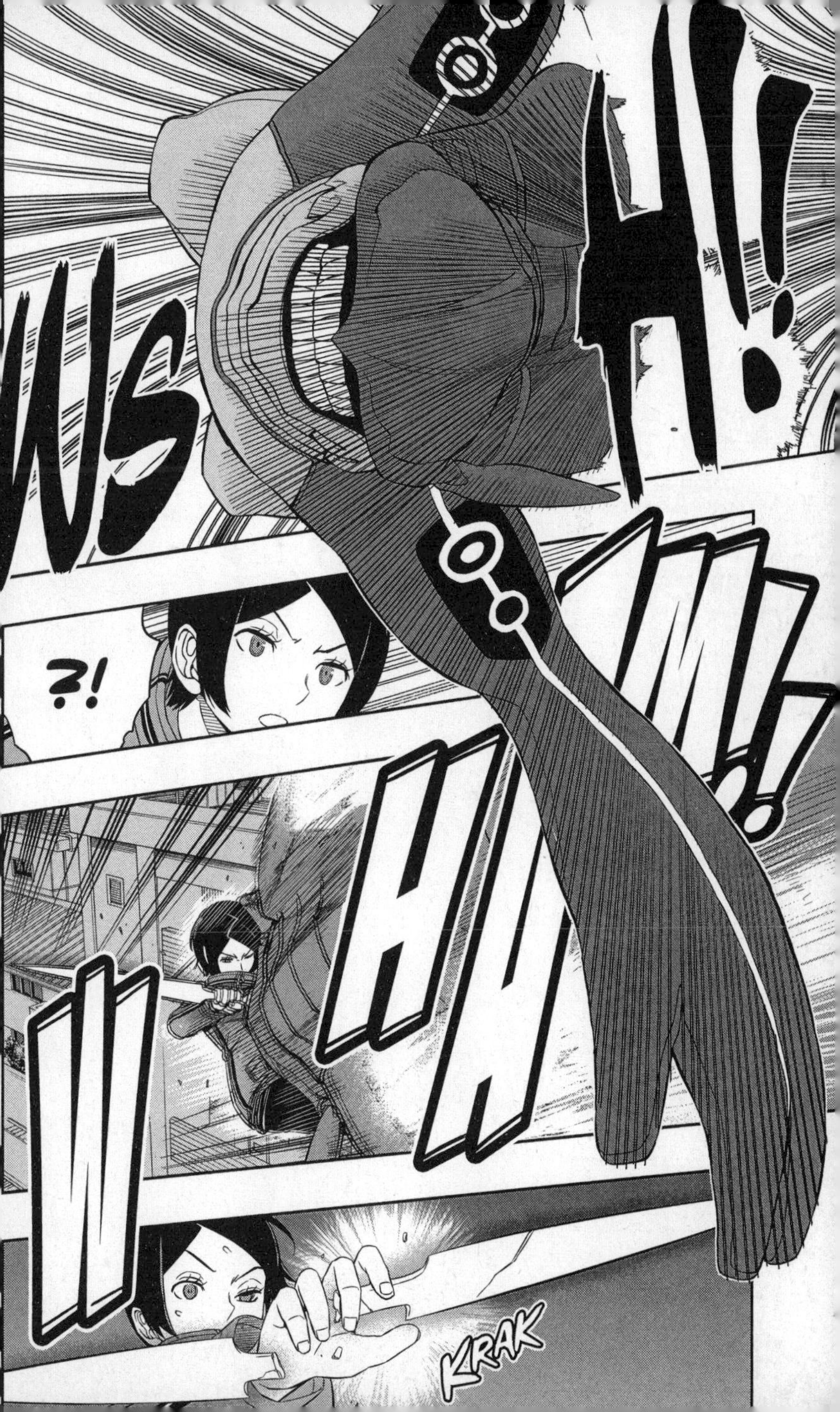
WS H!!
?!
WHAM!!
KRAK

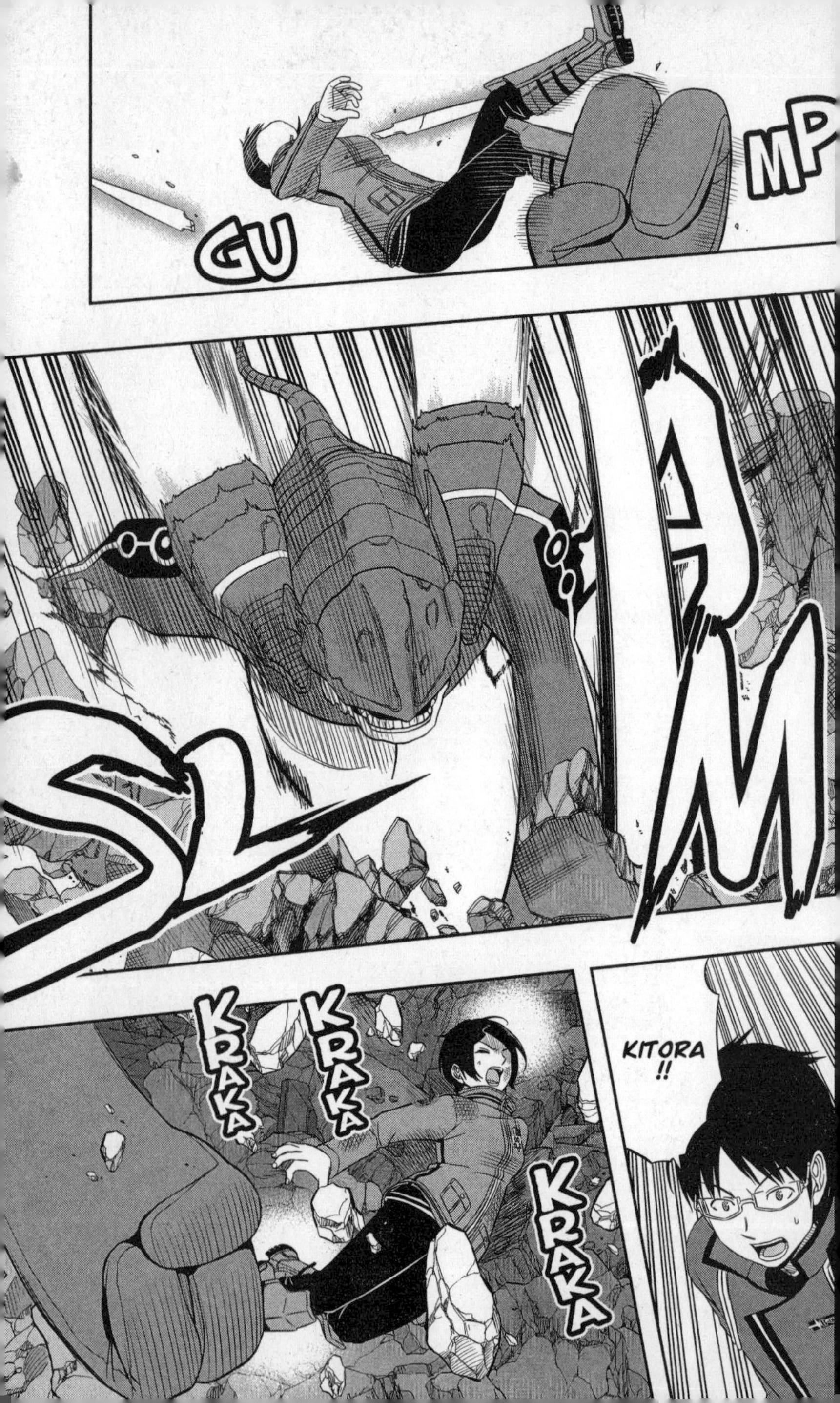
GU MP
SLAM
KITORA!!
KRAKA
KRAKA
KRAKA

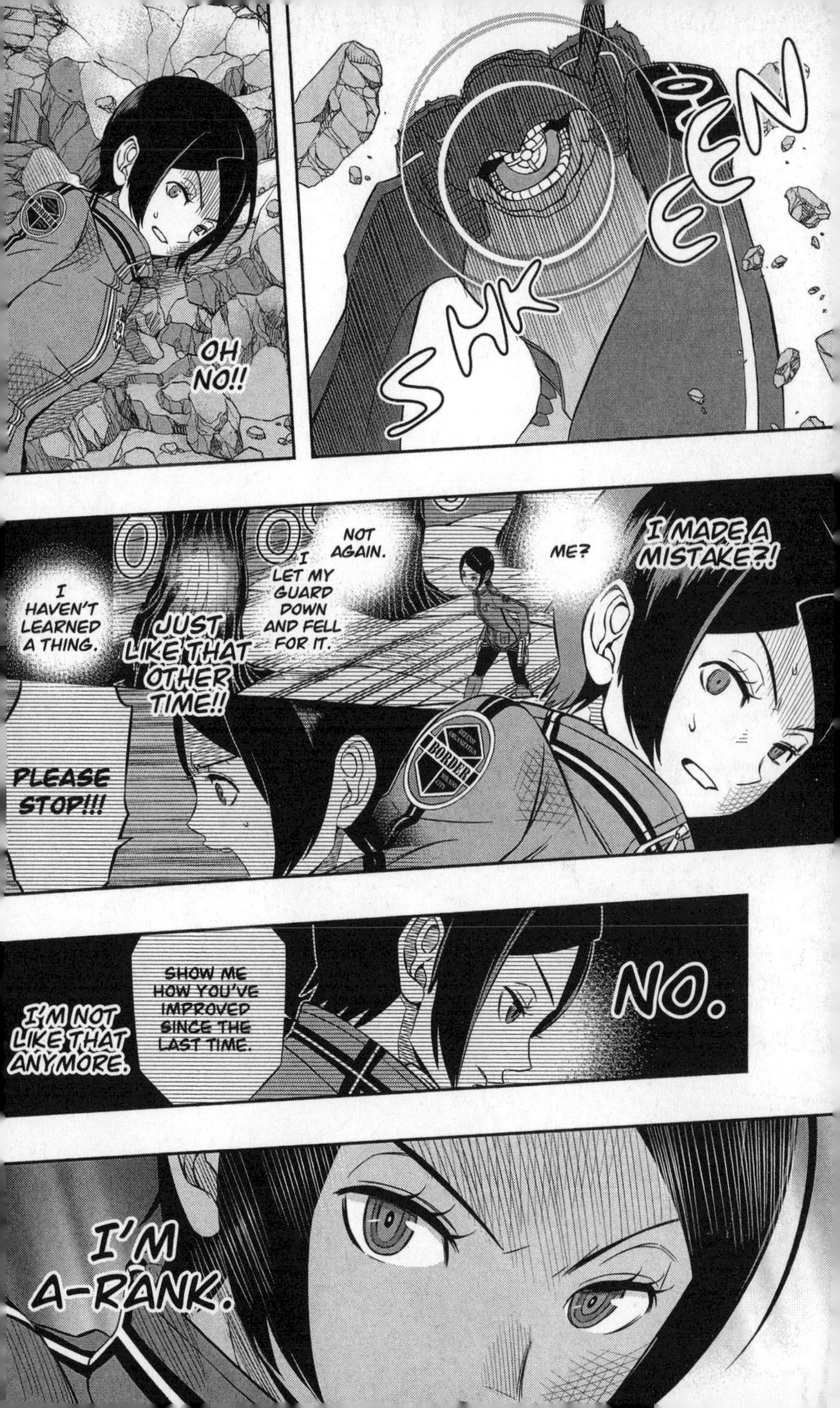
SHK
EEEN
OH NO!!
I MADE A MISTAKE?!
ME?
NOT AGAIN.
I LET MY GUARD DOWN AND FELL FOR IT.
JUST LIKE THAT OTHER TIME!!
I HAVEN'T LEARNED A THING.
BORDER
PLEASE STOP!!!
NO.
SHOW ME HOW YOU'VE IMPROVED SINCE THE LAST TIME.
I'M NOT LIKE THAT ANYMORE.
I'M A-RANK.

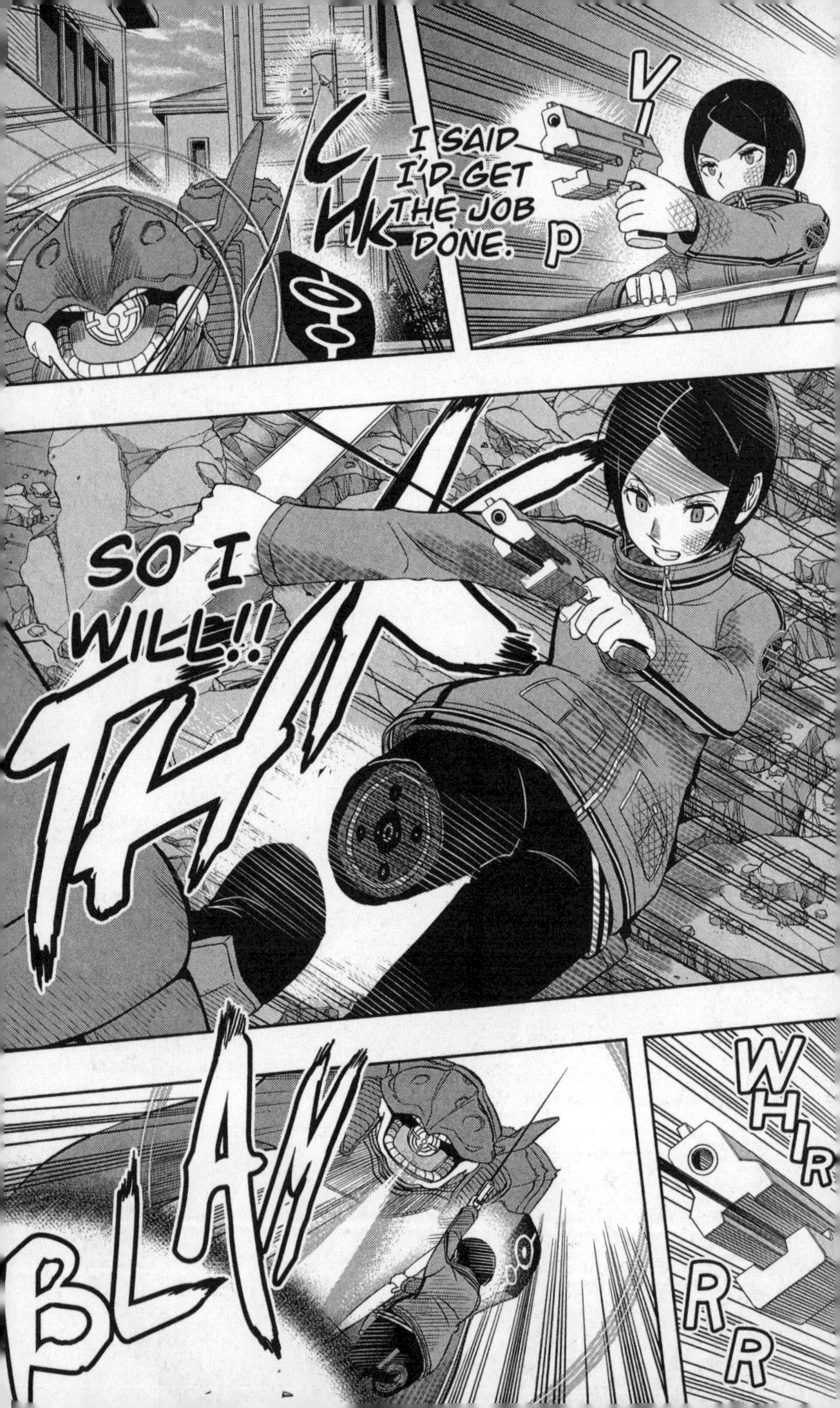
VP
I SAID I'D GET THE JOB DONE.
CHK
SO I WILL!!
WHIRRR
BLAM

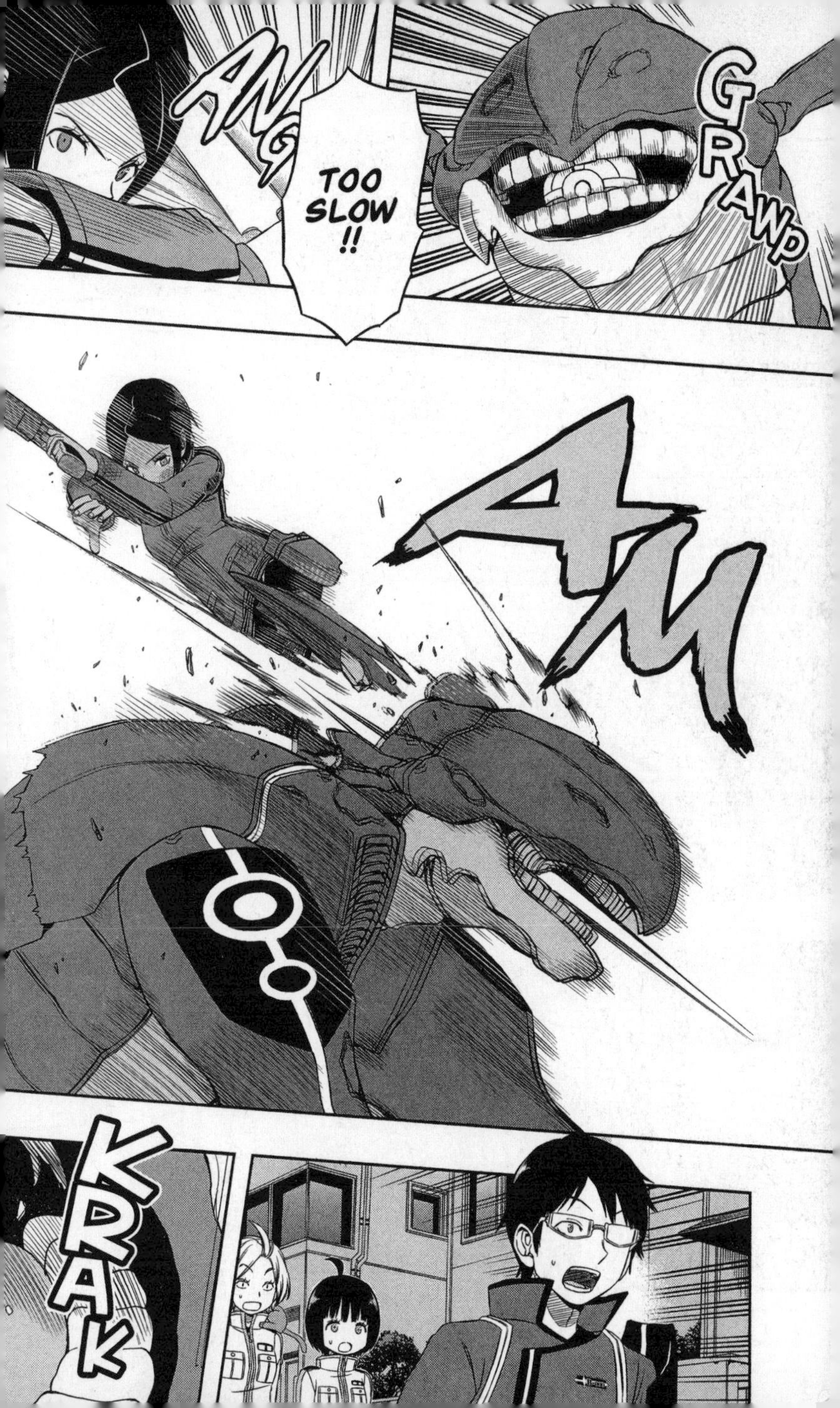
GRAWP
TOO SLOW !!
ANG
AM
KRAK

READ THIS WAY

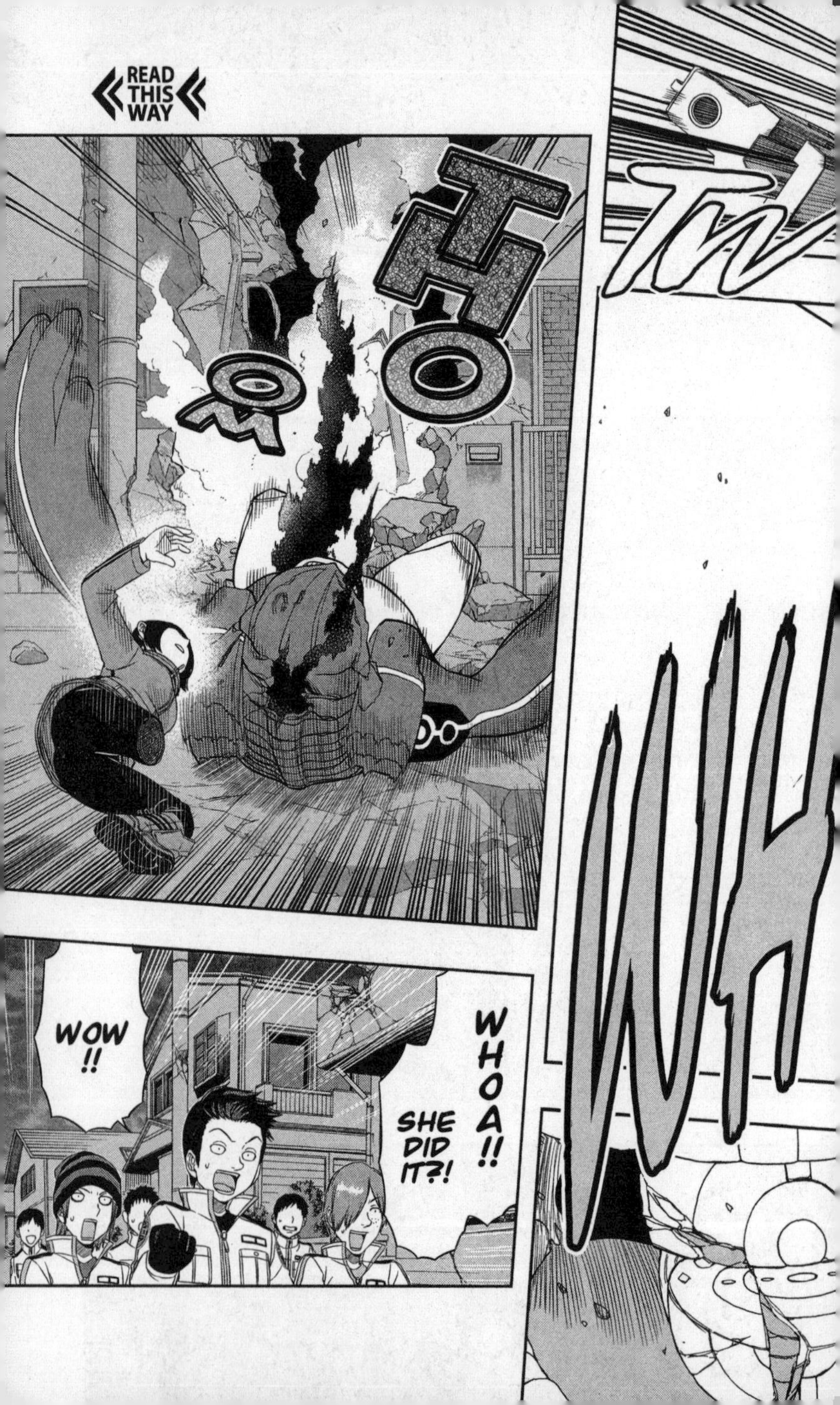
WHOA!!
SHE DID IT?!
WOW!!

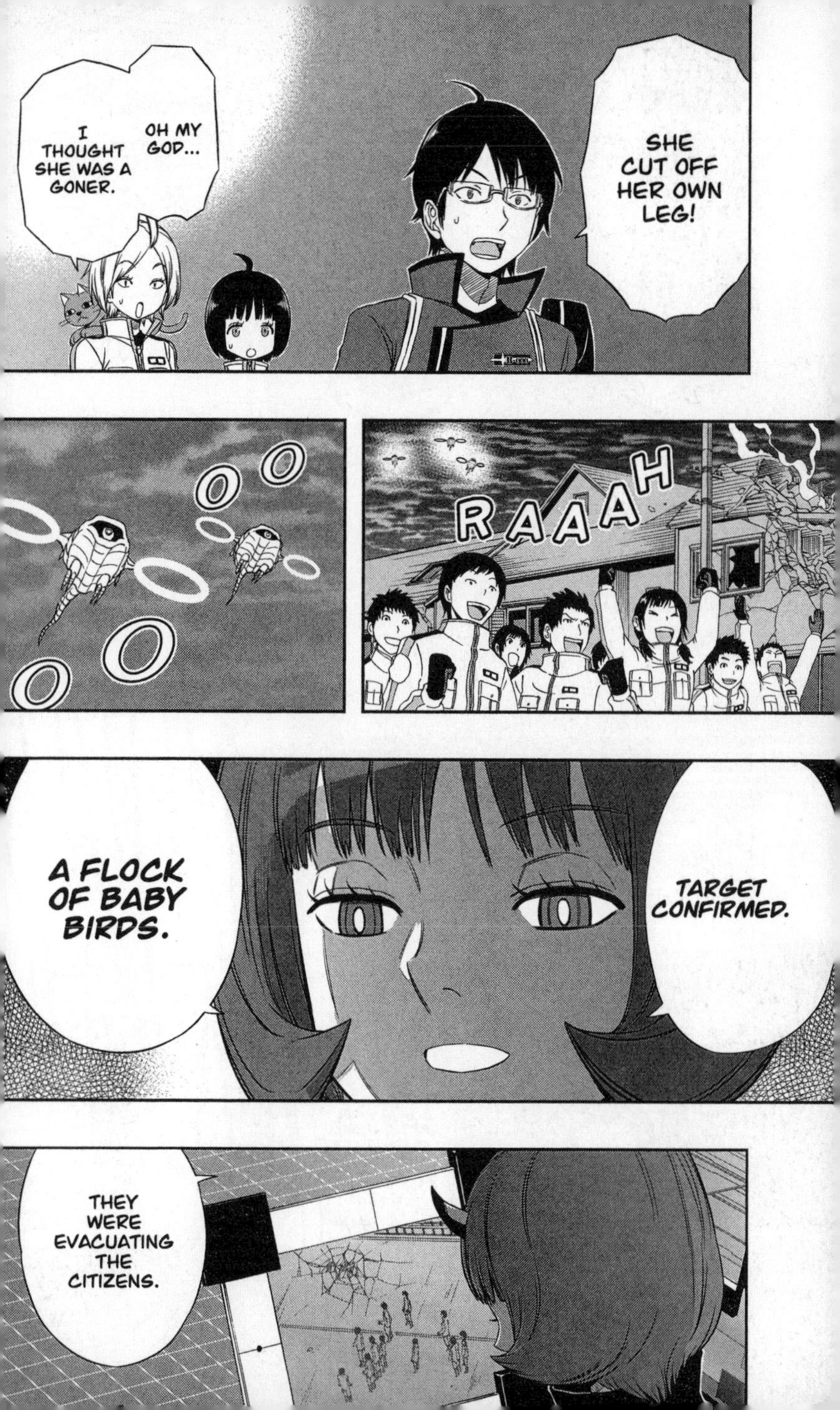
SHE CUT OFF HER OWN LEG!
OH MY GOD...
I THOUGHT SHE WAS A GONER.
RAAAH
TARGET CONFIRMED.
A FLOCK OF BABY BIRDS.
THEY WERE EVACUATING THE CITIZENS.

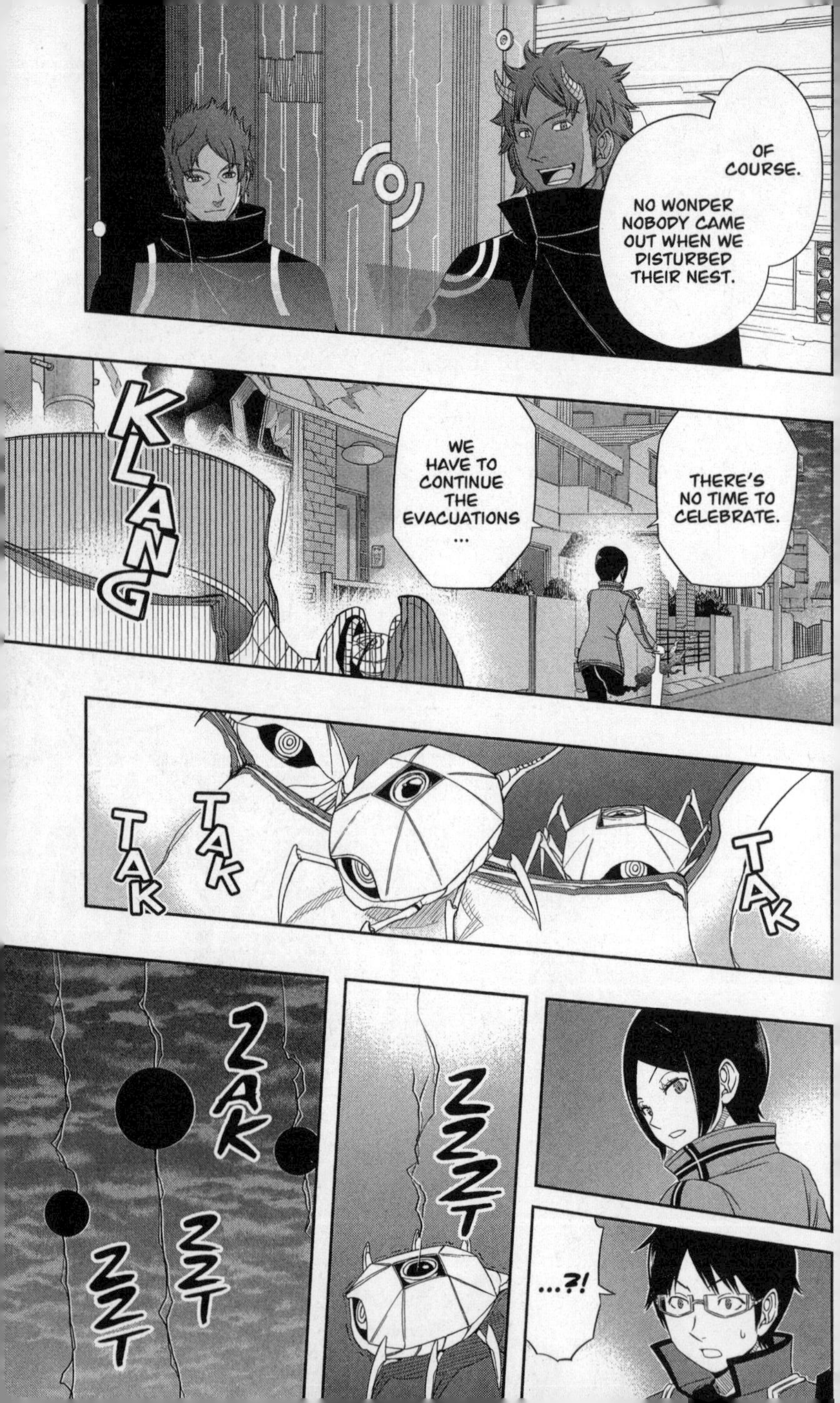
OF COURSE.
NO WONDER NOBODY CAME OUT WHEN WE DISTURBED THEIR NEST.
THERE'S NO TIME TO CELEBRATE.
WE HAVE TO CONTINUE THE EVACUATIONS ...
KLANG
TAK
TAK
TAK
...?!
ZZZT
ZAK
ZZT
ZZT

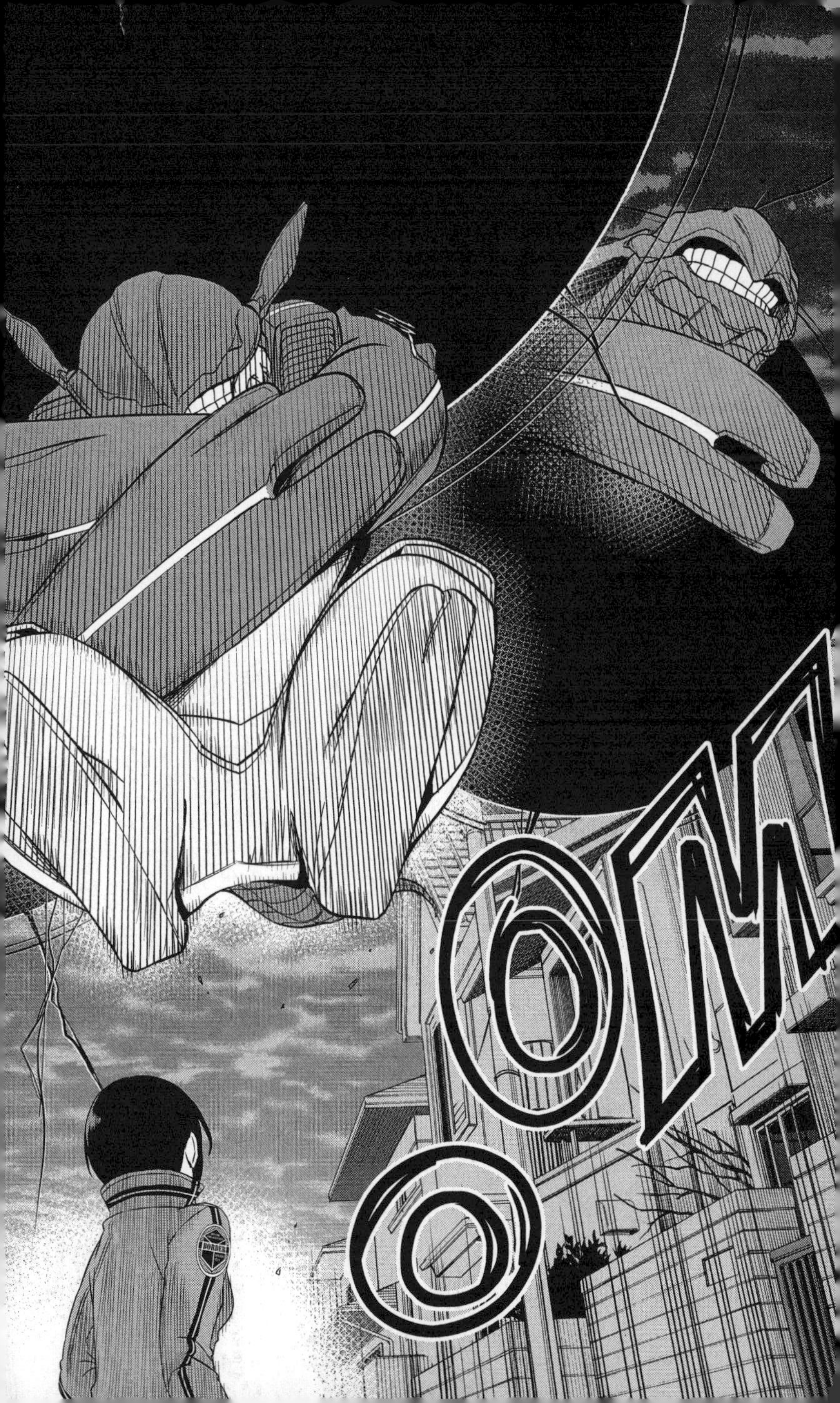
OOM
BORDER

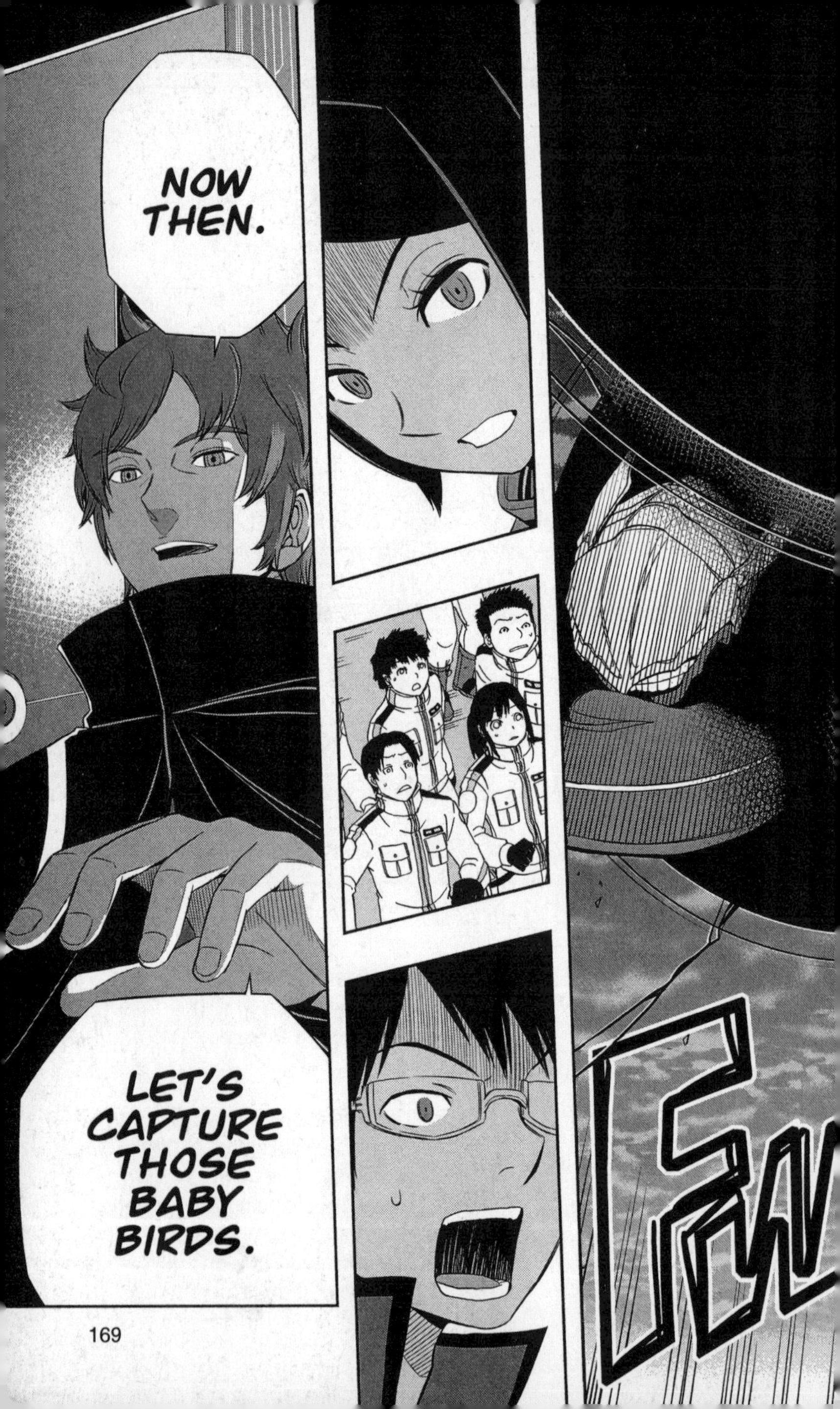
NOW THEN.
LET'S CAPTURE THOSE BABY BIRDS.

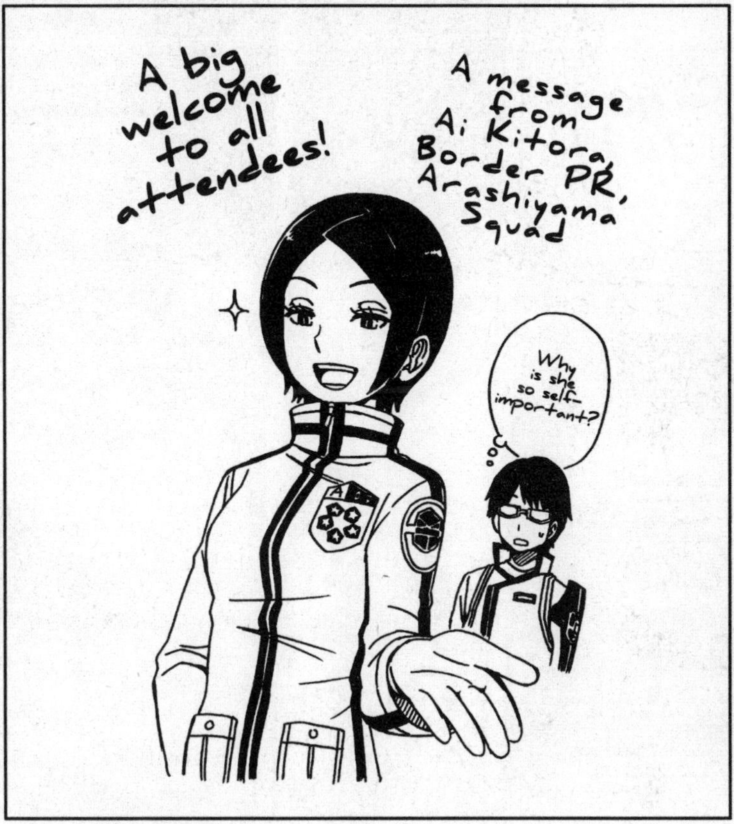
A big welcome to all attendees!
A message from Ai Kitora, Border PR, Arashiyama Squad
Why is she so self-important?

■ 2014
Jump Festa
Welcome Board

They wanted a sketch-style piece to display on the wall of the Jump Festa venue. Kitora came forward as PR representative. I apologize to anyone who was looking forward to Yuma and got disappointed. I couldn't quite imagine Yuma saying, "Thanks for coming!"

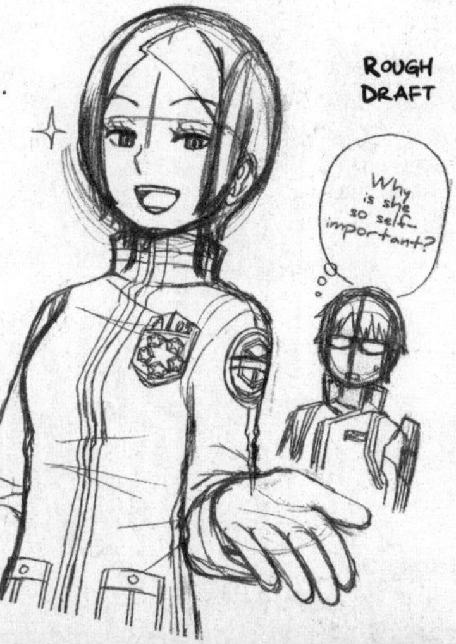
Why is she so self-important?

ROUGH DRAFT

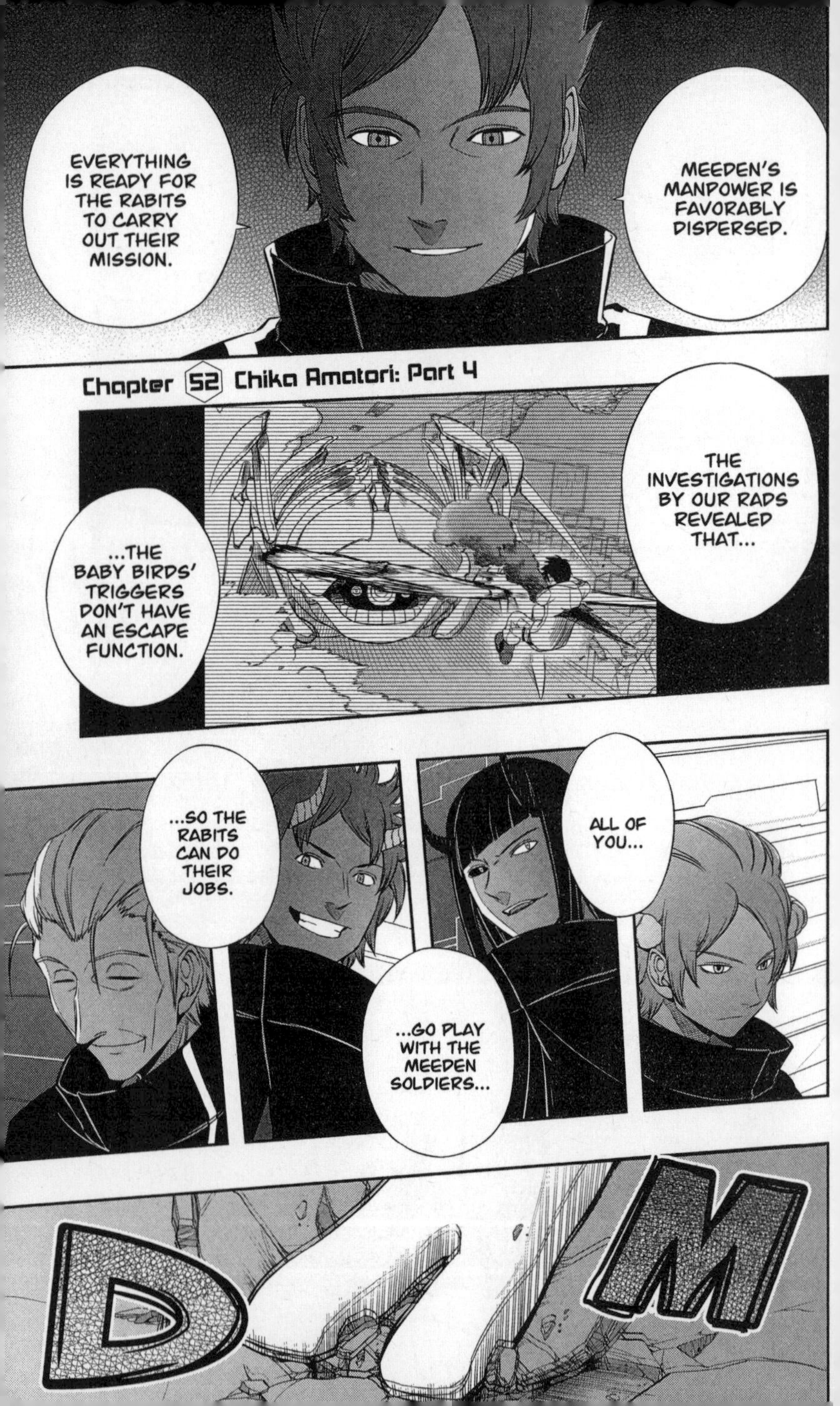
MEEDEN'S MANPOWER IS FAVORABLY DISPERSED.
EVERYTHING IS READY FOR THE RABITS TO CARRY OUT THEIR MISSION.
Chapter 52 Chika Amatori: Part 4
THE INVESTIGATIONS BY OUR RADS REVEALED THAT...
...THE BABY BIRDS' TRIGGERS DON'T HAVE AN ESCAPE FUNCTION.
ALL OF YOU...
...GO PLAY WITH THE MEEDEN SOLDIERS...
...SO THE RABITS CAN DO THEIR JOBS.
D M

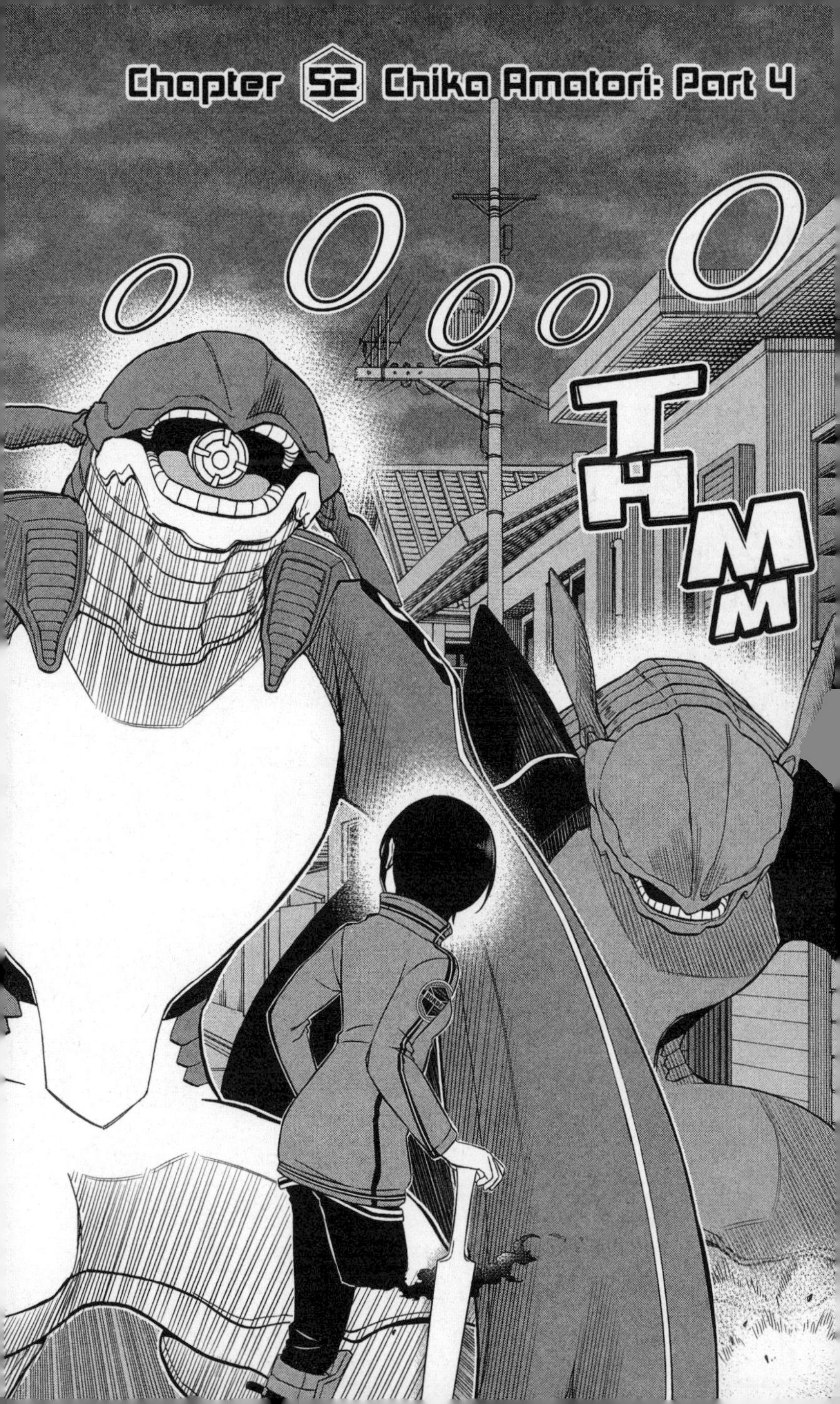
Chapter 52 Chika Amatori: Part 4
THMM

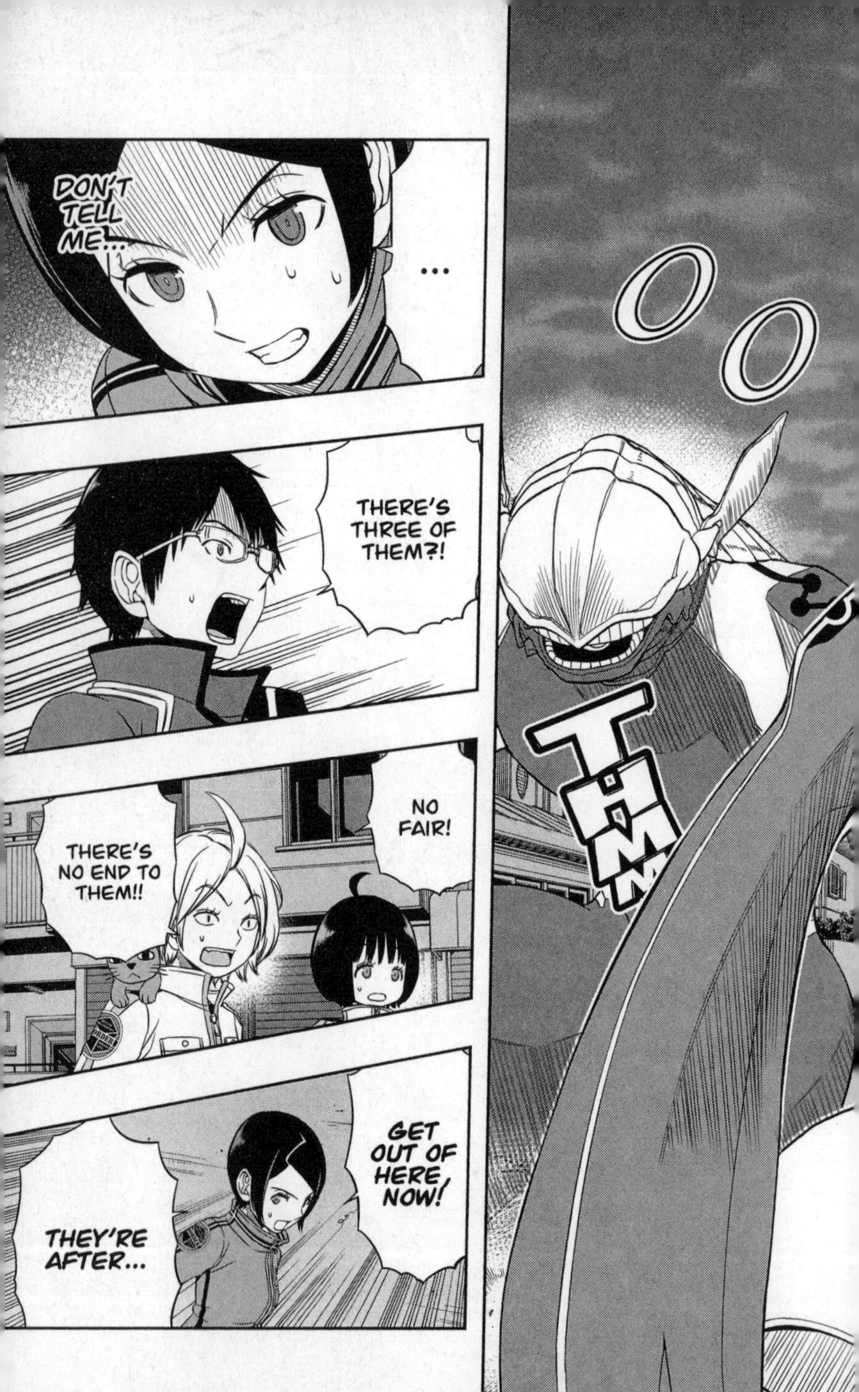
OO
THMM
...
DON'T TELL ME...
THERE'S THREE OF THEM?!
NO FAIR!
THERE'S NO END TO THEM!!
GET OUT OF HERE, NOW!
THEY'RE AFTER...

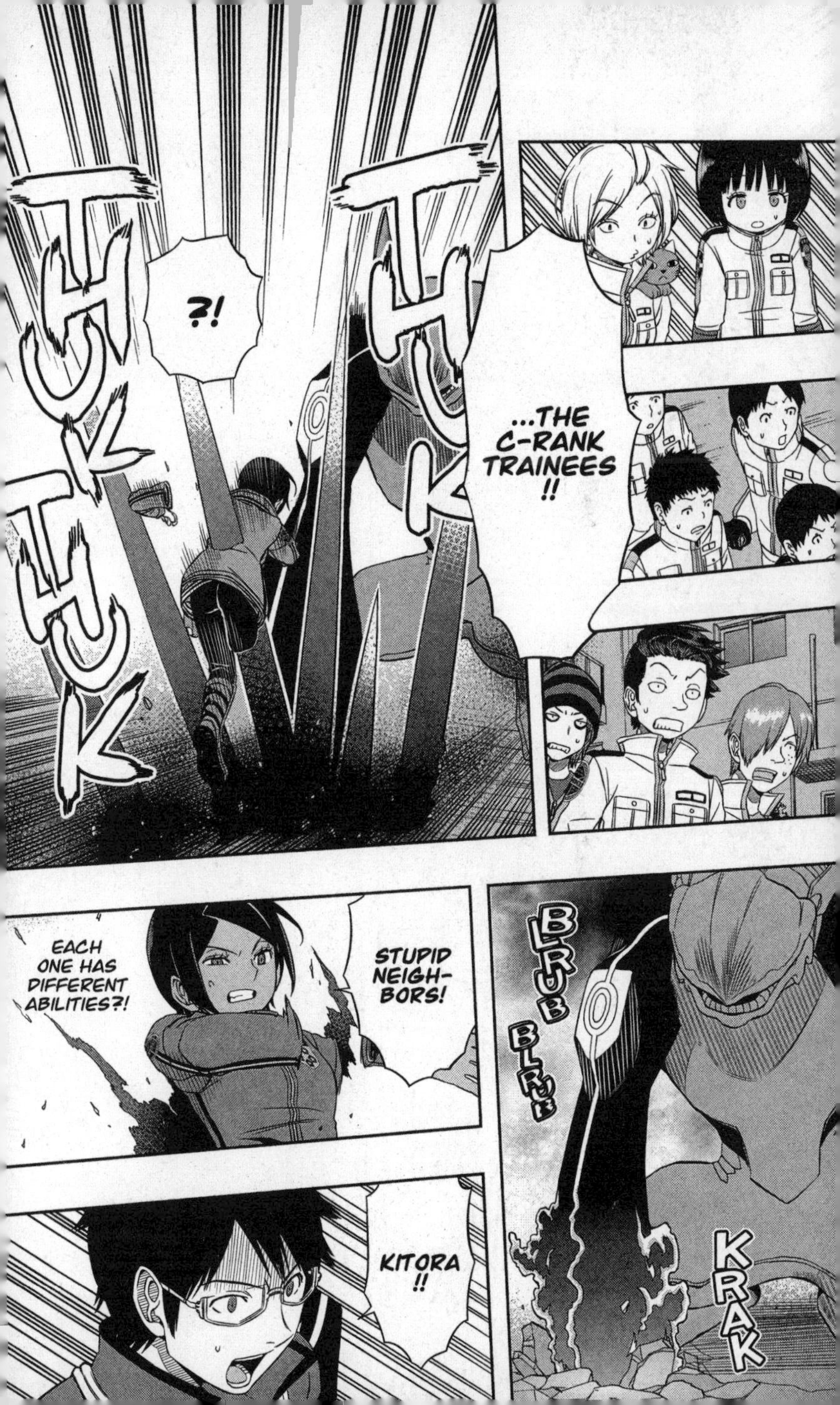
...THE C-RANK TRAINEES !!
THUCK
?!
THUCK
BLRUB
BLRUB
KRAK
STUPID NEIGHBORS!
EACH ONE HAS DIFFERENT ABILITIES?!
KITORA !!

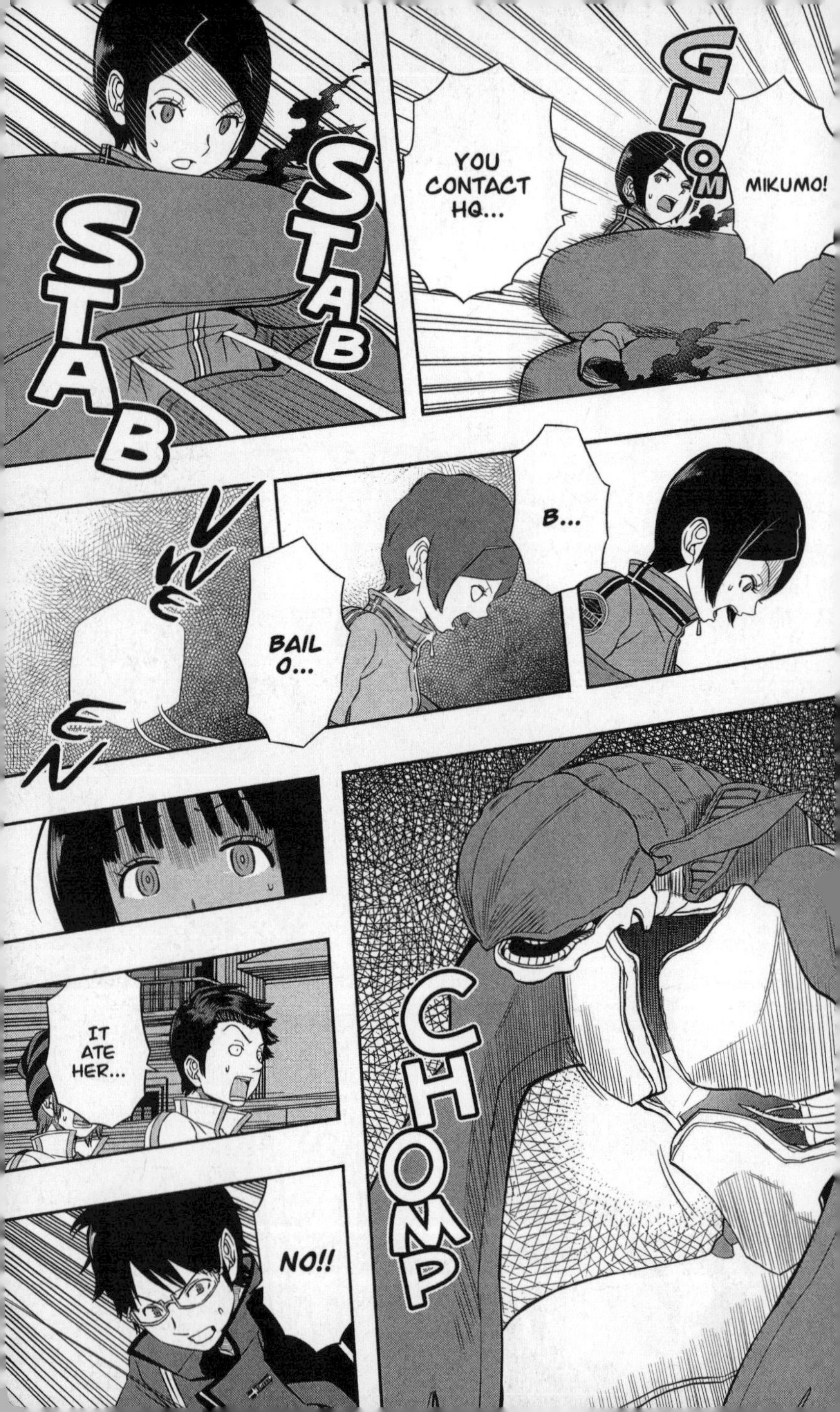
GLOM
MIKUMO!
YOU CONTACT HQ...
STAB
STAB
B...
BAIL O...
VWEEN
CHOMP
IT ATE HER...
NO!!

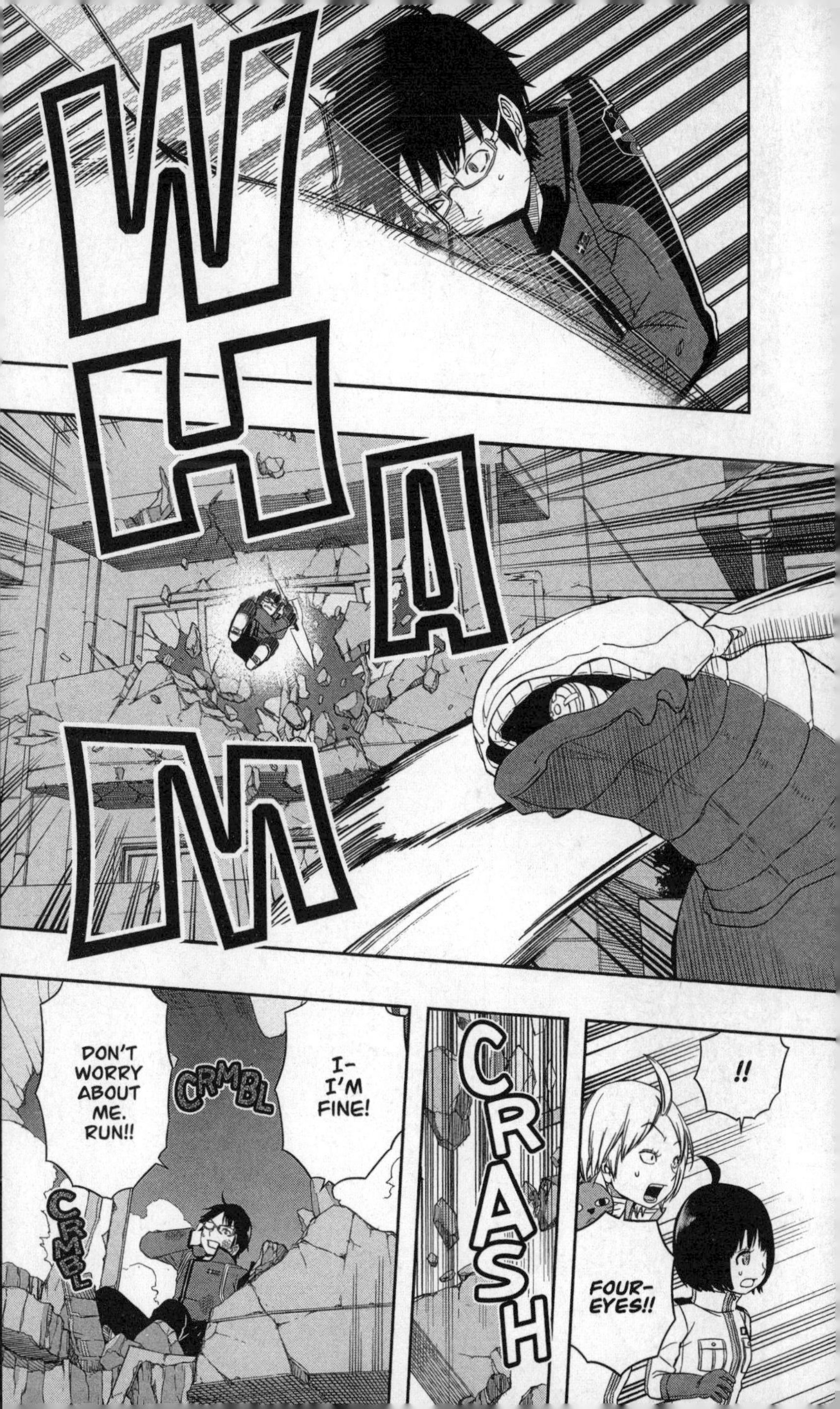
WHAM
!!
FOUR-EYES!!
CRASH
I- I'M FINE!
CRMBL
DON'T WORRY ABOUT ME. RUN!!
CRMBL

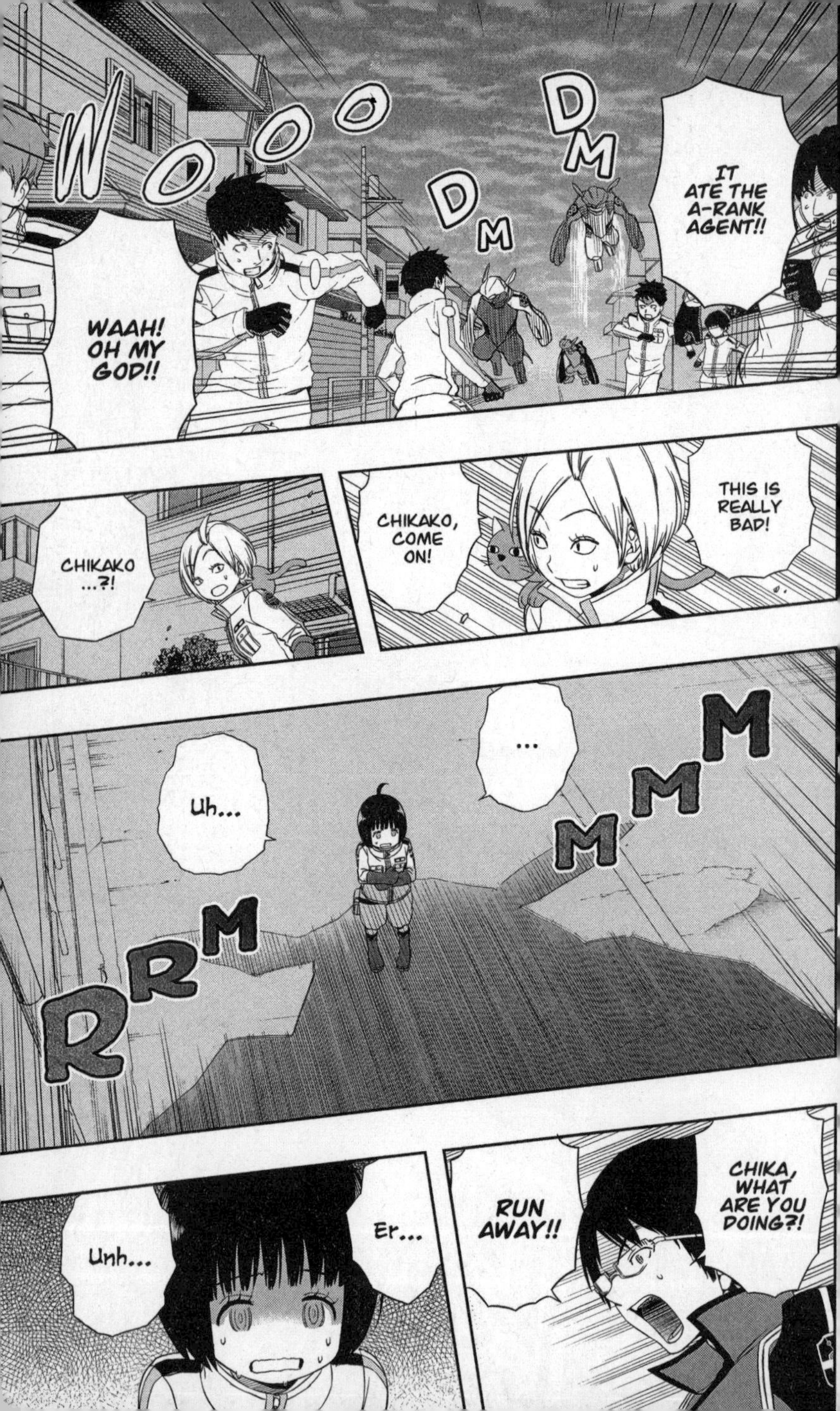
IT ATE THE A-RANK AGENT!!
DMDM
WOOOO
DM
WAAH! OH MY GOD!!
THIS IS REALLY BAD!
CHIKAKO, COME ON!
CHIKAKO ...?!
...
MMMM
Uh...
RRM
CHIKA, WHAT ARE YOU DOING?!
RUN AWAY!!
Er...
Unh...

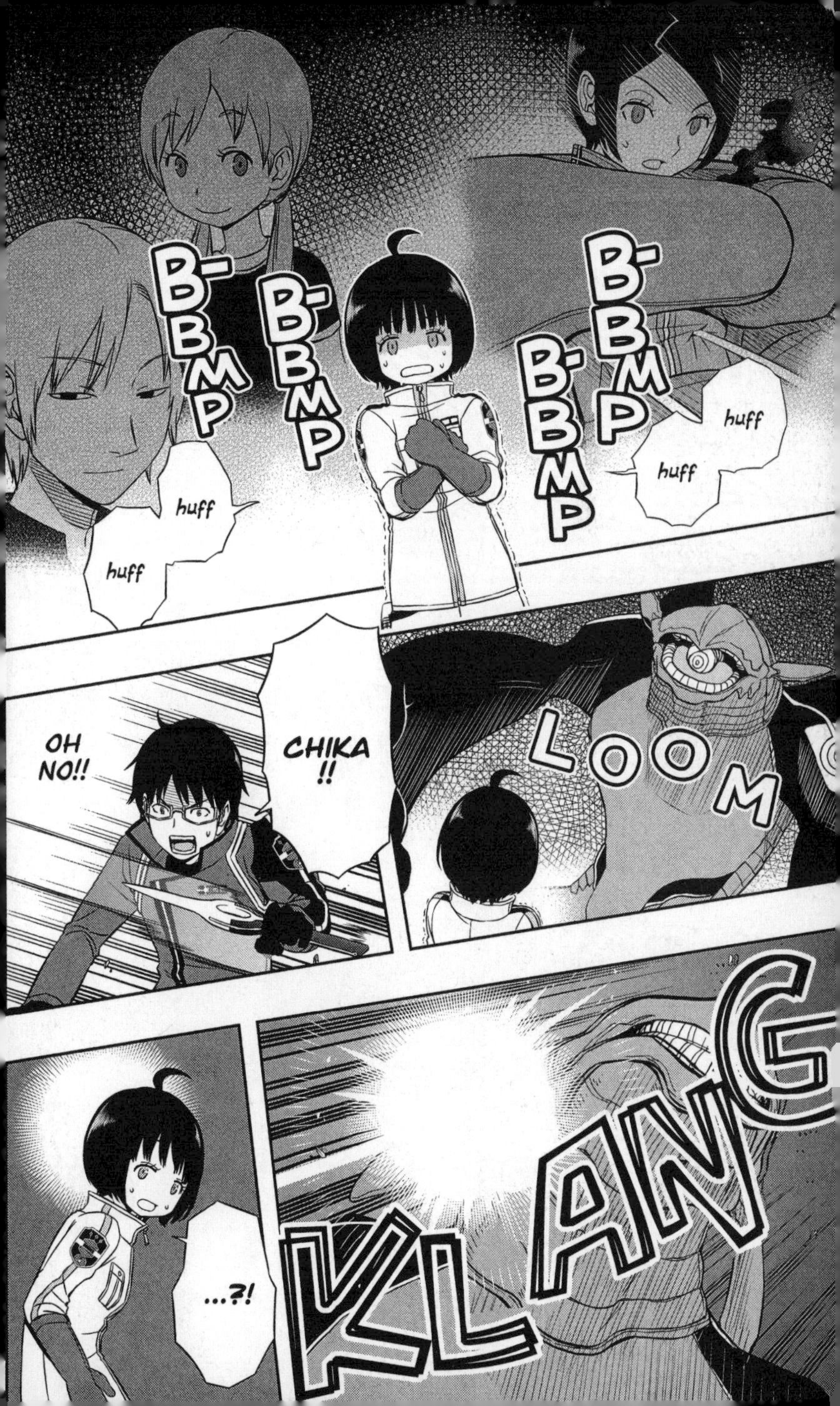
B-BMP
B-BMP
huff
huff
B-BMP
B-BMP
huff
huff
LOOM
CHIKA!!
OH NO!!
KLANG
...?!

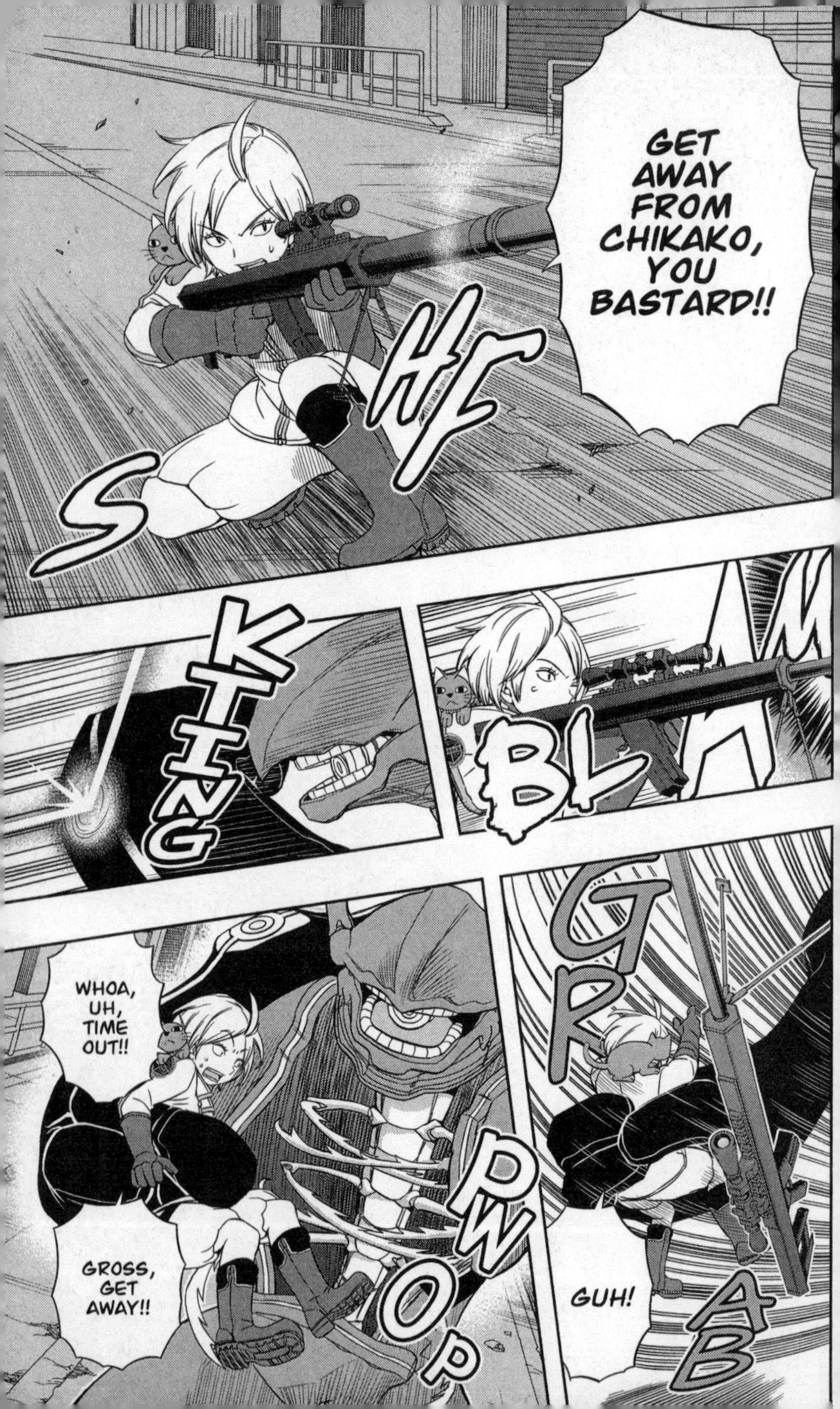
GET AWAY FROM CHIKAKO, YOU BASTARD!!
BLAM
KTING
GRAB
GUH!
WHOA, UH, TIME OUT!!
PWOP
GROSS, GET AWAY!!

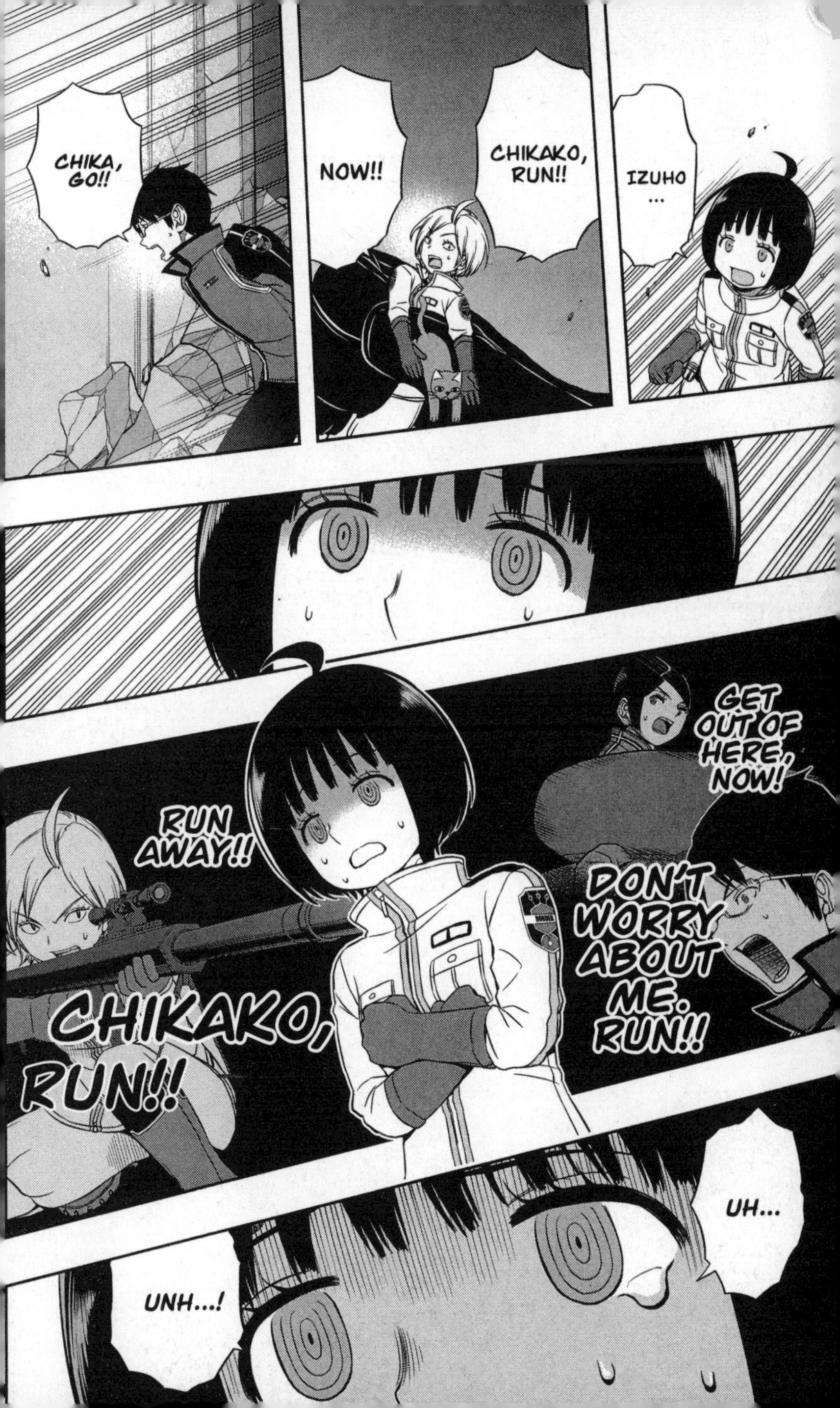
IZUHO ...
CHIKAKO, RUN!!
NOW!!
CHIKA, GO!!
GET OUT OF HERE, NOW!
DON'T WORRY ABOUT ME. RUN!!
RUN AWAY!!
CHIKAKO, RUN!!
UH...
UNH...!

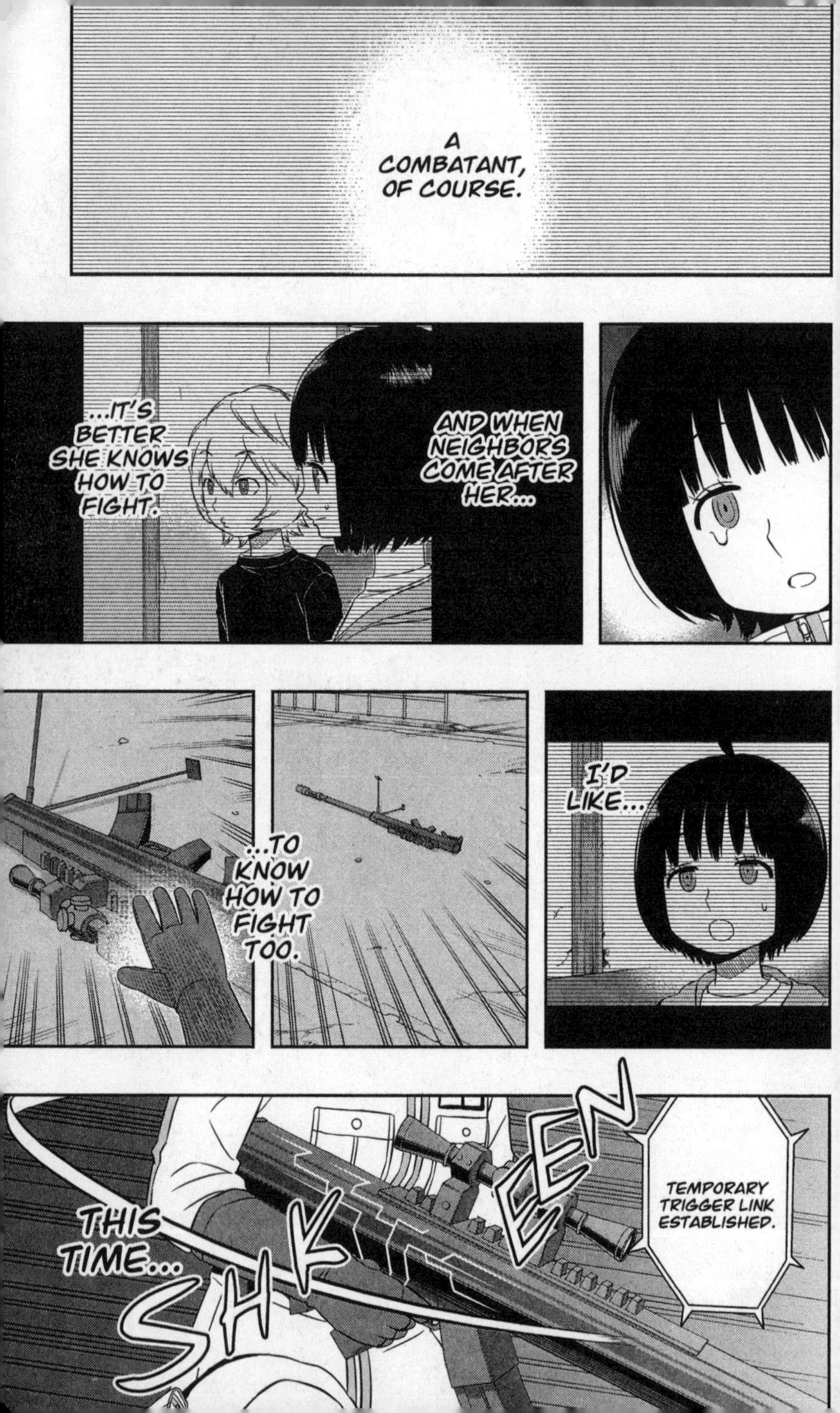
A COMBATANT, OF COURSE.
AND WHEN NEIGHBORS COME AFTER HER...
...IT'S BETTER SHE KNOWS HOW TO FIGHT.
I'D LIKE...
...TO KNOW HOW TO FIGHT TOO.
TEMPORARY TRIGGER LINK ESTABLISHED.
SHKEEN
THIS TIME...

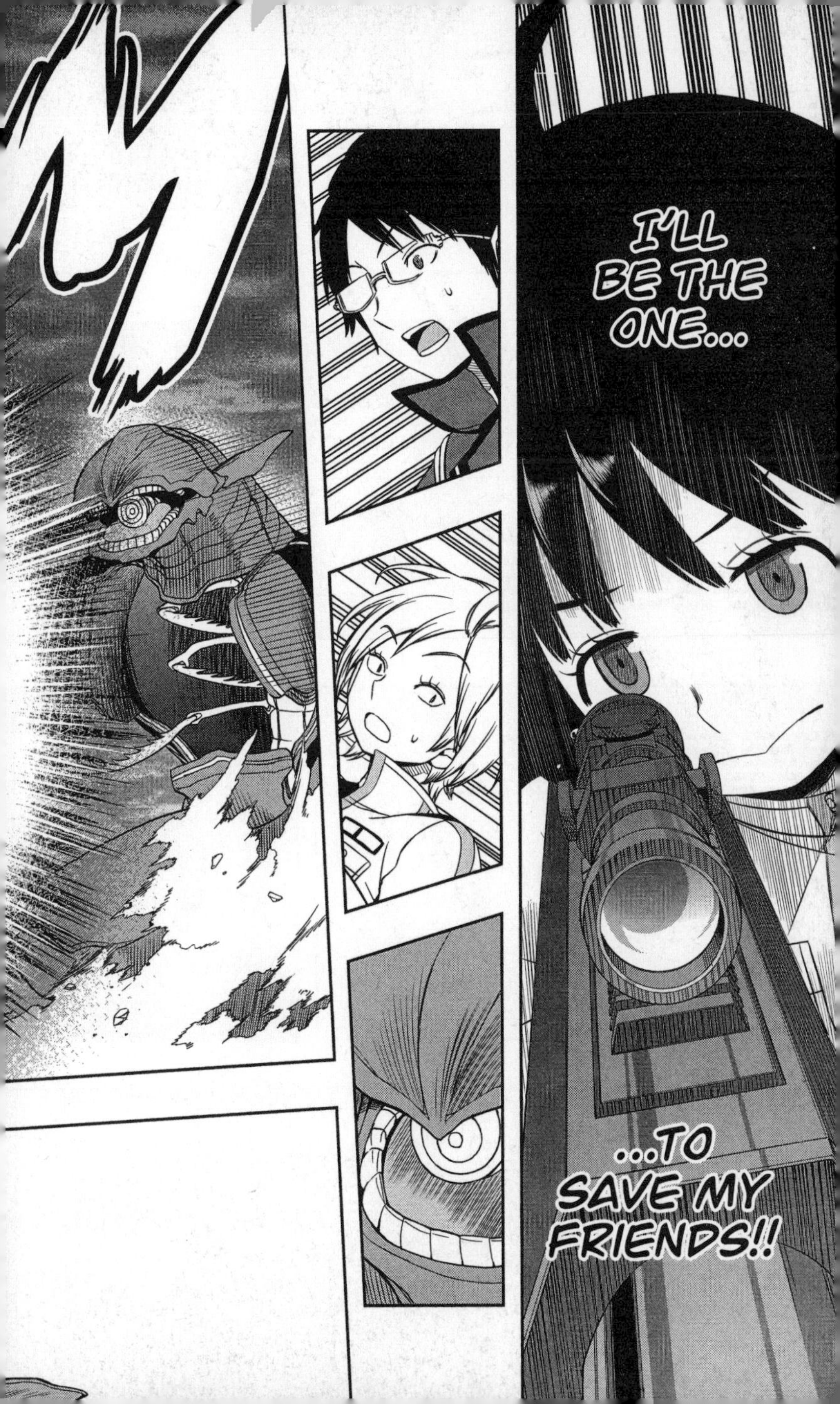
I'LL BE THE ONE...
...TO SAVE MY FRIENDS!!

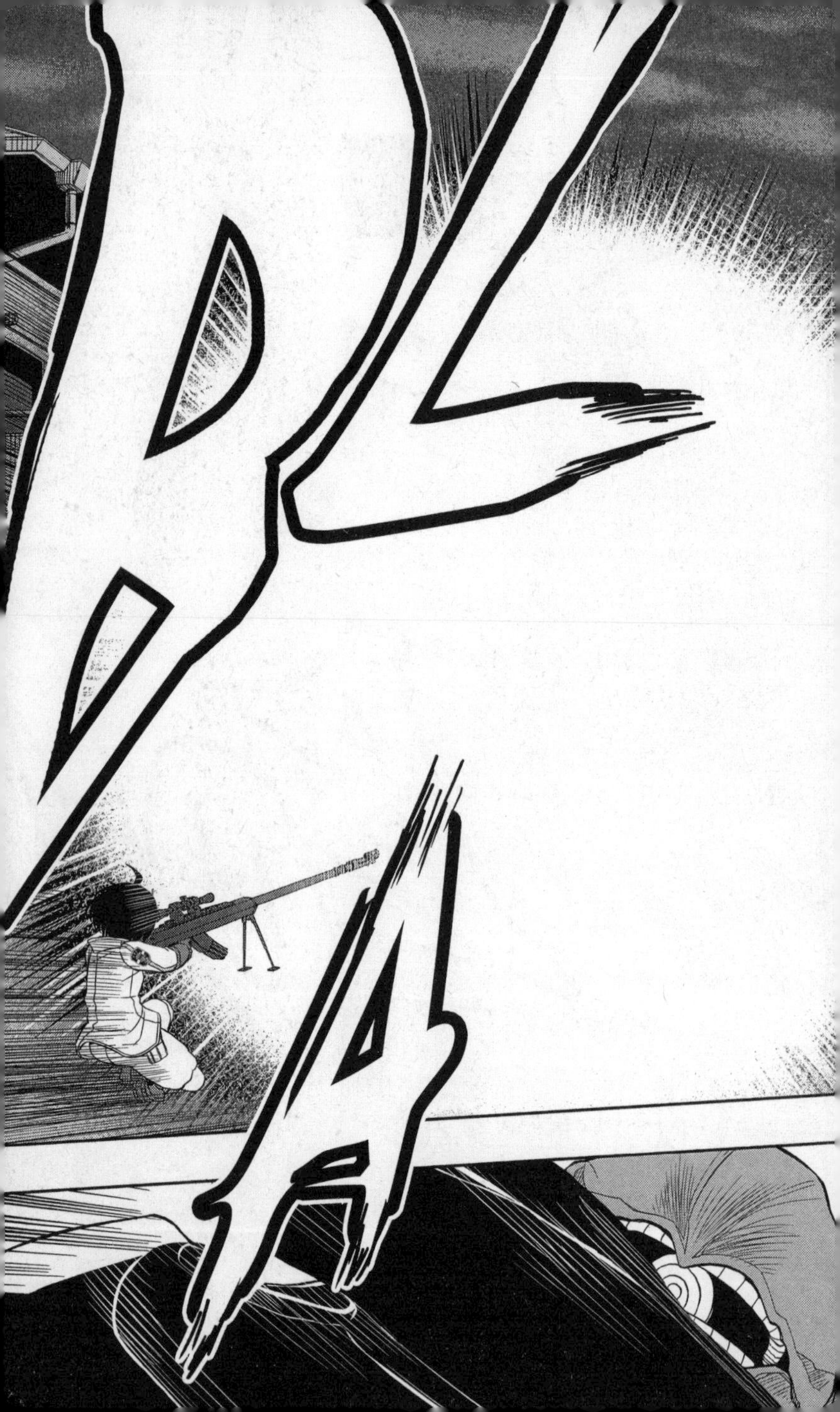

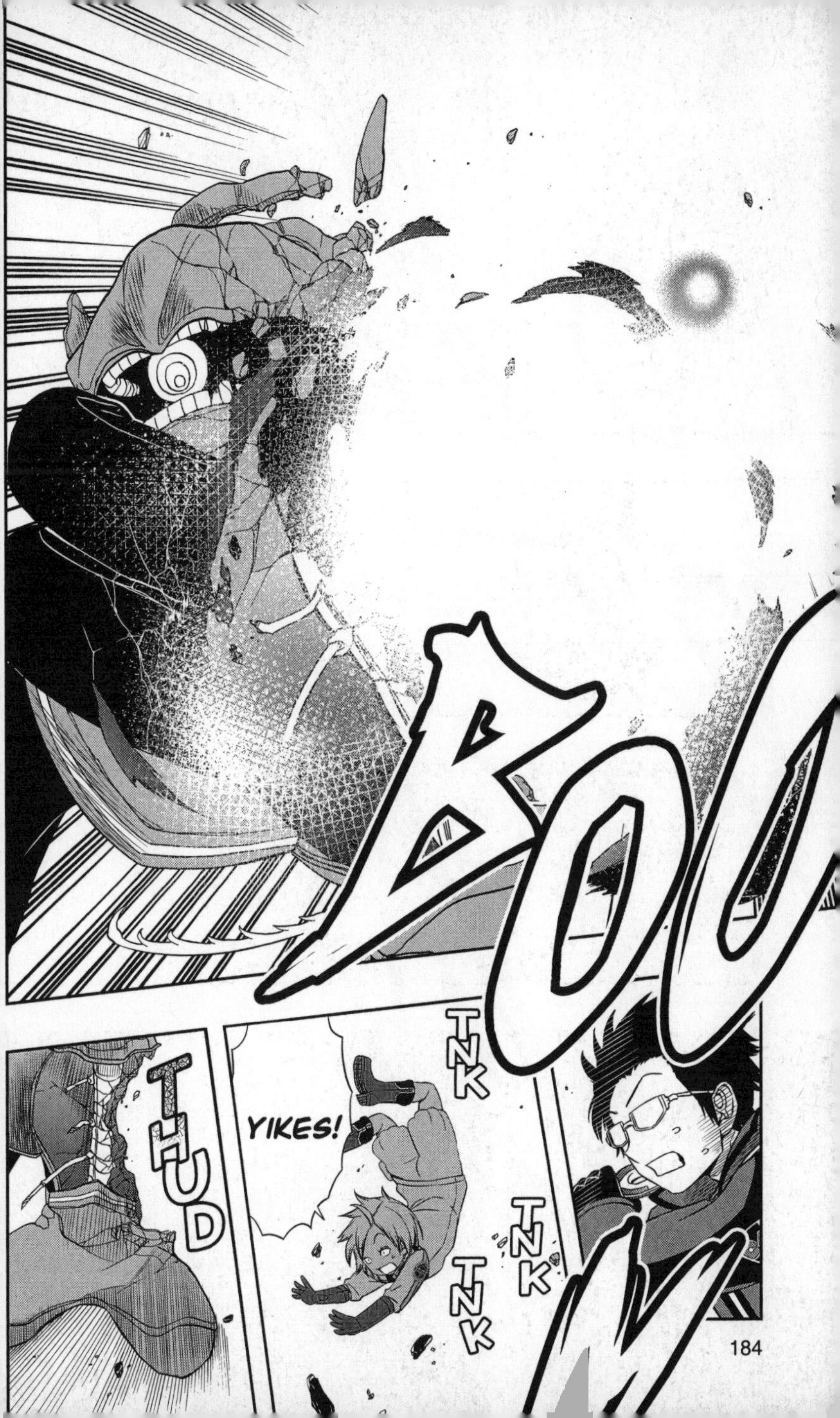
BOOM
TNK
TNK
YIKES!
TNK
THUD

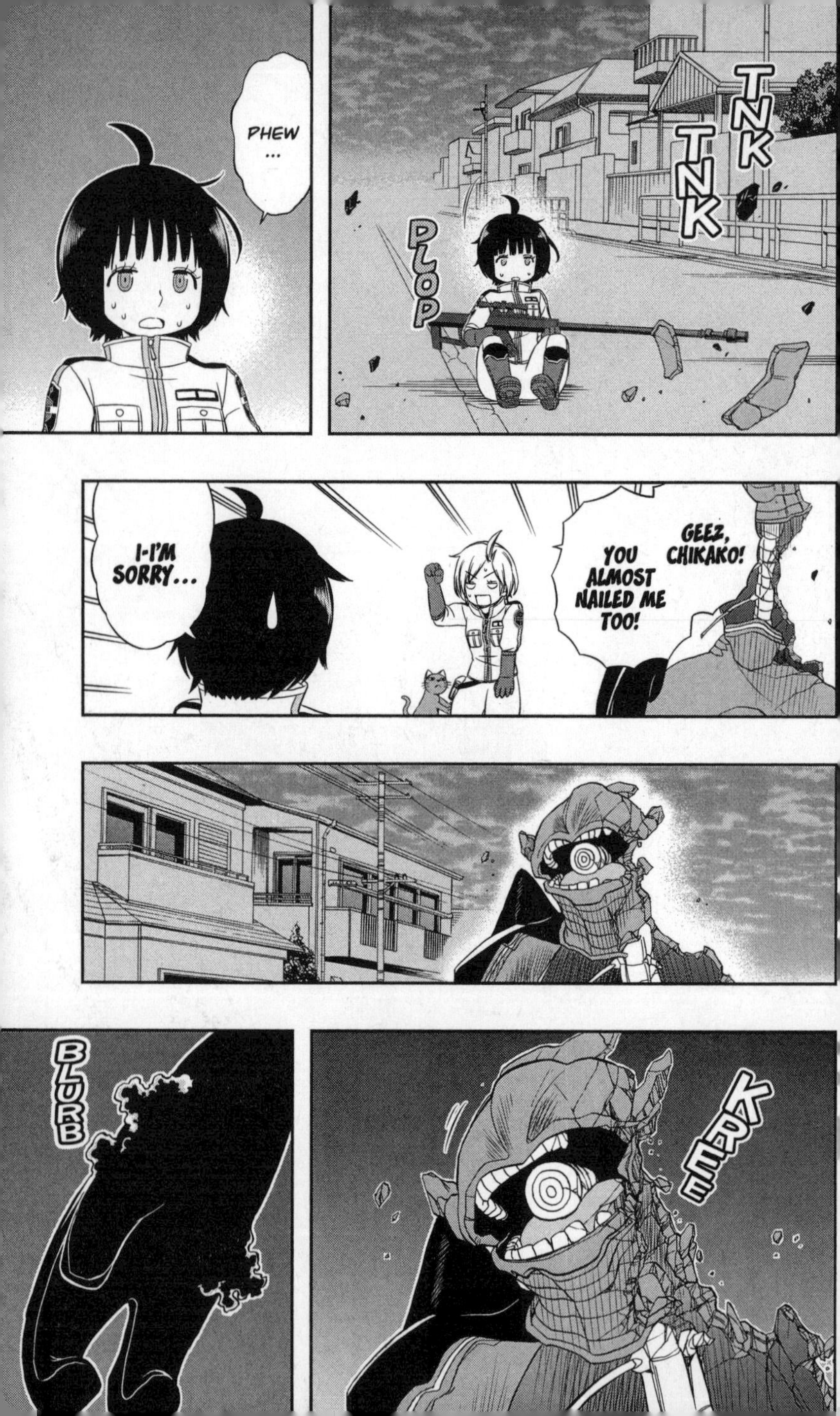
TNK
TNK
PLOP
PHEW ...
GEEZ, CHIKAKO!
YOU ALMOST NAILED ME TOO!
I-I'M SORRY...
KREE
BLURB

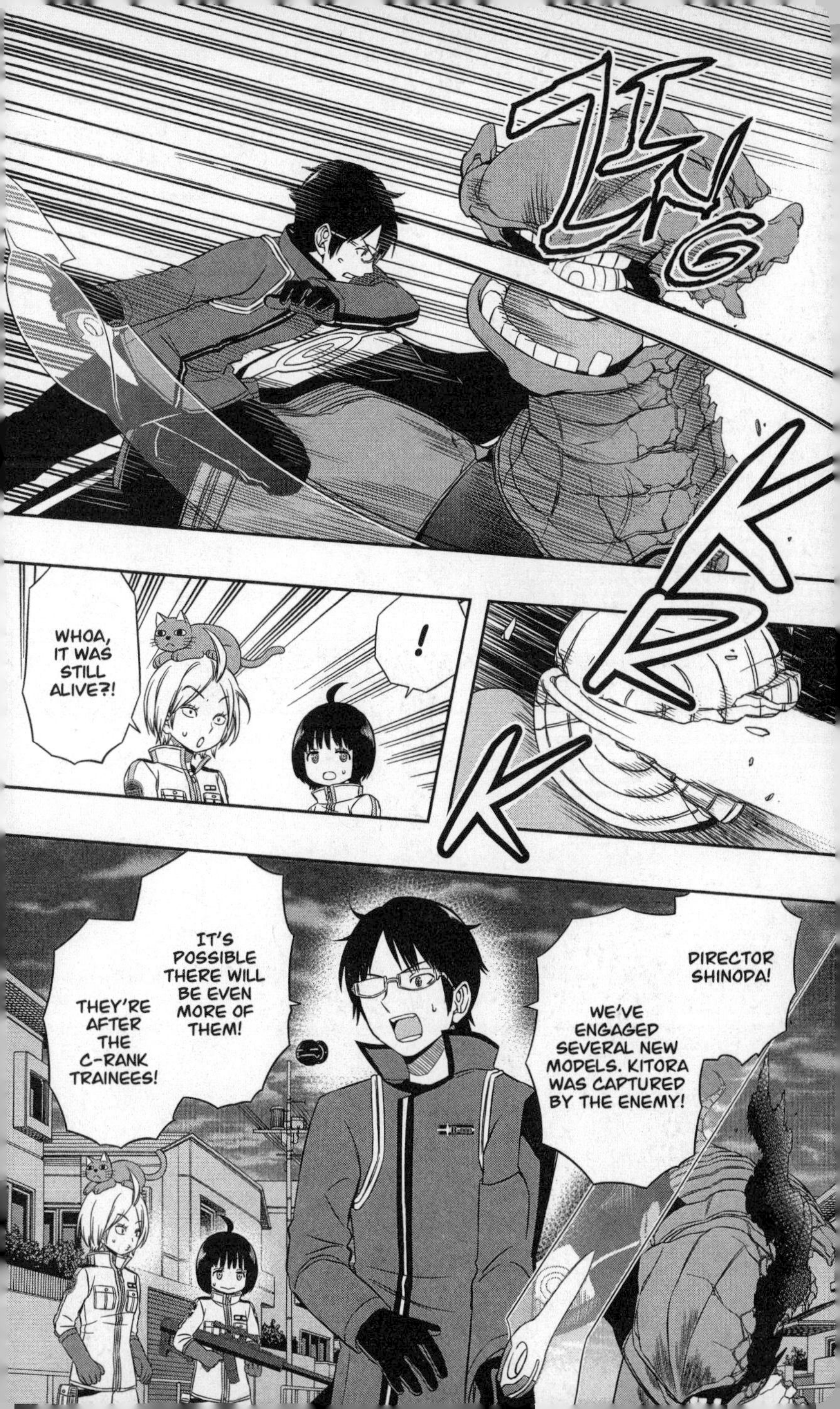
ZING
KRAK
!
WHOA, IT WAS STILL ALIVE?!
DIRECTOR SHINODA!
WE'VE ENGAGED SEVERAL NEW MODELS. KITORA WAS CAPTURED BY THE ENEMY!
IT'S POSSIBLE THERE WILL BE EVEN MORE OF THEM!
THEY'RE AFTER THE C-RANK TRAINEES!

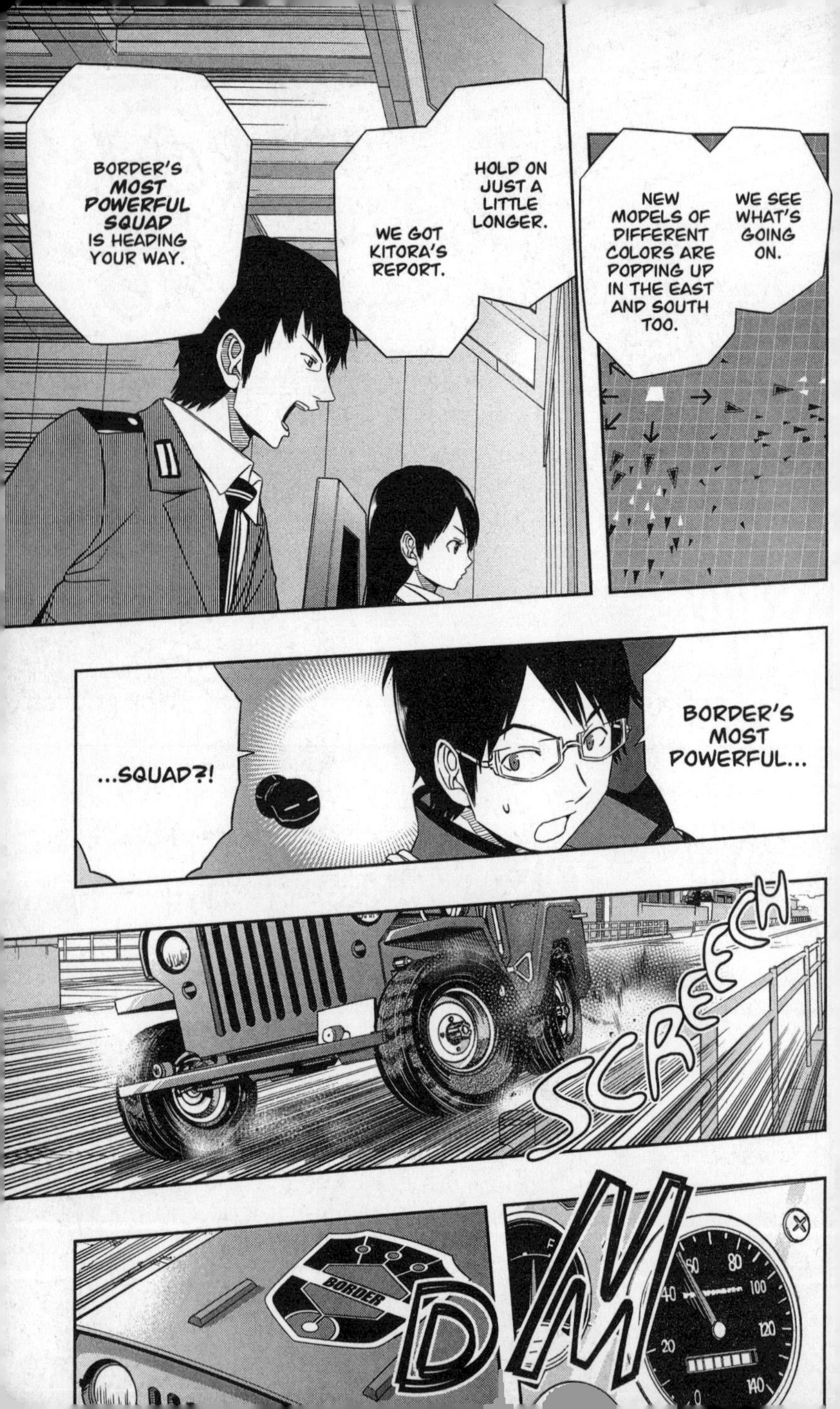
WE SEE WHAT'S GOING ON.
NEW MODELS OF DIFFERENT COLORS ARE POPPING UP IN THE EAST AND SOUTH TOO.
HOLD ON JUST A LITTLE LONGER.
WE GOT KITORA'S REPORT.
BORDER'S MOST POWERFUL SQUAD IS HEADING YOUR WAY.
BORDER'S MOST POWERFUL...
...SQUAD?!
SCREECH
BORDER
DM

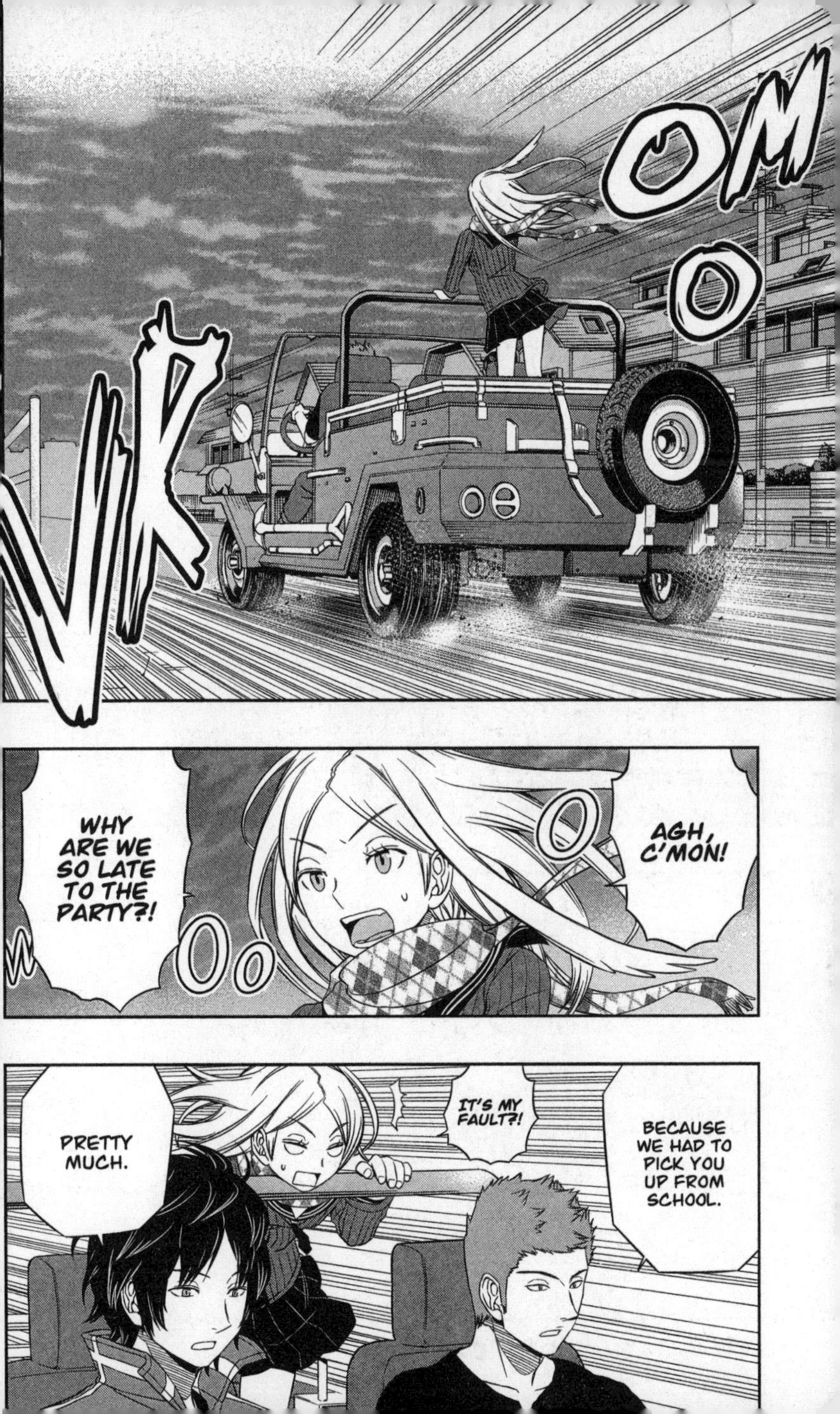
VROOM
AGH, C'MON!
WHY ARE WE SO LATE TO THE PARTY?!
BECAUSE WE HAD TO PICK YOU UP FROM SCHOOL.
IT'S MY FAULT?!
PRETTY MUCH.

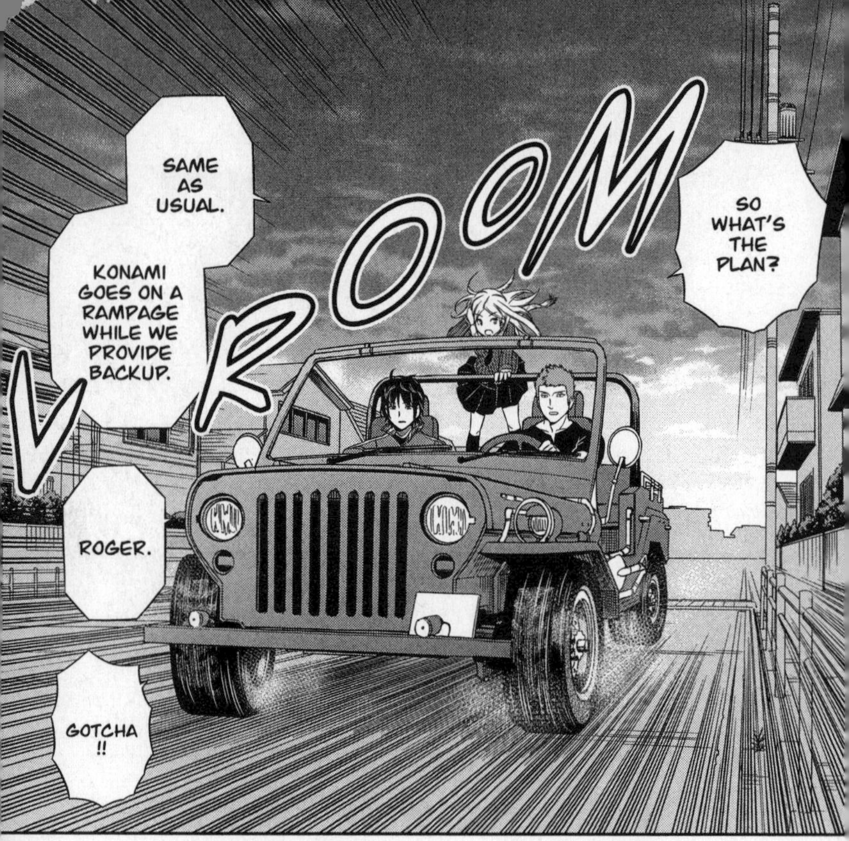
SO WHAT'S THE PLAN?
VROOOM
SAME AS USUAL.
KONAMI GOES ON A RAMPAGE WHILE WE PROVIDE BACKUP.
ROGER.
GOTCHA!!

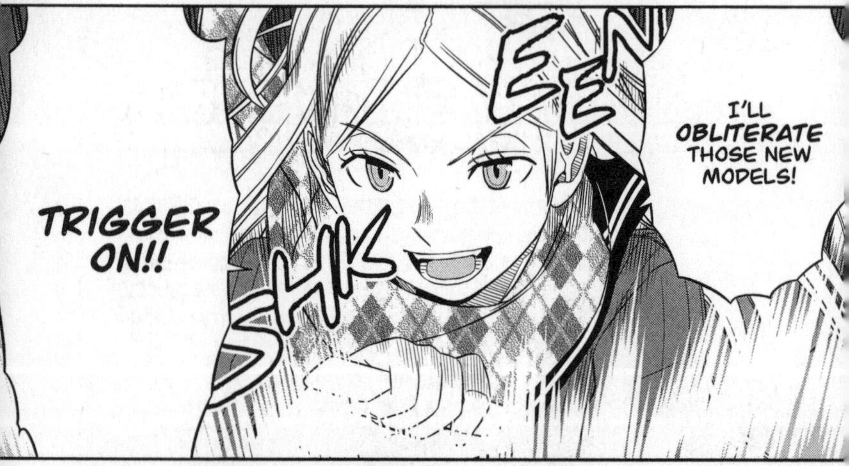
EEN
I'LL OBLITERATE THOSE NEW MODELS!
SHK
TRIGGER ON!!

To Be Continued In **World Trigger** 7!

WORLD TRIGGER

Bonus Character Pages

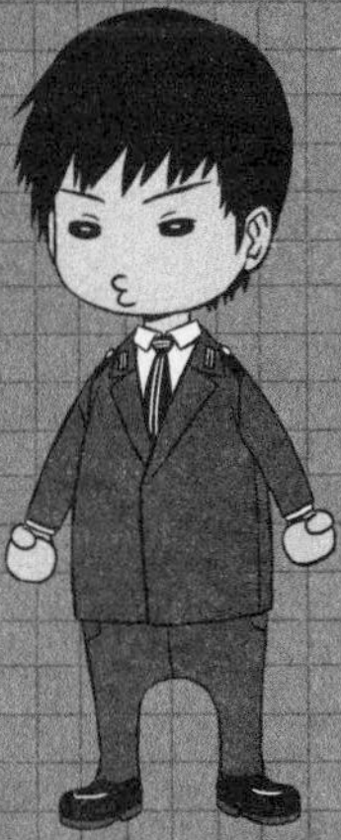

MR. SHINODA

Warm-hearted Tiger

HQ's top tiger. Mr. Kido gives him a hard time in every meeting. He increases his defense with such techniques as the "Tiger Arm-Folding" and the "Tiger Disapproving Look," which make the fox and the tanuki break into a cold sweat. He's so serious that people thought he'd be an anxious worrywart, but this volume shows how flexible and coolheaded he is in battle. The same age as Mr. Karasawa at 33.

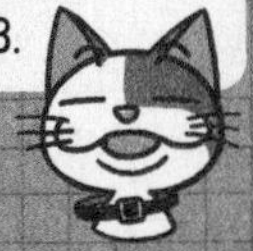

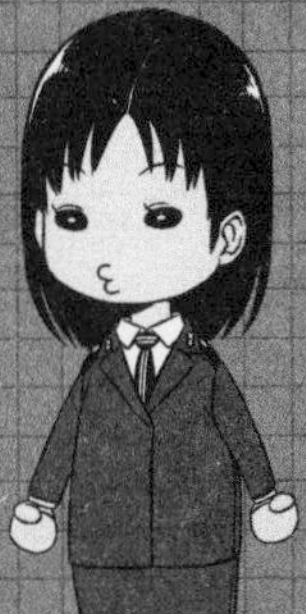

MISS SAWAMURA

Low Kick on First Appearance

Enlisted at the same time as Azuma, now 25 years old. Used to have short hair, but since that was too similar to Chika and Kitora, her hair became long. Too bad. She loves Mr. Shinoda, but she's a plucky woman who hides those feelings to carry out the mission. She's going to confess her love when this battle is over...

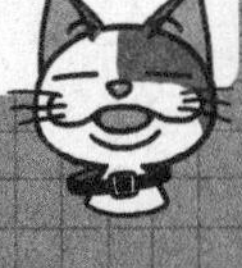

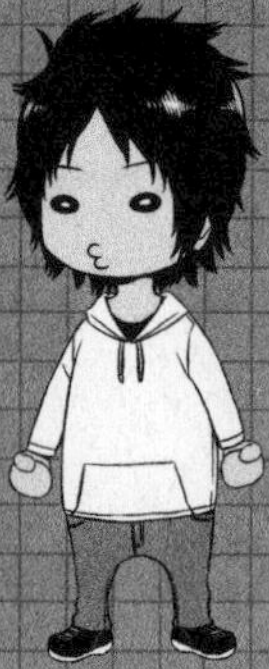

AMO

"Let's put an empty lot here."

An artisan of the battlefield who dramatically arranges open spaces. The city abandoned after the Trion soldier attack was reborn by his hand into, oh my goodness, a wide-open field with nothing to obstruct the view. No matter how you look at it, he's wrecking the city more than the Neighbors. My design concept for him was a stray dog.

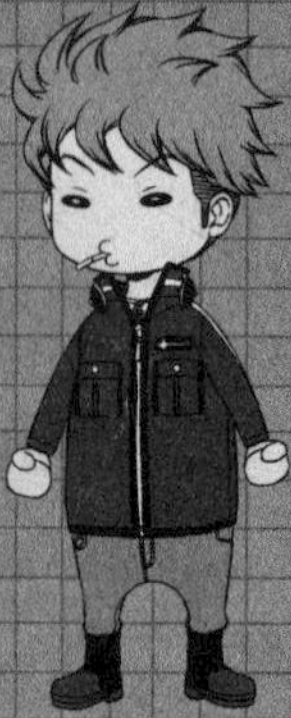

SUWA

Mr. Cube

One of the regular polyhedrons, a solid surrounded on six sides by a square. Used to be human, but now composed of 12 edges and 8 points. Personality-wise, he's actually no square—he's a fun character who does what he wants. A male version of Izuho. He's one of my favorite B-Rank agents. Really.

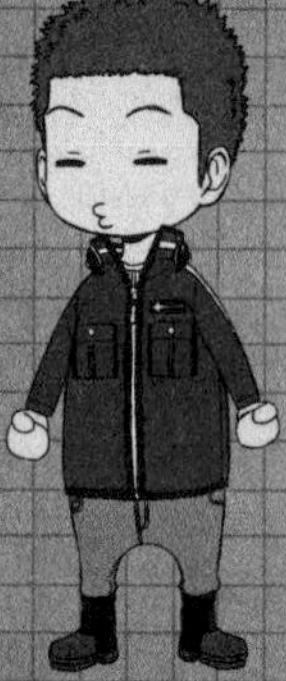

TSUTSUMI

Narrow-eyed Buzzcut with a Shotgun

The person who presumably said "Mikumo down" 25 times in volume 5. Quite the gambler, he believed in Osamu even after the 24th loss. He has a kind face, and his weapon is a close-range shotgun, but he's wavering between using that and summoning Suwa from the cube to make him fight.

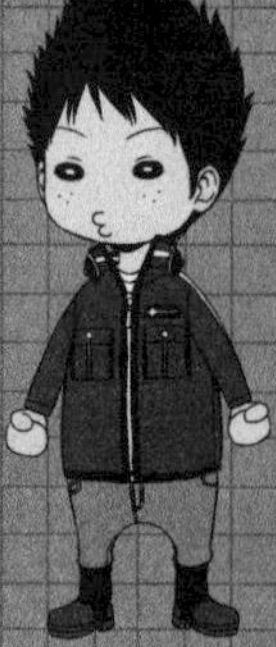

SASAMORI

Discouraged Avenger

The rare appearance of a hot-blooded freckled guy in *World Trigger*. The strategic lynchpin of Suwa Squad who pries open the enemy defense. He was beaten to the first cubing by Suwa, then he got chewed out by Kazama when he tried to avenge him. Poor thing. I like Suwa Squad a lot, so I hope he'll get a chance to shine soon...

YOU'RE READING THE WRONG WAY!

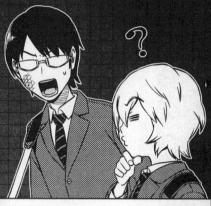

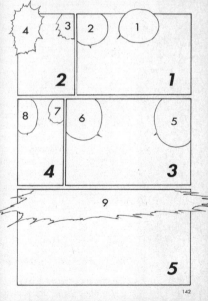

World Trigger reads from right to left, starting in the upper-right corner. Japanese is read from right to left, meaning that action, sound effects, and word-balloon order are completely reversed from the English order.